WOMEN of the Old Testament

WOMEN *of the* Old Testament

CAMILLE FRONK OLSON

Paintings by ELSPETH YOUNG

DESERET BOOK

SALT LAKE CITY, UTAH

Library of Congress Cataloging-in-Publication Data
Olson, Camille Fronk.
    Women of the Old Testament / Camille Fronk Olson ; paintings by Elspeth Young.
        p.   cm.
    Includes bibliographical references and index.
    ISBN 978-1-59038-791-7 (hardbound : alk. paper)
    1. Bible. O.T.—Biography.   2. Women in the Bible—Biography.   I. Title.
    BS575.O48 2009
    220.8'3054—dc22   2009014038

Printed in the United States of America
Worzalla Publishing Co., Stevens Point, WI

10   9   8   7   6   5   4   3

To my granddaughter, Kate,
and a new generation of women
who will know and love
the scriptures

CONTENTS

ACKNOWLEDGMENTS

*M*any individuals have contributed in a variety of ways to this volume. I gratefully acknowledge the review of the manuscript and academic suggestions by Donald W. Parry, professor of Hebrew and Semitic languages at Brigham Young University, and Rachel Cope, a recent Ph.D. recipient from Syracuse University in history and women's studies.

I also acknowledge the insights and meaningful questions posed by enthusiastic students in the multiple classes I have taught on the subject of women in scripture since the fall of 1991, particularly the students in a BYU class in the fall of 2005. This small group of bright women and men was selected to participate in research and exploratory questions that aided me in the initial approach to the book. Although the design and content of the project has changed dramatically and has expanded in scope since that time, I owe deep gratitude to the following students for their patience during the most serious transition period and for their insightful inquiries into the lives of many women in scripture. My thanks to Amy Bennion, Camille Buma, Susan Centeno, Karlin Coombs, Alicia Farrar, Kate Finlinson, Tyler Gibb, Natalie Hansen, Jaime Hauglid, Andrea Jolley, Jessica Kendrick, Michelle Larsen, Camille Madsen, BG McGill, Maren Payne, Letty Preston, Kathryn Ricks, Mary Robertson, Crystal Roper, Amy Soto, Ryan Stewart, Heather Thomas, Natalie Valentine, Meredith Veatch, Susan Walker, Elizabeth Watt, Elisabeth Westwood, Allyson White, Daile Wilson, Becki Wright, and Ariel Wootan. I add to these students the names of BYU students who worked for me on the project: Natalie Hansen, BG McGill, Mindy Nabrotzky, and Claire von Nieda as research assistants; Emil Pohlig in map design; and Steve Shorten in graphic design.

In fulfilling my desire for the book to be visually supportive of the scriptural text, I elected to focus on local talent and contributions. Photographs were taken and contributed by BYU colleagues David Whitchurch and Jeffrey Chadwick; a friend in Palestine, Sahar Qumseyeh; fellow travelers Ruth Ann Hubbard and Susan Y. Porter; our son David P. Olson; and a local dermatologist and friend, Dr. Steven Eyre. A BYU colleague, Richard N. Holzapfel, provided the line drawings for Israel's Tabernacle and

Solomon's temple, which had been created by Michael Lyon. Fellow faculty member D. Kelly Ogden suggested improvements for the maps.

I will forever be grateful for my friendship with the talented and gracious Elspeth Young, who agreed to collaborate with me on this project from the beginning; for her brother, Ashton, who created the exquisite line drawings for the book; and for her father, Al R. Young, who produced the painting of Eve. A dear friend, Kathy Jensen, has been a source of encouragement. She has a pulse on what will communicate to the intended audience and suggested ways to present the material graphically. Perhaps most important to my ability to stay focused and complete this work is my husband, Paul F. Olson. His constant encouragement, proofreading, and enthusiasm for my work compels me to improve in my research and writing and to better understand what it means to be a disciple of Jesus Christ. Additionally, Paul was an amenable photographer of many of the scenes included in the book, which we saw during our 2008 visit to the Holy Land.

Individuals at Deseret Book gave suggestions beginning with the earliest drafts of the first chapters and continuing until the manuscript was a stunning finished product. I am grateful to Jana Erickson for her trust in me and her wise advice that expanded the initial vision I had for the book and to Suzanne Brady for her excellent editorial skills and excitement for the book. I also acknowledge the contributions of art director Shauna Gibby and typographer Rachael Ward.

INTRODUCTION

*N*early twenty years ago, the magic of studying scripture through the lives of the women therein was opened to me through the compassion and genius of Margot Butler. Margot developed a course on women in the scriptures while teaching at the LDS Business College at the same time that I was employed there as an administrator. Whenever I passed by her office, I stopped to hear a brief insight or to be introduced to another story I had missed in the Old Testament.

Because the tendency is nearly universal to focus more on the prophets and political leaders in our formal scripture discussions, women's roles and contributions are often marginalized and even ignored. I was both amazed and thrilled to learn that more than 170 women are named in all the standard works, and hundreds more unnamed women are mentioned. Because only three women are named in the Book of Mormon and two women in the Doctrine and Covenants, it is clear that the great majority of scriptural women are found in the Bible.

When I left administration and returned to teaching, this time at the institute of religion near the University of Utah, I received permission to introduce a course on women in the scriptures. During regular meetings, Margot and I developed a packet for the course and a listing of all the women in scripture. In a way, this book represents a promise I made to Margot years ago that I would write something that invited others, men as well as women, to discover the scriptures through the lens of women's experiences and testimony.

No two are alike among this large number of women in scripture. Women in the Bible are young, old, and middle-aged. Some are affluent, others live in poverty, but most live in economic conditions somewhere in between. Most of the women in scripture are married, but some are single. Some are born in the lineage of the prophets, and others come from the cultures of the world. Some make their contributions from within a loving and supportive marriage; others bring about much good while being married to an abusive, absent, or unfaithful husband. Some have children; others do not. All of them have challenges. Rescuing others without thought of their own danger or sacrificing their lives to give life to another, many of these women are also types of Christ. They were encouraged and enabled to do what God asked them to do. When we consider the scriptural message through the experiences of women, we find that many women should be added to our list of outstanding men as examples of people who inspire us to greater discipleship.

To find the women in scripture, however, requires today's women and men to be *in* the scriptures. We cannot merely depend on retold paraphrases of these stories or hope that they come up in Sunday lessons. Rather, we must be diligent in accessing them for ourselves directly from the canon of holy writ to find the context, scriptural detail, and clues to each woman's influence. Because of space limitations, the decision was made not to include the scriptural texts in this book. Therefore, I hope you will have your own scriptures open beside you and study the scriptural accounts as the primary text as you read the discussions here. By examining the stories of these women in your own copy of the Bible, you will more likely appreciate and recognize new insights along the way. You may want to note these clarifying and edifying insights in your copy of the scriptures to enrich your teaching these stories to others and to inform your own future gospel study.

This book represents much of what I have learned through research, personal scripture study, and numerous classroom discussions with curious, bright university students. Faced with a different culture and centuries of history that separate us, I soon realized that the greatest stumbling block to accessing insights from the lives of these women is often a lack of knowledge about the ancient customs, history, languages, and geography. With some background in each of these areas, a dynamic new perspective is opened to us, unlocking the potential for multiple new insights and gospel connections. Before finding personal applications for our day, we must visualize and appreciate their day, including their different challenges and customs.

Twenty years ago, the best book to consider every woman in the Bible was one written by a Texas journalist, Edith Deen, who had no academic training but plenty of love for the scriptures. Her work, *All of the Women of the Bible,* was originally published in 1955 and is still in print. Since then, multiple biblical scholars have picked up Deen's passion for the study of women in scripture and added the details and corrections that were not available to a journalist in the 1950s. Academics such as Carol Meyers of Duke University, Tikva Frymer-Kensky of University of Chicago, Phyllis Trible of Wake Forest University Divinity School, Ross S. Kraemer of Brown University, Donald W. Parry of Brigham Young University, Susan Ackerman of Dartmouth College, and many others have explored new ways to consider familiar biblical stories about women by asking different questions, analyzing word meanings, and considering a different angle, all the while remaining true to the scriptural text.

Because no book of scripture or extrabiblical text from ancient Israel has been found to have been created by a woman, we are left to find women's voices amid the narratives and observations of men. That so many women were included in those narratives is indication that the stories of the people of the covenant cannot be told without reflecting the contributions of women. Further, as more ancient Israelite villages are excavated, archaeological findings reveal more about the presence of women—their world, their places of work, their vessels for food, and their articles of adornment. In short, women were not invisible in those ancient days. It is time to bring them out of the shadows today.

We gain valuable insight into the world of the Old Testament by augmenting stories from it with clues from archaeological discoveries, comparative writings from the same general era and location and other Bible translations, such as the Septuagint and the Dead Sea Scrolls. Josephus, a first-century Jewish historian, often offers added clarification to these stories by reporting what was understood and accepted about these Old Testament women shortly after the time of Christ. Additionally, Jewish traditions, or *Midrashim*, were recorded by rabbis and handed down for generations to supply rabbinic commentary and apologetics for Old Testament stories. Each chapter of this book draws on some of these primary sources.

Because many women seem to feel intimidated participating in scriptural discussions, my dream in producing this book is to encourage all its readers to share insights gleaned through personal scripture study and develop greater confidence in studying the Old Testament. Furthermore, because women frequently see different lessons in scripture than men do, it is my hope that men and women will hear and appreciate others' perspectives in shaping their own gospel understanding.

Questions surrounding these women rarely produce a single answer, given that many facts surrounding the lives of Old Testament women are missing and few of their stories define doctrine. Therefore, two or more people sharing their individual insights often produce a multiplicity of possibilities that collectively reveal the unparalleled depth and breadth of scripture. In this way, each of us can discover a personal application from the scriptures that is not dependent on another's interpretation. The Points to Ponder at the end of each section are intended to encourage such discoveries.

This volume focuses on women in the Old Testament. Only a sampling of the hundreds of women referred to in that great work of scripture is explored and discussed. Some are visibly absent. The length and unique circumstances of the Esther text preclude a separate chapter for her in the present format, but she is briefly discussed in the introduction to the section "Women Who Influenced Law." Tamar, Rahab, Ruth, and Bathsheba are not included here because they will be discussed in a forthcoming volume on women in the New Testament, "Women in the Savior's Lineage," as chronicled in Matthew 1.

The women chosen for this volume are from every time period in the Old Testament, which provides background information to apply to other women of the same era. For example, by knowing the general setting, culture, and history of Abigail's day, we can also visualize much of the world of Michal, Bathsheba, David's daughter Tamar, and the Queen of Sheba. For the brief time line included in each chapter, I consulted the chronology outlined in *The Cambridge Ancient History*, volumes 2 and 3 (Cambridge University Press, 1970).

The women discussed in this volume are presented in categories. An introduction to each category provides names of additional women who could also fit in the same section. To encourage continued study, a full listing of named and unnamed women in the Old Testament, with accompanying scriptural references, is found in Appendix B. Because a person's name and its meaning held significance in ancient Israel, that information is included for each woman highlighted in the book. A discussion of the significance of names is found in the introduction to the section entitled "Unnamed Women."

From the beginning of this project, I knew that visual images were needed to bring a feeling of reality to these biblical women. Elspeth Young was a student in a 2002 New Testament class of mine. She heard me give a presentation on women in the scriptures when I made a plea to art students to consider creating an informed portrayal of some of the biblical stories that have long been forgotten or inaccurately told. Elspeth accepted my invitation and has been finding unique ways to bring these women to life ever since. When I decided to begin this book, she was the first person I called to see if she would join me in the endeavor. Her enthusiasm and inspiring portrayals of these women often sustained and encouraged me in my research and writing. I believe that Elspeth's visual interpretation of these women will also contribute to the reader's ability to appreciate that these women of the Old Testament are real.

The Mother of All Living

The Joy of Our Redemption

EVE
חַוָּה

"Life Giver"

As "the mother of all living," Eve is connected to each of us (Genesis 3:20; Moses 4:26). Her use of reasoning and agency initiated life in a fallen world where her children would encounter pain, sorrow, and joy beyond anything she and Adam could imagine in the Garden of Eden. Although divinely designated to be a heroine and role model for her daughters, Eve is one of the most misunderstood and criticized women in history.

Appreciation for our first mother's virtue and purpose shapes our consideration of other women in scripture, and our interpretation of Eve's role in the Fall likely influences the manner in which we regard women in general. For example, if we scorn mother Eve as the cause of the world's woes and the loss of paradise for humankind, we are apt to see women as weak, incapable, overly emotional, reactive, vulnerable, and less intelligent than men. If, however, we consider Eve's decision in the Garden of Eden as coura-geous and faith-driven and the results of that decision to be conducive to God's plan, we are more likely to recognize intelligence, strength, rational thinking, and great ability in women in general. With cultural and gender biases and blinders removed, we can value "our glorious Mother Eve" (D&C 138:39) as an effective precedent to studying other women in scripture and seeing more clearly their respective challenges, contributions, and in-teractions with others.

Archaeological, historical, and geographical back-grounds do not provide access to Eve's world as they do for later women in the Bible, but a careful study of scripture does. Unfortunately, centuries of Christian and Jewish interpretations and traditions have frequently

GENESIS 2–3; 4:1, 25
MOSES 3–5; 6:2, 9
ABRAHAM 5:16–19
2 CORINTHIANS 11:3
1 TIMOTHY 2:13–15
1 NEPHI 5:11
2 NEPHI 2:17–26; 9:9
ALMA 12:21–26
DOCTRINE & COVENANTS 138:38–39
LDS BIBLE DICTIONARY, 668

VARIOUS BIBLICAL TRANSLATIONS OF GENESIS 2:18 COMPARED

I will make him an help meet for him (King James Version)

I will make him a helper as his partner (New Revised Standard Version)

I will make him an helper—as his counterpart (Young's Literal Translation)

I will make him a help like unto himself (Douay-Rheims translation)

I will make him a help like him (Latin Vulgate translation)

Let us make for him a help suitable to him (Septuagint)

colored our perceptions of Eve far more than the scriptures have done. Rather than relying on tradition or paraphrasing lessons from Eden, we should give close attention to the scriptural narrative, which reinforces God's love and divine attributes accorded His daughters and His sons. Neither sons nor daughters are blessed less than the other. Hebrew word meanings and the book of Moses, which is the first portion of the Joseph Smith Translation of the Genesis narrative, are especially helpful in exploring a positive and consistent understanding of Eve and her contributions.

CREATED IN GOD'S LIKENESS

The equal significance to God of man and woman is apparent from the Creation. The word *adam* in Hebrew is a generic term referring to all of humankind, implying those created from the earth. God created "man," that is, "male and female," in His own image and declared them both "very good" (Genesis 1:26–27, 31; Moses 2:26–27, 31). A reference in the book of Moses supports the Hebrew meaning: "In the image of [God's] own body, male and female, created he them, and blessed them, and called *their name Adam,* in the day when they were created" (Moses 6:8–9; emphasis added). Awareness of this meaning of the Hebrew word helps us to remember our first parents every time we speak of humankind or mankind. Furthermore, as descendants of Adam and Eve, each of us is created in the image of God's body with the capacity to develop Christlike attributes. Each of us carries a continual reminder of our divine heritage in our countenances and honorable desires.

Indicating another shared characteristic of those created in His image, God gave "them" dominion over all living things (Genesis 1:26, 28; Moses 2:26, 28). In this scriptural passage, "them" specifically refers to men and women. Given the responsibility to be stewards over God's other creations, all children of Adam and Eve are to use and care for His creations, remembering that they ultimately belong to God. Nowhere in scripture is man given dominion over woman, nor is woman given dominion over man.

WOMAN AS A HELP MEET FOR MAN

The apostle Paul taught that "neither is the man without the woman, neither the woman without the man, in the Lord" (1 Corinthians 11:11). From the beginning, God reinforced that truth with His initial appellation for Eve.

God referred to Eve as a "help meet" for Adam (Genesis 2:18; Moses 3:18), an expression that has suffered a variety of questionable translations, which are often uncomplimentary to Eve. For example, the expression has been incorrectly transliterated to *helpmate,* thus creating the false perception that God created woman to be subservient to man and important only as man's assistant.

The morphological units that make up the Hebrew expression *help meet,* however, communicate a much richer meaning. The first word (*'ezer*), translated "help," implies not a subordinate but rather someone who has strength to do what another cannot do for himself. Hebrew scholar Donald W. Parry has argued that the woman's unique strength, or "help," is as a "life giver" or a "life force" ("Eve's Role"). Therefore, Eve was blessed with tremendous power and strength to provide Adam with a life-giving power that typifies God's help. This same Hebrew word, *'ezer,* translated "help," appears numerous times in the Bible. The root is the basis for the name of the scribe Ezra and frequently appears in reference to God. For example, God is the One who rescues us in our distress (Psalm 70:5) or He has strength and power to save (Deuteronomy 33:7, 26, 29). In this way, women are types of Christ. It should come as no surprise that one of the stated purposes of the Relief Society is "to save souls" (*History of the Church,* 5:25).

The second word (*kenegdo*), translated "meet," is a compound of three common words that collectively appear in this form only in the Eden account (Genesis 2:18, 20; Moses 3:18, 20). The root word within this compound is the middle word, *kgd,* which means "to be conspicuous" or "to be apparent." The word is used in the noun form only in these two verses, allowing for such suggested meanings as "in front of, opposite, or counterpart." In Jewish Midrashim, the word means "equal," as in the well-known saying, "The study of Torah is equal (*keneged*) to all the other commandments" (Freedman, "Woman," 57–58). The collective meaning of the term suggests that Eve was an appropriate and worthy partner for Adam. God's description of marital companionship in Genesis 2 indicates no hierarchical dynamic between Adam and Eve.

The scriptural text gives further evidence that Adam and Eve were truly partners. Figuratively speaking, Eve was created from Adam's rib, not his head or his foot (the Hebrew word translated "rib" literally means "side"). The imagery of the rib, or side, symbolizes that man and woman are made of the same substance and are to exist together, side by side, not beneath or above. Furthermore,

Adam and Eve lived among the remarkable creations of God in their Garden of Eden paradise.

Eve was Adam's wife; they were married in the Garden and cleaved to each other (Genesis 2:23–25; Moses 3:23–25).

Through latter-day revelation, we learn that God established the patriarchal order of the priesthood with Adam and Eve in the Garden of Eden after they were married and before their mortality commenced. This ideal form of governing is patterned after God's government, which He, as our Father, operates through families here on earth. He established Adam and Eve as a family, sealed together for eternity, to have children and to perform His work throughout their mortality, as guided by the Holy Spirit. Today, this patriarchal priesthood is received in temples when a man and woman are sealed in eternal bonds of marriage.

In the patriarchal order, home is the center of the community, and religion is woven into the family's daily life. Children are viewed as a divine gift, and parents are stewards for God in rearing their children

THE PATRIARCHAL ORDER OF THE PRIESTHOOD

Church leaders have often spoken concerning the patriarchal order that commenced with Adam and Eve. The following are a few of their statements.

"Adam and his descendants entered into the priesthood order of God. Today we would say they went to the House of the Lord and received their blessings. The order of priesthood spoken of in the scriptures is sometimes referred to as the patriarchal order because it came down from father to son. But this order is otherwise described in modern revelation as an order of family government where a man and woman enter into a covenant with God—just as did Adam and Eve—to be sealed for eternity, to have posterity, and to do the will and work of God throughout their mortality" (Benson, *Ensign*, Aug. 1985, 9; paragraphing altered).

"A man who holds the priesthood accepts his wife as a partner in the leadership of the home and family with full knowledge of and full participation in all decisions relating thereto. Of necessity there must be in the Church and in the home a presiding officer (see D&C 107:21). By divine appointment, the responsibility to preside in the home rests upon the priesthood holder (see Moses 4:22). The Lord intended that the wife be a helpmeet for man (*meet* means equal)—that is, a companion equal and necessary in full partnership. Presiding in righteousness necessitates a shared responsibility between husband and wife; together you act with knowledge and participation in all family matters. For a man to operate independent of or without regard to the feelings and counsel of his wife in governing the family is to exercise unrighteous dominion" (Hunter, *Ensign*, Nov. 1994, 50–51).

"There is a difference in the way the priesthood functions in the home as compared to the way it functions in the Church. In the Church our service is by call. In the home our service is by choice. . . . In the Church there is a distinct line of authority. We serve where called by those who preside over us. In the home it is a partnership with husband and wife equally yoked together, sharing in decisions, always working together. While the husband, the father, has responsibility to provide worthy and inspired leadership, his wife is neither behind him nor ahead of him but at his side" (Packer, *Ensign*, May 1998, 73; paragraphing altered).

to love and serve Him. Family, rather than the priesthood holder or the primary caregiver, is the foundation of the patriarchal order.

SATAN BEGUILED EVE

The Bible provides no introduction to Eve's tempter, the serpent. The book of Moses, however, clarifies that Satan, "the father of all lies," was the mind and voice behind the serpent and that his ultimate purpose in attempting to beguile Eve was to destroy the world (Moses 4:1–6). Moreover, the book of Moses reveals that Satan "knew not the mind of God" (Moses 4:6). Spiritual things can only be understood by the Spirit. Satan was bereft of spiritual companionship, of faith in God, and was therefore limited in his understanding of God's plan, including the need for the Fall and a Redeemer. The scriptural text gives a sense that Satan falsely assumed that Eve would be foolish to partake of the Tree of Knowledge. His attempts to entice Adam and Eve to transgress the law suggest that he mistakenly supposed that God wanted Adam and Eve to forever remain in the Garden. The Savior and the prophets drew a connection between obedience to God and understanding His mysteries (John 7:17; Alma 12:9–10). President Ezra Taft Benson taught that no one can understand "why he needs Christ until he understands and accepts the doctrine of the Fall and its effect upon all mankind" (*Ensign,* May 1987, 85). The capacity of Satan's mind is incomparably inferior to the omniscience of God and to those who are taught and led by the Holy Spirit.

With his restricted understanding, Satan tempted Eve with a question that presupposes more is always better and that a restriction from God means He is withholding valuable opportunities. Satan asked Eve why she could not "eat of *every* tree of the garden" (Genesis 3:1; Moses 4:7; emphasis added). Satan seemed to suggest that a loving God would certainly allow His children access to *every* experience. Does Satan use a similar tactic to lure us into sin? Does the same skewed philosophy lead us to suppose that God curtails our agency and the need to know whether something is good or evil when He forbids us from experiencing everything firsthand? In one of his favorite modes of temptation, Satan would have us think that God selfishly withholds blessings and power by not giving us unconditional access to every option at all times.

Satan, the father of lies, next implied that God is a liar by claiming that Adam and Eve would *not die* should they partake of the tree of knowledge of good and evil (Genesis 3:4; Moses 4:10). Satan scores a victory whenever we distrust God and His counsel. Others have successfully used Satan's tactic by taking out of context something a believer has said, looking at the selected phrase from a different perspective

VARIOUS INTERPRETATIONS OF EVE'S CHOICE

Latter-day Saint Viewpoints

Latter-day Saint General Authorities have often spoken of Eve's wisdom in the Garden and the vital importance of the Fall. Following are some of their insights:

"It was Eve who first transgressed the limits of Eden in order to initiate the conditions of mortality. Her act, whatever its nature, was formally a transgression but eternally a glorious necessity to open the doorway toward eternal life. Adam showed his wisdom by doing the same. And thus Eve and 'Adam fell that men might be' ([2 Ne. 2:25]). Some Christians condemn Eve for her act, concluding that she and her daughters are somehow flawed by it. Not the Latter-day Saints! Informed by revelation, we celebrate Eve's act and honor her wisdom and courage in the great episode called the Fall.... Modern revelation shows that our first parents understood the necessity of the Fall" (Oaks, *Ensign*, Nov. 1993, 73; paragraphing altered).

"We and all mankind are forever blessed because of Eve's great courage and wisdom. By partaking of the fruit first, she did what needed to be done. Adam was wise enough to do likewise. Accordingly, we could speak of the fall of Adam in terms of a *mortal* creation, because 'Adam fell that men might be' (2 Ne. 2:25) [see also Moses 6:68]" (Nelson, *Ensign*, Nov. 1993, 34).

"There is the difference between the various religious sects of the Christian world and the Latter-day Saints. We ... understand ... why God permitted Mother Eve to partake of the forbidden fruit. We should not have been here to-day if she had not; we could never have possessed wisdom and intelligence if she had not done it.... We should never blame Mother Eve, not the least. I am thankful to God that I know good from evil, the bitter from the sweet, the things of God from the things not of God" (Young, *Journal of Discourses*, 13:144–45).

"I never speak of the part Eve took in this fall as a sin, nor do I accuse Adam of a sin.... This was a transgression of the law, but not a sin ... for it was something that Adam and Eve had to do!" (Smith, *Doctrines of Salvation*, 1:114–15).

"Adam and Eve could have remained in the Garden ... to this day, if Eve had not done [what she did]" (Smith, *Seek Ye Earnestly*, 4).

Other Interpretations

Awareness of other ways Eve's choice in the Garden is interpreted often increases appreciation for modern revelation, whether others' views disagree or agree with that revelation. The following are a few examples:

"Like her husband Adam, Eve rebelled against God and put her own plans and wisdom ahead of God's. Her disobedience triggered Adam's, and produced the chain reaction of anxiety and guilt in every person, and the estrangement between man and God, man and woman, brothers, nations and races, that continues to this day" (Barker, *Everyone in the Bible*, s.v. "Eve," 103).

"The woman sees that the tree is good for food and ... a delight to the eyes. Deceived by the serpent, she is now deceiving herself. All that she wants to do, she tells herself, is to satisfy two legitimate desires, for food and for beauty. By what right has God forbidden their satisfaction? Her real desire, however, is for power" (Terrien, *Interpreter's Bible*, 1:505).

"The figure of Eve lies at the heart of Christianity's understanding and estimation of women. Today she demands and achieves the closest attention of all scholars who wish either to revise that estimation of women or to uphold it. . . . Perhaps applying the model of resurrection to Eve might yield better fruit. Let us put to death the Eve of patriarchal fantasy, and raise up in her stead the Eve who, created in the image of God, takes responsibility for human progress, liberates herself and her husband from the playground of paradise and engages with the real world" (Sawyer, "Resurrecting Eve?" 274, 288; paragraphing altered).

than the speaker intended, and thereby encouraging his audience to question the believer's integrity and God's reality. Adam and Eve did not experience mortal death the instant they ate the fruit from the tree of knowledge; but after living in a fallen world where they had a probationary time to learn, repent, and grow outside God's presence (called spiritual death), they did die physically (Alma 12:21–26). God is Truth—always (John 1:17; Ether 3:12; D&C 93:36).

How long this conversation lasted between Satan and Eve or how often it occurred before Eve acted is not known. The text simply states that Eve now saw the tree of knowledge "was good . . . and it became pleasant . . . and . . . to be desired" (Moses 4:12). The italicized word in the Genesis account, "it *was* pleasant," communicates the translators' suggestion for clarity. In the book of Moses, however, the verse reads "it *became* pleasant," an equally valid proposition in the Hebrew, which implies the notion that Eve evolved in her realization that the tree was good. By placing the tree of knowledge in the center of the Garden with the warning "Thou shalt not eat of it, nevertheless, thou mayest choose for thyself, for it is given unto thee" (Moses 3:17; 4:9), God created an environment in which Adam and Eve were free to discover the only way they and their posterity could access the power of Christ's Atonement and thereby reach their divine potential.

So Eve willingly ate from the tree. Exercising her budding agency, she acted, "[seeing] that the tree was good" (Genesis 3:6; Moses 4:12). She also offered the fruit to her husband, who likewise accepted it (Genesis 3:6; Moses 4:12). Adam and Eve's choice to pursue the course of the fallen world enabled God's plan for all of His children to proceed (2 Nephi 2:25). Nowhere in scripture did God punish Adam and Eve's decision to leave the Garden. Moreover, He did not require them to repent after partaking of the tree of knowledge but, rather, announced, "Behold I have forgiven thee thy transgression in the Garden of Eden" (Moses 6:53).

COVERING THEIR NAKEDNESS

After choosing to eat from the tree of knowledge, Adam and Eve began to perceive what they had previously not been able to comprehend. The first new truth they recognized was that their bodies were not covered. *Nakedness* suggests being unclothed, unprotected, ashamed, and ill-equipped to succeed. Even more than what they saw in the present, the book of Moses relates that "they knew that they *had been* naked" (4:13; emphasis added), suggesting that they finally realized they had always been in a vulnerable condition. Only after eating the fruit from the tree of knowledge could they acknowledge their need for a covering. In truth, Christ's perfect love is the only complete covering. The Hebrew word for "atonement" (*kaphar*) literally means "to cover" or "a covering." The imagery evoked of the Savior's sacrifice being symbolized by a covering indicates what could have been the first blessing of the Fall: awareness of the absolute need for a Redeemer.

Adam and Eve's initial reaction to their exposed and helpless state was to use their own ingenuity to resolve their deficiency by making themselves a covering. When they heard God's voice, however, they seemed to know instinctively that the aprons of fig leaves were not sufficient covering; they tried to find additional cover by "hid[ing] themselves from the presence of the Lord God amongst the trees of the garden" (Moses 4:14).

Their self-confident response to their helplessness may also apply to us. How often do we try to save ourselves through our own ingenious means, only to discover that our best ideas and efforts are pitifully inadequate? Among our greatest discoveries is the personal realization that we need Jesus Christ as more than a Friend, Teacher, or Confidant. We need Him as our Savior and Redeemer—always.

Not surprisingly, the Lord God did not send Adam and Eve out of the Garden uncovered. He provided them clothing made from animal skins, a covering that requires the sacrifice of life (Genesis 3:21; Moses 4:27). Truly a life was sacrificed to provide the only sufficient covering for Adam and Eve. Being clothed in such a reminder of the Sacrifice of the Only Begotten, literally encircled in the love of God, Adam and Eve were blessed with the knowledge that they alone could not protect themselves in their vulnerable condition in a fallen world. They would need to live by faith in the Redeemer. Whether in the days when Christ lived in mortality, in the centuries since His resurrection, or in the Old Testament era extending back to Eve and Adam,

As Adam and Eve departed from the garden, the Lord provided them with a covering made from an animal skin (Moses 4:27).

Artwork by Joseph Brickey

the Savior's Atonement and His gospel are time-less and efficacious for all. Furthermore, because both Adam and Eve were covered by the Lord's enabling power, all men and all women can be similarly clothed by His infinite grace.

What happened to the garment in which the Lord covered Adam and Eve? No further specific mention of it is made in scripture, but many curious parallels emerge. Noah's sons recognized the seriousness of their father being uncovered on one occasion (Genesis 9:20–23). Joseph was given a coat that his brothers envied (Genesis 37:3–4). Elijah and John the Baptist also wore animal skins

Adam and Eve "sewed fig leaves together, and made themselves aprons" (Genesis 3:7).

(2 Kings 2:8; Matthew 3:4). If the garment indeed represented authority and divine protection, as indicated in the Nag Hammadi texts (Robinson, *Nag Hammadi Library, Gospel of Philip,* 57; Mead, *Pistis Sophia* 1:9–10), knowledge of it would have understandably compelled others to secure it for themselves.

Reporting that the garment contained powerful properties that made the bearer invincible, Jewish Midrashim include tales of Adam passing the garment to Enoch, who bequeathed it to Methuselah, who in turn gave it to Noah. According to these Jewish traditions, Ham stole the same garment from his father and passed it down to his descendants. The various traditions do not agree on what happened to the garment after Nimrod possessed it; one legend suggests it was recovered by Shem or Melchizedek, who gave it to Abraham (Ginzberg, *Legends,* 1:177, 332; see also Tvedtnes, "Priestly Clothing"; Ricks, "Garment").

Did God's prophets wear similar garments as a symbol of their discipleship? The Bible contains clues to suggest that they did. In Old Testament times, a true prophet cautioned that evil men were wearing "a rough garment to deceive" (Zechariah 13:4). During His mortal ministry, Christ also warned "of false prophets, which come to you in sheep's clothing, but inwardly they are ravening wolves" (Matthew 7:15). Do some or all of these passages refer to the covering given to Adam and Eve as they left the Garden? At the very least, they can each remind us that nothing but the Atonement of Jesus Christ can truly cover us.

CURSES AND BLESSINGS

The consequences that God pronounced after Adam and Eve's transgression underscore our knowledge that He had always intended them to leave the Garden. Everything He does is "for the benefit of the world" (2 Nephi 26:24). A careful reading of the text shows that two things were cursed, and neither one was Adam or Eve. God cursed the serpent and the ground—and He specifically cursed the ground "for [Adam's] sake" (Genesis 3:14, 17; Moses 4:20, 23).

In contrast to His cursing the ground and the serpent, God strengthened and empowered Adam and Eve. Because of their transgression in the Garden, Eve and Adam received from God opportunities for growth, not punishments. God bestowed a blessing of natural aversion, or "enmity," between Satan and the woman and between Satan and "her seed" (Genesis 3:15; Moses 4:21). Instinctively, the woman and her seed would be warned of evil. Discerning evil is a divinely bestowed blessing on all of Eve's children but is even more poignant when first applied to Jesus Christ, the only child born to a mortal woman rather than to a mortal man and woman. Only the Son of Mary had the wisdom and power to crush Satan's work of evil and then to rescue us. The apostle Paul explained that because of the Savior's grace and victory over sin and death, the "God of peace shall bruise Satan under your feet" (Romans 16:20). Adam and Eve, and their children through all subsequent generations, are blessed by the Seed of the woman as a result of the Fall.

God further rewarded Adam and Eve with recurring difficulties, hard work, and a strengthened partnership in the future. Appreciating the Hebrew meaning for words in God's response to Eve reinforces our understanding of His intent to bless her. He told her that He would "greatly multiply thy sorrow" (Genesis 3:16; Moses 4:22). The Hebrew word translated "sorrow" does not imply feeling sorry over something; it means pain or hurt. Furthermore, "multiply" in this passage means repetition or something happening over and over again, not something being added to or increased. Therefore, God promised Eve that life in the fallen world would require her to do painful things over and over again. He also told her, "I will greatly multiply . . . thy conception. In sorrow thou shalt bring forth children" (Genesis 3:16; Moses 4:22), meaning that she would repeatedly experience pain associated with bearing and rearing each of her children.

As a type of Christ, Eve was a "help" (*'ezer*) and magnified the supernal gift of life, provided only through the grace and merits of Jesus Christ, when she and her daughters gave mortal life to all of God's children who come to earth. Professor Parry observed that it was not until after Adam and Eve were expelled from Eden that Eve's role of life giver was intensified *because* they were cut off from the life-giving

THE VALUE OF WORK

"I believe in the gospel of work. Work is the miracle by which talent is brought to the surface and dreams become reality. There is simply no substitute under the heavens for productive labor. It is the process by which idle visions become dynamic achievements. I suppose that we are all inherently lazy. We would rather play than work. We would rather loaf than work. A little play and a little loafing are good. But it is work that spells the difference in the life of a man or a woman or a boy or a girl. Children who are taught to work and to enjoy the fruits of that labor have a great advantage as they grow toward maturity. The process of stretching our minds and utilizing the skills of our hands lifts us from the stagnation of mediocrity" (Hinckley, *Standing*, 80).

tree ("Eve's Role"). In other words, only when God removed access to the tree of life did Eve's important role as life-giver become apparent.

Adam was also obligated to work hard, "by the sweat of [his] face," to produce food from the thorn-infested ground. Adam *and* Eve would produce life with sweat, pain, and boundless joy. Neither would have an easier life than the other.

Most great inventions, literature, and other contributions in this world are born of working hard and surmounting difficulties. No satisfaction compares with achieving results after enduring challenging times. Childbirth, rearing children, and eking out nourishment from the barren ground require prolonged commitment and times of discomfort. The results, however, are often miraculous—with the repeated acknowledgment that growth is possible only with God.

God also blessed Eve that "thy desire shall be to thy husband, and he shall rule over thee" (Genesis 3:16; Moses 4:22). Although blessed with equal power (*kenegdo*), Adam and Eve complemented each other with their diversity. God gave each of them different gifts, challenges, and weaknesses (Ether 12:27). Such diversity reminded them that neither was enough alone. Just because some marriages since Adam and Eve's union have not reflected this interdependency does not mean that God's plan from the beginning is flawed. His teachings to our first parents underscore that man and woman need each other—and they need Him. His design is grounded in family and necessitated that Adam and Eve be united. By turning Eve's desires toward her husband, God fostered an interdependent companionship in which the woman needs the man as much as the man needs the woman. In addition, their resultant partnership created a healthy environment to sustain and support her multiple conceptions.

God's charge that Eve's husband shall "rule over her" elicits questions in a world plagued by unrighteous dominion. Selfish interpretations of this statement have allowed countless men over the centuries to justify debasing, humiliating, and abusing women. This consequence of partaking of the tree of knowledge may therefore say more about Adam's responsibility than any intended punishment for Eve. God assigned high standards for Adam and his sons in their responsibility to lead. President Gordon B. Hinckley interpreted the word *rule* to mean "that the husband shall have a governing responsibility to provide for, to protect, to strengthen and shield the wife" (*Ensign*, Nov. 1991, 99). With the wife's desires turned to strengthen and support her husband, and his desires focused on protecting and strengthening his wife, we see a formula for mutual approbation and progression. Furthermore, Professor Parry has suggested that the Hebrew preposition marked by the letter *bet* in the word translated "*over*" in the phrase "rule over" is often translated "*with*" in the Hebrew Bible ("Eve's Role"). Adam and Eve could rule together, in a partnership. Eve's unique role in that partnership was a help. This fact sets Eve apart from all others except God Himself.

AFTER THE GARDEN

Adam and Eve's equal yet complementary responsibilities are evident in their relationship and activities after their departure from the Garden. The book of Moses alone records these truths, providing us a glimpse of the partnership God inspired in our first parents.

Together Adam and Eve worked the soil (Moses 5:1), reared children (v. 2), prayed to God (v. 4), heard His response (v. 4), received His commandments concerning sacrifice (v. 5), and taught their children (v. 12). Never is it implied that Eve worked *for* her husband or *against* him or *around* him or *because* of him. But Eve "did labor *with* him" (v. 1; emphasis added). Both Adam and Eve expressed joy at the consequences of their choice to leave the Garden, notwithstanding the hardships. The scriptures do not show that either of them communicated even a whisper of regret. Eve felt what Adam felt; she knew what he knew. Neither blamed the other.

True to his God-given assignment to "rule," Adam's prophetic witness to his family reflected his role as provider and protector. He said, "Blessed be the name of God, for because of *my* transgression *my* eyes are opened, and in this life *I* shall have joy, and again in the flesh *I* shall see God" (Moses 5:10; emphasis added). Adam spoke of *his* transgression and *his* future joy, signifying that he acknowledged his leadership responsibility among the families of the earth.

According to the next scriptural verse, Eve "heard all these things and was glad," suggesting that she concurred with her husband's testimony (Moses 5:11). Still united with her husband, Eve also bore witness of their blessed state after leaving the Garden. She declared, "Were it not for *our* transgression *we* never should have had seed, and never should have known good and evil, and the joy of *our* redemption, and the eternal life which God giveth unto *all the obedient*" (v. 11; emphasis added). In contrast to

After leaving the Garden of Eden, Adam and Eve called upon the name of the Lord and offered the firstlings of their flocks in sacrifice (Moses 5:4–7).

Adam's speech in first-person singular, Eve spoke in first person plural, referring to *their* transgression, *their* children, and *their* redemption. Reflecting her divinely assigned desire to nurture, Eve spoke for her husband and children in her testimony. With an inclusive voice, she focused on the partnership between husband and wife and their joint responsibility to teach their children to love and obey their God.

EVE AS EXEMPLAR FOR ALL WOMEN

Far from cursing Adam and Eve, God blessed them to be equal and complementary partners for each other. Each was initiated into mortality as an individual creation with an independent voice and a divine purpose to unite with each other and with God.

Elder Bruce R. McConkie wrote, "The Lord never sends apostles and prophets and righteous men to minister to his people without placing women of like spiritual stature at their sides." Our first parents provided the pattern of partnership between husband and wife that happy and effective marriages in the future would follow. Elder McConkie continued, "Adam stands . . . to rule as a natural patriarch over all men of all ages, but he cannot rule alone; Eve, his wife, rules at his side, having like caliber and attainments to his own." Elder McConkie observed that "in all dispensations and at all times when there are holy men there are also holy women. Neither stands alone before the Lord. The exaltation of the one is dependent upon that of the other" (*Commentary,* 3:302). An acceptance and appreciation for the mutual dependence that God designed to exist between man and woman is one of the most important purposes of the scriptural record. Adam and Eve's example from the beginning ranks as a hallmark of marital partnership.

Clothed in Christ's enabling power and obedient to His will, "our glorious Mother Eve" gave direction and purpose to all of "her faithful daughters" (D&C 138:39). In their unique way, in their own time, and amid their own challenges, other women whose stories are related in scripture show that the principles learned from Eve are timeless and just as essential today as in the beginning.

POINTS TO PONDER: APPLICATIONS FOR OUR LIVES

1. Consider Satan's insinuation that God is selfish and distrustful because He did not allow Adam and Eve to eat from *every* tree without consequences. In what ways do you see Satan still trying to tempt us to judge God as unloving when He gives us restrictions?

2. How has doing something that is hard been a blessing to you? Why would you choose to pursue a challenging school schedule when you could graduate with easy courses? After experiencing the pains of childbirth, why choose to have another child? What blessings come from forgiving someone who has seriously offended you? What do we learn from experiencing pain that we cannot learn if we avoid hard work?

3. How does your perception of Eve influence your view of women in general? How can it shape your hopes for your own potential?

4. What insights into successful marriages do you recognize by considering the meanings of "help meet" and the patriarchal order?

5. In your personal scripture study, look for other passages of scripture that imply a "covering" in ways that could symbolize Christ's Atonement. For example, apply the concept to the Savior's plea, "How often would I have gathered thy children together, even as a hen gathereth her chickens under her wings" (Matthew 23:37; see also 3 Nephi 10:4–6; D&C 10:65).

6. Considering Eve's God-given covering, how can righteous women and their families be spiritually clothed today? (see Proverbs 31:21–25).

WIVES OF THE PATRIARCHS

Chronicled in the book of Genesis, the era of the patriarchs extended from the time of Adam and Eve through multiple generations to the twelve sons of Jacob (Israel). After the account of the Fall, the scriptural narrative quickly delineates several generations of patriarchs before it slows down with the introduction of Abraham and Sarah and the covenant God made with them and their righteous posterity.

Within these concluding generations of the patriarchal era is perhaps the most extensive portrayal of individual women in scripture. The wives of the patriarchs—namely Sarah, Rebekah, Leah, Rachel, and, to a lesser degree, Joseph's wife, Asenath—are often given center stage in the Genesis account and favorably remembered in New Testament writings. The narratives are particularly conversant in showing the humanness manifest by the patriarchs and their wives. Each is portrayed as possessing strengths and shortcomings; each requires a Savior.

FATHER ABRAHAM'S FAMILY TREE

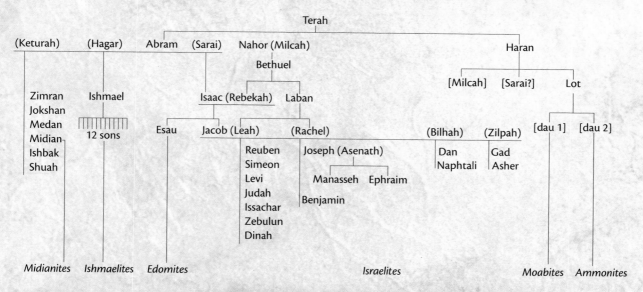

WHEN WAS THE PATRIARCHAL ERA?

Although more scriptural data accompany the four generations from Abraham to Joseph than most other biblical personalities, none of the patriarchs' lives was written as a full biography. Their stories and those of their families were clearly more complex than existing records portray.

Several challenges prevent assigning even approximate dates to the patriarchal era. No archaeological artifact makes reference to any of the Hebrew patriarchs or specific events chronicled in the biblical narrative. Similarly, accounts of the early patriarchs are retold without connecting them to recognizable individuals in the greater civilization, making it difficult to specify which of the surrounding rulers were contemporary with Abraham's clan. Without much mention of historically contiguous events and individuals, it is easy to incorrectly assume that anyone living in the larger region would have been keenly aware of the patriarchs. Moreover, we can develop an inaccurate picture that the patriarchs and their families alone occupied the greater Canaan area. More likely, the remarkable events chronicled in Genesis, and the patriarchs who participated in them, would have been largely unnoticed and unknown by their numerous neighbors.

Numerous findings, however, facilitate insight into the world of the patriarchs. Although no outside sources prove that the patriarchs and their wives actually lived, no extrabiblical text or artifact has

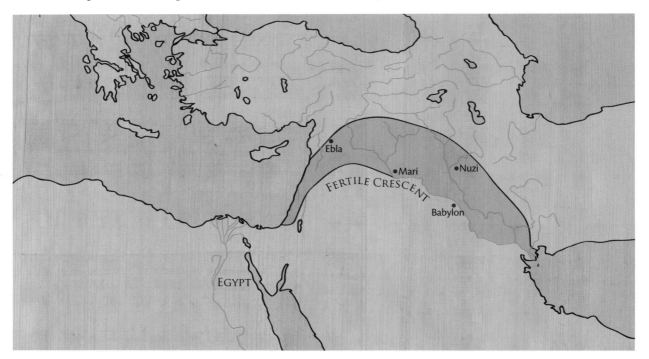

Texts dating from the Middle Bronze Age of peoples living in the same general geographical area as Sarah and Abraham have been discovered. These texts offer clues to the customs and laws followed by the patriarchs and their wives.

been found to nullify their reality. Descriptions of ancient peoples whose civilizations were akin to those of the patriarchs can therefore be meaningful.

Texts that date from the Middle Bronze Age (ca. 2100–1550 B.C.) in the general geographical area associated with the patriarchs reflect the strongest likeness to the biblical world. The Mari texts from the Euphrates River region (1700 B.C.); the Hammurabi Law Code from Babylonia (1700 B.C.); Ebla tablets from northern Syria (3000 B.C.); the Execration texts from Egypt's Middle Kingdom (2000–1700 B.C.); the *Story of Sinuhe* (popular Egyptian literature that was copied and circulated for a thousand years is set in the Middle Bronze Age); and the Nuzi texts of the Hurrians from the upper Fertile Crescent (1400 B.C.) are particularly noted for reporting laws, politics, customs, locations, and circumstances that parallel or echo parts of the patriarchal narratives. Considering archaeological and literary evidences of change in the area's social and legal environment by the Late Bronze (1550–1200 B.C.) and Early Iron (1200–1000 B.C.) Ages, the patriarchal narratives most authentically fit the Middle Bronze Age.

The law of Moses, reported in the books of Exodus, Leviticus, Numbers, and Deuteronomy, is not included as a meaningful source to explain customs and laws of the patriarchal era because it was delivered to the Israelites *after* the Middle Bronze Age. Pronounced upon descendants of the patriarchs who were recently released from Egyptian bondage, the law of Moses was far more dogmatic and unequivocal than the cultural mores of the patriarchs. In fact, the patriarchs and their wives practiced customs that were strictly forbidden under the Mosaic law, again indicating that the law was incongruent with the patriarchal era. For example, Abraham married his half-sister (Genesis 20:12), which was prohibited in Leviticus 18:9, 11 (see also Deuteronomy 27:22). Jacob was married to

Artwork by Ashton Young

Wedge-shaped writing in clay made by using the triangular cross-section of a reed is known as cuneiform. This form of writing was adopted from the ancient Sumerians by several later peoples, such as the Akkadians, the Hurrians, and the Elamites.

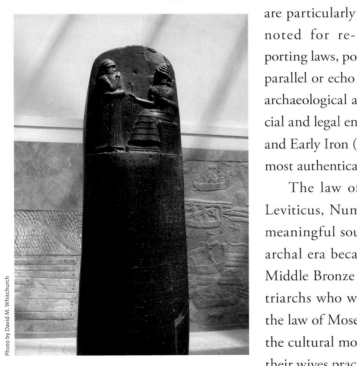

Photo by David M. Whitchurch

The stele of Hammurabi, inscribed with his Law Code, which consisted of 282 laws from the reign of the Babylonian king in the seventeenth century B.C. The scene at the top of the stele depicts Hammurabi worshipping the sun god Shamash.

two sisters at the same time (Genesis 29:21–28), in opposition to Leviticus 18:18. And finally, Jacob chose Joseph, his eleventh son but the firstborn of his beloved wife Rachel, as the birthright son (Genesis 37:3; 48:21–22), a practice later forbidden under the law of Moses (Deuteronomy 21:15–16).

THE INHABITANTS OF THE WORLD OF THE PATRIARCHS

A variety of peoples, collectively called Semites (a name derived from Noah's son Shem), populated land between Mesopotamia and Egypt during the first half of the second millennium before Christ. Later known as Assyrians, Babylonians, Hebrews, and others, Semites in the Middle Bronze Age spoke Akkadian, a Semitic language written in the cuneiform syllabic script borrowed from the Sumerians. The dynamics and configuration of these tribal societies reflect the world of the patriarchs.

Among their numbers were urban settlers who lived in multiple small and large city-states that dotted the area. Inhabitants of these city-states were under the power and protection of city lords, or kings. Damascus, Sodom, Hebron, and Jerusalem (literally, "city of Salem") are a few examples of these early urban centers.

Other inhabitants of the land elected to trade in shuttling necessities and luxuries back and forth between Mesopotamia and Egypt. Where no centralized government yet existed in Canaan, these traders were either independent entrepreneurs or agents for one of the city lords. The absence of conquering empires also facilitated peaceful travel and free trade in all directions. Trade routes were well-known and included settlements approximately every seventeen miles or so along the route. The patriarchs resided near many of these caravan stations. Haran ("caravan station"), Shechem, Bethel, Hebron, and Beersheba were each located along a major trade route.

A relatively small number of people resisted inclusion with any of the various groups living at large in the land. Best described as outlaws and bandits, these individuals picked off the flocks, crops, and goods of others to survive.

More of the population, however, was composed of independent seminomadic pastoralists who roamed less populated areas in the central hill country of Canaan down to the Negev, pasturing their flocks and settling long enough to farm the land. The biblical patriarchs and their large clans appear most closely akin to these seminomadic populations. Consulted on all family matters, the father or patriarch of the clan was its leader or chieftain. He identified the clan's new territory, controlled grazing rights and access to water, and determined the length of their stay.

In addition to sizable herds of sheep and goats, these family clans included numerous lifelong servants and retainers for short-term work. At one time Abraham is reported to have owned 318 servants available to join him in battle (Genesis 14:14), suggesting a community as large as two thousand people. Jacob's clan contained merely seventy men at one time, indicating a much smaller community (Genesis 46:27). The Beni Hasan tomb painting, from the nineteenth-century before Christ, is thought to depict a seminomadic clan being led by a patriarchal chieftain as they traveled from Canaan to Egypt.

Artwork by Ashton Young

BENI HASAN PAINTING

This is a reproduction of a detail from the Beni Hasan painting, from a nineteenth-century B.C. tomb of an Egyptian nobleman. It depicts a group of thirty-seven people from the land of Canaan entering Egypt to trade or resettle there. In contrast to the clean-shaven Egyptians in solid white skirts, the foreigners wore multicolored tunics or skirts (probably made of wool), which are longer on the women than on the men. The men all have a full head of hair and are bearded. Most are wearing sandals. The women's feet are covered with a type of slipper, and their long hair is adorned with headbands. The men carry a variety of weapons, donkeys are laden with tools and supplies, and the children are near the women. The actual figures are approximately eighteen inches in height.

For the most part, pastoral groups settled near major population areas, peacefully coexisting while retaining autonomy. They would also have frequently encountered other traveling groups. A family burial ground was likely a clan's only permanent land acquisition. Before passing through their grazing land, caravan leaders and other travelers negotiated with the clan leader for access to water and grazing. Jacob's gifts to Esau before being led through Esau's territory is a biblical example of such negotiations (Genesis 33).

THE PATRIARCHAL SOCIETY

Families within pastoral societies shared strong kinship ties and looked to the greater needs of the community rather than to individual pursuits. Marriage within the clan was preferred in order to maintain the family's integrity. The patriarch and matriarch of the clan were granted chief leadership status. Their children and grandchildren remained with them in one united community as long as the oldest common ancestor lived. The assumption was that every healthy young man and woman would marry.

The home, rather than a commercial center, was the hub of the community. Each family lived in tents clustered near all the other families' tents in the community. No physical evidence remains of these ancient tents because they were made of organic material, probably woven goat and/or camel hair, which eventually decomposed without a trace. These animal skin fabrics allowed pinpoints of light to show through the loose weave for interior illumination and ventilation. The fibers shrank to provide a waterproof covering when it rained. Family tents were divided by a sheet of tent cloth to form separate quarters for men and women. During moderate weather, the front wall of the tent could be extended and upheld by two additional poles to form an awning for a covered porch. The tent floor was covered with woolen or goat's-hair mats.

A woman who had wife status typically owned her own property, probably given to her by her parents when she married. Responsibility for protection of her inheritance then passed from her father to her husband. She often possessed a personal tent or private partition of a tent for her own quarters. Ancient marriage contracts, bills of sale, and court records indicate that frequently women also owned female slaves. The origin of the slavery that was clearly practiced in the patriarchal period is not known; however, it was an obvious departure from the ideal society taught by God and modeled by Adam and Eve when they left the Garden. Perhaps the custom began as a way to care for the poor and needy rather than any attempt to demean certain members of a community. Whatever the case, female slaves did not have the same rights and privileges as did free women who held wife status. Of more importance than individual rights in a patriarchal society was strengthening the entire household. No caste system or subordination of women resulted because every person was necessary in order for the community to survive and flourish.

Every member of the patriarchal community had responsibilities for the progress and welfare of the clan. Although distinct, the mother's authority and responsibility were not inferior to the husband's authority and duty. Women were responsible for the domestic sphere, especially the care and teaching of children and the preparation of food. Teaching daughters was especially important, because a daughter had to be prepared to leave her natal home and adjust to unfamiliar family customs and dynamics in her future

A PARALLEL ANCIENT STORY

The *Story of Sinuhe* reflects a patriarchal society similar to that of the Genesis narrative. This ancient literary treasure tells of a high-ranking Egyptian official named Sinuhe, who fled Egypt in fear for his life. As an isolated traveler, he was vulnerable but found safety in Canaan among a series of different pastoral clans. He eventually arrived in Retenu, an area of Syria, where he settled in the tents of a powerful chieftain with a Semitic name. There Sinuhe married the chieftain's daughter, farmed a portion of his wife's familial territory, and served his father-in-law as commander for the clan. He mentions an array of weaponry (bows and arrows, spears, battle-axes, daggers, javelins, and shields) in his encounters with plunder, captivity, attack, and banishment from pasture land and wells. Preparing to return to Egypt in his old age, Sinuhe turned his property over to his eldest son. He then traveled back to Egypt, where he died and was buried.

husband's home. Olives, goat cheese, figs, and lemons preserved in salt were staples in their diet. Coupled with food preparation was a woman's authority over the food resources, with the responsibility to appropriately ration the supply until the next food disbursement. Women were also likely to weave and to make pottery. Perhaps because they gleaned perspective from living in the household of their parents and later the household of their husbands, women were frequently the

Men, women, and children in patriarchal families cared for their animals.

mediators in settling family disputes, including defusing conflict over appointing an heir.

Men, women, and children were all responsible for the care of their animals. Men of the community assumed official roles in the community and responsibility in metallurgy and farming preparations, such as clearing the land, digging wells, building terraces, and plowing the land. Children were particularly valued in such societies. They were the promise of economic stability for the family's future and protective care for elderly parents.

RELIGION IN SEMINOMADIC CLANS

Religion in patriarchal societies was far simpler than the complex pantheon of gods and accompanying rituals observed by neighboring peoples from Mesopotamia to Egypt. In patriarchal communities, religious practices and beliefs were transmitted through family life rather than through a priest or other religious figure. Marriage and family were considered sacred and foundational in a person's relationship with God. Children were perceived as divine gifts, and parents were stewards for God in caring for them.

God was the unseen head of the family who taught, guided, rebuked, and provided. The patriarch, by proxy, was divinely directed to protect and provide for the clan. Each individual family member had direct access to God, without a need to go through the patriarch. For the most part, the father rather than a priest performed animal sacrifice.

One could argue that, as keepers of the home in this society, the chief wife of the patriarch enjoyed status and privilege as great as women have ever been afforded in the history of the world. God gave Abraham his name that means "father of many nations" and Sarah her name that means "princess" and called her a "mother of nations" (Genesis 17:16), underscoring both the family focus and the royal respect given chief women. Similarly, God covenanted that He would bless Abraham's *children* with the gospel and assigned Abraham's children the responsibility to take His gospel to all the *families* of the earth.

Is Anything Too Hard for the Lord?

SARAH AND HAGAR

שָׂרָה   הָגָר

"Princess," female "Ruler"   *"Flight," "Wanderer"*

Sarah and Hagar came from dramatically different backgrounds and divergent social classes. Yet they shared a moment in history that established God's covenant as a means to bless every family on the earth. Their names, complex story, and influence are therefore known throughout the world but not without a variety of interpretations and concerns.

The simple fact that two women seemingly in competition for the same blessings from opposing angles appear in the same story is enough to invite serious debate and unfair comparisons. A common argument contends that because Sarah and Hagar disagreed at times and were dissimilar in many ways, they were the complete opposite of each other. Therefore, the argument concludes, one of them was righteous and loved by God, whereas the other made bad choices and was spiritually rejected.

Because Hagar was an integral part of the family for less time than Sarah and bore a son who was not foreordained to be the covenant leader, the temptation is to paint her as the nemesis, the intruder, the foreigner to faith. The biblical text, however, does not allow such an interpretation. Hagar directly communed with God, received inspired directions, and was promised eternal blessings. Unquestionably, God loved Hagar and acknowledged her goodness. But so was Sarah loved, cherished, and commissioned by God for a great mission. And even though more column inches of scripture pertain to Sarah than to any other woman in the Bible, there are not enough verses to satisfy all our questions and concerns about her.

Furthermore, the Genesis narrative shows that the

> GENESIS 11:27–13:1; 16:1–23:20;
> 24:36, 67; 25:10–16; 49:31
> ISAIAH 51:2
> ROMANS 4:19; 9:9
> GALATIANS 4:21–31
> HEBREWS 11:11
> 1 PETER 3:6–7
> 2 NEPHI 8:2
> DOCTRINE & COVENANTS 132:34–37, 65
> ABRAHAM 2
> LDS BIBLE DICTIONARY, 698, 769

greatness and blessedness of the patriarchs and their wives was not due to their own intellect and power. As with each of us, neither Abraham nor Sarah nor Hagar was free from weakness and vulnerability. They experienced serious family conflict, separation, and disappointment; suffered from feelings of envy, isolation, and unfulfilled expectations; and repeatedly bore the weight of tests of their faith. None of them alone possessed what God required of them at the dawn of a new dispensation. They needed each other. But partnership was not all they required. Time and time again, the lives of Hagar, Sarah, and Abraham, individually and collectively, communicate the necessity for a Redeemer.

SARAI'S PREPARATION

After Sarai and Abram (as they were known before God gave them new names) married, they resided with Abram's father's clan in the city of Ur in the area known today as northwestern Syria. On account of famine, customs that encouraged the worship of foreign gods, and commandments from God, the clan moved a short distance east to Haran (Genesis 11:26–31). Located in Padan-aran, the area between the two rivers in northern Mesopotamia, Haran became the homeland for Abram's brother's family and the place where the next two generations of patriarchs found God-fearing wives.

But God had other plans for Sarai and Abram in a land where their newly created clan would be strangers. Subsequently, when Abram's father, Terah, returned to his practice of worshipping idols, God directed Abram, Sarai, their nephew Lot and his wife, and "the souls that [they] had won in Haran" to move again (Abraham 2:15). This time God directed them southward, to a land that He chose for their land of inheritance—the land of Canaan (Genesis 12:4–7).

A Midrash, or rabbinic tradition or legend, speaks of Abram devoting himself for two years in "turning the hearts of men to God and His teachings," suggesting one scenario for how they may have "won souls" in Haran. Sarai was equally involved in this missionary endeavor, according to the Jewish tradition. "While [Abram] exhorted the men and sought to convert them," the Midrash reads, "[Sarai] addressed herself to the women. She was a helpmeet worthy of Abraham. Indeed, in prophetical powers she ranked higher than her husband. She was sometimes called Iscah, 'the seer,' on that account" (Ginzberg, *Legends,* 1:203). God's ideal for partnership in marriage had survived from Eden to the patriarchal era.

The Hebrew term used in Genesis 11:28 to identify Abram's "land of nativity" is also used in Genesis 24:4 to indicate "my country," the area where Abram's servant was sent to find a wife for Isaac. Therefore, Abram's Ur was near Haran, which we know to be in northwestern Syria. Latter-day scripture also gives support for Syria as the location of Abram's Ur rather than the larger city-state named Ur in the Persian Gulf area (Abraham 1:10, 20). Furthermore, the area called "Chaldees" was not named such until several centuries after Abram's time, suggesting that "Ur of the Chaldees" in the patriarchal era is anachronistic and thus an editorial gloss to the biblical account (Hoskisson, "Chaldees?" 127–30; Lundquist, "Ebla?" 226–27).

Because of famine, the clan of Abram and Sarai continued their travels southward, briefly establishing settlements with their tents and livestock, until they eventually came to Egypt (Genesis 12:8–10).

For much of their lives, Sarah and Abraham and their clan lived a nomadic existence in the wilderness similar to that of these twentieth-century tent-dwelling Bedouin.

TIME LINE

Abram is born to Terah (ca. 2000 B.C.)

Sarai is born (Abram is 10)

Death of Abraham's brother Haran due to the famine in Ur; Abram and Sarai marry

Terah's clan moves to Haran (place)

Abram (75) and Sarai (65) move to Canaan

Abram and Sarai go to Egypt

Abram and Sarai return to Canaan, bringing Hagar

Hagar becomes a second wife to Abram (85)

Hagar gives birth to Ishmael (Abram is 86)

Abram pays tithes to Melchizedek

Names changed to Abraham and Sarah

God makes His covenant with Abraham (99) and Sarah (89)

Abraham and Ishmael (13) are circumcised

Sarah (90) gives birth to Isaac (Ishmael is 14)

Hagar and Ishmael (17) are sent away; God blesses them

Hagar finds Ishmael a wife from Egypt

God commands Abraham to sacrifice Isaac

Sarah dies (127) when Isaac is 37 years old

Isaac (40) marries Rebekah

Esau and Jacob are born to Isaac (60) and Rebekah

Abraham dies (175); Ishmael (89) and Isaac (75) bury him

SARAI IN EGYPT

Abram and Sarai arrived in Egypt some time during the Middle Kingdom period (ca. 2200–1700 B.C.), an era known for its enlightenment and prosperity. Due to unusually long reigns of the pharaohs of the Middle Kingdom, fewer rulers reigned, and the nation saw relative peace and generosity. Pharaohs and their officials manifested unusual concern and support for their subjects and freely traded with Canaan and Mesopotamia. Foreigners were welcomed to Egypt to experience a superior society and were invited to reside in the mainly undeveloped area of Goshen in the eastern delta of the Nile.

A curious dilemma, well attested in two books of scripture, occurred as Abram and Sarai approached Egypt. Abram asked Sarai to tell the Egyptians that she was his sister as a safeguard for his life (Genesis 12:11–20; Abraham 2:22–25). Apparently, protocol of the day would not allow a powerful ruler to take another man's wife, and so the death of the husband was required to free the woman to marry the king. For Sarai to be merely Abram's sister would not necessitate his death in order for the pharaoh to take Sarai into his household. A similar circumstance and response transpired after Abram and Sarai left Egypt to return to Canaan when Sarai and Abram told Abimelech, king of the city-state Gerar, that they were brother and sister. As in the case of Pharaoh, their claim coincided with Abimelech's desire to marry Sarai (Genesis 20:1–18). One difference emerges between the cases of these two men wanting Sarai: her beauty was a key explanation for Pharaoh's desire but is not mentioned at all in the case of Abimelech.

Abram's claim of sibling relationship with his wife appears duplicitous and cowardly. The book of Abraham contributes the important clarification that God commanded Abram to tell Sarai to present themselves as brother and sister rather than as husband and wife (Abraham 2:22–25). This single added insight changes the question from, Why did they hide their marriage from Pharaoh? to Why did God lead them into

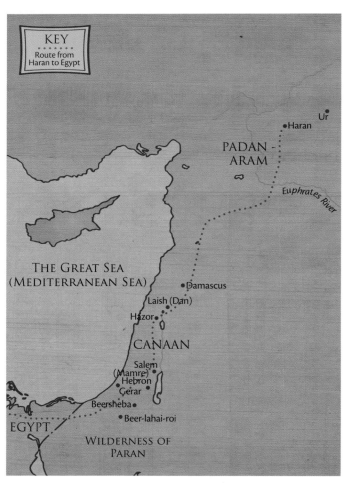

Sarah and Abraham made their home in various locations over their long lives, including a time in Egypt. The distance between Dan and Beersheba, Abraham's covenant land, is about 150 miles.

SHE IS MY SISTER

At two different times Abram and Sarai claimed to be brother and sister. A variety of sources indicate how they may have been closely related, indicating that their claim of kinship was valid.

From the Bible: "And yet [Sarah] is my sister; she is the daughter of my father, but not the daughter of my mother; and she became my wife" (Genesis 20:12).

From a Midrash: Rabbinic tradition identifies "Iscah" as Sarah in the following verse: "And Abram and Nahor took them wives: the name of Abram's wife was Sarai; and the name of Nahor's wife, Milcah, the daughter of Haran, the father of Milcah, and the father of Iscah" (Genesis 11:29; Ginzberg, *Legends,* 1:203).

From the Jewish historian Josephus: "Now Abraham had two brethren, Nahor and Haran; of these Haran left a son, Lot; as also Sarai and Milcha his daughters. . . . Nahor married Milcha, and Abram married Sarai" (Josephus, *Antiquities,* 1.6.5). If Haran died before Sarai and Abram married, Terah may have adopted Sarai, a common practice at the time.

From the Pearl of Great Price (editions before 1981): "And it came to pass that I, Abraham, took Sarai to wife, and Nahor, my brother, took Milcah to wife, who were the daughters of Haran" (Abraham 2:2).

From the Nuzi texts: These records of the Hurrians, a people who share numerous parallels with the patriarchal clans of Genesis, describe an augmented social status that was created by linking marriage to a legal recognition that the wife is also a sister to her husband. The designation may have been important to the husband as verification of the woman's lineage to guarantee a pure posterity. The long-standing Hurrian society in northern Syria surrounded the city of Haran, where most of the patriarchs and their wives resided for a time. A brother who gave his sister to another in marriage also gave her the legal status of sister-wife, reminiscent of the biblical story of Laban giving his sister, Rebekah, for Isaac to marry (Genesis 24:29–67). The legal standing of "sister-wife" had the highest social status for a woman in Hurrian society.

such a dilemma? Furthermore, Why did Pharaoh desire to marry Sarai? Certainly, Sarai was "a very fair woman to look upon" (Abraham 2:22), but we can't help remembering that Sarai is aging and that innumerable young, beautiful women surrounded Pharaoh in Egypt.

The scriptures do not contain answers to these questions, suggesting that either the author had forgotten or no longer understood the explanation, or that portions of his account are missing. Several possibilities, however, suggest a variety of viable explanations for the story.

GOD'S PURPOSE IN EGYPT

Perhaps God led Abram and Sarai into life-threatening situations because He wanted the learned Egyptians to hear the gospel preached to them. The book of Abraham relates lessons the Lord taught Abram when he gazed into the night sky—lessons in astronomy that led to doctrinal teachings about premortality and the Creation (Abraham 3–5). With this divine tutelage came the Lord's assignment to Abram: "I show these

The oldest of the great Egyptian pyramids, the Step Pyramid at Saqqara, was likely seen by Sarah and Abraham during their time in Egypt.

things unto thee before ye go into Egypt, that ye may declare all these words" (Abraham 3:15).

Echoing the book of Abraham, Josephus explained that Abram went to Egypt "to partake of the plenty [the Egyptians] enjoyed" because of the famine in Canaan but also to hear their priests' views concerning their gods and "to convert them into a better way, if his own notions proved the truest." As a result of Abram's superior reasoning with the learned Egyptians, Josephus continued, "he was admired by them . . . as a very wise man, . . . persuading other men also to assent to him. He communicated to them arithmetic, and delivered to them the science of astronomy" (*Antiquities,* 1.8.1–2).

The Lord's commission to "take the gospel to every nation" is well documented in the New Testament but is largely lost from the Old Testament. Sending Abram to preach the gospel to the Egyptians comfortably fits the Lord's pattern of missionary work for His people in other eras. Identifying this important role in Egypt for Abram, however, does not explain the purpose of Sarai's precarious and dangerous position.

SARAI'S ROLE

How Sarai created such desire in powerful leaders, particularly when she was no longer in her youth, is uncertain. Some have wondered whether Sarai was fairer in coloring than the Egyptians and Canaanites and thereby attracted attention for her beauty. Others have argued that her wealth and position made her attractive as a means to advance Pharaoh's or a city-king's political or commercial power. Still others refer to an ancient Near Eastern custom of cementing friendships between two peoples by trading women for that purpose. A further opinion states that as "sister" to Abram, Sarai may have presented a guarantee to Pharaoh and Abimelech that she would bear them a pious and favored posterity. On the other hand, political leaders may have recognized Abram's unusual power and glory and sought to access it through Sarai. Finally, the scriptural explanation may simply be the only reason—Sarai was very beautiful (Abraham 2:22–23). If additional characteristics made her attractive, no definitive answer is available.

More important than Pharaoh's desire to marry Sarai is the extent to which the unusual circumstance affected her. Recall that Sarai learned of God's command to say that she was Abram's sister not directly from God but from Abram, who reported it to her. Furthermore, Abram did not command Sarai but entreated her with a plea, allowing her to make her own decision. Granted, Sarai's choice to follow Pharaoh into his house apparently saved Abram's life and provided him opportunity to teach Egypt's scholars about God, but it left her vulnerable without any apparent promise or specified mission.

Paralleling Sarai's nightmare in Pharaoh's house is the story of three young women of royal birth, the daughters of Onitah, who refused to compromise their virtue and were consequently sacrificed on an altar to an Egyptian god (Abraham 1:11). Ancient Egyptian culture suggests that Sarai faced the same outcome if she refused Pharaoh's advances. Because the command to profess to be Abram's sister came neither from Sarai's understanding of morality nor from her husband's fears but from God, faith was her only support as she faced an unknown future, "not knowing beforehand the things which [she] should do" (1 Nephi 4:6).

Sarai's test ultimately reveals that no one could save her but God. As wise and articulate as her husband appeared before the Egyptians, he was powerless to save his wife. Sarai's test also underscores Sarai's great importance in God's eyes. No other woman could take her place. She had a unique mission to fulfill, albeit decades later. So God intervened in a dramatic and powerful way—and Sarai was saved. The biblical text suggests that God stopped Pharaoh in his advances to Sarai by afflicting him with a debilitating disease (Genesis 12:17). The *Genesis Apocryphon*, a Dead Sea text written in Aramaic, reports that Pharaoh suffered from the scourge for two years until finally he learned that his afflictions came because he had taken Sarai from her husband. Abram was summoned, berated for not telling the truth about Sarai, and was asked to heal Pharaoh. The *Genesis Apocryphon* account, written in Abram's voice, reads, "So I prayed [for him] . . . and I laid my hands on his [head]; and the scourge departed from him and the evil [spirit] was expelled [from him], and he lived" (1QapGen, 20). Latter-day Saint scholar Hugh Nibley suggested that God might have saved Sarai by sending a rescuing angel, as He had earlier saved Abram and would later save Isaac when each was presented as a sacrifice on an altar (Nibley *Old Testament*, 99).

Although Sarai's faith matched that of Onitah's daughters, Sarai was rescued and Onitah's daughters

A SELFLESS PARTNERSHIP

"It was . . . a pharaoh who sought the hand of Sarah, the true princess, in order to raise up a royal progeny by her. Upon a royal bed identical in form with the altar of Abraham, she too prayed for deliverance and was rescued by an angel while the king was constrained to recognize Sarah's true marriage and heritage, bestowing upon her regal insignia and a royal escort. At God's command, Abraham humbled himself to ask Sarah as a favor to declare herself to be his sister, eligible to marry another and thus save his life. This is only part of the deference that Abraham had to make to his wife, and it left no place for his male pride. Sarah, on the other hand, with equal humility, went to Abraham confessing God's hand in her childlessness and actually begging him to have children by another woman. Can one imagine a greater test of her pride? When both sides of the equation are reduced, the remainder on both sides is only a great love" (Nibley, *Old Testament*, 99).

God Liveth and Seeth Me (Hagar)

were sacrificed. Similar dramatic discrepancies in outcomes among believers occur today. Faith in Christ is therefore intertwined with patience and an eternal timetable rather than tangible proofs in the immediate present. Sarai's test of faith included a specific outcome in preparation for her unique mission, just as our mortal tests and outcomes prepare us for ours.

SARAI AND HAGAR

Abram and Sarai returned to Canaan from Egypt wealthier than when they had left (Genesis 13:2). In addition to cattle, gold, and silver, Pharaoh is thought to have given Sarai a personal maid named Hagar. A Midrash claims that Hagar was Pharaoh's daughter and royalty in her own right, "for he preferred to see his daughter the servant of Sarah to reigning as mistress in another harem" (Ginzberg, *Legends,* 1:223). It seems more likely that Hagar was either an Egyptian child sold by her parents into slavery or a slave born to other Egyptian slaves within Abram and Sarai's household.

After Sarai had endured years of infertility, the catalyst that sparked her decision to inaugurate an alternative plan for a child is not given (Genesis 16:1–4). The Nuzi texts include a law that considered a similar dilemma and the required solution. This Hurrian law stated that should a woman not bear a child, she was required to provide her husband a concubine. The wife was to retain authority over the concubine's child. Since the Hurrian and patriarchal societies shared many similarities, Abram and Sarai may have been influenced by a common law.

The decision for Abram to marry an additional wife, however, may not have been theirs alone to make. Extrabiblical sources support the idea that Sarai and Abram acted in obedience to God in this matter. The Jewish historian Josephus indicated that "Sarai, at God's command, brought to [Abram's] bed one of her handmaidens, a woman of Egyptian descent, in order to obtain children by her" (*Antiquities,* 1.10.4).

A Midrash describes Sarai as Hagar's spiritual teacher in preparing her for marriage to Abram. It reads: "Taught and bred by Sarah, [Hagar] walked in the same path of righteousness as her mistress, and thus was a suitable companion for Abraham, and, instructed by the holy spirit, he acceded to Sarah's proposal" (Ginzberg, *Legends,* 1:237). Finally, through revelation given to Joseph Smith, we learn from the Lord that "[Sarah] administered unto Abraham according to the law when I commanded Abraham to take Hagar to wife" (D&C 132:65). Knowing that God willed Hagar to be included in this marriage trio and that she must have therefore believed in Abram's God directs us to consider her with equal acceptance.

In scriptural text, Hagar is referred to as a "concubine" (Genesis 25:6; D&C 132:37). With none of the immoral overtones inherent in the label today, a concubine in the ancient Near East was a legal wife who was elevated from servant status by her marriage. Her increased status did not, however, equal that of the chief wife, who was always a free woman. Although a legitimate wife to her husband, a concubine remained a servant to her mistress, who could discipline or sell her at will. Receiving free status and giving birth

The traditional site of Abraham's well in biblical Beersheba illustrates an element of life for the families of the patriarchs.

often added confusion to her status in the family and threatened to reverse her importance with that of the chief wife. The ancient Babylonian law, the Code of Hammurabi, rescinded freedom and status should a concubine assume equality with her mistress. The regulation reads, "If a man take a wife and she give this man a maid-servant as wife and she bear him children, and then this maid assume equality with the wife: because she has borne him children her master shall not sell her for money, but he may keep her as a slave, reckoning her among the maid-servants" (no. 146). The ancient Babylonian custom parallels the dynamics between Sarai and Hagar when Hagar knew she had conceived a child (Genesis 16:4–6). Sarai's remorse after Hagar became pregnant may have been out of fear that Hagar would supplant her as chief wife. Likewise, Hagar's "despising" of Sarai suggests that Sarai's importance and status had diminished in Hagar's eyes. The distinction between authority and possession was beginning to blur.

Although Hagar did not receive the high calling in the covenant that Sarai was given, Hagar's importance to God and that of her unborn son are attested in the Genesis narrative. An angel of the Lord found Hagar where she had fled into the wilderness and instructed her to return and submit—not to her husband—but to Sarai, her mistress (Genesis 16:7–9). God required Hagar to voluntarily return and confront the source of her pain rather than run from it. Often God gives us answers to our problems not by eliminating the problem but by giving us strength to face them. As Eve also learned, God blesses us with greater wisdom and endurance when we accept His invitation to do what is difficult. Hagar chose to follow that invitation, and as a result she and her son were blessed by the covenant and her own personal promise from God (Genesis 16:10–11).

A longstanding tradition locates the place of God's communication with Hagar at a fountain or well about fifty miles south of Beersheba. Reminiscent of Hagar's awe that God saw her in her afflictions and her reverence for God's prophetic message, the well was called *Beer-lahai-roi* (Genesis 16:14), meaning "the well of the Loving One who sees." As a reflection of the miracle Hagar experienced at the site, the angel announced that her son would be named Ishmael, which means "God hears" (Genesis 16:11). Isaac and Rebekah established their home near the well Lahai-roi (Genesis 25:11), suggesting that the area remained important to later patriarchs. For the well to retain its name throughout subsequent generations indicates that God's concern for Hagar was not forgotten.

THE COVENANT

God's covenant with Abram was the constant that sustained the patriarchs and their families during a series of challenges and uncertainties throughout their lives. At first glance, the covenant promised the patriarch of a seminomadic community that which he would most desire—land and posterity. Upon further consideration, however, we see that Abram and Sarai's journey to the promised land was more than a search for an earthly homeland; it was a spiritual quest that led them to God's greatest gifts and power.

Establishing the covenant with Abram and Sarai commenced with their receiving a new identity, which is symbolized in changed names. Abram became known as Abraham, and Sarai was called Sarah (Genesis 17:5, 15). The significance of these new names was not so much in changed meaning but in the fact that God assigned them. Under the covenant, "father" Abraham and "princess" Sarah accepted a new responsibility and relationship with God, the definitive Father and King.

Covering countless generations, Abram and Sarai's sons and daughters would become God's people, according to the covenant, by taking the gospel to every nation and extending the blessings of eternal life to every family (Abraham 2:9–11). Isaiah invited all Israel, past and present, to look to Abraham and Sarah as the rock of the covenant (Isaiah 51:1–2). Beginning with an individual (Abraham), the covenant expanded to his wife (Sarah), then to his family (Isaac), then to a people (house of Israel), and from them to the entire world.

Every patriarchal blessing includes validation that the recipient is a son or daughter of Abraham, either literally or by adoption. Our responsibility to stand as a witness for God and the potential for eternal life likewise accompany that great lineage. Missionaries going two by two to the nations of the world, faithful Church members striving to lead others to Christ by their walk and talk, officiators and patrons of temple service are among those who carry on the great work of the Abrahamic covenant.

As an outward symbol and a personal reminder of their promise to God, Abraham and all the men in his community were circumcised (Genesis 17:23–27). In Hebrew, one "cuts a covenant," rather than "makes a covenant," which also explains at least in part why Abraham received this promise from God by cutting sacrificed animals in half (Genesis 15:9–10; Jeremiah 34:18). Similarly, a custom of the Mari society, an ancient people who lived near the Euphrates River during the patriarchal era, was to cut an animal into pieces to signify the consequence should a covenant member become unfaithful in his promise (Falk, *Hebrew Law,* 26).

Further evidence suggests that the covenant extended beyond the direct lineage of Abraham and Sarah. Abraham would marry yet another woman, Keturah, presumably after Sarah's death. Six sons blessed that marriage, including one named Midian (Genesis 25:1–2). Generations later Moses married

Zipporah, a daughter of Jethro, a descendant of Midian. Through revelation, Joseph Smith learned that Moses received the higher priesthood from his father-in-law (D&C 84:6). Additionally, we remember that thirteen-year-old Ishmael was circumcised with his father (Genesis 17:23–26). Even though Hagar's and Keturah's sons would not have the authority and leadership among the covenant people that Sarah's son would be given, these other sons of Abraham had access to the blessings of the covenant and the power of the priesthood, the same as Isaac.

ANNUNCIATION AND BIRTH OF ISAAC

When three holy men entered his community, Abraham followed the customs of hospitality in providing guests with refreshment and a place to rest (Genesis 18:1–5). The obligation of preparing food did not rest solely on Sarah. She made the bread while Abraham cooked the meat and prepared side dishes (Genesis 18:6–8).

Similar hospitality customs, including the types of foods served, were long practiced in the Middle East among Bedouin peoples. During the late nineteenth century, a British scholar was hosted by some Bedouin tribes. Her description of the food preparation is meaningful in visualizing the manner of Abraham and Sarah's cooking. "[The Bedouins] had dug two broad, shallow pits in the ground, in which they had made fires of wood and thorns. In one a lamb was being baked whole, and over the other a cauldron of rice was boiling." Sarah, who was expected to make bread quickly (Genesis 18:6), likely used a method that continued to be practiced by the Bedouin well into the twentieth century. The same British scholar observed: "A brisk wood-fire was kindled in the open air, on a small circular hearth, formed of smooth round pebbles, spread evenly and close together. When this primitive hearth was sufficiently heated, the embers were carefully removed, and the well-kneaded paste, flattened out by the hand, was thrown on to the hot stones, and quickly covered with the burning ashes. In this way several large cakes of unleavened bread were soon made ready. . . . They were about half an inch in thickness, and had received the impression of the pebbles of which the hearth was composed." The full Bedouin dinner consisted of lamb served on a large metal tray; "mountains of rice, yellow with butter"; wooden bowls

Artwork by Ashton Young

The most primitive manner of cooking bread was on hot stones over a fire, as this woman is doing.

filled with sweet clotted cream, new milk, or a yogurt substance; and flat cakes of bread served hot (Rogers, *Domestic Life,* 203, 220).

Abraham entertained the guests while Sarah remained in her tent, but she was fully aware of what they discussed. The message they delivered had everything to do with her and was probably spoken for the primary purpose of informing her, because Abraham had already heard it through revelation (Genesis 17:15–17). From inside the tent, hearing the messengers tell Abraham that she would bear a son, Sarah laughed (Genesis 18:9–12).

Everyone else involved seemed to react to the news in much the same way—at first with almost a fearful disbelief and then with the doubt quickly changing to pure glee. Anyone who has long sought fulfillment of a righteous desire, daily praying and at times pleading with God to grant a miracle, can relate to Sarah's waiting a lifetime for a child. The most feasible time to be granted the promised desire passes and no scenario that even approximates the dream can be imagined. Then, at the least probable time, when every circumstance underscores that fulfillment is impossible, the Spirit whispers that God has kept His promise and will now bestow the blessing. The first emotion is typically a combination of fear and doubt. Nothing in our rational world can explain it. Then the boundless joy sets in, with the realization that the promised blessing is all the sweeter for the wait and much grander even than imagined. God may not answer when we claim we need Him, but He is always on time.

The biblical text is delightful in this regard. When God revealed to Abraham that Sarah would bear a son in her old age, Abraham "laughed" (Genesis 17:17). When Sarah overheard the three holy men tell Abraham that she would yet bear a child, she likewise "laughed" (Genesis 18:12–15). Wanting everyone to join the rejoicing at this miracle, Abraham and Sarah chose to call their son *Isaac,* a name derived from the same Hebrew root meaning "laugh" and "laughter" (Genesis 21:3–6). This Hebrew word reflects a harmony of rich emotions—including *smile, jest, sport,* and *play*—sparked by an unexpected, unbelievable, and yet pleasant turn of events. The Joseph Smith Translation renders the word simply as *rejoice* (JST Genesis 21:5; KJV Genesis 17:17).

That the Lord responded to Sarah's laugh and ignored Abraham's identical response to the news may be further evidence of Sarah's importance to God's covenant. On numerous occasions throughout Sarah's life, God taught her that she was preserved and prepared for a unique calling. With the announcement that the fulfillment of her promise of motherhood was imminent, Sarah needed to acknowledge that truth and again reach for God's unparalleled assistance.

Whatever fear or doubt Sarah experienced when she first heard the news was short-lived. Her ability to conceive, bear a child, and nurse that babe is not a reflection of Sarah's physical strength or perpetual agelessness. She was enabled beyond her natural ability only through the grace of Jesus Christ. Commending Sarah, the apostle Paul avowed that the miracle of the ninety-year-old matriarch giving birth is explainable only through her tremendous faith in the Savior (Hebrews 11:11).

EQUAL LOVE

President Howard W. Hunter, as a member of the Quorum of Twelve Apostles, taught: "*All* men are invited to come unto [Christ] and *all* are alike unto him. Race makes no difference; color makes no difference; nationality makes no difference. . . . No nation or people or individual could expect to be favored above another. . . . We need to discover the supreme truth that indeed our Father is no respector of persons. Sometimes we unduly offend brothers and sisters of other nations by assigning exclusiveness to one nationality of people over another. . . . [W]ords from the lips of the Master know no national boundaries; they are not limited to any race or culture" ("All Are Alike unto God," 32, 33, 35; paragraphing altered).

SENDING HAGAR AND ISHMAEL AWAY

Because of high infant mortality, families celebrated the milestone of a child's survival at his weaning. The ceremonial event has long been marked in parts of the Middle East by feasting and a ritual offering of soft, solid food to the child. Records of ancient contracts show that wet nurses were hired for as long as three years, indicating Isaac's approximate age when Sarah weaned him (Genesis 21:8). An apocryphal source cites a mother telling her son, "Have pity on me that bare thee nine months in my womb, and gave thee suck three years" (2 Maccabees 7:27). Postponing a child's weaning for three years may also reflect a mother's attempt to strengthen her child to survive the perilous diseases of infancy.

Sarah's strong opinion that Hagar and Ishmael should leave the clan appears stark and selfish. The only background in the text to her perspective is that teenaged Ishmael "mocked" young Isaac (Genesis 21:9–10). According to the apostle Paul, Ishmael "persecuted" Isaac (Galatians 4:29). In his history of the Jewish people, Josephus claimed that Sarah loved Ishmael "with an affection not inferior to that of her own son" until she feared that, due to the significant difference in the two boys' ages, Ishmael should "do [Isaac] injuries when their father should be dead" (*Antiquities,* 1.12.3). Perhaps Sarah's servitude in Pharaoh's house years before heightened feelings of distrust for Hagar the Egyptian rather than forming a bond of sympathy.

Whatever the circumstances that led Sarah to this high level of concern for her son, God did not object. Again the Lord directed Abraham to "hearken unto [Sarah's] voice" concerning Hagar and Ishmael (Genesis 21:12). Ancient law suggested three different options were available to a chief wife who saw cause to reprimand her servant who was elevated to concubine status. She could free the concubine and send her away, brand her a slave and return her to servitude, or punish her. The first option is arguably the most generous course of action. Freed slaves were usually given a legal document verifying their emancipated status.

Thomas Cardinal Cajetan, a Catholic leader in the early sixteenth century whose main focus in scriptural commentary was capturing the intent of the original language, rather than citing the Church Fathers or other commentators, suggested four arguments for a kinder reading of Hagar's manner of exile. Because Abraham was a decent man, Cajetan reasoned, he would not treat his wife and son heartlessly. "Next, from the sex and condition of Hagar: she was, after all, his wife. Then, from the age of his own son. And lastly, from the bread, that is, from the provisions to be carried. Indeed, all these things together indicate that pack animals were needed to carry them and, consequently, their servants and all the other necessities. Surely Abraham did not treat Ishmael worse than the other sons whom he later begot from his concubine [Keturah], on whom he lavished rewards [see Genesis 25:1, 6]" (Thompson, *Writing*, 73 n. 241).

Whatever gifts Abraham bestowed upon Ishmael and the sons of Keturah, however, did not rob Isaac of his spiritual and temporal inheritance. The Genesis narrative relates that "Abraham gave all that he had unto Isaac" (Genesis 25:5). Likewise, Isaac's favored status as Abraham's heir did not preclude the other sons from achieving prosperity and greatness. God not only promised Hagar, "I will make [Ishmael] a great nation," but he also "was with the lad" as he grew to manhood (Genesis 21:18, 20).

HAGAR'S BLESSINGS

Ishmael was about seventeen years old when he and his mother left Abraham's camp. The word translated "wilderness" where Hagar and Ishmael wandered connotes the edge of civilization or the community. Some traditions tell of Abraham visiting Ishmael's camp and becoming acquainted with Ishmael's wife and family over the ensuing years. The Bible suggests that good feelings existed between Ishmael and his father at the time of Abraham's death, with the report that together Ishmael and Isaac buried their father (Genesis 25:9).

When Hagar was expelled from Abraham's camp in Beersheba, she was not sold as a slave but left as a free woman. As evidence of her free status, Hagar alone chose a woman from her homeland to be the wife of Ishmael (Genesis 21:21).

In a symbolic sense, Hagar typifies the future nation of Israel. She was freed from Egyptian slavery, directed to safety through God's intervention, and required to return to the place of her challenges to be purified and strengthened by covenant. Finally, just as Israel left Mount Sinai as a covenant people, so Hagar departed with God's covering, symbolic of the enabling power of His Atonement. She was spiritually free to receive His greatest blessings.

In additional ways, Hagar prefigures Israel. When both Israel and Hagar were freed from their bondage, they fled into the wilderness and required God's divine assistance to assuage their thirst. A foreshadowing of Jacob's twelve sons, Hagar would become a mother of the twelve tribes of Ishmael, divinely destined to bless the earth. Centuries later, the apostle Paul drew on this symbolism to teach the restrictiveness of the law of Moses in contrast to the Lord's higher law. In the allegory, Hagar and her descendants represented the lesser law while Sarah and her descendants symbolized the law of Christ (Galatians 4:21–31). Both the higher law and the law of Moses came from God, but the higher law promises something greater. Ishmael's descendants, although great, would need to come to Isaac's descendants for the promises of the covenant and the Savior's greatest blessings.

One possible meaning for Hagar's name is "flight," reflecting in her a desire to run away from problems. But God allowed her to turn around and receive His power that enabled endless "flight" to the highest heavens. As her blessing indicates, Hagar's inheritance included the covenant's promise of eternal life. Though an outsider to Abraham's community, Hagar was not outside the saving grace of Christ.

Hagar's eternal destiny is likewise taught in modern scripture. Revelation to the Prophet Joseph Smith indicates that all the wives of the patriarchs will enjoy the blessings of exaltation with their husbands. The specific mention of "concubines" is a reminder that Hagar, Keturah, and later Bilhah and Zilpah are included in this promise. "Abraham received concubines, and they bore him children; and it was accounted unto him for righteousness, because they were given unto him, and he abode in my law; as Isaac also and Jacob did none other things than that which they were commanded; and because they did none other things than that which they were commanded, they have entered into their exaltation, according to the promises, and sit upon thrones, and are not angels but are gods" (D&C 132:37).

To be gods in the eternities is to receive the highest heaven or degree, and that necessitates marriage blessed by the patriarchal priesthood (D&C 131:1–3). Abraham, Isaac, and Jacob do not receive exaltation alone. Each must have a "help meet for him" (Genesis 2:18). An eternal companion with appropriate strength to rescue or save is essential for God's ultimate blessings.

SACRIFICE OF ISAAC

The apostle Peter named Sarah and Abraham to exemplify how husbands and wives should honor each other through their obedience and conduct "as being heirs together of the grace of life" (1 Peter 3:7). Much of Sarah and Abraham's story contains tests of their faith and a willingness to sacrifice in order to discover that which is essential. Young Abraham's dramatic escape from being sacrificially offered to strange gods (Abraham 1:12–16), Sarah's deliverance from Pharaoh's and Abimelech's advances, and Sarah's giving her handmaid as a wife to Abraham could have challenged their loyalty to God and to each other. Through these and other difficult times, they were partners.

So when God presented a test by directing Abraham to "take now thy son, thine only son Isaac, whom thou lovest, and get thee into the land of Moriah; and offer him there for a burnt offering upon one of the mountains which I will tell thee of" (Genesis 22:2), did the test include Sarah? She is not specifically mentioned in the scriptural account of Abraham and Isaac's journey to Mount Moriah, but Sarah is never forgotten in the background. Would God have asked Abraham's obedience to sacrifice Isaac without also requiring Sarah's willingness?

Their life's pattern of complete partnership logically argues that as Abraham's partner and help meet, Sarah would have been privy to God's command of sacrificing their son and likewise strengthened by her exercise of faith. President Spencer W. Kimball suggested that Sarah was tested along with her husband in this command. "Father Abraham and Mother Sarah knew—knew the promise would be fulfilled. How? They did not know and did not demand to know. Isaac positively would live to be the father of a numerous posterity. They knew he would, even though he might need to die. They knew he could still be raised from the dead to fulfill the promise, and faith here preceded the miracle" (*Faith Precedes*, 7; see also Hebrews 11:17–19).

The story of Sarah and Abraham records tests of their faith and a willingness to sacrifice to discover that which is essential. As a young man, Abraham was dramatically rescued from being sacrificially offered to strange gods (Abraham 1:12–16). Sarah had her own confrontations with sacrifice.

A Jewish Midrash sees Abraham as loving equally both of his sons. Abraham was therefore confused when God commanded him to "take thy son" because he didn't understand which son He meant. The traditional tale continues with God clarifying for him, "Thine only son. . . . Whom thou lovest." Abraham's confusion persisted in his response, "I love this one and I love that one." Finally the Lord stated, "Even Isaac" (Ginzberg, *Legends*, 1:274). The Joseph Smith Translation also shows sensitivity and acknowledgment of Ishmael as Abraham's son by changing "thine only son" to "thine only Isaac" (JST Genesis 22:2). Another addition to the story from a different Midrash indicates that Ishmael accompanied his father and Isaac to Mount Moriah. These suggestions combine to reinforce an image of a loving and continued interaction with Ishmael after he was expelled.

SARAH'S DEATH AND BURIAL

Sarah is the only woman in scripture whose age at death is recorded (Genesis 23:1). No clue is given to indicate how long she lived after Isaac and Abraham departed for Mount Moriah. Some traditions assert she died while they were gone; others claim she died shortly after their return. Considering that Sarah may have said good-bye to her only son without any guarantee that she would see him again in mortality may be one example of how this family "all died in faith, not having received the promises, but having seen them afar off, and were persuaded of them, and embraced them" (Hebrews 11:13).

In purchasing the cave of Machpelah for Sarah's burial plot, Abraham established the closest thing

A Herodian edifice was built around the cave of Machpelah, the traditional burial site of Sarah, in Hebron. Today it houses a mosque on one side and a synagogue on the other.

to a homeland that his clan would know. Archaeological excavations of societies in the Middle Bronze Era in Canaan provide insight into events described in Genesis 23. Several people were buried in one common cave or burial chamber. Presumably the chamber was reopened each time a member of the clan died. The Bible chronicles that the cave of Machpelah also became the burial place for Abraham (Genesis 25:9), Isaac, Rebekah, and Leah (Genesis 49:31–32), and Jacob (Genesis 50:13).

In the *Story of Sinuhe,* the Egyptian tale that reflects aspects of the patriarchs' culture, the Egyptian author compares what he sees as superior burial customs in Egypt to rudimentary practices of the "foreigners" in Canaan. In Egypt, elaborate burial rituals and burial clothing of "royal linen, myrrh, and prime oil" prepared the dead for a final resting place on a comfortable "bed" buried in the sand. By contrast, the dead in Canaan were simply covered in "sheepskin" before burial. The foreigners' practice of giving the dead a covering of sheepskin is at least reminiscent of the covering of Adam and Eve made of animal skin when they left the Garden of Eden (Genesis 3:21). The image of covering the dead in the Atonement of Christ in contrast to the riches of the world is powerfully symbolic.

The manner in which Abraham secured the property at Machpelah from the landowner Ephron is also paralleled in material culture. Bills of sale, legal documents, and other ancient texts indicate that a foreigner negotiated a land purchase for his clan by presenting his request at a village meeting, usually held at the town's main gate. According to their hospitality customs, the landowner might offer the foreigner the desired real estate as a generous gift. His offer, however, was likely not expected to be accepted (see Genesis 23:8–13). In the presence of witnesses, all agreements and stipulations were reached by spoken assent.

In the case of Abraham's purchase of a burial plot for Sarah, Ephron included the entire field connected to the cave in his negotiations and at an excessively high price of 400 shekels (or about ten pounds) of silver. Abraham paid the full amount, weighed on the scales and transferred to Ephron, in the presence of witnesses (Genesis 23:14–16). In comparison to Jacob's purchase of land in Canaan for 100 shekels, Abraham paid an excessively generous amount (see Genesis 33:19). No written contract is mentioned in Abraham's purchase of the cave.

Shortly before the birth of Christ, Herod the Great enclosed the traditional site of the cave of Machpelah with a magnificent building that stands today. The edifice has been alternatively used as a church, a mosque, and a synagogue, depending upon who controls the area. Christians, Muslims, and Jews all reverence the traditional burial plot of their father Abraham. Within the edifice, cenotaphs honor the memory of those reportedly buried in the area: Sarah, Abraham, Isaac, Rebekah, Leah, and Jacob.

Most of the world population today looks to either Sarah or Hagar as their maternal ancestor. With deeper knowledge and appreciation for Sarah's and Hagar's courage amid staggering opposition, our shared legacy inspires greater emulation of active faith in the Lord.

POINTS TO PONDER: APPLICATIONS FOR OUR LIVES

1. After noting the familiar maxim "If it's fair, it is not a true trial," Elder Neal A. Maxwell explained that "without the added presence of some inexplicableness and some irony and injustice, the experience [or trial] may not stretch us or lift us sufficiently" (*All These Things,* 31). How does a significant delay in receiving the desire of our heart alter the way we see God, His promises, and the world around us?

2. What added challenges and blessings come when we receive the fulfillment of a promise from God later than we expected (such as delayed parenthood, marriage, education, or career)?

3. What does Sarah teach us about parenting? What does Hagar exemplify for parents? From Ishmael's perspective, who was the best mother? From Isaac's perspective?

4. In what way is each of us an outsider like Hagar?

5. How is Sarah an equal partner to her husband? What qualities of a good marriage are modeled in Sarah and Abraham's relationship? What did the apostle Peter want us to see as exemplary in their relationship? (1 Peter 3:1–7).

6. How do these stories surrounding Sarah and Hagar bear witness of Christ and His Atonement?

7. Which principles of the gospel do we see illustrated in the stories of Sarah and Hagar?

The Struggle Within

REBEKAH

רִבְקָה

"Ensnarer," "Knot"

Rebekah is unique among the wives of the patriarchs in at least two ways. First, she alone has a consistently monogamous marriage; we know of no other woman who married Isaac. Second, she plays a more active role in the Genesis narrative than her patriarch husband; her individuality and vitality among the covenant people is striking in stories of her qualifying as Isaac's wife, receiving revelation from God for their sons, and ensuring the bestowal of the birthright on Jacob, as God intended. In a further evidence of her distinctiveness, Rebekah's birth as a lone daughter is listed among the multiple sons of Nahor and Milcah in the middle of the Abraham-Sarah narrative (Genesis 22:20–24).

By contrast, Isaac is remarkably passive in the narrative. Rather than highlighting Isaac's actions, the narrative focuses on other family members. Isaac's older brother, Ishmael; his father, Abraham; Abraham's servant; and Isaac's son all had more active roles than Isaac. Although seemingly quiescent, Isaac provided the important link that perpetuated God's covenant in antiquity: Isaac continued the patriarchy from Abraham to Jacob.

Consideration of ancient culture and traditions, modern revelation, and a careful regard for the biblical text provide a more complete picture and additional insight into Rebekah's challenges and victories. Being married to a prophet of God did not protect her from heartache and uncertainty. Her plea for divine assistance was sincere, and the Lord's direct response to her was profound. Resolute in her duties, Rebekah demonstrated her faith in God by an unflinching commitment to act on what she knew to be right. Beginning with a servant's inspired mission to identify the wife of soon-to-be-patriarch Isaac, the Rebekah narrative is dynamic and rich.

GENESIS 22:23; 24:29; 28:5; 29:12;
35:8; 49:31
ROMANS 9:10–13
DOCTRINE & COVENANTS 132:37
LDS BIBLE DICTIONARY, 760

49

ABRAHAM'S SERVANT AND THE OATH

The servant who was entrusted to find Isaac a wife is unnamed, although tradition identifies him as Abraham's steward named Eliezar (Genesis 15:2–4). The biblical text reports that he was Abraham's "eldest servant," meaning he was the attendant with the highest authority, the servant who had responsibility over all that Abraham owned. The designation was a reflection of the servant's intellect and loyalty to the patriarch rather than an indication of his age (Genesis 24:2).

In preparation for his departure to Haran, the servant made a formal vow to Abraham in an unusual manner: He placed his hand under Abraham's thigh (Genesis 24:2–3, 9). The most generally accepted explanation for the custom is derived by considering the proximity of the thigh to the organ of procreation, reflecting that the oath was important as it pertained to Abraham's posterity and the continuation of the covenant. But the Joseph Smith Translation changes *thigh* to *hand,* rendering the oath "Put, I pray thee, thy hand under my hand" in both references in Genesis 24. In this context, then, the description of making an oath by placing one's hand under another's hand may be suggesting the modern-day equivalent of shaking hands to seal an agreement.

The seriousness of Abraham's command to his servant and the accompanying oath resemble a final request, as though he believed he would soon die (Genesis 24:1–9). The Bible gives evidence that Abraham lived decades after Rebekah joined the family; he died at age 175 (Genesis 25:7–10). On the other hand, later indicators in the story support the suggestion that Abraham died while the servant was away. During marriage arrangements with Laban, the servant referred to Isaac as my "master's son" (v. 51), but when he returned to Canaan with Rebekah, the servant called Isaac "my master" (v. 65). Furthermore, after sending his servant to find Isaac's wife, Abraham is noticeably absent from the narrative. If in fact he died before the servant's return, the events discussed in Genesis 25, including Abraham's marriage to Keturah, must have occurred before Rebekah was brought into the clan.

Importantly, Abraham stipulated to his servant that the woman he chose for Isaac must "be willing" to journey to Canaan and marry Isaac (Genesis 24:8). In other words, even if the woman's family desired to negotiate for the marriage, Abraham would

To fulfill his duty to find a wife for Isaac, Abraham's servant took ten camels, laden with goods, from Hebron to Nahor.

not accept their agreement unless the bride herself also accepted the offer. By contrast, later laws among the Israelite tribes do not reflect the same respect for a woman's voice in marriage decisions. For example, the law of Moses allowed a father to sell his daughter to the man who married her (Exodus 21:7–11). The same law allowed a man to take a wife from the spoils of military victory (Deuteronomy 21:10–14). In neither of these later cases is found any indication that the "bride" was consulted for her approval of the proposed marriage.

THE SERVANT'S JOURNEY

Travel from Hebron to Nahor would likely have taken the servant and his entourage nearly a month to complete, covering a distance of some 850 miles. The city of Nahor was likely either another name for Haran or a community near Haran that was located in the larger area of Aram-Naharaim (Syria or "Aram of the two rivers"), translated in the biblical account as "Mesopotamia" (Genesis 24:10). Aram-Naharaim is later called "Padan-aram" (Genesis 28:5–6), or the plain of Aram/Syria.

The ten camels that Abraham's servant conducted to Nahor imply that other servants accompanied him and the large quantities of supplies and gifts being transported (Genesis 24:32). The impressive caravan gives further evidence of Abraham's wealth, generosity, and serious intent to secure an appropriate wife for his son. Most likely the camels were dromedaries, one-hump camels that thrived in the hot deserts of northern Africa and western Asia. An exceptional pack animal that can travel some one hundred miles in twelve hours while carrying up to four hundred pounds of goods, the dromedary consumes about twenty-five to thirty gallons of water in a single session and stores it in its three-chambered stomach. Considering remnants of pots discovered from the Middle Bronze Era, Rebekah's "pitcher" would likely have held at most five gallons of water. That being the case, she would have carried her filled jar more than fifty times to

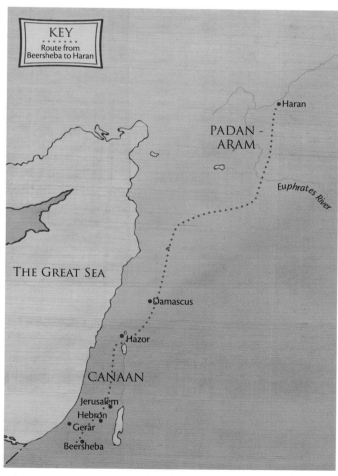

Abraham's servant traveled from Beersheba to Haran, a distance of about 850 miles, to find a wife for Isaac.

The dromedary camel can consume twenty-five to thirty gallons of water in a single session to store in its three-chambered stomach.

complete her service to the servant, giving some indication of Rebekah's offering when she watered all ten camels.

Some scholars have argued that the reference to camels in the Genesis era is anachronistic because no depiction of dromedaries has been found in Egyptian tomb paintings (Köhler-Rollefson, "Camels," 180–88). Such a conclusion is still debatable, because in the 1970s archaeologists found evidence that camels may have occupied a small island off the Arabian peninsula during the third millennium before Christ. Bones from approximately two hundred camels that date back to 2700 B.C. have been uncovered, providing the earliest evidence of camels in the ancient Near East (Ripinsky, "Camel," 134–41). Because Arabia's archaeological record is extremely scarce for the third and second millennia, scholars often warn that any specifically assigned use or role of the camel at the time of the patriarchs is speculative.

FINDING REBEKAH

Without receiving any hint of what the servant was seeking, Rebekah approached the well near Nahor and exhibited characteristics that immediately attracted his attention. With no feigned attempt to impress a stranger who had come to town, she demonstrated her true compassionate nature and closeness to the Spirit by being at the right place, at the right time, and engaging in the right activity. At least twice a day, women of all ages went to the well from surrounding areas to draw water for cooking, washing, and watering their livestock. Josephus recorded that many maidens at the well were drawing water at the time Abraham's servant arrived but that the others all refused to give the stranger any water before Rebekah came forward "in an obliging manner" (*Antiquities*, 1.16.2).

Although Rebekah's age is not mentioned in the biblical account, the fact that she was yet unmarried suggests she was still youthful. A Jewish Midrash claims she was married at age fourteen (Ginzberg, *Legends*, 1:311), probably in reflection of the ancient custom that girls married soon after reaching puberty; however, no other source confirms that she was so young.

Rebekah was willing, eager, and energetic in her service to a stranger. She "hasted" to give the visitor water after he requested a drink (Genesis 24:18), volunteered to water all his camels and then "hasted" and "ran" until she completed the task (vv. 19–20), and finally "ran" to notify her family of the stranger's coming (v. 28). The servant's instant approval of Rebekah is further noted in Joseph Smith's translation of the text: "And the damsel, being a virgin, very fair to look upon, such as the servant of Abraham had not seen, neither had any man known the like unto her" (JST Genesis 24:16). Rebekah's instinctive compassion, vitality, and work ethic likely made her more attractive to Abraham's servant than her appearance alone. She was also of the right lineage and single, as revealed through answers to the servant's questions about her father and whether she was still living in her "father's house" (Genesis 24:23–25).

MARRIAGE CUSTOMS

During the patriarchal era, marriages were skillfully negotiated with deference to political and economic ramifications that would be created by the arrangement. The patriarch agreed on alliances that would benefit the entire clan and maintain the community. The criteria Abraham's servant incorporated in his test to identify Isaac's future wife suggests those characteristics valued in Abraham's society. She should be God-fearing, from the right clan, industrious, compassionate to both strangers and animals, and wise in her care of property.

Different from the western practice of marrying the person one loves, the biblical world more often exemplified the eastern custom of learning to love the person one marries. Parental approval and arranged marriages were therefore the norm. For example, Hagar found Ishmael a wife without negative ramifications (Genesis 21:21; 25:12–18), but Esau seriously disappointed his parents when he married without their approval (Genesis 26:34–35; 27:46). No mention is made of Isaac's concern or disapproval for his father's plan to find him a wife. The scriptures indicate that he readily accepted the servant's choice for his wife.

When the servant began negotiations for Isaac's marriage, he possessed "all the goods of his master . . . in his hand" (Genesis 24:10), probably meaning that he held a document that verified Abraham's ownership of property, servants, livestock, and other wealth that would become Isaac's inheritance. When the groom's financial circumstances promised a comfortable lifestyle, the bride's family would be more inclined to agree to a marriage.

Rebekah watered all ten camels from a community well such as this one, which is similar to the numerous ancient wells found throughout biblical lands.

But recompense in the form of gifts from the groom's family to the bride and her family was also customary during marriage arrangements. Abraham's servant would be expected to pay a bride-price to the bride's family as compensation for their loss of a daughter and as an indication of the groom's ability to support a family. The bride-price also reinforces the value of a daughter to the family and indicates the substantial work women contributed for the good of the clan. Although

Artwork by Ashton Young

Abraham's servant lavished jewelry upon Rebekah, including gold bracelets and a nose ring. The earrings and bracelet depicted here are based on several found in Canaan that date to the second millennium before Christ.

we have no specifics, the "precious things" given to Rebekah's brother and mother were likely a substantial bride-price (Genesis 24:53).

Almost immediately, the servant began dispensing gifts of jewelry to the selected bride, with additional jewelry and clothing presented to her after the marriage agreement was complete (Genesis 24:22, 53). The initial gift translated "earring" was most likely a nose ring, reflecting a fashion of that era (v. 47; footnote 47a). Nose rings, typically one to two inches in diameter, were pinched on the right nostril. The two bracelets or bangles given to Rebekah were "a pair" of bracelets (v. 22), a symbolic wedding gift signifying a man and woman becoming bound in marriage. The weight in gold of these initial gifts was the equivalent of several years' wages. For example, the ten and a half shekels' weight of gold jewelry the servant gave Rebekah could have purchased five slaves. By offering these lavish gifts, the servant promised the family that Rebekah would be generously accommodated in her marriage to Isaac.

REBEKAH'S WILLING CONSENT

Verification of the bride's parentage was clearly important for the servant's final approval of Rebekah. A heritage that valued Abraham's reverence for God would have been particularly essential. Rebekah was a granddaughter of Nahor, Abraham's brother, and his wife Milcah, who was possibly Sarah's sister. Rebekah's father, Bethuel, is frequently mentioned in the account without ever being present, suggesting that he may have been deceased. Several clues bear out this idea: Rebekah took the servant to "her mother's house," not to her father's house (Genesis 24:28); Laban, Rebekah's brother, negotiated the marriage arrangement rather than her father; gifts were given to Rebekah's "brother and to her mother" with no mention of her father (v. 53); and final exchanges were made between Rebekah and her brother and mother (vv. 55–60). The isolated mention of Bethuel as a participant is therefore suspect, suggesting an editorial gloss or perhaps a reference to a younger brother to Laban named Bethuel (v. 50). Josephus clearly reported that Rebekah told the servant that her father, Bethuel, had died (*Antiquities*, 1.16.2).

Laban, as eldest son, appears to have assumed the role of family patriarch in the absence of his father. Importantly, however, the authority and approval of the clan's matriarch was not diminished by the death of her husband. The presence of Rebekah's mother during the marriage negotiations was as important as the participation of Laban, the new male leader of the clan.

The servant did not receive Rebekah's spoken consent to the marriage until arrangements were being made for her departure to Canaan. Interestingly, the servant asked the family's permission, and the family sent for Rebekah, saying, "We will call for the damsel, and enquire at her mouth" (Genesis 24:57). Her response is profound in its simplicity: "I will go" (v. 58). In a parallel instance, the Nuzi texts contain a report of a proposed bride being asked whether she was willing to accept the marriage proposal. Although the proposal was arranged by others, the bride's acceptance or rejection of it was honored.

"I WILL GO"

The Genesis narrative is filled with acknowledgment that Rebekah's proposed marriage to Isaac was the Lord's will. Latter-day Church leaders have noted Rebekah's agency and obedience in this regard:

"We have . . . examples from the scriptures of how we should consider and evaluate the commandments of the Lord. If we choose to react like Joshua, and Abraham, and Rebekah and Rachel, our response will be, simply, to go and do the thing that the Lord has commanded.

"[We should] make our decision *now* to serve the Lord. . . . We should decide now, in the light of the morning, how we will act when the darkness of night and when the storms of temptation arrive" (Hunter, *Ensign*, Nov. 1982, 58).

"We each have to say to ourselves, *What will I create of my life? My time? My future?*

"First, go where the Spirit directs. Be still and listen. Your Heavenly Father will guide you as you draw near to Him. Immerse yourself in the holy word of the prophets, both ancient and modern, and the Spirit will speak to you. Be patient, ask in faith, and you will receive guidance in your creative efforts.

"Second, don't be paralyzed from fear of making mistakes. Thrust your hands into the clay of your lives and begin. I love how Rebekah of old responded to Abraham's servant who came in search of a wife for Isaac. Her answer was simple and direct, 'I will go,' she said.

"Rebekah could have refused. She could have told the servant to wait until she had the proper send-off, a new wardrobe, until she lost a few pounds, or until the weather was more promising. She could have said, 'What's wrong with Isaac that he can't find a wife in all of Canaan?' But she didn't. She acted, and so should we.

"The time for procrastination is over. Begin! Don't be afraid. Do the best you can. Of course you will make mistakes. Everyone does. Learn from them and move forward" (Smoot, *Ensign*, May 2000, 65).

At Rebekah's departure, she was given a dowry as an inheritance from her family. The family's gift to a bride always belonged to the woman and therefore was hers to sell or bequeath to another as she deemed necessary or desirable. As part of her dowry, Rebekah received a maidservant, her nurse named Deborah (Genesis 35:8). A child and her nurse were bound by nearly as close a tie as the child and her mother, making a fast friendship when the now adult Rebekah was preparing for marriage. The text notes that Rebekah received additional servants at her parting, and most likely other valuables, although they are not mentioned (Genesis 24:61). These would have also been included in her dowry. Her family's final gift was the pronouncement of a blessing; they prayed that she would have a numerous posterity and protection from enemies (v. 60). Rebekah would never again see her family members or return to the land of her birth.

REBEKAH AS A TYPE OF THE CHURCH

As much as any of the ancient prophets, Isaac is viewed as a type of Christ when he willingly complied with the sacrifice on Mount Moriah. The Book of Mormon prophet Jacob taught, "It was accounted unto Abraham in the wilderness to be obedient unto the commands of God in offering up his son Isaac, which is a similitude of God and his Only Begotten Son" (Jacob 4:5). Additionally, the relationship between God and His people is compared to the bond between husband and wife. In this way, Isaac can also be viewed as a type of the Savior in His role as the Bridegroom. Just as Christ's bride is the Church (Revelation 21:2, 9), and Isaac's bride was Rebekah, so can Rebekah typify "the Church," or those who come to Christ and receive His covenant. Prophets often referred to the people of God in such female terms as "daughter" (Jeremiah 49:4), "daughter of Zion" (Isaiah 52:2; 62:11; Lamentations 2:1, 4), "daughter of Jerusalem" (Zechariah 9:9), "daughters of Jerusalem" (Luke 23:28), "daughter of Judah" (Lamentations 2:2, 5), and "daughters of Judah" (Psalm 48:11; 97:8).

Rebekah's characteristics noted by the servant are therefore meaningful to men and women who consider themselves part of "the Church." Like Rebekah, a true follower of Christ is willing to serve without being asked,

"Isaac went out to meditate in the field at the eventide" (Genesis 24:63), and he saw the camels that were transporting Abraham's servant and Rebekah.

responding to others' needs without hesitation. Single-handedly watering ten camels could symbolize God-given assignments that are beyond our natural ability to perform. Yet Rebekah completed the task without hesitation, a witness that the Church and its members can accomplish whatever God requires by the enabling power of Christ. The Savior's Atonement gives us strength and wisdom to succeed in ways that exceed our imagination and clearly go beyond anything we can do alone. Next, a true disciple is virtuous and obedient to the Father's servants, as Rebekah sincerely exemplified to Abraham's servant. Finally, a sincere Christian is worthy and desirous to become part of the covenant family and live as a witness for Christ.

CHRONOLOGY

Isaac is born to Abraham (100) and Sarah (90)

Isaac is offered as a willing sacrifice

Isaac (37) loses his mother, Sarah (127)

Abraham sends his servant to find a wife for Isaac

Isaac (40) and Rebekah marry

Abraham marries Keturah; they have six sons

Esau and Jacob are born to Isaac (60) and Rebekah

Isaac (75) and Ishmael (89) bury their father, Abraham (175)

Esau (40) marries two Hittite women (Isaac is 100)

Rebekah guides Isaac to give Jacob the birthright blessing

Jacob departs for Padan-aran to find a wife

Esau marries a daughter of Ishmael

Ishmael dies (137)

Isaac dies (180)

Continuing this analogy, Isaac's anticipation of Rebekah's arrival points to the Savior's love and concern for each of us. Christ is aware of our coming toward Him long before we clearly recognize Him. Before the servant told Rebekah that the stranger coming towards them was her future husband, she rapidly descended from her camel (Genesis 24:64). Why did she react with such deference to a stranger? Perhaps her instinctive response was evidence of God's revelation to her concerning this man.

In preparation for meeting her bridegroom, Rebekah displayed a natural inclination to cover herself with a veil (Genesis 24:65). Considering that Sarah's beauty was observable to strangers (Genesis 12:14) and that Eli could see Hannah's mouth when she was praying (1 Samuel 1:12–13), women did not always wear a veil for modesty. Tammi J. Schneider of Claremont Graduate University suggests that Rebekah's decision to veil herself could just as easily have been to allow her to view her future husband without being observed or even that Rebekah did not want Isaac to have his first glimpse of her when she was travel weary (*Mothers*, 55). Additionally, in the metaphor of the bride and bridegroom, Rebekah's covering could symbolize the Church's need for the Savior's Atonement as He clothes His beloved ones with His perfect love and protection (Genesis 24:63–67). In this way, Rebekah's veil is another reminder of the covering God gave to Adam and Eve (Genesis 3:21).

Still today, the practice of a bride's wearing a veil symbolizes purity, signifies that the woman is unmarried, or gives a general indication of her good character. In contradiction to these interpretations, another woman who lived among the ancient patriarchs, Tamar, is often accused of posing as a harlot because she wore a veil to trap Judah, her father-in-law (Genesis 38:14–15). Whatever the intended symbolism behind Rebekah's veiling herself to meet an intended bridegroom, the custom of veiling the bride at her wedding has become widespread.

MOTHER OF ESAU AND JACOB

Twenty years pass without direct detail concerning Rebekah and Isaac, except to note that their home was near the well where Isaac first met Rebekah, the same well where God spoke to Hagar in her distress—Lahai-roi (Genesis 16:13–14; 24:11; 25:11). Rebekah and Isaac's experiences in Gerar, including King Abimelech's desire to marry Rebekah, may have occurred during these twenty years (Genesis 26). Although the biblical text provides no explanation of significance for Rebekah's encounter with King Abimelech of Gerar, the account clearly parallels Sarah's earlier experience. The repetition reinforces the suggestion that outsiders witnessed, admired, and strongly desired a unique endowment of power and success that they recognized in God's covenant family. Did these outsiders believe that this unique something could be accessed through marriage to a leading woman in the clan? The Genesis narrative encourages such questions without supplying answers.

When the Isaac-Rebekah narrative resumes, we learn that Rebekah was barren, an echo of her mother-in-law's heartache, and Isaac "intreated" the Lord to bless her with a child (Genesis 25:21). According to Jewish Midrash, Rebekah united her prayers with her husband's pleas to the Lord for a child. God answered their petitions, and Rebekah conceived (Ginzberg, *Legends,* 1:312–13).

Concerned over struggles she felt in her womb, Rebekah did not go to family or friends for help but turned first to God to receive understanding and comfort. Furthermore, the biblical text is clear that Rebekah spoke directly to God and God responded directly to her, without her prophet-husband's intervention (Genesis 25:22–23). That she recognized God's multifaceted revelation suggests that fervent prayer was not a novelty for Rebekah. She had already developed a close relationship with the Lord and the spiritual sensitivities necessary for clear communication. In response to her prayer, Rebekah learned prophetic truths: she would give birth to twin boys, each son would be a leader of a nation, and the second-born would lead the firstborn (Genesis 25:23). In time, all three prophecies were fulfilled.

The apostle Paul referred to Rebekah's revelation about her two sons as evidence for the doctrine of election, God's practice of choosing specific missions for individuals and peoples before their mortal birth. The prophetic nature of the answer Rebekah received to her prayer underscores that Esau and Jacob were called to their earthly responsibilities before they were born, that is, before they had "done any good or evil" to *earn* a divine calling in mortality (Romans 9:11).

Reflecting his initial appearance, the firstborn was named Esau (meaning "hairy") but was also called Edom (meaning "red"; Genesis 25:25, 30). The second-born was called Jacob (from the Hebrew "may God

---

A MOST NOBLE AND GLORIOUS WOMAN

A latter-day apostle noted Rebekah's exemplary faith and important role as the recipient of revelation:

"Rebekah is one of the greatest patterns in all the revelations of what a woman can do to influence a family in righteousness [Genesis 25:22]. . . .

"Now note it well. She did not say, 'Isaac, will you inquire of the Lord. You are the patriarch; you are the head of the house,'" which he was. She went to inquire of the Lord, and she gained the answer: [Genesis 25:23].

"That is to say, 'To you, Rebekah, I, the Lord, reveal the destiny of nations that are to be born which are yet in your womb.' . . .

"Rebekah—truly she is one of the most noble and glorious of women!" (McConkie, *Ensign*, Jan. 1979, 62).

---

protect"; or "supplanter" in reference to his act of supplanting or unseating his brother as the firstborn; or "heel").

THE BIRTHRIGHT

Within the patriarchal order, every son was entitled to a share of his father's estate. One son, however, was named the "birthright" son with particular responsibilities and privileges beyond those his brothers received. The birthright son inherited presiding authority as the clan's patriarch and double the wealth that his brothers were given. His responsibilities and additional resources extended to the care and sustenance of his mother, any childless wives of his father, unmarried sisters, or sisters returning home either divorced or widowed without children. As Rebekah's brother Laban acted in proxy for their father before her marriage to Isaac, the birthright son would act in proxy for his father in helping any unmarried sisters find husbands and providing them a dowry.

The firstborn son was traditionally the recipient of this birthright, but ancient texts written by neighboring peoples suggest that another son could just as easily receive it. Hurrian law, as recorded in the Nuzi texts, indicated that a patriarch could designate any of his sons as the eldest, regardless of birth order. These texts also gave legal authorization for one son to sell his share of the inheritance to another brother, even when the traded commodity did not equal the value of the inheritance or birthright.

The Genesis narrative portrays Esau as having little regard for his responsibilities as the firstborn. He "despised his birthright" (Genesis 25:34), which was demonstrated by his selling it to Jacob for food and by marrying two Hittite women who were not God-fearing and therefore outside the blessing of the covenant (Genesis 25:29–34; 26:34–35). The Prophet Joseph Smith taught that Esau had the legal claim to the birthright "but through unbelief, hardness of heart, and hunger," he relinquished it to Jacob, just as God knew "beforehand that he would do . . . of his own free will and choice" (*History of the Church*, 4:261–62).

The legal declaration of the birthright son was often made by the father in a formal, official manner, such as a patriarchal blessing. The scene in which Isaac bestowed his father's blessing on each of his sons is dramatic, with Rebekah featured at center-stage.

BLESSINGS FOR JACOB AND ESAU

Questions and conjecture accompany the biblical account of Jacob's receiving Isaac's birthright blessing. Because details and explanations are absent, it is easy to make accusations of deception and manipulation.

At the time of the blessing, Isaac was nearly incapacitated, described as "old, and his eyes were dim, so that he could not see" (Genesis 27:1). He was unable to distinguish his sons from each other and considered his mortal life nearly at its end (v. 2). Yet, at the beginning of the next chapter, Isaac is portrayed as alert, with no difficulty recognizing his second son, and capable of delivering lengthy counsel for Jacob's imminent journey to Padan-aran (Genesis 28:1–5). The two settings invite a possibility that the chapters are not presented in chronological order. Perhaps Isaac pronounced the birthright blessing years later, or else he died shortly after blessing his sons rather than when his death is reported several decades later (Genesis 35:28–29). The fact that Isaac is mentioned only indirectly after he blessed his sons provides no additional clues to correct this seeming inconsistency. We do know, however, that Isaac was chosen by God to pronounce blessings and enact ordinances. A description by Joseph Smith supplies helpful insight into Isaac's character that is otherwise absent in the biblical text. Joseph Smith wrote that "[Isaac] was more holy and more perfect before God and came to him with a purer heart and more faith than men in this day" (Jessee, *Writings,* 299).

Without denigrating Isaac's authority and pure heart, Rebekah's leadership in orchestrating the birthright blessing is undeniable. As soon as she heard Isaac's instruction to Esau to "make me savoury meat . . . that I may eat; that my soul may bless thee before I die" (Genesis 27:4), Rebekah sprang into action, advising Jacob to likewise bring fresh meat that could be prepared in the manner that his father loved.

All women have similar opportunities to open up a way that allows God's will to be made known. "Women are appointed, Rebekahlike, to be guides and lights in righteousness in the family unit," Elder Bruce R. McConkie taught, "and to engineer and arrange so that things are done in the way that will result in the salvation of more of our Father's children" (*Ensign,* Jan. 1979, 63).

After hearing his mother's plan, Jacob feared that Isaac would know he was not Esau because the two brothers differed in appearance. Rebekah's confidence in pursuing her plan must stem in part from the revelation she received before her sons were born. She knew that God had chosen her younger son to receive the birthright.

Rebekah's preparation of Jacob included covering him in Esau's "goodly raiment" and putting animal skin over Jacob's skin (Genesis 27:15). Even as hairy as Esau reportedly was, it is difficult to imagine a man as hirsute as a goat. According to a Jewish Midrash, Esau's "wonderful garments . . . were the high-priestly raiment in which God had clothed Adam" which had been handed down to Noah, Shem, Abraham, Isaac, and finally to Esau, as Isaac's firstborn son (Ginzberg, *Legends,* 1:332). The resultant image is that the covenant son was covered with the skins of a sacrificed animal in preparation of inheriting all that his father had. Was Esau's goodly raiment symbolic of presiding priesthood authority and guardianship for the covenant that was originally given to Adam and Eve? Perhaps the covering was an outward reminder that the wearer was dedicated to the Lord to "bear this ministry and Priesthood unto all nations" (Abraham 2:9)?

Whatever the clothing's significance, Isaac became confused when the son before him smelled like Esau but sounded like Jacob. In the end, the feel of the goodly raiment, not the son's voice, determined the rightful recipient of the blessing. Rebekah's plan created the environment where Isaac, without his eyesight, received revelation to bestow the birthright on the foreordained son.

Isaac's blessing to Jacob echoed Rebekah's revelation that she received before Jacob's birth as well as portions of the Abrahamic covenant (Genesis 27:28–29; 28:4). Esau also received a remarkable blessing. Isaac promised his elder son "the fatness of the earth, and of the dew of heaven from above" and reiterated what Rebekah knew before he was born, that "thou . . . shalt serve thy brother," but made no mention of the covenant blessings (Genesis 27:39–40).

A New Testament epistle confirms that Isaac acted in faith and not manipulation or deception when he blessed Jacob and Esau (Hebrews 11:20). Similarly, Jewish Midrashim assert that both Isaac and Rebekah were guided by the Spirit on this occasion (Ginzberg, *Legends,* 1:330, 334). Furthermore, an early Latter-day Saint apostle cautioned against judging Rebekah and Jacob harshly because the Holy Ghost was working to bring about God's purposes. "There was neither unrighteousness in Rebekah nor in Jacob in this matter; but on the contrary," Elder Erastus Snow taught, "there was the wisdom of the Almighty, . . . knowing as He did that Jacob and his seed were, and would be, more deserving of the birthright, and would magnify it in its true spirit. . . . The Lord therefore saw fit to take it from [Esau], and the mother was moved upon to help the younger son to bring about the purpose of the Lord, in securing to himself the blessing through the legitimate channel of the Priesthood" (*Journal of Discourses,* 21:371).

Rather than depicting Isaac as foolish and deceived, this event indicates his wisdom and commitment to follow God's commands. And rather than characterizing Rebekah as manipulative and conniving, the account shows her sagacity and efforts to enhance the power of their partnership.

REBEKAH'S GREAT HOPE

Our final glimpse of Rebekah is at the time of her plea that Jacob leave their home in Canaan to live with her brother's family in Haran. She was concerned about Jacob's physical safety in light of Esau's anger over the birthright blessing and about Jacob's spiritual safety should he, like his brother, marry outside the covenant (Genesis 27:42–46).

The principal issue surrounding marriage in the patriarchal clan appears to have been more a matter of faith and of reverence for the covenant, than race or nationality. With God's approval, Abraham married the Egyptian Hagar and also Keturah, who most likely was from Canaan. Later, Joseph, the birthright son, would marry Asenath, the daughter of the priest of On. Two theories have been presented about Asenath's lineage. She may have been a Semite woman from the Hyksos people who may have ruled Egypt at the time of Joseph (Ivins, *Improvement Era,* Aug. 1931, 571), or she may have been an Egyptian woman and a daughter of the priest at the pagan temple at On (Jackson, *Restored Gospel,* 162–63). Whatever the case, the marriage between Joseph and Aseneth was considered to be approved by God, if only because we know the birthright passed from Joseph to his and Aseneth's son.

After seeing his parents' pleasure in Jacob's willingness to marry a believing wife, Esau married Ishmael's daughter (Genesis 28:6–9). Was this marriage to add further hurt to his parents or was it to regain their favor and God's? The record does not explain. A Jewish Midrash claims it was to garner Ishmael's support to destroy Jacob (Ginzberg, *Legends,* 1:344). Later interactions between Esau and Jacob suggest the more positive motive. Jacob and Esau were amicable when Jacob returned to Canaan with his wives and children (Genesis 33) and were cooperative and united when burying their father (Genesis 35:29). Nothing in the biblical text prohibits a repentant Esau.

Rebekah hoped that Jacob would be away in Haran only "a few days" (Genesis 27:44). In actuality, it would be a lengthy twenty years. The Bible narrative reports that Isaac was living in Hebron upon Jacob's return (Genesis 35:27), but no mention is made of Rebekah. Did she ever see Jacob again? Did she see her numerous grandchildren and further hope of her family's marriage blessing that she would be a "mother of thousands of millions"? (Genesis 24:60). Perhaps most important, did she see her two sons reconciled and commencing the creation of two remarkable nations? The biblical account tells us nothing more about Rebekah except to report that she was buried in the cave of Machpelah, alongside Abraham, Sarah, and Isaac (Genesis 49:31).

Much about Rebekah's life is unknown. Her joys and moments of contentment are largely eclipsed by accounts of her struggles and tests of faith. But the surviving scriptural accounts instill a belief in the ever-present need for God—for Rebekah and for each of us. Rebekah said, "I will go," and she seems never to have looked back. Her trust in the Lord amid uncertainties was a blessing to her entire family. Additionally, Rebekah's role in preserving and affirming God's will pertaining to the covenant underscores a woman's importance as help meet for her husband and for the larger community.

POINTS TO PONDER: APPLICATIONS FOR OUR LIVES

1. What does Rebekah teach us about the need for a Savior?
2. When Rebekah was asked whether or not she would depart immediately with Abraham's servant, she said, "I will go." Can you think of other scriptural examples of individuals who responded likewise? When have you felt the unhesitating urge to quickly act in obedience to the Spirit?

3. With Rebekah as a type of the Church, what "Rebekahlike" characteristics could you adopt in an effort to encourage your own diligence as a disciple of Christ?

4. Do you think Rebekah told Isaac about her prophetic revelation about their unborn sons? Why or why not? When is it appropriate to speak of personal revelation? When is it not appropriate? Have you ever been present when someone inappropriately tried to share a personal spiritual experience?

5. Does the image of Rebekah wearing a nose ring, culturally acceptable at the time, bother you? Why or why not? How may our interpretation of outward appearances color our perceptions of a person's spirituality or worth in God's eyes?

6. What modern-day examples do you know of women who have accepted revelation from God concerning their families or community responsibilities and appropriately acted to incorporate it for the good of all? How have such examples strengthened your confidence to receive and act upon personal or family revelation?

7. What principles of the gospel does Rebekah illustrate through her life's example?

With Her Father's Sheep (Rachel)

LEAH AND RACHEL

לֵאָה

"Cow"

רָחֵל

"Ewe"

The story of the patriarchs continues with Jacob arriving in Haran. After receiving the birthright blessing from his father and threats on his life by his brother, Jacob escaped to his mother's homeland in hopes of finding a believing wife. A popular stop on a caravan route through upper Mesopotamia, Haran offered many opportunities for worldly pursuits, greed, and idol worship. In Haran, Jacob continued to be haunted by episodes of deception and integrity, evident at his departure from his parents' home. His mother's brother would test every ounce of his integrity, answering with trickery and deceit Jacob's honest attempts to succeed. But this community also instilled great faith and devotion to God in untold numbers of inhabitants, ever since Abram and Sarai had lived there. In Haran, Jacob found more than his match in Laban's two daughters, Leah and Rachel.

As pawns in their father's strategy to exploit Jacob's favor with God, Rachel and Leah found themselves married to the same man. In addition to being used as a mere bargaining chip for her father's financial gain, Leah was hated by her husband. Rachel, on the other hand, was fortunate to have an adoring husband, but she could not bear children, the achievement that gave women value in her society. Through deepening trials, each was stretched to the realization that only God validates and enables. His infinite balm, offered to each of us, provides healing, comfort, and pure love that exceeds any mortal attempt to succor. The sisters' individual responses to God in the midst of their unexpected circumstances helped to shape the foundations of God's covenant people.

As long as Leah and Rachel interpreted the birth of children and Jacob's attention as evidence of their individual worth, their feelings of inadequacy, worthlessness, and selfish pride were reinforced. Their deepest pains

> GENESIS 29–35; 46; 49:31
>
> RUTH 4:11
>
> 1 SAMUEL 10:2
>
> JEREMIAH 31:15
>
> MATTHEW 2:18
>
> DOCTRINE & COVENANTS 132:37
>
> LDS BIBLE DICTIONARY, 723, 759
>
>

came by excluding and envying the other and by competing for outward signs of superiority. When they forgot their personal fears, their greatest strength came by working as a family unit to obey God's commands. Known as the mothers of the twelve tribes of Israel, Leah's and Rachel's circle of partnership expanded to include their handmaids, Bilhah and Zilpah.

JACOB AND RACHEL'S FIRST MEETING

Jacob's journey from Beersheba to Haran, a distance of approximately 850 miles over well-marked trade routes, was not without incident. In Bethel, Jacob received God's reconfirmed promise that "in thee [Jacob] and in thy seed shall all the families of the earth be blessed" (Genesis 28:14). Expectations of marriage and children would have intensified as he neared Haran.

Seeing men watering their flocks at the well and learning that they were from Haran, Jacob immediately inquired about his mother's brother, Laban. Yes, the men knew of Laban, and the woman approaching the well with her flock of sheep, the men informed him, was his daughter Rachel (Genesis 29:1–8). Men and women in that day shared the responsibility of caring for livestock. Why was Leah, the older sister, not also working with the sheep? Perhaps she was working elsewhere on her father's lands, or perhaps she was given more duties in the home, while Rachel was assigned duties with the livestock. Or perhaps Rachel was simply more capable in those duties than was Leah. Whatever the reason, Rachel's obvious abilities in this regard prefigure Laban's loss of laborers when his daughters left his clan.

When Jacob first observed Rachel at the same well where his mother had met Abram's servant, it is possible that he recalled Rebekah's story of commencing her path to a successful marriage there. How much of Jacob's conviction that Rachel was to be his wife occurred by perceiving similarities in Rachel to his mother? Whatever the deciding

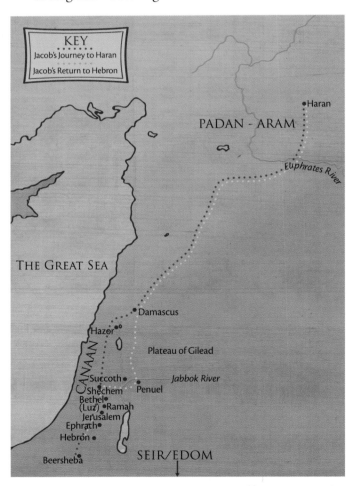

Jacob's journey from Hebron to Haran and his return trip to Hebron with his wives, children, and livestock would probably have followed well-marked travel routes.

factor, Jacob identified Rachel as his future wife almost immediately. He had yet to win the approval of Rachel's parents, however. Jacob's worth to Rachel's father became clear during the month of hospitality that Jacob enjoyed with Laban's clan. Laban could see that Jacob was wealthy, favored of God, and a profitable and honest laborer (Genesis 29:15).

LABAN'S TWO DAUGHTERS

A herdsman, Laban may have named his two daughters to reflect his appreciation for his source of material success. The elder was called Leah, "young cow." The younger was named Rachel, "female sheep." Jewish Midrash claims the girls were fraternal twins and that their marriages to their twin cousins Esau and Jacob were arranged by Rebekah and Laban from the time of the girls' births (Ginzberg, *Legends,* 1:327, 358). Another Jewish tradition explains that Leah's "tender" or weak eyes (Genesis 29:17) were the result of continual weeping over a marriage contract that promised her to the wicked Esau (Ginzberg, *Legends,* 1:359). By contrast, many modern Bible translations suggest that Leah's eyes were strikingly attractive and her most distinguishing physical asset.

The biblical text is clear, however, that Rachel was the more beautiful of the two sisters. Her physical appearance and perhaps other characteristics attracted greater marriage possibilities than her older sister received. For example, when Jacob requested marriage to Rachel in remuneration for his labors, Laban implied that other marriage offers for Rachel were expected (Genesis 29:19). By contrast, during the seven years that Jacob worked to pay the bride-price for Rachel, no indication is given to suggest that Leah's hand in marriage was sought by a suitor. Jacob's love for Rachel preceded their marriage rather than being fostered after marriage, as was the case with Jacob's parents.

The Bible gives no suggestion that any jealousy existed between the two sisters before their marriages. The implication is that Leah and Rachel were close confidantes who shared hopes and dreams for their future families. Did they see virtues in each other that men typically missed? Did they envision raising their families near each other, expecting to

Leah and Rachel worked in the fields and cared for the flocks on their father's vast lands. No wonder Laban resisted their desire to depart with their husband.

Blessed (Leah)

secure husbands who lived in the same clan that would allow the sisters to remain close during the remainder of their lives?

Although no clues are given in the text concerning the sisters' relationship during the first seven years that Jacob worked for their father, Jacob's awareness of the calendar, the fulfillment of his seven-year-agreement to Laban, and his imminent marriage to Rachel was apparent.

LEAH AND RACHEL MARRY JACOB

The week-long wedding celebration began with a feast attended by members of the larger clan and community. The scriptural narrative does not furnish any clue for whether Leah had the role of bride all week long or just before the official ceremony. Most likely, the dark of night and the bride's veil prevented Jacob from detecting Laban's strategy of substituting his elder daughter for the younger as the bride until after their first night together.

The biblical text reports Jacob's anger and dismay when he discovered the deception, but no mention is made of the response of Leah or Rachel (Genesis 29:25). What did they think about their father's marriage schemes for them? Why did the sisters go along with the plan? Did they have a choice? As an imposter at her own wedding, how did Leah feel when she knew her husband would soon discover that she was not his beloved Rachel? Where was Rachel during the ceremony? Was this an act of unselfishness on her part to allow her elder sister also to enjoy the blessings of marriage? Or was Rachel opposed to her father's chicanery?

Whatever the case, Leah and Rachel became burdened with considerable confusion produced by the men closest to them. Only by trusting in the Lord could their subsequent pain and disappointment be removed and their souls healed. Their individual struggles to let go of burdens created by those who should have been their protectors, while learning to rely on the grace of God, affords us a great lesson for our day.

Written marriage contracts were customary throughout the ancient Near East. Before the wedding day, the groom and the bride's father (or his representative) signed the contract containing all the accepted negotiations. Consequently, Jacob held a solid legal claim against Laban for failing to meet his commitments in the contract and therefore could have been released from his marriage to Leah. Reflecting his weakened position, Laban proposed an appealing solution the moment Jacob accused him of duplicity. If Jacob would give Leah her due attention during the full bridal week, he could also marry Rachel. Furthermore, Laban did not require Jacob to wait until the negotiated seven additional years of labor were completed before relinquishing his second daughter to him, again indicating Laban's awareness of his vulnerable position.

The only evidence of dowries for Leah and Rachel from their father at the time of their weddings was the gift of a handmaid to each of them. Laban gave his servant Zilpah as a handmaid to Leah and his servant Bilhah to Rachel (Genesis 29:24, 29). No mention is made of any inheritance for them. Years later, when Jacob and his family finally left Haran, Leah and Rachel's lack of inheritance became an important issue.

BARRENNESS, CHILDBIRTH, AND TWO HANDMAIDS

In recent translations of Genesis 29:31, Leah is described as "unloved" rather than "hated," suggesting that Jacob did not feel animosity against her but more likely ignored or discounted her in Rachel's shadow. The Hebrew term in the text, however, has a stronger meaning than loving someone less; it is most accurately translated as "hate" (Schneider, *Mothers,* 66). In this way, Leah represents those whom God loves, even if no one else seems to. Others may not have been sensitive to Leah's rejection, but God certainly was. His compensatory care and blessing led her to deeper faith and greater reliance on Him. Leah eventually bore six sons and one daughter. The names she chose for her sons reflect her growing realization that she needed the Lord's grace and enduring love more than her husband's attentions and an elevated position in the family. Her sons' names also serve as reminders of our need for Christ, the *Son* who opens our communication so that God *hears* us, *joins* us to the Father with His At-one-ment, and deserves our eternal *praises* for His sacrifice on our behalf.

By contrast, the beautiful Rachel was surrounded by Jacob's love and attention but bore no children. Her cry, "Give me children, or else I die," gives painful reality to the void in her life (Genesis 30:1). Her husband's love and visible gifts did not provide an escape from serious disappointment and trials of faith. As He did

TIME LINE

Esau and Jacob are born to Isaac (60) and Rebekah

Abraham dies (175); Esau and Jacob are about 15

Esau (40) marries out of the covenant

Jacob receives the birthright blessing

Jacob goes to Padan-aran to find a wife

Jacob marries Leah and Rachel

Leah gives birth to Reuben, Simeon, Levi, and Judah

Jacob marries Bilhah

Bilhah gives birth to Dan and Naphtali

Jacob marries Zilpah

Zilpah gives birth to Gad and Asher

Leah gives birth to Issachar, Zebulun, and Dinah

Rachel gives birth to Joseph

Jacob departs Haran with four wives, eleven sons, and one daughter

Rachel dies after giving birth to Benjamin

Jacob and Esau are reconciled; Jacob's clan settle in Hebron

Joseph (17) is sold into Egypt

Joseph (30) is made a ruler in Egypt and marries Asenath

Isaac dies (180); Esau and Jacob (120) bury him

Joseph and his brothers are reconciled

Jacob's family moves to Egypt

Jacob dies (147)

MANDRAKES

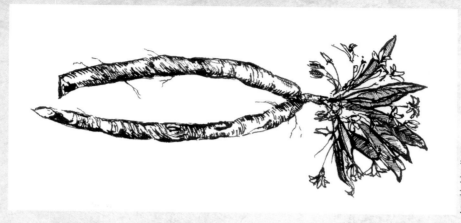

Artwork by Ashton Young

A folk remedy for barrenness, the roots of the mandrake plant were believed to contain fertility-inducing powers. Mandrakes are an eastern plant that produces dainty purple flowers and roots that may have the appearance of a human body, or, to some analysts, the form of a newborn baby. Mandrake roots were probably boiled to prepare a tonic that was often taken as an aphrodisiac.

for Leah, the Lord would also lead Rachel to where only He could help her. Jacob's angry response to his beloved wife indicates his realization of the same truth (Genesis 30:2). Rachel, Leah, and Jacob all endured uncertainties and adversities which led them to acknowledge that God was their foundation.

Rachel's initial solution to her barrenness was to achieve motherhood through her handmaid, Bilhah. Perhaps prompted by Sarah's decision to give Hagar as a wife to Abraham, Rachel gave Bilhah to Jacob as his third wife. Rachel's statement that Bilhah would "bear upon my knees" (Genesis 30:3) is an idiomatic expression suggesting that any child Bilhah bore would be acknowledged as Rachel's own child.

Assuming she could bear no more children, Leah gave her maid, Zilpah, to Jacob to marry and thereby add children to her tally (Genesis 30:9–10). Given the high infant mortality rate of the times and the early death of men in warfare, polygamy was probably not unusual among these ancient peoples. And although less is known of Bilhah and Zilpah than of Rachel and Leah, their position as handmaids did not preclude them from receiving the legal title and status of "wives," as the biblical narrative clearly recognizes (Genesis 37:2).

As Leah gave birth to four sons and concluded that she "had left bearing" (Genesis 30:9) and as Bilhah and Zilpah each bore two sons, Rachel continued to yearn for her own child. When she saw Reuben take mandrakes to his mother, Rachel pleaded with her sister to give them to her. In exchange, Rachel would ensure that Jacob stayed the night in Leah's tent. The barter produced another son for Leah but further disappointment for Rachel.

THE TRIAL OF BARRENNESS

Throughout the patriarchal era, chief women faced trial and refinement through a period of barrenness. For a significant length of time, all except Leah feared they might never bear a child. The wives of the patriarchs viewed barrenness as even more disastrous than did women generally and Hebrew women specifically. For the patriarchs, a son was the assurance of the continuation of God's covenant with Abraham. Even after giving birth, these wives of the patriarchs were still responsible to ensure that the son that God had chosen inherited the birthright, that he married a woman who likewise reverenced the birthright, and properly perpetuated the covenant through a worthy heir. The trial of barrenness served to underscore the value of children in general and the birthright son in particular. They knew that no one else in that generation could assume the birthright's role, but through the faith and obedience to God of the birthright son, he could become an instrument to perpetuate God's ultimate blessings to all of humankind. Rachel's plea, "Give me children, or else I die" (Genesis 30:1) was more than an instinctive maternal desire but was a profound longing to fulfill her responsibility to continue the Abrahamic covenant.

Furthermore, the matriarchs' trial was exacerbated by living near women who quickly and frequently conceived. A Jewish Midrash suggests that Rachel began to connect unrighteousness with her inability to conceive a child, concluding that her sister must be more righteous and more beloved of God than she (Ginzberg, *Legends,* 363).

Like Rachel, we may see trials as punishments from God rather than as divine gifts to strengthen and polish us. Although difficult circumstances differ significantly from one person to another, such as those faced by Rachel and Leah, challenges are one of the humbling conditions of mortality that include persuasive invitations to draw closer to God. Rachel had an ideal marriage but no children. Leah had a difficult marriage but a great family. Both situations posed a temptation for the women at times to feel worthless and forgotten by God or at other times to feel superior and more chosen by God. Each situation, however, also became the vital soil from which the sisters developed unshakable testimonies of God and divine strength to nurture the future leaders of the House of Israel.

In many ways, barrenness is symbolic of any unrealized righteous desire or unforeseen difficulty that strikes everyone sooner or later. When such blessings as marriage, health, education, a home, or believing family members elude us, we may better relate to these wives of the patriarchs during their trial of barrenness. The irony presents itself when one receives God's promise of the desired blessing but current circumstances deny any foreseeable manner that the blessing could be realized. But "faith is the assurance of things hoped for, the evidence of things not seen" (JST Hebrews 11:1). When no evidence exists to show how the promised blessing will be realized, a person of faith acts with certitude as though the blessing had already occurred. Having "an eye of faith" (Alma 32:40), we can see God's promises "afar off" (Hebrews 11:13) and live today with the confidence and assurance that God's plan for us will be better than our greatest dreams. In the imagery of barrenness, each of us is unfruitful without Jesus Christ. It is by His grace we are saved, no matter how great our works may appear to be. After listing Christlike attributes that make up our divine nature, the apostle Peter wrote, "For if these things be in you, and abound, they make you that ye shall neither be barren nor unfruitful in the knowledge of our Lord Jesus Christ" (2 Peter 1:8).

The Lord stretched Rachel's faith in a different way from the way He tested Leah's and Jacob's faith. We may also assume that Zilpah and Bilhah had their share of difficulties that led them to further trust in the Lord. None was exempt; each was beloved of God. Each had pains that could only be assuaged by the healing grace of Jesus Christ.

Another Jewish Midrash adds drama to the story by portraying a compassionate Rachel assisting Leah in her disguise on her wedding night and remaining silent during the ceremony that allowed Leah the blessing of marriage and family that she might not have received otherwise. In turn, Leah, Bilhah, and Zilpah later joined Rachel in her

A monument remembering Rachel, who "weeps for her children . . . because they are not" (Matthew 2:18), is found at the Kibbutz Ramat Rachel, named in her honor, located between Jerusalem and Bethlehem.

petitions to God for a child (Neusner, *Genesis Rabbah,* 3:60–65). The imagery is powerful, suggesting that our sensitivity and compassion for others when we are "barren" can go far to engender greater faith.

Kadya Molodowsky, a twentieth-century poet, penned in Yiddish a sublime set of poems named *Froyen-Lider (Women's Songs).* The sixth poem of the set tells of the compassion that Sarah, Rebekah, Rachel, and Leah have for women who fear they will not marry or bear a child. The wives of the patriarchs are shown to have great sensitivity to ordinary women whose hearts are breaking. Specifically, Sarah cries a goblet full of tears for those who are barren; Rebekah supplies a lovely dowry delivered on the backs of camels for those who have only "patched wash" to begin their married life; Rachel brings the barren "healing leaves," probably mandrakes; and Leah silently acknowledges the pain of single women by covering her eyes (Hellerstein, "Word," 65–69). With a poignant reminder of the desired blessing, the poetess assigned the name "mother" to each of the wives of the patriarchs.

A Book of Mormon prophet acknowledged that most of us need multiple difficulties and hardships to turn us to Christ. "And thus we see that except the Lord doth chasten his people with many afflictions," Mormon observed, "they will not remember him" (Helaman 12:3). A recurrence of mortal trials is evidence of a divine continuing-education program that includes objectives of building greater faith in the enabling power of Christ and a deeper sense of our profound indebtedness to Him.

RACHEL'S SACRIFICE

The number of years that Rachel waited for her righteous desire is not given in scripture. We know only that it was a long time. For some of us the time of uncertainty is even longer—beyond this mortal life. But the same principle applies. God hears. He keeps His promises. Rachel eventually gave birth to two sons and died in giving life to her last born. Her earlier exclamation, "Give me children, or else I die," carries sobering reminders of the potential sacrifice a woman accepts every time she chooses to bear a child. The estimate now is that one in four women died in childbirth in the ancient Near East. Certainly a yearning to bring a child into the world was a life-threatening wish.

It is worthy of note that Rachel's midwife was with her when she died, but Jacob was not (Genesis 35:17). Furthermore, Jacob rejected Rachel's deathbed name for her son. "As her soul was in departing" (Genesis 35:18), Rachel selected the name for her newborn son, often witnessed as the mother's privilege in the Bible, but Jacob changed it. Finally, Rachel is the only one of the wives of the patriarchs who was not buried at Machpeleh (Genesis 49:31). Claremont professor Tammi J. Schneider suggests that these observations may be evidence that the love affair initially enjoyed by Rachel and Jacob had subsided (*Mothers,* 92).

Prophets long remembered Rachel's sorrowing for children, recounting the name she chose for her last born—Ben-oni—which reflected her distress and sorrow (Genesis 35:18), as well as stories of her numerous descendants, living in Israel's northern kingdom, who would be scattered by the conquering Assyrians and lose their covenant identity (Jeremiah 31:15–21). In New Testament times, Matthew portrayed Rachel as weeping again, this time over the children of Bethlehem who were slain in answer to Herod's jealous rage over prophecies of the Messiah's birth (Matthew 2:16–18). The image of Rachel portrayed by these prophets is one of motherly love that knows no bounds and continues throughout the eternities.

Although a traditional burial monument for Rachel stands today near the city of Bethlehem, the biblical text indicates a location farther north. Jacob's clan had traveled only "a little way" from Bethel when Rachel died (Genesis 35:16), and her burial

Traditional burial place of Rachel, just outside Bethlehem. It is more likely, however, that Rachel was buried near Bethel in the territory that would later be inherited by the descendants of her son Benjamin.

site was noted to be within the border of Benjamin during the era of the judges (1 Samuel 10:2). Both of these references suggest that Rachel died near the town of Ramah (in the territory assigned to the tribe of Benjamin) rather than in Bethlehem (in the tribe of Judah's territory).

Unfortunately, the sacred text does not contain Rachel's confirming witness of the Lord's enabling power. We do, however, sense her growing love for God and reliance on Him through her trials. Her sense of individual worth deepened far beyond the ability to attract a husband. Rachel learned that she was known, loved, and entrusted by God with a unique and very important mission. Through God's validating power, she became a mother of Israel, with a testimony of faith and endurance that continues to inspire her daughters today.

DEPARTURE FROM HARAN

Rebekah urged Jacob to "flee thou to Laban my brother to Haran; and tarry with him a few days" (Genesis 27:43–44), which turned into twenty years. In addition to the fourteen years Jacob worked for Laban to earn the bride-price for his two wives, he served six years for wages in livestock and servants (Genesis 30:43; 31:41). Despite Jacob's honest labor over these many years, Laban was loath to see Jacob's family depart. Jacob, Leah, Rachel, and their servants were a significant workforce to him and collectively contributed incredible wealth for Laban. Clearly, the Lord had blessed Laban's clan since Jacob's coming (Genesis 30:30). Should they depart, Laban's holdings and potential for expansion would be dramatically reduced. When Laban changed his payment agreement with Jacob for the tenth time and his agenda against Jacob became more transparent, the Lord directed Jacob to return to his homeland in Canaan.

Laban's sons feared their inheritance would walk away with Jacob should he leave Haran (Genesis 31:1). Because this is the only mention of children of Laban other than Leah and Rachel, the reference is likely to other relatives who anticipated inheriting Laban's wealth in the absence of a son.

Jacob's clan had claim upon a portion of Laban's estate in two ways: Jacob's six-year work contract and his wives' dowries. The text substantiates both claims. Jacob's accusation that Laban frequently changed his wages implies that each time Jacob should have been paid for his labors, Laban paid him less than they had agreed. Jacob testified that he had kept his part of the bargain (Genesis 31:6).

Likewise, Rachel and Leah found dishonesty in their father's dealings with them. Rather than providing each with a dowry, derived at least in part from the bride-price paid to the bride's family, Laban had "quite devoured" it, or spent their share of the inheritance (Genesis 31:14). The dowry was compensation for their separation from the family property and was a critical part of establishing a new household, including an inheritance for the next generation. Losing their dowry was likely facilitated by Leah and Rachel remaining residents of their father's clan, under his protection and decisions, for the first thirteen years of their marriages.

Betrayed by their earthly father, Leah and Rachel faced the temptation to distrust others close to them.

Most of all, they needed to learn that despite others' mistreatment of them, God never hurts or betrays. As difficult as that lesson was under their circumstances, Leah and Rachel exemplify that it can be learned.

Here we see Rachel and Leah at their best. Their finest moment in scripture occurs when their voices combine to give inspired counsel. The Lord commanded Jacob to depart from Haran, but before acting upon the command, he counseled with his wives. Jacob was aware that obedience to God would anger his father-in-law and likely damage relationships between Leah and Rachel and their father. The decision required partnership—the involvement of a "help meet" for him. Surrounded by a flock of sheep in their father's fields, Rachel and Leah were united and grounded in their reverence for God as they counseled their husband, "Whatsoever God hath said unto thee, do" (Genesis 31:16). Whatever instances of rivalry had previously passed between the two sisters, they were exemplary when the moment of decision came; they were a family—bonded together in love and devotion to God and His purposes.

Aware of Laban's patriarchal hold on them in Haran, Jacob's family departed without warning and took their claimed inheritance with them. Jacob's astounding abundance upon departure is in stark contrast to his arrival twenty years before—alone and empty-handed. The Lord kept His promise: "I will be with thee" (Genesis 31:3).

RACHEL'S THEFT OF THE *TERAPHIM*

That Laban did not discover Jacob's absence for three days is indication of his large property holdings and the size of his household (Genesis 31:22). Without livestock, cargo, and children to transport, he could travel faster and eventually overtake Jacob's company. Exhibiting his incredulity against his son-in-law, Laban met Jacob with a flood of accusations and feigned regrets (vv. 25–30). Jacob justified his clandestine departure by explaining his fear that Laban would forcibly withhold Rachel and Leah from him had he openly declared his plans (v. 31).

In the short time Laban needed to organize his pursuit of Jacob, he must have quickly surveyed the security of his greatest valuables, only to find that his *teraphim,* or household gods, were missing. (*Teraphim* is translated as "images" in the King James Version of the Bible.) Scripture records that "Rachel had stolen the images that were her father's" while Laban was away shearing his sheep (Genesis 31:19). Jacob was apparently ignorant of Rachel's role in removing the teraphim, as evidenced in his proclamation of death for the person who took them (v. 32).

Teraphim were small, portable figurines in human shapes. Anciently, they were consulted as oracles for purposes of divination and represented the family's prosperity and divine protection. Terephim were often installed in a family shrine and thought by some to be ancestral images that were worshipped. The city of Haran was a center for the worship of the Mesopotamian moon god named Sin or Nanna. Sin was believed to control the night and see into the darkness to reveal a person's destiny and answers to life's difficult decisions. Believers imagined a plethora of gods and demons encircling the earth ready to pour out disaster and pain on the unprotected. Teraphim were believed to guard a household and ensure protection against the evil forces that surrounded them. Many believed that their gods' protection extended to foreign lands when they carried their teraphim with them during their travels.

Both Abraham's father, Terah, and Laban were idol worshippers and may have been among such believers. Laban said that it was by "experience" (Genesis 30:27)—or divina-

Household "images," called teraphim, were believed to keep a family safe and prosperous.

Artwork by Ashton Young

tion through omens rather than from God—that he knew the Lord favored Jacob. Was this one way that Laban used his teraphim? Interestingly, Laban referred to the figurines as "gods," whereas the Genesis narrator calls them by the more secular word *teraphim,* translated "images" (compare Genesis 31:30 with 31:19, 34). Later, Jacob required his clan to dispose of "all the strange gods which were in their hand, and all their earrings which were in their ears" before they entered Bethel (Genesis 35:4). The episode suggests that Rachel was not the only one to take teraphim before departing, including some who wore a potential reverence to a foreign god in the form of an earring.

In searching for the teraphim, Laban first looked in Jacob's tent and then in the tent of each woman, concluding at Rachel's tent. Going last to Rachel suggests that Laban suspected her least of all. Rachel hid the teraphim in "the camel's furniture," perhaps in a compartment under the saddle, and was sitting upon the furniture when Laban entered (Genesis 31:34). Her pretense of female incapacitation afforded her an excuse not to move away from the hiding place in order to allow her father to search the furniture (Genesis 31:35). The scene suggests that a woman was granted particular privacy and protection from disturbance during her menstrual period. Taking advantage of what may have been Laban's view that female descendants were unworthy heirs to his wealth, Rachel used a symbol of her womanhood to deflect detection of her "theft." Perhaps she wanted to render the deities ritually impure by sitting on them to show that they held no power. Whatever the case, she succeeded in keeping Laban's teraphim away from him.

A complex and confused man, Laban was not consistent in his teachings to his daughters and what he

WHY DID RACHEL TAKE THE TERAPHIM?

The significance of the teraphim and Rachel's motive for taking them remain uncertain. Several explanations have been proposed, including the following:

According to Josephus, Rachel took them as a precaution to obtain her father's forgiveness in the event that he pursued and caught them (Josephus, *Antiquities*, 1.19.9).

A Midrash paints Rachel as a loving daughter who was trying to deter Laban from future idolatry by removing the teraphim from his household (Ginzberg, *Legends*, 1:373).

Another Midrash suggests Rachel was removing Laban's source of divination so he could not discern their whereabouts and return them to Haran (Ginzberg, *Legends*, 1:371).

The Nuzi texts explain that the chief heir was the one who possessed the teraphim, particularly in unusual cases where legal title was given to someone other than a son, such as a daughter, son-in-law, or adopted son. This ancient custom has encouraged additional explanations for Rachel's motive, such as the following:

1. To secure the title for inheritance that was legally hers
2. To establish authority over Leah as the chief wife, who produced children before Rachel did
3. To establish her son, Joseph, as the birthright son in place of Reuben
4. To change Jacob's status as a servant in Laban's household to that of an adopted son and heir who married the master's daughters

The custom was apparently complex yet commonly understood to have been practiced in the era it is historically situated in by the Genesis narrative. That knowledge of the practice has survived in more than one society, but not the explanation of its significance, is further attestation of the custom's authenticity.

allowed in himself. His greed justified him to lie to his son-in-law and daughters and to be untrue to his God. As Rebekah's brother, he would have been taught to reverence God and not the deities of his neighbors. He wanted his daughters to honor the true God but was not willing to do so himself. Do the sins of the father, however, preclude his daughters from embracing the true faith? Many children of errant parents are more adamant in their religious principles, expressly because they have seen the trappings of sin and therefore want lives different from their parents'. Such were Rachel and Leah.

Laban acknowledged defeat in retrieving his teraphim when he blessed his daughters and bade them farewell (Genesis 31:55). Rachel and Leah would never return to Haran. As Jacob's company turned again toward Canaan, one senses the tremendous spiritual and temporal wealth that accompanied them, leaving Laban and his household emotionally and spiritually destitute in their wake.

JACOB'S REUNION WITH ESAU

A highlight of the journey back to Canaan was Jacob's reunion with his brother, Esau, in the "land of Seir, the country of Edom" (Genesis 32:3), a territory that reflected names by which Esau was known from birth. Esau's brotherly affection and generosity indicated that Jacob was not the only one who changed in the intervening twenty years. What happened in Canaan during Jacob's absence? Was their mother, Rebekah, yet alive? Did she ever know of her sons' reconciliation?

Both brothers had prospered since they had last seen each other. Jacob's accrued wealth was manifested by his proffered gift to Esau (Genesis 32:13–15). Indicative of his parallel success, Esau had four hundred fighting men in his clan (Genesis 32:6). Both men showed spiritual strength and gratitude for their increase by acknowledging "I have enough" (Genesis 33:9, 11) and crediting their good fortune to God.

Demonstrating that their reconciliation continued beyond this reunion, Jacob and Esau later met in Hebron at the cave of Machpelah to bury their father (Genesis 35:29; 49:31). These incidents show the scriptural unsoundness of blaming today's animosity between Israelis and Arabs on an unresolved hatred between Jacob and Esau.

MOTHERS OF THE TWELVE TRIBES OF ISRAEL

Centuries after the patriarchal era, community leaders would bless a new bride named Ruth, praying that she would be a woman "like Rachel and like Leah, which two did build the house of Israel" (Ruth 4:11). Different in appearance from each other as well as in their challenges, Rachel and Leah are known most by what they accomplished together. Along with Zilpah and Bilhah, Leah and Rachel are the mothers of the twelve tribes of Israel.

THE TWELVE TRIBES OF ISRAEL

Name	Meaning	Expanded Meaning
Mother Leah		
1. Reuben	"Look, a son"	"Surely the Lord hath **looked** upon my affliction; now therefore my husband will love me" (Genesis 29:32).
2. Simeon	"Hearing"	"Because the Lord hath **heard** that I was hated, he hath therefore given me this son also; and she called his name Simeon" (Genesis 29:33).
3. Levi	"Joined"	"Now this time will my husband be **joined** unto me, because I have borne him three sons: therefore was his name called Levi" (Genesis 29:34).
4. Judah	"Praise"	"Now will I **praise** the Lord: therefore she called his name Judah" (Genesis 29:35).
Mother Bilhah		
5. Dan	"Judge"	"God hath **judged** me, and hath also heard my voice, and hath given me a son: therefore called she his name Dan" (Genesis 30:6).
6. Naphtali	"Wrestlings"	"With great **wrestlings** I have wrestled with my sister, and I have prevailed: and she called his name Naphtali" (Genesis 30:8).

Name	Meaning	Expanded Meaning
Mother Zilpah		
7. Gad	"Good fortune" or "troop"	"A **troop** cometh: and she called his name Gad" (Genesis 30:11).
8. Asher	"Happy" or "blessed"	"**Happy** am I, for the daughters will call me **blessed**: and she called his name Asher" (Genesis 30:13).
Mother Leah		
9. Issachar	"Recompense"	"God hath **given me my hire**, because I have given my maiden to my husband: and she called his name Issachar" (Genesis 30:18).
10. Zebulun	"Lofty, high, exalted," from the same root as *endued* (Hebrew *zbd*)	"God hath **endued** me with a good dowry, now will my husband dwell with me, because I have born him six sons: and she called his name Zebulun" (Genesis 30:20).
Mother Rachel		
11. Joseph	"To add; to take away; to gather"	"God hath taken away my reproach: And she called his name Joseph; and said, The Lord shall **add** to me another son" (Genesis 30:23–24).
12. Benjamin	"Son of the right hand"	"His father called him Benjamin" (Genesis 35:18). Jacob expected to depend on his youngest son as "his right hand" in his declining years.

After Rachel's death, no further mention is made of Leah in the Genesis narrative. Did she also die prematurely? The text merely records that she died before her husband and that he buried her (Genesis 49:31). Were the many later problems among the twelve sons and one daughter evidence of the absence of a mother? Whether she lived much longer or not, Leah's invisibility after Rachel's death in the Genesis account suggests unity and equality between the two sisters' contributions. For example, although Leah was buried next to Jacob in the cave of Machpelah (Genesis 49:31), Rachel is listed first in biblical references of the sisters (Genesis 31:4, 14; Ruth 4:11). Additionally, Rachel was the ancestress of many of Israel's leaders from the time of the conquest of Canaan, including Joshua; the judges Deborah, Samuel, Gideon, and Jephthah; and Saul, the first king of Israel. One of her sons also received the birthright blessing, which includes important responsibilities in the latter day (2 Nephi 3). Leah's posterity was every bit as impressive. She was the ancestress of Moses and Aaron and the administrators of the lesser priesthood down to John the Baptist. Most important, through her son Judah, Leah was an ancestress of Jesus Christ.

God does not measure greatness in number of children, age at marriage, titles, or material wealth. He looks at the heart and the commitment to respond as Rachel and Leah did: "Whatsoever God hath said unto thee, do" (Genesis 31:16). After facing frequent threats to their familial relationships, Rachel and Leah had reason enough to complain of life's injustices. Subsequent generations, however,

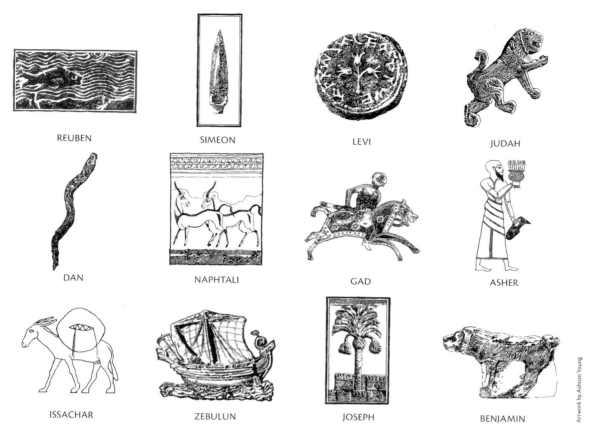

REUBEN   SIMEON   LEVI   JUDAH

DAN   NAPHTALI   GAD   ASHER

ISSACHAR   ZEBULUN   JOSEPH   BENJAMIN

Artwork by Ashton Young

Symbols for each son. In the days of Moses, the high priest's breastplate contained twelve precious gemstones representative of the twelve tribes (Exodus 28:17–21), and each tribe carried a standard, or "ensign," indicating their "father's house" when they traveled (Numbers 2:2). The emblematic insignia for each of the twelve sons, as designed by Ashton Young, is based on the respective son's blessing as recorded in scripture.

would bear witness of the sisters' unique role in establishing God's covenant people. Looking beyond immediate desires and selfish demands allows a glimpse of God's promises and the Spirit's witness of a reason to hope.

As the sisters learned to rely on their Redeemer rather than on status, appearance, or family circumstance, they developed strength and wisdom beyond their natural abilities. They discovered the validating and enabling power that can only come from God. With their deepened understanding and faith, they could receive the healing balm of Christ to overcome the scars of betrayal and abuse meted out by their father. Consequently, Rachel and Leah built a healthier sense of individual worth that in turn enabled them to build stronger and more meaningful family relationships. Most important of all, through their serious and long-term trials, they gained a witness that God lives and loves them. With God to sustain and lead them, no force could destroy them.

POINTS TO PONDER: APPLICATIONS FOR OUR LIVES

1. When no one else seems to notice or appreciate your presence, how do you know God sees and cares about you? How has the Lord compensated your faithfulness to Him when individuals in your life ignore or patronize you?

2. Life is unpredictable. Have you judged another person who appears to have escaped any disappointment or challenge? Considering Leah's and Rachel's vulnerable condition when facing fears and uncertainties, how might you retract your judgment of that person?

3. When have you experienced a time of barrenness? In retrospect, what divine truths were illuminated for you as a result of that difficult time?

4. What can we learn from Leah and Rachel about being better sisters, wives, and mothers?

5. What principles of the gospel are illustrated through the lives of Rachel and Leah?

6. Do you relate to one of the sisters more than the other? Why? How does she inspire you in your faith in Jesus Christ?

7. How has your individual worth been shaped by your relationship with God and reliance on Christ's Atonement?

8. How has the Lord shown you His enabling power and enduring love during your recurring trials?

PROPHETESSES

$\mathcal{B}$etween the time the children of Israel wandered in the wilderness and the Savior's birth, the Bible refers to several women as prophetesses, a term that can be troubling to those who restrict the meaning of *prophet* to a man whom God authorizes to declare doctrine, relay His will to His people, and lead them back to Him. But authors of the accounts in the Bible often use *prophet* in a more general sense that easily includes women. Biblical prophets and prophetesses possess the gift of prophecy, one of the numerous gifts of the Spirit, but are not authorized with keys to direct the affairs of God's church. The apostle John taught that "the testimony of Jesus is the spirit of prophecy" (Revelation 19:10). Joseph Smith taught that a prophet is anyone who possesses a testimony of Jesus Christ (*Teachings,* 119, 160, 269). Therefore, prophetesses and prophets are endowed with the spiritual knowledge that Jesus is the Christ; they then bear that witness by the same Spirit. More than predicting future events, prophets and prophetesses deliver God's message of warning or direction pertaining to current situations, a message that can also have a profound effect on an entire people.

Other Church leaders have reiterated that the gift of prophecy is not conditioned on gender or priesthood authority. Elder James E. Talmage of the Quorum of the Twelve Apostles observed, "No special ordination in the Priesthood is essential to man's receiving the gift of prophecy. . . . The ministrations of Miriam and Deborah show that this gift may be possessed by women also" (*Articles of Faith,* 228–29). President Gordon B. Hinckley told the women of the Church that the spirit of prophecy may be theirs, "as much so as any man in the world." He also recognized that some women are blessed with added discernment for future events. "Can anyone doubt that many women have a special intuitive sense," he observed, "even a prescient understanding of things to come?" (*Ensign,* Nov. 1985, 88).

All Israelite women were not given the title of prophetess, nor was the title assigned because a woman was married to a prophet or other important man in society. Only one of the seven biblical women called "prophetess" in the Bible was married to a prophet, as we use the term today. That woman was Isaiah's wife, as he indicated in the following verse: "And I went unto the prophetess; and she conceivd, and bare a son. Then said the Lord to me, Call his name Maher-shalal-hash-baz" (Isaiah 8:3). Nothing in the verse explains why Isaiah referred to his wife as a prophetess. The boy's name is prophetic, meaning "to speed, spoil, hasten, plunder," as explained in 8:4.

Considering the other women who were given the title "prophetess" and the way the term has been used by both ancient and modern prophets, Isaiah's wife also must have received a personal witness of the Savior and may have been given a confirming witness to that of her husband's concerning the prophetic name for their son. In the other examples of Old Testament prophetesses, either no husband is mentioned or little is known of the woman's husband. Thus the title of prophetess speaks more about the woman herself. Women were qualified as true prophetesses by their faith in the Savior's Atonement rather than by marriage to a righteous man.

Some women purposely misused their positions of trust to teach false prophecies and doctrines with the intent to thwart God's work. Two of the seven women named as prophetesses in the Bible—Noadiah in Old Testament times and Jezebel in New Testament times—were among those considered *false* prophetesses (Nehemiah 6:10–14; Revelation 2:20). The prophet Ezekiel warned of women who used divination to "prophesy out of their own heart" rather than by the Spirit. He accused these women of teaching "lies [that] have made the heart of the righteous sad; whom [God has] not made sad and strengthened the hands of the wicked, that he should not return from his wicked way, by promising him life" (Ezekiel 13:17, 22).

Briefly consider the five women regarded in the Bible as true prophetesses. Miriam was called a prophetess when she led the children of Israel in singing and praising the Lord after their deliverance from Egypt (Exodus 15:20). Known as one of Israel's judges, the prophetess Deborah rekindled her people's faith in the Lord to rise up against their oppressors (Judges 4:4). By declaring the veracity of the Lord's word in scripture, Huldah inspired Judah's king to deeper religious reform before the Babylonian invasion (2 Kings 22:14; 2 Chronicles 34:22). Reflecting her role as prophetess, Isaiah's wife gave their sons names that bore witness of the Lord's promise to scatter and then gather the tribes of Israel (Isaiah 8:3–4, 18; 7:3; 2 Nephi 18:3–4). And while numerous couples brought their firstborn infant sons to the temple during the reign of King Herod, the prophetess Anna recognized one of those babies as the Son of God and bore witness of that fact (Luke 2:36–38).

By giving them the label of prophetess, biblical authors imply that these women devoted time to testify of the Messiah. The label does not preclude other women from having a similar commitment and devotion, even though they are not specifically called prophetesses in the biblical record. Under our definition of the term, could not Eve, Sarah, Hagar, and Rebekah have been considered prophetesses? Can you find qualities in them or circumstances they encountered that allow for such recognition? After the resurrection, for example, one of the first Christian leaders by the name of Philip had four daughters "which did prophesy" (Acts 21:9). These young women appear to possess characteristics of a prophetess, although they are not called by the title. Descriptions of Hannah, particularly in 1 Samuel 1 in the Septuagint and the Dead Sea Scrolls, fit the characteristics of a prophetess even though she is not specifically labeled as such.

The biblical women called prophetesses were women who lived under the law of Moses, from its inception almost to the day it was fulfilled through Christ's atoning sacrifice. Certainly this portrays an impressive length of time that prophetesses were recognized. It may, however, suggest something more. The era of the lesser law often shows the Israelites either meshing the law with the surrounding pagan practices or viewing it as the end rather than the means of coming to Christ. When the need for a Redeemer is marginalized by desires for power, wealth, and lasciviousness, we cannot hear too many witnesses of God's reality and purposes from prophets and prophetesses. Is that one reason why we find them during this era?

Numerous teachings, both scriptural and from latter-day leaders, remind us that we can be prophetesses and prophets, too. Feeling the incredible weight of his responsibility to the children of Israel, Moses complained to God, "I am not able to bear all this people alone" (Numbers 11:14). In response, the Lord called seventy others to assist Moses. When the Spirit rested on the seventy, they all prophesied, drawing concern and criticism from the camp. To these concerns, Moses replied, "Would God that all the Lord's people were prophets, and that the Lord would put his spirit upon them" (v. 29).

Joel 2:28 quotes the Savior's promise, "I will pour out my spirit upon all flesh; and your sons and your daughters shall prophesy," to testify of how we may know the Lord is in our midst. Similarly, the Book of Mormon prophet Alma taught that all can receive the Lord's revealed truth, independent of age or sex. "[God] imparteth his word by angels unto men, yea, not only men but women also. Now this is not all; little children do have words given unto them many times, which confound the wise and the learned" (Alma 32:23). Without explicitly using the words *prophets* and *prophetesses,* these passages reinforce the meaning of the titles by describing the qualifying credentials.

In the early days of the restored Church, President Heber C. Kimball stressed the reality that this gift is found in more than the First Presidency and Quorum of Twelve: "There is not a man or woman in this congregation," he explained, "if they live their religion and have the Holy Ghost upon them, but what are prophets, every one of them. . . . I wish to God you, brethren and sisters, were all prophets and prophetesses; you may be, if you live your religion; you cannot help yourselves" (*Journal of Discourses,* 5:88).

More recently, Elder Dallin H. Oaks shared one way we may become what Moses so desired: "Latter-day Saints revere our prophets and respect what they have said about the meaning of various scriptures. But what we are seeking to accomplish through the authority and knowledge received in the Restoration is *not to magnify the standing of the prophets but to elevate the spirituality of our rank and file members.* Like Moses, we declare, 'would God that all the Lord's people were prophets, and that the Lord would put his spirit upon them!' We encourage everyone to study the scriptures prayerfully and seek personal revelation *to know their meaning for themselves*" ("Scripture Reading," 1; emphasis added).

This section focuses on four biblical prophetesses who lived in very different circumstances: Miriam, after Israel's Egyptian bondage; Deborah, near the beginning of the rule of judges; Hannah, at the end of the rule of judges; and Huldah, in Jerusalem after the northern kingdom had fallen.

By the River's Brink

MIRIAM

מִרְיָם

Meaning uncertain, perhaps "Bitterness," "Exalted"

The prophetess Miriam entered the stage of biblical history at the dawn of one of its most dynamic periods. During her lifetime, a people were divinely tutored to become disciples of Abraham's God and heirs of the Abrahamic covenant. In her generation, a multitude was delivered from long centuries of Egyptian slavery, gained distinctiveness as the nation of Israel, and received a forty-year, spiritually designed education of essential values and behaviors that shaped them into God's peculiar people.

Although Miriam's younger brothers, Moses and Aaron, were the priesthood leaders of this miraculous movement, several women played prominent roles that exemplified unshakable benevolence and established a foundation from which a God-fearing people could develop. Parallel to the twelve sons of Jacob are twelve women introduced in the opening two chapters of the book of Exodus. The midwives Shiphrah and Puah (Exodus 1), Jochebed, Miriam, the daughter of Pharaoh, and Zipporah with her six sisters (Exodus 2) showed great courage, leadership, and morality in oftentimes life-threatening circumstances.

Early in her life, Miriam responded with mature bravery and wisdom as she risked her own life to save her infant brother. After her people miraculously crossed the Red Sea and watched their mighty pursuers drown in their wake, Miriam was the prophetess who bore witness of their Deliverer in a prophetic hymn of praise and view of their future. Finally, Miriam invites us to learn deeper respect for God's authority and revelation after the chastisement she suffered because she criticized God's prophet.

Miriam is unique among biblical women in being portrayed in scripture from childhood to burial. Her life includes evidences of remarkable strengths in leadership and also a weakness in judgment that drew the Lord's fierce displeasure. As a result of the completeness in her story, we can see ourselves in Miriam. Her greatness, like ours, lies neither in one glorious hour of success nor in a

EXODUS 2:4–8; 15:20–21
NUMBERS 12:1–16; 20:1; 26:59
DEUTERONOMY 24:9
1 CHRONICLES 6:3
MICAH 6:4
LDS BIBLE DICTIONARY, 733

TIME LINE

18th century B.C.	Jacob's family moves to Egypt
17th to 14th century B.C.	Hebrews enslaved in Egypt
1370 B.C.?	Birth of Miriam
1363 B.C.	Birth of Aaron
1360 B.C.	Birth of Moses
	Miriam orchestrates the wet-nurse agreement with the daughter of Pharaoh (Moses 3 months old)
1357 B.C.	Moses (3 years old) moves to the palace
1320 B.C.	Moses (40) flees from Egypt and resides in Midian; marries Zipporah
1280 B.C.	Moses (80) returns to Egypt as the prophet of Jehovah to deliver the Israelites
	First Passover
	Miraculous crossing of the Red Sea
	Miriam's hymn of praise
	Law given from Mount Sinai
1279 B.C.	Second Passover
	Miriam and Aaron criticize Moses (81); Miriam's leprosy
1242 B.C.	Miriam dies at Kadesh
1241 B.C.	Aaron dies
1240 B.C.	Moses (120) is translated
	Joshua leads the children of Israel into the promised land

Dates are approximations based on the late date theory for the Exodus (see pages 173–74).

moment of public failure but rather over the ledger of our lives. Repeatedly, day by day, we learn to trust that Christ is the only Source of healing and empowerment.

In the New Testament record, more Israelite women are known by the Greek version of Miriam's name than by any other name. As many as seven women named Mary are part of the early Christian church. Although the exact meaning remains uncertain, the name has been shown to mean both "exalted" and "bitterness," a reflection of emotions, challenges, life in the fallen world, and hope of God's eventual promise. With this insight, all women can share her name. Indeed, Miriam is Everywoman.

HEBREW LIFE IN GOSHEN

Miriam lived in the area of Goshen with the other Hebrew slaves (Exodus 9:26), close to the treasure cities they were building for Pharaoh. If the pharaoh of this period was indeed Rameses II, many brilliant edifices and colossal statuary remain today as a witness of the sacrifices and hard labor of the slaves who built them.

Miriam was the eldest child of Amram and Jochebed. Her brother Aaron was a few years younger and brother Moses three years younger still (Exodus 7:7). Not only did both parents belong to the tribe of Levi, but they were even more closely related: Jochebed was Amram's aunt (Exodus 6:20; Numbers 26:59; see also 1 Chronicles 6:3). Under the law of Moses, a man would later be forbidden to marry his father's sister (Leviticus 18:12–13), but no stigma seemed to accompany it before God's instructions from Mount Sinai.

Although Miriam's family is identified with the tribe of Levi early in the story, it is uncertain how long and how carefully the descendants of Israel strictly traced their lineage or absorbed the patriarchs' beliefs. The few clues we have suggest that the Hebrew multitude in Egypt maintained little if any of the pure gospel of Abraham. Moses received a strong Egyptian education before he fled to Midian. Not until he lived among the Midianites, where he was taught by his wife's family and by the Lord

The grandeur and power of Egypt are reflected in numerous monuments throughout the land. Miriam and her people left all this behind to live in dramatic simplicity in the wilderness.

Himself, did Moses learn of God, the priesthood, and the covenant. Jehovah taught Moses face to face, revealing His identity as Jehovah, the Creator of worlds without number, the God of Abraham, Isaac, and Jacob, His infinite power to deliver them from Egyptian bondage, and the continuation of His covenant with Abraham's descendants (Exodus 3–4; Moses 1). Moses' father-in-law, a descendant of Abraham through Keturah, ordained him to Melchizedek Priesthood authority, and his wife, Zipporah, taught him the importance of the covenant and circumcision (D&C 84:6; JST Exodus 4:24–27).

Shortly before the plagues began, Moses began to teach the Hebrew multitude back in Goshen. Were these Miriam's first doctrinal instructions and first encounter with a testimony of the true God? The brief narrative suggests that Moses addressed gospel beginners, not seasoned believers. Even then, the enslaved people struggled to believe his message, on account of the bitter and hopeless state of their bondage (Exodus 4:27–31; 6:9). Finally, at Mount Sinai, the Israelites made their covenant with Jehovah and thereafter referred to Him as the One who came from Sinai, further underscoring His origin as far as their experience dictated (Judges 5:4; Psalm 68:8). Miriam's great service as a child was likely inspired by her parents' ethical teachings and the light of Christ (Moroni 7:16).

MODERN-DAY JOCHEBEDS AND MIRIAMS

"Like Jochebed, we raise our families in a wicked and hostile world—a world as dangerous as the courts of Egypt ruled by Pharaoh. But, like Jochebed, we also weave around our children a protective basket—a vessel called 'the family'—and guide them to safe places where our teachings can be reinforced in the home and at church. . . . Along the way, at times when our children are away from us, the Lord provides inspired 'Miriams' to watch over them—special third-party helpers such as priesthood and auxiliary leaders, teachers, extended family, and worthy friends" (Hales, *Ensign*, May 2004, 89–90).

SAVING HER LITTLE BROTHER

Sometime during the three years between the births of Aaron and Moses, Pharaoh decreed that "every [Hebrew] son that is born ye shall cast into the river" (Exodus 1:22). Josephus reports that the consequence for Israelite parents who disobeyed Pharaoh's decree and saved their infant sons from death was that "they and their families should be destroyed" (*Antiquities,* 2.9.2). The early Christian apostles taught that Jochebed and Amram "were not afraid of the king's commandment" because of their faith (Hebrews 11:23).

The Exodus narrative highlights courageous solutions that several women took to thwart Pharaoh's edict. By contrast, the men—whether Israelite or Egyptian—are invisible, as though nothing could be done by them to thwart the royal command.

Fearful of attracting Pharaoh's attention, Jochebed hid her newborn son for three months as a temporary solution to preserving the baby's life. Her subsequent plan required her daughter's assistance. Although the daughter is not named until later in the record (Exodus 15:20; Numbers 26:29), Jochebed is certainly referring to Miriam. To keep the baby afloat in the river, Jochebed used a small ark made of bulrushes. Interestingly, the Hebrew word translated "ark" here (*tebah*) is the same word used to describe Noah's ark, also a vessel of divine protection and deliverance (Genesis 6:14).

And just as Noah's ark was covered, inside and out, with pitch (Hebrew *kaphar*), so Jochebed daubed, or sealed, her small vessel with slime and pitch. Remembering that another rendering of the Hebrew word *kaphar* is Atonement, referring to Christ's covering of our sins, we glimpse a correlation with the Savior. Although the Hebrew word for *pitch* used to describe Jochebed's sealing element is different from the word that appears in the description of Noah's ark, the parallel invites discovery of Christ's Atonement in the rescue of Moses.

Once Jochebed sent the basket floating down the Nile, carrying her precious cargo, Miriam's responsibility began. Not knowing beforehand where the basket would stop, Miriam watched, ready to devise a plan that would protect her little brother, no matter what circumstance unfolded (Exodus 2:4). If she were discovered, Pharaoh would certainly condemn Miriam to death.

What thoughts flashed through young Miriam's mind as she watched Pharaoh's daughter retrieve the infant from the ark? Was that the plan from the beginning? Certainly it was the plan from God's perspective. Generations before, Joseph had prophesied that a daughter of Pharaoh would assist in Israel's future, saying that Moses "shall be nursed by the king's daughter, and shall be called her son" (JST Genesis 50:29). Although the Egyptians despised the Hebrews and treated them as less than human, something stirred within the princess's heart so that God's plan and promise could move forward.

The daughter of Pharaoh was bathing in the Nile River, undoubtedly a common ritual, considering the Egyptians' views of the river's sacredness and its power to impart longevity and fruitfulness. Perhaps that is what evoked her immediate acceptance of the baby drawn from the sacred life source. She recognized right away that the infant was Hebrew. Was that a deduction purely from the circumstances of finding him in the river? Was the baby wrapped in a customary Hebrew cloth that additionally identified him as a Hebrew child? A Jewish tradition claims that Moses was circumcised in accordance with the Abrahamic covenant, revealing his Israelite lineage (Ginzberg, *Legends,* 2:267). Whatever the clues, the Egyptian princess knew what was at stake; she instinctively reached out to save the child in defiance of her father's command.

Miriam's quick thinking and wise timing created a way for the baby to have a continued relationship

WHO WAS THE DAUGHTER OF PHARAOH?

The name of the daughter of Pharaoh never appears in scripture, and the name of her father is also absent. Josephus calls her Thermuthis/Thuoris, indicating his belief that she was the daughter of Rameses II. Josephus further explains that Thermuthis's desire to adopt the infant Moses grew out of the impossibility that she could produce a legitimate heir of her own because she was married to the infant heir of the throne of Lower Egypt when she was an adult woman. Josephus's account also explains how her royal marriage provided sufficient independence from her father's demands, allowing her to keep a Hebrew baby (*Antiquities,* 2.9.5–7; see also Ginzberg, *Legends,* 2:266).

If the pharaoh who declared the edict against the Hebrew babies was Thutmoses, scholars have surmised that the daughter may have been the great Hutshepsut, the princess of the Eighteenth Dynasty who became queen over Egypt.

Other legends suggest that the daughter of Pharaoh eventually married a Hebrew man, rejected her father's wicked beliefs and her privileged life of royalty, and joined the Israelites in the wilderness. Jewish tradition claims that she married Caleb and changed her name to Bithiah, whereas 1 Chronicles records that the daughter of Pharaoh named Bithiah married Mered (see 1 Chronicles 4:17–18; Ginzberg, *Legends,* 2:270–71).

In fact, however, nothing more is known of the daughter of Pharaoh after Moses first leaves Egypt.

with his birth family (Exodus 2:7–9). Wet-nursing agreements are common in ancient Near Eastern documents. The agreement Miriam suggested to Pharaoh's daughter allowed the infant Moses to live in his parents' home until he was weaned, at about the age of three years. As an older sister living in the same home, Miriam would have undoubtedly been involved in Moses' early care and guidance. Seeing her as an obedient, courageous, and bright child adds understanding for Miriam's preparation to become one of Israel's great leaders.

Again, showing respect for the child's cultural origins, the daughter of Pharaoh gave her adopted son a name that had meaning for both Egyptians and Hebrews. *Moses* is an Egyptian name that means "is born," as found within the names of such pharaohs as Thutmose and Rameses. But the daughter of Pharaoh explained that she chose the name for its Hebrew meaning, "to draw out" (see Exodus 2:10). She also provided her adopted son an outstanding education, and he became "learned in all the wisdom of the Egyptians, and was mighty in words and in deeds" (Acts 7:21–22).

DELIVERANCE FROM EGYPT

Although no mention of Miriam appears in scripture while Moses lived in Midian or during his later negotiations with Pharaoh, a general idea of her life can be extrapolated from the Exodus narrative. As a Hebrew slave in Lower Egypt, Miriam would have grown up amid continual poverty, injustice, adversity, and prejudice against her people. Whatever specific hardships she faced daily with her assigned labor, she would have felt added stress and affliction created when taskmasters required that the Hebrews make their standard quota of bricks without supplying them with straw (Exodus 5). Without straw as a binder to prevent mud bricks from splitting as they dried, the slaves were compelled to find an alternative material, such as hair, dried reeds, or slender sticks, to bind the bricks, or to make additional bricks to compensate for those that broke. Such requirements, added to an already demanding burden, create a test that builds either faith or bitter feelings toward God. Was turning the Israelites away from hope of divine deliverance Pharaoh's objective in this stratagem?

Miriam's hardships in slavery would have been further exacerbated when Moses brought down the plagues upon Egypt. Remembering that the first three plagues afflicted the slaves as well as the Egyptians assists us in visualizing Miriam's chaotic and confusing life during those ten days. First, blood flowed through the Nile River and its tributaries for a full week, contaminating the Egyptians' deified source of life but also polluting the slaves' source of water (Exodus 7:14–24). Next came frogs, made additionally repulsive by their sheer number, continually emerging from the Egyptians' glorious Nile and invading the homes of Egyptians and slaves alike (Exodus 7:25–8:11). Finally, every person in the land was plagued with lice, as dust everywhere moved with the saturation of this vermin (Exodus 8:12–15). The horrors of these afflictions were especially troubling to the Hebrews, who must have felt deeply confused if not betrayed by the God of Moses. How did Miriam cope? How did she sustain her faith?

Even though the remaining seven plagues did not directly affect the Hebrew slaves, the crisis would have created considerable unrest throughout the area. Did the Egyptians increase persecution against the Hebrews because of Moses and the wretched plagues? Were Miriam and her people ad-

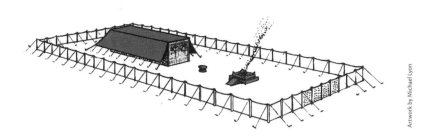

The tabernacle in the wilderness covered an area 150 feet by 75 feet within the outer fence. The sanctuary floor measured 45 feet by 15 feet. Gifts to Israelite women from their Egyptian neighbors contributed significantly to its glorious appearance.

ditionally tempted to reject their newfound God? Certainly God did not expect those He was molding to be His people to merely sit back and watch the manifestation of His power. Miriam and each of the Hebrew slaves were humbled until they recognized that no one could deliver them but God Himself.

As He expects of each of us, God required the children of Israel to act, participate, and begin building a firm foundation of faith in Him. First, He commanded the Hebrew men and women to collect silver and gold jewelry, clothing, and metals from their neighbors, not with the suggestion that these items were a loan but rather given to them as a gift. All the Hebrew women were instructed to go to their female Egyptian neighbors and the men to the male neighbors, signifying that gender associations had already been established (Exodus 11:2; 12:35–36).

Some of the word choices in this passage in the King James Version may add confusion to this part of the story. To clarify that the goods were given rather than lent, a better translation for "borrow" in Exodus 11:2 and 12:35 would be "ask," and "let them have" would be more accurate than "borrowed" in Exodus 12:36. Similarly, "despoiled" or "divested" are better word choices than "spoiled" in Exodus 12:36, suggesting that the Egyptians were bereft of their finery because they chose to give it to the Israelites rather than continue to suffer plagues. These fine linens, metals, and jewels would later be used to construct and adorn the portable tabernacle in the wilderness after the children of Israel donated them with willing hearts for that purpose (Exodus 35:22–29).

The Israelites also changed their daily diet the week before the tenth and final plague struck the Egyptians. God forbade them to eat anything containing leaven, such as bread, or to store any yeast or leavening in their homes during that entire week (Exodus 12:18–20). Instructions for the preparation of the first Passover feast were explicit, requiring specific elements that bore witness of their True Redeemer from bondage. As the Israelites offered an animal sacrifice through the shedding of blood, they were reminded that the family of Abraham escaped bondage and death only because the Savior, the Lamb of God, gave His perfect life to redeem them.

Knowing the meal was to be observed in families rather than as a community, every man and woman among the Israelites needed to know God's requirements in order to be in perfect compliance for the sacred

THE FIRST PASSOVER FEAST

Although men slaughtered the lambs, other requirements accompanied the feast preparation. Consider the critical role of the women in preparing and serving the feast. God's instructions included the following:

A yearling male lamb (taken in his prime), without blemish, and slaughtered by the shedding of blood at the close of the day (Exodus 12:5–6; see also 1 Peter 1:19).

The lamb was roasted whole on a spit over an open wood fire, not boiled in water, not undercooked, and without breaking any bones (Exodus 12:8–9, 46).

The lamb was to be served with unleavened bread, probably cooked in the simplest manner. Women built a fire on a flat stone and then removed the hot ashes and placed the bread dough on the heated stone. They covered the dough with the hot ashes until the dough was cooked through, cleared off the ashes, and served the bread.

The lamb was also served with a pungent condiment of bitter herbs such as endive, chicory, or other edible herbs grown in Egypt (Exodus 12:8).

The family must consume all the lamb by morning, without taking any leftovers to neighbors (Exodus 12:3–4, 10, 46).

Hyssop, an herb of the mint family with aromatic white flowers, was used to spread the symbol of life, the blood of a perfect lamb, around the doors (Exodus 12:22; see also John 19:29 for its use when Jesus was on the cross). The plant holds liquids well and was also used in rituals for cleansing lepers according to instructions in the law of Moses (Leviticus 14).

feast. Meat was rarely part of the Israelites' diet in ancient times because cows, sheep, and goats were more valuable for what they produced alive. The command for every family to provide a lamb, therefore, required a significant level of faith and sacrifice, especially for this initial Passover commemoration. Because eating lamb was a rarity, the animal was already held in symbolic reverence and appreciation by the people. The men were responsible for slaughtering the lambs and then collecting the lambs' blood as the symbol of life. Using a hyssop plant as a brush, the men were assigned to paint the blood of the lamb around the doors to their homes in a symbolic act to bring the Lord's protection from death (Exodus 12:21–22).

But who was responsible for preparing the Passover meal with exactness? Every step and each ingredient was designed to bear witness of Christ. Careful attention to every detail was never more important in food preparation than for this sacred meal. We assume the women took this role, even though the scriptural text does not specifically assign it. Each woman who was responsible for the meal would discover Christ for herself in the preparation, and she would teach her children about Him through the elements of the feast (Exodus 12:26–27).

Furthermore, every family was required to remain indoors throughout the entire night of the Passover and tenth plague. Wouldn't the women also be the most alert to be sure that no child, whether inadvertently or out of curiosity, would step outside to watch the chaos associated with the final plague? (Exodus 12:22).

Much more than just a meal for a hungry family, the Passover feast was designed to teach the Israelites of their Redeemer and His sacrifice for them. Obedience to Him was required at every step, by every man, woman, and child. The success of this divinely designed lesson depended in large part on the vigilance and faith of the women.

Where was Miriam in all of these dramatic events? Who trained and taught the women these important principles and precise directions? Miriam was long remembered as a leader among the Israelites (Micah 6:4). Because this critical act of symbolic significance required exceptional leadership, Miriam was likely a director among the women. As with modern-day Relief Society presidents, she could inspire, instruct, and encourage the other women to value and succeed in their essential contribution. And also as in our day, these women's remarkable acts were largely unreported and undetected in the text.

A MIXED MULTITUDE DEPARTS FROM EGYPT

God had revealed to Abraham that his descendants would "come out [from the nation they had served] with great substance" (Genesis 15:14). The remarkable fulfillment of that prophecy is well-known. The children of Israel, adorned with all the vestments and jewels of Egyptian finery, simply walked away from Egypt and their lives of bondage. The actual events of their departure and subsequent wanderings, however, were doubtless more complex than the account recorded in the Bible indicates.

Imagine the mighty Egyptian army, with their hundreds of speeding chariots, charging closer and closer to the sprawling menagerie of men, women, children, and livestock harnessed with whatever belongings they could carry. The Exodus narrative reports that the trauma of this departure caused the fleeing multitude to fear for their lives and even rue their decision to escape (Exodus 13:18; 14:6–12). Memories of their inferior status and helplessness among the Egyptians and the dominion held by Egypt throughout the ancient Near East must have tested their budding faith in Jehovah, an unfamiliar and unseen Power.

Evidence suggests that those who made up the Israelite host were not all direct descendants of Jacob's twelve sons. The narrative reads, "A *mixed multitude* went up also with them; and flocks, and herds, even very much cattle"

Artwork by Ashton Young

Hundreds of speeding chariots drawn by horses and driven by Egyptian warriors descended upon Miriam, Moses, and the rest of the fleeing Israelite multitude.

(Exodus 12:38; emphasis added; see also Numbers 11:4). In addition to the Israelites, the slaves conscripted by the Egyptians likely included other Semitic people from Canaan who came to Egypt at various times for numerous reasons such as famine and greater opportunities available under the Hyksos' regime. Egyptian texts and art portray a variety of Semitic peoples and Nubians (from south of Egypt) among their enslaved groups.

Whether or not Midianites were among the original group leaving Egypt, many of that ethnic group quickly joined the nomadic community. Descended from the son of Abraham and Keturah named Midian, the Midianites lived around the Gulf of Aqaba, the Sinai Peninsula, and northwestern Arabia. By the time of Moses, they were a large, seminomadic amalgamation of tribes that frequently controlled trade routes throughout the area. Moses' wife, Zipporah, her father, Jethro, and her six sisters were Kenites, one of the Midianite tribes (Judges 1:16). Because of marital ties and priesthood leadership connections, we know that this family was numbered among the Israelites almost from the beginning.

Eventually noted as Israelite heroes, Caleb and his brother Othniel were Kenezites, an Edomite clan, but they were later associated with the tribe of Ephraim (Joshua 14:14; 15:17; Genesis 36:11, 15). Surprisingly, some Egyptians also appear to have been included in the Israelite camp (Leviticus 24:10). For example, Asenath, wife of Joseph, was likely an Egyptian, though she may have been of Semite lineage. Undoubtedly, many converts to the camp of Israel were picked up after they encountered Moses' people in the wilderness. Disenfranchised people, attracted by the stability, unity, religion and leadership in the Israelite camp would also have contributed to the diversity and potential strength of the "mixed multitude." Lacking unifying beliefs and a strong tribal identity, this host of people began the transformation from a conglomeration of slaves to an organized covenant community led by Moses.

One suggested route for the Israelites' exodus from Egypt and their subsequent travels in the wilderness.

Logistical issues suggest that the number

of people involved would have been closer to a few thousand men, women, and children rather than the six hundred thousand men of fighting age, plus women and children, noted in the biblical narrative (Exodus 12:37). It is difficult to imagine the area of Goshen and later Sinai supporting a population in the millions. Furthermore, an army of six hundred thousand could have overthrown any opposing force in that day, including the Egyptians. Instead of stand-

The oasis at Rephidim is thought to have been one of the campgrounds where Moses, Miriam, and the Israelites pitched their tents soon after they left Egypt.

ing up to Pharaoh's army, we see the Israelites cringe before them (Exodus 14:10). Similarly, a caravan of two to three million people with their flocks and herds and other belongings would extend over a greater distance than the miles between their starting place and the Red Sea, and yet the entire multitude crossed the Red Sea in one night, all the while staying out of reach of an army of speeding chariots (vv. 22–25). More likely the recorded number of six hundred thousand men of fighting age is hyperbole, a scribal error, or an indication of Israel's future numbers when they would become the great empire of the ancient Near East (Bright, *History,* 133–34; for an argument to support a literal reading of Israel's population at the Exodus, see Keil and Delitzsch, *Commentary,* 1:337–38).

God led the Israelites "through the way of the wilderness of the Red sea" rather than the more direct route to Canaan, knowing their fear could entice them to "repent," or turn around, and return to Egypt (Exodus 13:18, 17). The first day the multitude traveled on foot from Rameses to Succoth (Exodus 12:37). They made it to Etham the second day (Exodus 13:20). With a maximum two days' lead on Pharaoh's army, the whole host could not have traveled much farther before reaching "the sea," where the army overtook them (Exodus 14:9).

The location of the famous crossing has long been in dispute, including arguments that the Israelites crossed a lake called the "sea of reeds" (negated in 1 Kings 9:26), a body of water farther north in the Bitter Lakes region, or a northern leg of the Red Sea called the Gulf of Suez (which may have extended farther north in antiquity). The debate is compelling when the distance from the Egyptian capital to the Red Sea is considered. The extra mileage for the Israelites to reach the main body of the Red Sea seems unnecessary. Furthermore, unless the distance was considerable, a trained army in chariots could catch up to a large, unwieldy mass of people and flocks fairly quickly.

THE SONG OF MIRIAM

After walking through the sea on dry ground and witnessing the Egyptian army drowned in its depths, the Israelites lost all fear of the Egyptians. In awe of God's power and Moses' divine calling, they were confident that God was with them (Exodus 14:26–31). Clearly, by this time in Miriam's life, she was honored as an inspirational leader among the people.

Full of exultation and praise to the Lord for His defeat of Egypt at the Red Sea, the children of Israel sang a hymn. It is in the context of this musical tribute to Jehovah that Miriam is called "prophetess." Even without reading the words to the hymn, we know that as a prophetess she would have testified of the Lord's reality and power, knowledge of which she had gained through personal revelation. The lyrics of a hymn deserve analysis different from that used on the narrative of ancient texts. Words of songs survived indefinitely as a memorized passage whereas narrative accounts were retold in numerous ways, highlighting and discounting various facts, explanations of custom, or significance. For this reason, biblical scholars have posited that the lyrics of this Israelite hymn may be the earliest written text to survive in our Bible, especially the verse of lyrics specifically attributed to Miriam (Exodus 15:21).

Many scholars also argue that the attribution of leadership of the song to Moses is false, probably inserted into the text by later editors (Exodus 15:1). More likely, Miriam was author of the words of rejoicing and led the entire song. That suggestion fits the ancient Near Eastern pattern of women being the musicians, dancers, and vocalists for the community, except when music was performed in the tabernacle or temple, where the male priests and Levites were the singers and musicians. Outside the temple, however, musicians came from the ranks of the women, whether during times of sorrow or times of rejoicing (Judges 11:34; 1 Samuel 18:6–7). The suggestion also reflects evidence for Miriam's role as a prophetess because the song is filled with praises to the Lord and testifies of His might, mercy, and wisdom.

Sung as a hymn to praise God for delivering them, the lyric poem contains numerous insights to the miracle the Israelites had just experienced, as well as a prophecy for their future as a people. The name of Jehovah appears ten times in the hymn (rendered as LORD in the King James Version). Mention of His right hand (Exodus 15:6, 12) and His nostrils (v. 8) reinforce the Israelite belief that Jehovah was a corporeal God. In contrast to the mighty Egyptian empire or any emerging empire whose power appears invincible one day but dissipates the next, they knew the Lord's power is eternal (v. 18).

The next stanzas are prophetic in their nature. Again, they are a fitting testimony of the prophetess Miriam, if she indeed is the author rather than Moses. While acknowledging God's great love and kindness to His covenant people, the song notes the terror and awe that the peoples of Canaan or Palestina, Moab, and Edom will feel as Israel approaches (Exodus 15:13–16). It prophesies of Israel "passing over," bringing to mind the dramatic entrance into the promised land through the Jordan River, forty years in the future (v. 16). Finally, the hymn sings of God "plant[ing] them," an allusion to a permanent residence, "in the mountain . . . in the Sanctuary" that is established by the Lord, prefiguring the temple to be constructed in Jerusalem some two hundred years later (v. 17).

TIMBRELS

Miriam and all the women of the camp danced and played disc-shaped musical instruments called timbrels. These were hand-held, hoop-shaped drums whose diameter was wider than the depth of the instrument. They were played by striking them with the flat of the hand. More accurately described as drums than tambourines, timbrels are the only percussion instrument mentioned in ancient texts or depicted in their art,

Women were often depicted in ancient art as dancers playing a drum-like instrument called a timbrel.

and women are the only ones represented as playing them. For that reason, any mention of drum playing in biblical times assumes that women were the percussionists. Numerous Iron Age clay figurines of women playing drums uniformly depict them holding the instrument perpendicular to their bodies. Most frequently, artwork portrays women playing timbrels in celebration of their men's victory in battle and holding the attention and respect of the larger community. Because ancient Near Eastern music is believed to have been rhythmic rather than melodic, drums were likely the most important musical instrument, which further added status to women who were skilled in their use.

MOUNT SINAI

Three months after crossing the Red Sea and celebrating their deliverance with the song of Miriam, the Israelites came to Mount Sinai (Exodus 19:1). Their initial show of faith and praise to God did not endure the many challenges of wilderness living and travel. Complaints over the shortage of food and potable water, attacks from marauders, and regrets over leaving Egypt were frequent (Exodus 15:22–17:16). But during the three months they also witnessed numerous ways that the Lord remained patient with them.

The traditional site of the mount where God delivered His law to Moses is Jebel Musa, toward the southern tip of the Sinai Peninsula. Jebel Musa is within the area believed to have been inhabited by Midianites and near the location of several copper mines, which were important to the Kenites. Here, in the wilderness, the mixed multitude from Egyptian slavery came under covenant to transform into Jehovah's people.

In contrast to legal systems oriented toward a secular society, the law that God revealed to Moses

The majestic mountains of the Sinai wilderness to which Moses led his people. Miriam and the Israelites arrived in this area three months after crossing the Red Sea. Here at Mount Sinai they joined together to make a covenant with Jehovah.

at Mount Sinai communicates a distinctive religious orientation. Surprisingly, considering the Israelites' lengthy sojourn in Egypt, the law of Moses consists neither of abstract beliefs nor reflections of Egyptian polytheism and legend. It also differs sharply from all the surrounding legal and religious perspectives the Israelites encountered in the wilderness and in Canaan. For example, although the law of Moses contains many similarities to the then three-hundred-year-old Code of Hammurabi, distinctively different philosophies separate the two sets of rules. Under Hammurabi's code, the severity of punishment for a crime is determined by social class; the law of Moses assigns the same punishment for all people who commit a particular infraction. Hammurabi's code aimed to build civility among the Mesopotamian people under its guidelines; the law of Moses endeavored to build a relationship between the people and their God. The law of Moses was unusually farsighted, giving hope and responsibility to a people who would soon settle in a land of promise. It focused on their Creator, not on the things He created. Most powerfully, it pointed to Jesus Christ and His infinite Atonement.

WAS MIRIAM MARRIED?

The biblical text frequently mentions Moses' wife, Zipporah, his sons, Gershom and Eliezer, and his father-in-law, Jethro, but gives no reference to Miriam's husband and children. Consequently, many have surmised that she never married. One could argue, equally, that she naturally had married and bore children and that the absence of any details is further evidence that marriage was a given in that society.

Multiple traditions suggest the identity of Miriam's husband, but no reliable source gives greater support to one theory than another. Josephus claims that Miriam married Hur, a trusted companion to Moses and Aaron and the leader who resolved conflicts while Moses was receiving instruction on Mount Sinai (*Antiquities,* 3.2.4; Exodus 17:10, 12; 24:14). Another tradition suggests that Miriam married Caleb, one of the spies Moses sent into Canaan and who brought back an optimistic report (Numbers 14:6–38). The tradition relates that Hur was their son, and Bezaleel, the craftsman of the tabernacle, was their son or grandson (Ginzberg, *Legends,* 2:253–54; 3:121; 3:154; see Exodus 31:2). According to genealogical records of 1 Chronicles, however, Caleb and Ephrath (not Miriam) are the parents of Hur and the grandparents of Bezaleel (1 Chronicles 2:18–20).

CRITICISM AND CHASTISEMENT

The next scene in which we clearly see Miriam occurs about a year later, after the children of Israel observed their second Passover (Numbers 9:1). Scriptural accounts that depict Miriam at both her best and shortly thereafter in her chastisement breathe reality into her humanity. The Israelite congregation was camped at Hazeroth, a journey of some four or five days from Sinai (Numbers 10:33; 11:35; 12:16), after lusting for flesh instead of appreciating God's gift of manna and suffering a plague caused by gorging on quail (Numbers 11:31–34). At some time amid the drum of murmuring and negativity, Miriam's patience cracked. At their previous camp, Moses' exasperation with the chronic complaints reached a peak when he pleaded with the Lord, "I am not able to bear all this people alone, because it is too heavy for me" (Numbers 11:14). Perpetual negativity can have tremendous influence on the faith and hope of even the most fervent believers. Perhaps the same pressures broke Miriam's resolve.

Another development may have also eroded Miriam's faith and created the temptation to criticize and belittle her brother in his attempts to lead the people. In addition to Miriam and others who were clearly seen as leaders in the camp, the Lord gave spiritual enlightenment and prophetic voice to seventy elders (Numbers 11:14–26). When we are exhausted from complaints and criticisms over our best efforts to help, we are more likely to resent others who have success in their efforts. With the spirit of faith and hope diminished, we can easily become jealous of another's gifts.

Whatever the catalyst, Miriam and Aaron added their voices to the chorus of complaints. As indicated by the feminine singular form of the Hebrew verb translated "speak" in Numbers 12:1, Miriam instigated the grumbling. Apparently Aaron concurred. Rabbinic tradition labels their weakness as the sin of slander (Ginzberg, *Legends,* 3:261).

Their first objection was to Moses' Ethiopian wife (Numbers 12:1). Was this Zipporah or had Moses married another woman? The land of Ethiopia was also called "Cush" in ancient times and can refer to more than one location and people in the Old Testament. One possibility is the area south of Egypt along the Nile River called Nubia (today's nation of Sudan). But a "Cushite" also referred to a Midianite (Habakkuk 3:7). If the second possibility is correct, this wife is none other than Zipporah, the Midianite. In an interesting twist of the criticism, Jewish tradition tells of Zipporah complaining that Moses neglected her to attend to his religious duties, so Miriam and Aaron spoke to Moses on her behalf, asking him to give her more of his attention (Ginzberg, *Legends,* 3:255–56).

The second reason that Miriam and Aaron spoke out, however, points to the deeper problem. They questioned the preeminence of Moses' prophetic calling and his attendant leadership capabilities (Numbers 12:2). Moses had previously warned the people of the seriousness of criticizing him and other religious

MURMURING AGAINST THE LORD'S ANOINTED SERVANTS

Elder George F. Richards, as president of the Quorum of the Twelve Apostles, explained the effects of criticizing our leaders: "When we say anything bad about the leaders of the Church, whether true or false, we tend to impair their influence and their usefulness and are thus working against the Lord and his cause" (Conference Report, Apr. 1947, 24; see also Oaks, *Ensign*, Feb. 1987, 68–73).

Similarly, the Lord warned: "Cursed are all those that shall lift up the heel against mine anointed, saith the Lord, and cry they have sinned when they have not sinned before me, saith the Lord, but have done that which was meet in mine eyes, and which I commanded them" (D&C 121:16).

leaders. "What are we, that ye murmur against us?" Moses asked them. "The Lord heareth your murmurings which ye murmur against him: and what are we? your murmurings are not against us, but against the Lord" (Exodus 16:7–8). Among the children of Israel, Moses' relationship with God was unique, and his responsibility for God's people surpassed that of all the others in the camp. Moses was *the* prophet, whereas Miriam, Aaron, and the seventy elders were prophets. Prophets like Moses hold keys; those with the gift of prophecy may or may not hold keys. As a prophet or prophetess, our gift is to bear witness of Christ by the power of the Spirit, not direct the affairs of God's kingdom on the earth.

Older siblings may often view a baby brother or sister as less capable. They remember when he was completely dependent on others. In this particular family, Miriam had risked her life for Moses when he was a helpless infant. Like her brothers, she had received gifts from the Lord to lead and encourage the Israelites. She had experienced the thrill and empowerment of revelation, teaching with the Spirit, and Christlike leadership. But what occurs when we forget the source of our empowerment? What happens when we aspire to the honors of the world and strive to gratify our pride and vain ambition because of past God-given successes? (D&C 121:35–37). The Lord's lesson to Miriam, therefore, applies to all of us, whether we are caught as she was or not.

In a most impressive show of character, Moses resisted any temptation to lash back in defense of his position. While everyone around was finding fault and judging him, Moses remained silent: "Moses was very meek, above all the men which were upon the face of the earth" (Numbers 12:3). Meekness is becoming as little children; it is becoming like Christ, who was buffeted for his righteousness but suffered it patiently (Mosiah 3:19; Matthew 11:29; 1 Peter 2:20–21). Because Moses followed the Lord, God defended Moses and humbled his accusers (Numbers 12:4–9).

LEPROSY (*TZARA'AT*)

As further evidence that Miriam was the instigator and chief complainant against Moses, the Lord chastened her alone with a week-long bout of "leprosy," a condition that, under the law of Moses, required a seven-day purification process (Leviticus 13:32–37). Various impurities affecting the skin caused *tzara'at,* or "leprosy," as it is translated in the King James Bible. *Tzara'at* was a condition that differs substantially from Hansen's disease, the infection we call leprosy today. Symptoms of *tzara'at* included skin erosion that produced swelling, rash, or snow-white scales similar to those of psoriasis and eczema, or like vitiligo, which develops white spots without scales (Leviticus 13:6, 25–27, 42).

More meaningful than its physical symptoms are the spiritual connotations associated with *tzara'at.* Because Miriam sinned, God afflicted her with *tzara'at*—a condition that symbolizes sin, uncleanness before God, death, and being separated from God's presence. As *tzara'at* causes the skin to flake and degenerate, so sin eats away at the soul. Emblematic of life gradually oozing away as the skin disintegrates, a person afflicted with *tzara'at* was viewed as potentially dead unless God arrested the condition and

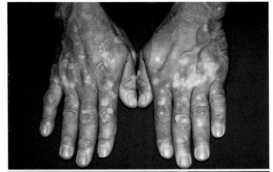

restored the outcast to full health (Numbers 12:12). Those afflicted were quarantined outside the camp or community until the condition disappeared and the inflicted underwent the proper rituals of cleansing (Leviticus 13:46).

No scriptural directives indicate that the disease was feared to be contagious, suggesting that expelling a victim from society was likely the result of an offensive appearance rather than a fear of spreading the disease. That victims were segregated from the rest of the community again invites a symbolic explanation. Only a priest could examine the condition to determine if the disease was *tzara'at* and later pronounce the afflicted person clean and free to return to society when all physical symptoms were gone and the proper rituals performed (Leviticus 13–14). Miriam's case illustrates that these dermatological conditions can change rapidly to bring full healing and purification in one week. After seven days (in Hebrew the number seven signifies completion and also covenant), she was again welcomed into God's presence as a whole and complete, clean and forgiven, covenant daughter of God.

In the Hebrew original of "Miriam became leprous," her afflicted condition came upon her immediately, or in other words, in a way that communicated to everyone in the camp that the *tzara'at* was a direct consequence of her judgmental behavior (Numbers 12:10). In addition to the

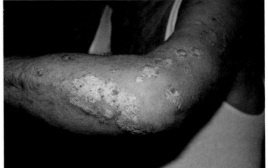

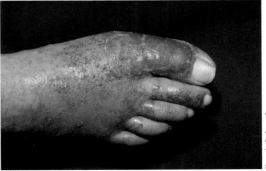

Photos by Dr. Steven Eyre

Modern-day skin affliction similar to tzara'at.

disease, Miriam's deep humiliation for her outburst may have been exacerbated by the fact that the entire community waited the seven days for her cleansing before moving on to the next camp (Numbers 12:15–16). Her public chastisement and the weakness that elicited her embarrassment would be remembered for years afterward (Deuteronomy 24:8–9). On the other hand, the week-long hiatus from travel may have been an outpouring of the company's love and support for Miriam. Waiting for her to be reinstated could have offered a similar repentance period for all the Israelites. Acknowledging their own sins of slander and criticism against their leaders, perhaps all the children of Israel willingly stopped in order to receive the Lord's cleansing and healing.

MIRIAM'S DEATH

After following Miriam through her courageous childhood, prophetic leadership, and humbling call to repentance, the Bible gives us a glimpse of the conclusion of her life. Shortly before the children of Israel entered the promised land during the fortieth year in the wilderness, Miriam died and was buried at Kadesh (Numbers 20:1; see also Josephus, *Antiquities,* 4.4.6). Later that same year, her brother Aaron also died and God took Moses from the people (see Numbers 20:22–29; 33:38; Deuteronomy 34:5–7).

Kadesh, meaning "holy," is the one site in the Israelites' wilderness sojourn whose location is largely uncontested by scholars. The area was the most permanent residence for the children of Israel and was probably their home for some thirty-eight of the forty years that they lived in the wilderness. Blessed by a natural supply of water from a series of spring-fed lakes, Kadesh includes a spring that generates as much as forty cubic meters of water per hour. Surrounded by the wilderness of Zin, the oasis of Kadesh could produce plenteous vegetation, including olive trees. It is located about 150 miles from Egypt, 140 miles from Mount Sinai, and 40 miles from Beersheba.

Jewish tradition relates that Miriam, Moses, and Aaron all died sinless (Ginzberg, *Legends,* 3:444). Similarly, centuries later the prophet Micah remembered Miriam and her brothers as national heroes (Micah 6:3–4).

Miriam's story is a gift. We can share in her victories as well as her shortcomings. Through the power of the Lord, she led her people in a song of praise and acknowledgment for His deliverance. Likewise, through the power of the Lord, she received correction, rebirth, and forgiveness when she stumbled over God's command to sustain and honor those called to lead her. In both circumstances she reminds us that we owe all that we are and can be to the Lord.

Although no further chapters of her life are recorded between her chastisement with leprosy and her death some thirty-eight years later, the silence testifies to her meekness, likely inspired by that of her "little brother." Rather than becoming distraught and withdrawn after her public humiliation, Miriam appears to have trusted in God's forgiveness by also forgiving herself. She discovered expanded ways to exercise her spiritual gift while sincerely sustaining the prophet. Returning to leadership and influence, she added deep humility to her strengths while giving all the glory to the Lord.

POINTS TO PONDER: APPLICATIONS FOR OUR LIVES

1. Without having to showcase our sick souls as publicly as Miriam did, how can we know if our attitudes and actions are displeasing to God? How can Miriam inspire us to humbly acknowledge a weakness and choose to repent?

2. What gospel principles are taught in Miriam's story?

3. How would you describe Miriam's role in establishing the children of Israel as the people of God?

4. How do you express gratitude and praise to God for your successes and deliverance from jeopardy?

5. Do we support and wait for the purification of others during their times of repentance? Do we rejoice with them when they again become clean through Christ's Atonement?

6. What does Miriam teach us about leadership for women? What does she teach us about increased power from sustaining those called to lead us, particularly when our leaders are related to us or are not as naturally capable of leadership as we are?

7. How does Miriam bring you closer to Christ?

I Arose a Mother in Israel

DEBORAH

דְּבוֹרָה

"Bee"

*K*nown for her wisdom and respected as a leader, Deborah is introduced in the biblical record with no indication that the fact of a woman's holding such influence was inappropriate or surprising. She rose to prominence as a "prophetess," judge, and "mother in Israel" among the splintered Israelite tribes during the chaotic era that followed Joshua's conquest of Canaan (Judges 4:4; 5:7). Although other individuals showed inspiring courage and faith in God to assist in Israel's victory, Deborah was the catalyst that ignited the Israelite surge. Her conviction that God would deliver His people from twenty years of Canaanite oppression inspired an army to rise up and win freedom for Israel.

As an exception to traditional roles, Deborah held and manifested unique titles and attributes, three of which are described in the book of Judges. First, she was the only woman in a long list of judges to rule Israel before the monarchy. Second, she was the only judge named in the book of Judges who also held the title of prophet, although no scriptural background explains her rise to prominence or her gift of prophetic wisdom. Finally, her appellation as a mother in Israel appears in a context that is unrelated to traditional motherhood and lacks evidence that she bore children. Deborah was a "mother in Israel" not because she gave birth to a child but because she reared up Israel and led them back to the Lord. Collectively, these roles prepared her to become a heroine and example of effective, female leadership both to her contemporaries and to us. As a tool in the Redeemer's hand, Deborah bore witness that the Savior is the true Deliverer.

The victory over the Canaanites that Deborah inspired occurred as early as 1200 or as late as 1125 B.C. Two accounts of Deborah's story are contained in the Bible, one in prose (Judges 4) and the other in verse, presumably written by Deborah and performed with the Israelite captain Barak after their military victory (Judges 5). The song of Deborah exhibits linguistic traits that mark it as very early Hebrew writing. Because words of

JUDGES 4–5
LDS BIBLE DICTIONARY, 655

107

song and poetry endured without revisions over time, it is likely that this song is one of the oldest pieces of text in the biblical canon. Similar to Miriam's song after God's deliverance of the children of Israel at the Red Sea, Deborah's composition is a hymn of thanksgiving in which she praises God for His gracious acts in their behalf.

The two versions of Deborah's story contribute unique and corroborative elements that together bring to life Deborah and her colleagues. For example, details surrounding the battle—the locations, peoples involved, and manner in which God wrought the victory—come into sharper focus when both chapters 4 and 5 are studied. Consequently, the two accounts are represented here.

THE PERIOD OF THE JUDGES

The Israelite era of the judges spanned the years between the conquest of Canaan and the commencement of the Israelite monarchy. Because the biblical account does not correlate stories of Deborah and the other judges to externally documented events, the chronology and historical years cannot be positively assigned. Material culture and related ancient texts strongly indicate that the age of the judges coincided with the archaeological period known as Iron Age I (1200–1000 B.C.), which coincidentally also contains more material evidence of women's presence than any other ancient era. According to the early date theory, judges led Israel from about 1375 to 1020 B.C.; the late date theory puts the period from 1200 to 1020 B.C. A brief survey of life in Canaan during this era provides a meaningful backdrop to visualize the tumultuous world that Deborah inherited, confronted, and changed.

Although Joshua had led his people to conquer significant territory in Canaan, much of the land remained under enemy control at his death. After their initial military success, the Israelites became complacent and weak in their loyalty to God and efforts to establish a new homeland. Disunity, shifting beliefs, and dwindling spiritual identity disrupted the Israelites' physical security and theological moorings. Instead of driving out the idolatrous people as God had commanded, the children of Israel married them and progressively incorporated foreign religious perspectives into their own beliefs (Judges 2:12). Deborah would have been accustomed to this chaos and disunity long before she roused a military response to their bondage (Judges 5:7).

Dealing with their own internal crises, previously powerful empires such as the Hittites, Egyptians, and Assyrians left the land of Canaan vulnerable to other invaders. The loose conglomerate of Israelite tribes maintained a precarious presence, surrounded by foes and separated by natural geographical boundaries. Without a central Israelite government, "every man did that which was right in his own eyes" (Judges 17:6). Perpetual unrest and disunity therefore defined life in Canaan as inhabitants enjoyed rare peaceful respites between skirmishes with their neighbors and their own communities. In the south, the tribes of Judah and Simeon battled with Philistia for control of the land. In the north, the remaining ten tribes clashed with Canaan for dominance. Without a standing army, tribal clans closest to a new conflict were the first and sometimes the only Israelite representatives to rally for battle.

Notwithstanding the constant threat of attack and destruction, Israel's economy, artisanship, and quality of life gradually improved as the Israelites acquired new skills and identified opportunities for commerce along trade routes in their new homeland. During the two hundred years of Iron Age I, the number of settlements in the central hill country of Canaan, for example, increased from less than thirty to more than two hundred, most of them small farming communities rather than urban centers, as the earlier settlements had been. New residents cleared forests in previously uninhabitable areas in the hill country and, by lining cisterns with baked lime plaster, secured a water supply where no natural spring or well existed. Presumably, the Israelites settled these new farming villages while the Canaanites controlled most of the established, fortified cities.

Geographical locations important in the story of Deborah.

The closest semblance of an Israelite tribal center during the period of the judges was the village of Shiloh (Joshua 18:1; Judges 18:31; 1 Samuel 1:3). Centrally located in territory assigned to Ephraim, Shiloh housed the tabernacle and the ark of the covenant for a time and beckoned Israelites from all the tribes to visit and worship. As a judge within the boundaries of Ephraim, Deborah would have been well acquainted with Shiloh and the tabernacle (Judges 4:5). Particularly in outlying areas, however, as many Israelites gradually absorbed Canaanite rituals and beliefs into their own religion, the power and importance of the tabernacle and Shiloh diminished.

In her song, Deborah described the dire conditions among the Israelites because they "chose new gods; then was war in the gates" (Judges 5:8). "The highways were unoccupied," she sang, perhaps a reflection of the danger created from enemy garrisons and marauding bands that patrolled the travel routes (v. 6). "The inhabitants of the villages ceased," she observed, suggesting that communities may have combined together in an undisclosed location for protection (v. 7). Additionally, the Canaanites might have disarmed the Israelites when they gained control because Deborah asked, "Was there a shield or spear seen . . . in

Israel?" (v. 8). From their fortified cities amid the numerous Israelite settlements, Canaanites banded together to terrorize the Israelites. Few in Israel had the heart to resist.

THE CANAANITES NEAR HAZOR

The various Canaanite peoples suffered from a similar crisis of identity and solidarity as did the Israelites. Primarily united by a mutual distrust and fear of the Israelites, the people of Canaan were otherwise a disconnected conglomeration of independent city-states, each ruled by its own leader. Likely one of these city kings was Jabin of Hazor. That the Bible calls him "king of Canaanites" indicates that Jabin may have organized a larger Canaanite confederation of cities to keep the Israelites in check for the twenty years leading up to Deborah's ascendancy (Judges 4:2–3).

Located about ten miles northwest of the Sea of Galilee, Hazor was a major fortified city that commanded an important trade route connecting Mesopotamia to Egypt. Whoever controlled Hazor controlled both the trade route and the various peoples who resided in the region.

Archaeological evidence indicates that Hazor was destroyed near the end of the thirteenth century before Christ. This documentation of destruction may correlate with Joshua's conquest of Hazor (Joshua 11:1–14) and indicates that Deborah lived in Canaan after the city was rebuilt and retaken by the Canaanites. Considering their geographic locations, the tribes of Naphtali and Zebulun would have been those most affected by Hazor's dominance in the area. The surrounding tribes of Asher, Issachar, and western Manasseh (on the west bank of the Jordan River) would also have experienced loss of freedom but less directly and intensely than those bordering Hazor's trade route.

THE PRIDE CYCLE

A cyclical pattern of forgetting God, suffering hardship, and pleading to God for deliverance occurred often during the era of the judges. An entire rotation of the cycle is evident in the story of Deborah.

First, the children of Israel "again did evil in the sight of the Lord" (Judges 4:1). Increasingly indifferent toward their God, they followed after other gods and consequently were left to their own strength. Then, unable to defend themselves without God's might, the Israelites in the north were overcome by the Canaanites and oppressed by Jabin, the king of Hazor (Judges 4:2–3). Subsequently, when their challenges became unbearable and they lacked wisdom and power to escape, the Israelites cried to the Lord for liberation (v. 3). God responded by enlivening their hope for deliverance through the testimony and witness of Deborah, a judge and prophetess in

THE ISRAELITE PRIDE CYCLE

1. The children of Israel did evil in God's sight (Judges 4:1)
2. The Lord sold them to an enemy nation (Judges 4:2)
3. The children of Israel cried unto the Lord (Judges 4:3)
4. God raised up a deliverer—Deborah (Judges 4:4)
5. Victory was won and peace restored (Judges 5:31)

The gate area of the Iron Age city of Dan in the northern kingdom of Israel retains the remnants of a place where a judge would sit to hold public court. A canopy, upheld by posts that were grounded in decorative stone anchors at each corner, covered a chair that rested on the stone dais. Deborah's judgment seat was under a palm tree rather than at this more common location.

Israel (v. 4). Finally, God gave Israel the victory and restored them to freedom and deeper faith in Him (Judges 5:31).

Although many individuals played important roles in Israel's regaining freedom, Deborah provided the motivation that changed hearts and prompted ready action among the Israelites. She is the central figure in the story and the deliverer who turned her people back to the Lord. To appreciate the details of Israel's victory over the Canaanites, Deborah's roles as prophetess, wife, judge, and mother in Israel require special exploration.

DEBORAH AS JUDGE

The era of the judges is not the first evidence that Hebrew leaders functioned as judges. During the patriarchal era, judges were the heads of the various clans, such as those of Abraham and Jacob. In the wilderness, Moses was the judge for all of the people in the camp until Jethro taught him to delegate the responsibility to others, who in turn judged segments of the population (Exodus 18:13–26; Deuteronomy 1:9–17). Thereafter, only the most important and difficult cases were brought to Moses (Exodus 18:26).

JUDGES NAMED IN THE BOOK OF JUDGES

Name of judge and tribe	Scriptural reference	Military conquest against
1. Othniel of Judah	Judges 3:8–11	Cushan-Rishathaim
2. Ehud of Benjamin	Judges 3:12–30	Eglon of Moab
3. Shamgar?	Judges 3:31	Philistines
4. Deborah of Ephraim	Judges 4–5	Canaanites (Sisera)
5. Gideon of Manasseh	Judges 6–8	Midianites; Amalekites
6. Tola of Issachar	Judges 10:1–2	
7. Jair of Gilead	Judges 10:3–5	
8. Jephthah of Gilead	Judges 10:6–12:7	Ammonites
9. Izban of Bethlehem	Judges 12:8–10	
10. Elon of Zebulun	Judges 12:11–12	
11. Abdon of Ephraim	Judges 12:13–15	
12. Samson of Dan	Judges 13–16	Philistines

The precedent set in the wilderness likely continued throughout the era of the judges and beyond. If the book of Judges reflects events and reigns of the various judges in chronological order, Deborah was the fourth judge to serve her people. Because it appears that the judges held authority not for the entire nation of Israel but rather for their own tribe and local community, two or more judges could have functioned concurrently in their respective territories. Furthermore, there is doubt whether the third on the list, Shamgar, should be identified as a judge in Israel because his name is Hurrian rather than Hebrew. If that is indeed the case, Shamgar's heroism was more likely inadvertent or in the role of a courageous mercenary who came to Israel's aid. Shamgar is mentioned twice in the book of Judges: once as a victor over the Philistines (Judges 3:31) and again in Deborah's song when she saw Jael's role in Sisera's defeat as a parallel to Shamgar's victory (Judges 5:6).

Called *shophet* in Hebrew, Israel's judges served the people by defending, avenging, delivering, and pronouncing punishment on the Israelites independent of economic status or race (1 Samuel 2:25; Deuteronomy 16:18–20). Most judges served in a significant military capacity and held both political and judicial influence. The title of judge assumed neither a line of succession, nor permanent assignment, nor absolute power. It is uncertain whether judges were called to serve by the Lord or by the voice of the people. Whatever the case, they appear to have been selected because of their particular wisdom, valor, leadership capacity, or trust in the divine. Individually and collectively, Israel's judges looked to God as the ultimate Judge.

Like earlier judges, Deborah would have opened her hearings to the public (Exodus 18:13; Ruth 4:1–2), allowed each party to present his or her view (Deuteronomy 1:16; 25:1), considered evidence given by witnesses, if any (Deuteronomy 17:6–7; 19:15; Numbers 35:30), and rendered her sentence after a thoughtful hearing of the case (Joshua 7:24–25). The scriptures note that Deborah held court under a palm tree somewhere between the villages of Ramah and Bethel, in the territory of the tribe of Ephraim (Judges 4:5). Located along the same travel route used by the patriarchs journeying from Haran to Hebron (Genesis 31:13), Deborah's judgment seat was also along the most commonly used route taken to visit the tabernacle in Shiloh. More specifically, Ramah was located on a hill at the crossroads of the north-south Way of the Patriarchs and the east-west route that linked the coast with Transjordan.

Considering another ancient text that tells of a judge's selection of the village threshing floor as his official site for deciding cases, Deborah may have chosen the palm tree location because it was a well-known site that was frequented by all her people (Pritchard, *Ancient,* 151). Because palm trees are not typical in the area between Ramah and Bethel, it is possible that Deborah's palm tree was a noted rarity and a natural landmark for her to meet those with disputes to settle.

DEBORAH AS PROPHETESS

The scriptures contain several indications that warrant Deborah's being called a prophetess. As one who bore fervent witness of the Lord, she communicated to the Israelite military leader and her people that God called them to rise up and fight off the Canaanite oppression (Judges 4:6; 5:2–3). In the King James Version, Deborah conveyed Jehovah's command to Barak (Judges 4:6–7). In the Septuagint, the prophetic command to muster the troops at Mount Tabor came directly from Deborah. As a prophetess, Deborah also showed respect for those she counseled by her willingness to listen to them. In her song, she acknowledged her people's awareness of their need for divine assistance because they came to her, crying for help, "Awake, Deborah" (Judges 5:12).

By remembering that God sustained and empowered their fathers in their journey through the wilderness and into the promised land, Deborah testified that He had not forgotten them and would bring them victory over the Canaanites (Judges 4:7). To further confirm that God's power would make them conquerors, Deborah noted previous miracles that included severe weather conditions that paralleled the manner in which the Lord would secure

Photo by David M. Whitchurch

Deborah judged under a palm tree on the route between Bethel and Ramah in Ephraim territory.

their own victory—a storm cloud in Edom/Seir and an earthquake and thunderstorm at Mount Sinai (Judges 5:4–5; see also Exodus 19:16–18).

In a striking evidence of Deborah's powerful testimony as a prophetess, Barak, the mighty military captain, agreed to go to battle only if Deborah accompanied them. "If thou wilt go with me, then I will go," Barak offered, "but if thou wilt not go with me, then I will not go" (Judges 4:8). Though vowing not to abandon him, Deborah further prophesied that God would empower a woman and not Barak to conquer Sisera, the Canaanite captain (v. 9). The prophecy was fulfilled, but the heroic conquering woman was not Deborah, as one might assume at that point in the story, but a Kenite woman named Jael.

Finally, Deborah was a prophetess on the actual day of the battle. When the frightened army of Israel looked down upon the heavily armed Canaanites awaiting them in the valley, Deborah again bore testimony of the Lord's ability to revive their faith and purpose. At her call, "Up; for this is the day in which the Lord hath delivered Sisera into thine hand: is not the Lord gone out before thee?" Barak's army advanced, and the battle began (Judges 4:14).

Throughout both accounts of the Israelites' victory over the mighty Canaanites, Deborah never forgot that her people's only hope for salvation and healing from their woes was the greatness of the Lord. Christ was the true Captain; Deborah, Barak, and Jael were His witnesses.

DEBORAH AS MOTHER IN ISRAEL

Referring to a woman today as a "mother in Israel" is generally akin to complimenting her as a kind, conscientious parent to her biological children. Such a definition is not the case in the song of Deborah, the text where the term originates. Rather than hearing others bestow the title upon her, Deborah called herself "a mother in Israel" (Judges 5:7). Additionally, she selected the phrase in response to her efforts in liberating the Israelites from oppression, not to portray herself in a parent-child relationship. Again, no mention of Deborah's having biological children appears in either chapter, nor would this information be germane to the story.

As a mother figure for her people, however, Deborah manifested characteristics that are equally valued in parenting. She loved the people she served as a mother loves her own children. As a mother gives tender care and tutelage of her offspring, Deborah nurtured, protected, taught, and inspired the people of Israel to trust in God, act in faith, and work with Him to restore freedom, peace, and opportunity in the land. Duties of mothers, in this context, are focused not on cleaning and cooking but on leading one's charges to the source of salvation. From this scriptural perspective, a mother sees beyond daily survival to eternal and spiritual progression. She recognizes that she can never save her children—but He can. Armed with this knowledge and conviction, she selflessly seeks to bring others to the same truth.

The phrase "mother in Israel" appears one other time in scripture, this time when King David ruled the nation (2 Samuel 20:19). In this later story, the narrator used the phrase to tell of a wise woman in the

LATTER-DAY MOTHERS IN ISRAEL

Parallels to "Mother" Deborah are found in Latter-day Saint religious tradition. Throughout 1916, a series of articles entitled "Mothers in Israel" appeared in the *Relief Society Magazine,* each one featuring a specific woman who exemplified qualities inherent in the title.

One was Lucy Mack Smith, mother of the Prophet Joseph Smith and nine other children, who was heralded in the first article of the series, not because she had such outstanding children but for her kindness and generosity toward all members of the Church. "'Mother Smith,' as she was lovingly called, was a dominating figure in any assemblage where she happened to be. She was commanding in appearance, keen in [intellect], dignified and gracious in manner, and she loved the sick, the poor, and the unfortunate, with an abiding tenderness. She was the soul of hospitality and generosity. Together with her noble husband, she ministered to all who came for help or shelter" (Jan. 1916, 3).

Eliza R. Snow "had no children of her own, but she was indeed by nature and grace, the mother of all mothers in Israel," the fourth article in the series reported. As a respected hymn writer, teacher, and "head of all organization work for women in the Church," Sister Snow's influence and leadership example continue to resonate today. "To her gifts as poet, writer, public speaker, high priestess in the temples, and ministering angel among women, she added the supreme gift of initiation," the article continued. "When she entered a room or an assembly, no matter what condition things may have been in before her entrance, she at once dominated the gathering, and order followed immediately. . . . In and through it all, she was a mother to all mothers. No night was too dark, no distance too great, for her to go out and administer to the sick child or to the discouraged mother" (Apr. 1916, 182–89).

Israelite town of Abel who defended her town and settled disputes for her people (vv. 16–22). It is debatable whether the title "a mother in Israel" in this case refers to the unnamed woman, who sounds a lot like Deborah, or to the town of Abel, in the way that cities were sometimes poetically viewed as a "mother" to the people. In either case, literally bearing and rearing children did not appear to be prerequisite to being a "mother" in biblical times.

This expanded meaning of *mother* suggests that a mother's love can be manifest outside the immediate family to eventually unite cities and nations. Such mothers see family in community where all are welcomed and offered nourishment and compassion. These women offer service to strangers outside their homes with the same level of gentle care and discipline that they give to those who share their homes. Certainly, Christ's perfect and infinite love has that boundless capacity to encircle all those who come to Him. In turn, when filled with His love and Spirit, we willingly and naturally reach out to lift others. The love of a woman for the children she has borne and the compassionate concern that Deborah had for her people emulate the selfless love that the Savior feels for each of us. In turn, these examples inspire us to develop love for neighbors and members of the larger community.

DEBORAH, WIFE OF LAPIDOTH

The final descriptive title given to Deborah is *'ešet lappidôt,* which is most frequently translated "wife of Lapidoth." Because no description or further mention of Lapidoth appears in the text, several alternative translations have emerged. Chief among the suggestions is that this phrase may say nothing about Deborah's husband, because the same Hebrew word can communicate both "wife" and "woman." Furthermore, nothing in the text specifies that Lapidoth is a person, let alone a husband. Because the word *Lapidoth* relates to "fire" or "light," the phrase could connote a place or function involving fire, such as lighting torches.

Considering these various possibilities, the passage may have intended to communicate that Deborah was "a woman from the town of Lapidoth," or to recognize her enlightened wisdom or her practice of carrying a torch by indicating that she was a "woman of light or torches," as much as to relate that she was the "wife of the man Lapidoth." In other words, Deborah may or may not have been married. In either case, her leadership role did not depend on the presence or status of a husband.

Because the abstract Hebrew ending of *Lapidoth* is clearly not feminine and because Barak's name means "lightning," a synonym of *Lapidoth,* rabbinic tradition named Barak as Deborah's husband. The legend describes him as an "ignoramus" who was capable only of carrying a torch to light the way for his wife, Deborah, as he accompanied her to the sanctuary. According to the legend, people therefore knew Barak by the pseudonym Flames (or Lapidoth) and Deborah as the wife of Flames (Ginzberg, *Legends,* 4:35). The tradition may have evolved because, as a military captain, Barak showed surprising humility in his request for Deborah's presence throughout the battle. Unfortunately, however, Barak's humility is perceived by some as a weakness. Nothing in scripture sustains this rabbinic interpretation of the phrase.

THE CALL FOR BATTLE

At Deborah's urging and with her promise of support, Barak called the people to prepare for battle. He gathered ten *alafim* (ten thousand troops, or ten units of troops) from Naphtali and Zebulun, the two tribes most directly affected by Hazor's domination (Judges 4:10). Other tribes from as far south as Benjamin eventually came to support the fledgling troops but with perhaps less enthusiasm than those immediately threatened by Sisera's grip. Not every community exploited by Hazor responded to Barak's call. The inhabitants of Meroz, a village in the land of the tribe of Naphtali, received Deborah's pointed denunciation "because they came not to the help of the Lord" (Judges 5:23).

Depending on how one translates Judges 5:14–18, either four more or all eight of the remaining northern tribes joined Zebulun and Naphtali in battle. Troops from the tribes of Ephraim, Benjamin, Manasseh (Machir), and Issachar are clearly acknowledged as aiding Barak's forces (vv. 14–15). Deborah either chastened the other four for making excuses not to come or praised them for their assistance when they could easily have remained at home to watch over their sheepfolds: Asher and Dan along the coast,

A view of Mount Tabor from the Jezreel Valley. Sisera's army of chariots, horsemen, and footmen stationed themselves near the Kishon River in the Jezreel Valley as they awaited the Israelite army that would have been visible on the slopes of Mount Tabor.

and Reuben and Gad (Gilead) even farther away, across the Jordan River (vv. 16–17). The two southern tribes, Judah and Simeon, are not mentioned at all, perhaps because they were involved in their own battles with the Philistines. The tribe of Levi is not cited, being exempt from military duty because of priesthood responsibilities.

Of all the tribes that participated, however, Deborah particularly lauded Zebulun and Naphtali for their courageous efforts in the battle (Judges 5:18). That may be the reason these two tribes alone are mentioned in the prose account of the conflict (Judges 4:6, 10). Additionally, Barak was likely from the tribe of Naphtali because he came from the village of Kedesh-naphtali (v. 6).

Meeting at the city gates, the troops turned to Deborah for confirmation that God was with them: "Awake, awake, Deborah: awake, awake; utter a song" (Judges 5:12). Their cry to Barak was filled with hope: "Lead thy captivity captive" (Judges 5:12). With weapons scarce, the only means of attack left to the Israelite army were likely slings, bronze swords, and bows and arrows (Judges 5:8). By contrast, spears and shields defined professional military men, such as the Canaanites commanded. Confidence in the Lord and reminders of His power and love for them would quickly become the Israelites' only hope for victory.

A view of the Jezreel Valley from atop Mount Tabor. Deborah, Barak, and the relatively small Israelite army held the high ground of Mount Tabor when Sisera's mighty Canaanite army advanced to fill much of the Jezreel Valley below.

Deborah commanded Barak to take the high ground. He marched his army to Mount Tabor, the highest elevation in the area, rising more than thirteen hundred feet above the surrounding plain and about ten miles from the origin of the Kishon River. From atop the hill, Barak and his men could see the Jezreel Valley as the Canaanite army with its nine hundred chariots readied for battle. On the slopes of Mount Tabor, the Israelites were safe from chariot attack; once they descended to the flat terrain, however, they would easily be destroyed by the speeding chariots.

THE CANAANITES PREPARE FOR BATTLE

The Canaanites received, possibly from a Kenite named Heber, the alarming news that the Israelites were preparing to revolt (Judges 4:11–12). The Kenites were one of the various Midianite tribes and known for their skill as silversmiths, coppersmiths, and traveling tinkers. By the era of the judges, most of the Kenites had annexed themselves geographically and politically to the tribe of Judah in the south (Judges 1:16). Heber and his wife Jael, however, lived in tents in a break-off Kenite community in the north, which apparently was neutral in the Israelite-Canaanite conflict. Their community of Kedesh appears to be different from the Kedesh-Naphtali where Barak lived. Heber's Kedesh was likely farther north and away from Israelite strongholds, considering that Sisera chose to seek refuge from his enemies there (Judges 4:11).

The scriptures also indicate that Heber made a peace pact between his household and Jabin (Judges 4:17). Perhaps this alliance developed over a business relationship that included Heber's metalsmith skills and an agreement to build and repair Jabin's iron chariots and weapons. When Heber learned that the Israelites were preparing for attack, he turned informant to warn his Canaanite ally. In response, Jabin commissioned Sisera to lead an attack against the Israelite rebellion.

Josephus reported that Jabin's army consisted of three hundred thousand footmen, ten thousand horsemen, and at least three thousand chariots (*Antiquities*, 5.5.1). Most likely, no one city at the time would have commanded such an enormous contingent or even nine hundred chariots. The song of Deborah indicates that the Canaanite army was sent by "the kings of Canaan," including Jabin of Hazor, to put down the Israelite rebellion (Judges 5:19).

With full view of Mount Tabor and the Israelite army positioned on its slope, Sisera arrayed his "nine hundred chariots of iron, and all the people that were with him," near the Kishon River in the Jezreel Valley (Judges 4:13). Along the flatlands beside the river, his chariots would have facility of movement and room to generate speed and force behind their blows.

No representation of the Canaanite chariots has been found in art or written description. The closest parallel would be the Hittite chariots depicted in Egyptian monuments. Like the Canaanites, the Hittites used chariots as their primary weapon. Three fully armed Hittites rode in each chariot box: one guided the chariot, one attacked with a sword or lance, and one guarded the occupants from enemy blows with a large shield. In all probability, the entire chariot would not have been made of iron, but the chariot box would have been plated with iron with, perhaps, iron scythes projecting from the axle on either side to protect the lower body of the soldiers who drove it.

THE LORD'S VICTORY

The Canaanites' possession and effective use of such chariots had previously halted the Israelites' military progress by prohibiting their access to the plains and valleys (Judges 1:19). This knowledge as well as the reality that combat was imminent must have tested every bit of bravery and faith the Israelites had. The scene that emerges from the scriptural pages is poignant in its dramatic contrasts. On one side was a heavily armed force of nine hundred chariots plus a great number of foot soldiers. On the other side was an untrained coalition of men with makeshift weapons. The reality would have been stunning. Only with divine power and wisdom could the Canaanites be defeated. The victory would be due to God's grace, not to the Israelites' strength, intelligence, or personal righteousness.

According to Josephus, Israel's army was "so affrighted at the multitude of those enemies, that they were resolved to march off, had not Deborah retained them, and commanded them to fight the enemy that very day for that they should conquer them, and God would be their assistance" (*Antiquities* 5.5.3).

Deborah bore witness of God's timing and communicated His military plan to Barak. "Up; for this is the day in which the Lord hath delivered Sisera into thine hand," she announced to Israel's captain. "Is not the Lord gone out before thee?" (Judges 4:14). At Deborah's command, Barak descended from Mount Tabor to confront the Canaanite chariots in the valley below. According to Judges 4, Deborah's contribution in the conflict was not to fight but to encourage and bear witness of the Lord's might and divine leadership. According to Judges 5, she was the chief commander of Israel's army, and Barak respectfully followed her directive (vv. 7, 12). In either case, Deborah was a leader and the inspiring genius behind Israel's remarkable victory.

The decisive battle occurred near the confluence of streams that make up the Kishon River, and near the pass between Taanach and Megiddo (Judges 5:19). Megiddo was a strategically located fortified city that had not yet been conquered by the Israelites. Taanach was a swampy, poorly drained area of the Jezreel Valley that easily flooded when the nearby Kishon River overran its bounds in a rainstorm. The ground was dry when the Canaanites positioned themselves near the river; it would not remain so for long.

According to the prose account of the battle, the Lord "discomfited" Sisera when the two armies met, causing the Canaanites to abandon their chariots (Judges 4:15). The word in Hebrew translated here as "discomfited" is also used to describe the panic the Egyptians experienced at the Red Sea (Exodus 14:24). Deborah sang of stars in the heavens that fought against Sisera (Judges 5:20), suggesting that God's heavenly power came to Israel's assistance. Her song continued with images of the Kishon River sweeping away their enemies, soldiers being trodden down, and horses becoming broken in the confusion and bad weather (vv. 21–22).

Most likely, the Lord caused a sudden rainstorm, which began a cacophony of disasters in rapid succession. The heavy rain caused the river to flood, which disabled the chariots in the muddy terrain, stranded the Canaanite troops or swept them away by the floodwaters, and allowed Israel's foot soldiers the advantage of attacking stationary targets. Josephus added that a fierce wind blew the storm into the faces of the Canaanites but was at the backs of the Israelites, thereby further favoring Barak's army (*Antiquities* 5.5.4).

Each chariot was drawn by two or four horses. According to one biblical scholar, the horses would not have been shod. "In consequence of the rapidity of their flight, their hoofs were, as Deborah mentions in her song, shattered and broken, and the horses becoming lame, left their riders an easy prey" (Jamieson, *Manners,* 242).

No details emerge in the scriptures to explain how all the Canaanite soldiers were destroyed, only that "all the host of Sisera fell upon the edge of the sword" (Judges 4:16). Did they fall on their own swords in the confusion? Did they drop their weapons, allowing the Israelites to claim them and use them against their former owners? The inability to explain how the enemy was destroyed underscores that God was their source of power and strength—and not any number of deadly weapons.

Reinforcing that the Lord is our enabling power, the apostle Paul noted that the "weapons of our warfare are not carnal" (2 Corinthians 10:4) and we must put on the "whole armour of God" (Ephesians 6:11) to succeed in life's battles. Similarly, the apostle John testified that we were victorious as an army of God against Satan's forces in premortality because we relied on "the blood of the Lamb, and . . . the word of [our] testimony" (Revelation 12:11). The combination of the unlimited power of the Savior's Atonement and our unflinching conviction and reliance on His love and promises makes every enemy conquerable.

With the Lord's power in a thunderstorm, Captain Barak ("lightning") and his army descended upon the mighty Canaanites. Only one of the enemy survived, the Canaanite captain Sisera, who fled the battle scene on foot to find refuge. Sisera's approaching demise would fulfill Deborah's prophecy. The credit for his death would not go to Barak or to any of his soldiers. That honor would go to a woman, just as Deborah had foretold.

JAEL'S HOSPITALITY

The peace pact between Heber and Jabin presented Sisera with what he must have supposed was a safe haven. He ran not to Heber's tent, however, but to the tent of Heber's wife, Jael (Judges 4:17). Heber's absence, along with no mention of other Kenite men around Jael's tent, may suggest that they were also involved in the fighting that day.

Visualizing the fleeing Canaanite captain entering the home of a woman alone, we might expect to find Jael the vulnerable one and fear for her safety rather than for that of the mighty warrior. Under ancient laws of hospitality, guests were received in the man's tent or his partition of the tent because the woman's partition was reserved for her personally. Questions of propriety could easily follow should a man who was not husband or brother be found in a woman's tent. But Jael showed no signs of fear when the captain arrived. She went out to greet Sisera and offered him protection even before he arrived at the camp (Judges 4:18).

Jael welcomed the battle-worn Sisera into her tent by covering him with a "mantle," perhaps a blanket or rug (Judges 4:18). After his long, intense flight from the battlefield, Sisera may not have appreciated a heavy blanket as

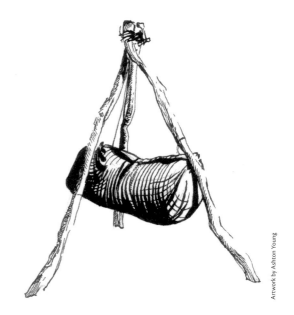

Animal skins functioned as containers for storing and processing milk into yogurt, cheese, and butter.

Artwork by Ashton Young

much for warmth as for a covering of concealment. Sisera had two requests of Jael: water to quench his thirst and surveillance for his pursuers. Should Barak come in search for him, she was to deny that he was there (v. 19). Jael's performance of hospitality exceeded both requests.

Instead of water, Jael offered Sisera milk from a "bottle," also described as "butter in a lordly dish" (4:19; 5:25). Jael's name means "mountain goat," and the milk she offered was likely goat's milk, which acts as a mild sedative. The bottle was no doubt an animal skin that functioned as a container for the milk. Because stored milk needs refrigeration, especially in warmer climates, the early Israelites processed it into different kinds of butter, cheeses, and yogurt. Milk was soured by shaking it in the animal skin container and allowing it to ferment with the bacteria remaining in the skin from a previous use. Milk in its processed curdled or yogurt form was a common drink.

And then Jael killed him. Her actions confound every expectation of how women should behave. Moreover, she delivered defeat to the mighty warrior in a manner considered most shameful—death at the hands of a woman. The two accounts portray Sisera's death differently. The narration in prose depicts Jael striking a nail or tent peg through Sisera's temples, fastening him to the ground, while he slept (Judges 4:21–22). In the song of Deborah, Sisera was standing when Jael attacked him, not motionless in sleep. In poetic verse, Sisera's death occurs in slow motion while he gradually bows deeper and deeper to eventually land at Jael's feet (Judges 5:26–27).

Jael's thoughts and motives in attacking Sisera are unclear. Did she slay him out of reverence and fear for Israel's God? Noting that Jael killed him in "her" tent, did she act to protect her honor, guessing that Sisera had a scheme to assault her or something worse after he had rested? Did she remain true to the Kenites' original alliance with Israel to nullify her husband's breach of it? Perhaps she considered Barak's response to her should he find Sisera protected within her tent. Or did she consider the bigger picture resulting from this battle, recognizing that Israel was obviously now the victor and opting to side with them?

Whatever the reason, Deborah called her "blessed," suggesting that Jael did God's work in killing Israel's enemy (Judges 5:24). An inspiration for all women when war invades their homes, Jael was likened to the war hero Shamgar in the narrative account (Judges 4:7; see also 3:31).

A vivid symbolic image emerges from Jael's story. A nail or tent peg (*yathaid*) was a stake that measured as long as three feet. It was to be driven deep into the sandy terrain with a large mallet to anchor tents in place. With a *yathaid,* Jael fulfilled prophecy and led the enemy captive. Israel was delivered from the grasp of oppression.

The mission of the Savior can be found within this imagery. Zechariah likened Jehovah to a *yathaid* and a cornerstone because He is the One who grounds and aligns us (Zechariah 10:4; see also Ezra 9:8). Likewise, Isaiah testified that the Savior's mission included providing His children with a glorious throne in His Father's house, as a *yathaid* that is fastened "in a sure place" (Isaiah 22:23). As Jael's tent peg brought a sure end to Sisera's life, so also Christ's mission of atonement certifies sure and certain blessings for eternity.

SISERA'S MOTHER AS CONTRAST

In contrast to Christ's victory through a mother in Israel, Deborah transitioned her song to consider Sisera's mother, a mother in Canaan, to highlight the depths of the enemy's defeat (Judges 5:28–30). Rather than feeling a natural sympathy for each other as women, Deborah's song indicates that women were emotionally involved in the conflict, even though they were not directly engaged in warfare.

In their royal surroundings with latticed windows, Sisera's mother and her attendant "wise ladies" expected Sisera's troops to speedily return as victors, as they always had. Accustomed to receiving luxuries from the war booty, the women greedily anticipated Sisera's triumphal entry, annoyed that they must wait so long.

Canaanite warriors had license to take what they wanted from those they defeated, including "a damsel or two" (Judges 5:30), a practice that the law of Moses allowed only if the Israelite warrior married her and cared for her (Deuteronomy 21:10–14; Numbers 14:3). In her song, Deborah did not call a woman captured by the Canaanites a "damsel," as the Hebrew term is translated in the King James Version, but a "womb," signifying that women were seized in battle specifically for their reproductive capacity. Due to high mortality during childbirth, many young widowers sought a wife among the girls they captured. Additionally, population growth through the offspring of "womb-girls" promised a future slave labor force and replacements to the male population decimated by years of fighting.

Deborah's song suggests that the women of Canaanite nobility were especially covetous of the colorful fabrics that they hoped to receive from the war booty. Because dyes were expensive and therefore colorful fabrics and clothing less common, colorful articles were prized. Deborah described a

Artwork by Ashton Young

Canaanite woman looking through window. Frequently a motif carved in ivory, the "woman at the window" design reflects the dream of seeing a soldier returning home from battle. One interpretation of the woman could be Sisera's mother, who waited at her window for her son to return with the victor's spoil.

particularly enviable fabric as one that conveyed a variety of colors on both sides (Judges 5:30). Sisera's mother, however, would never receive these anticipated spoils from the Israelites—and she would never again see her son alive. This time the Israelites were the victors, not the mighty Canaanites of Hazor. The Israelites listened to a prophetess call them to battle, thus allowing the Lord to be their Captain.

REST IN THE LAND

As a result of their triumph, Israel enjoyed freedom for the next forty years (Judges 5:31). Although their victory did not make them the undisputed landlords of the Jezreel Valley, it did allow the Israelites safe travel in the area and freedom to settle there.

Deborah's story shows that many Israelites played a part in overcoming the Canaanites. Barak as the military captain, Jael as Sisera's slayer, Deborah as the prophetess, and the ten thousand obedient soldiers were all vital to the outcome. No one of them, however, could have accomplished the victory alone. No one of them was the essential hero. The victory was the Lord's. Only with Him did they become conquerors.

The story also teaches that even though Israel pulled away from God, God never forgot Israel. In a completely unexpected way, the Lord built His offense behind the leadership and unwavering faith of a woman who directed the army with both the gentle compassion of a mother and the courageous forthrightness of a general. In this striking combination of characteristics, Deborah typifies Jesus Christ, the Captain and Savior of our souls. She reminds us that becoming like the Lord and learning His gospel are not a matter of gender.

Much like Deborah and Barak, we each face individual and collective battles against enemies that surround us and those that attack us from within. The key to victory is always the same, whether we are men or women. By redirecting our lives to align with the Savior, we put our faith into action and rely on His ample arm. Only then is victory sure.

Deborah's passionate appeals to the people in the name of the Lord awakened national unity and rallied a military response. With victory won, she described her people as those who had changed and now loved the Lord. Reconnected to their God, she likened them to the sun that was rising in might (Judges 5:31). By depending on the grace of the Lord in the use of her God-given talents and opportunities, she rose to heights that inspired others to similarly trust in God. Deborah the judge, the prophetess, and the mother in Israel became more than any of her titles suggest. In the strength of the Lord, she became the catalyst that inspired a mighty change of heart and led a people to rediscover their Redeemer.

POINTS TO PONDER: APPLICATIONS FOR OUR LIVES

1. How does Deborah's faith in Christ and willingness to act in the face of daunting odds help you see your challenges with renewed hope?

2. In the war in heaven, God and His followers defeated Satan and his followers with the use of two

weapons: the blood of the Lamb and the word of their testimony (Revelation 12:11). What evidence do you see that these same weapons aided Deborah and Barak in their victory? How do these weapons enable us to be successful in modern-day battles with evil?

3. In what ways was Deborah a mother in Israel? How does her example inform your understanding of the title of "mother"?

4. What Christlike attributes are exemplified in Deborah's story? How did Deborah bear witness of Christ?

5. What insight do Deborah and Barak supply into effective and appropriate ways that men and women can serve together in the Church or the community?

For This Child I Prayed

HANNAH

חַנָּה

"Grace"

Like several wives of the patriarchs, Hannah was barren "because the Lord had shut up her womb" (1 Samuel 1:6). Judgments against infertile women had not improved among the people of the covenant since the days of Sarah and Rebekah. Their society continued to see barren women as a disgrace to their husbands and without purpose in their communities. The Lord had an important mission and lesson for Hannah that became apparent to her only through her struggles with barrenness.

Before learning that lesson, however, Hannah manifested her sorrow in frequent crying and a loss of appetite. Her husband, Elkanah, cherished her, but his attention and love did not fill the void in her life. Her priesthood leader, the high priest Eli, misunderstood her and accused her falsely. Hannah came to realize that no one could assuage the emptiness in her life but the Savior. Her despondency and awareness of her nothingness therefore became an important catalyst that led Hannah to discover the Lord's teachings for her. Through His compassionate acceptance and limitless strength, God helped this Israelite woman recognize that she could contribute to the Lord's work and have a fruitful life whether she ever gave birth or not. In the apostle Peter's perspective, one is not barren or unfruitful if she abounds in faith, virtue, knowledge, temperance, brotherly kindness, and charity. These Christlike attributes are available to everyone and will fill every void in one's life (2 Peter 1:5–8).

No explicit scriptural mention is given that Hannah was a prophetess, but a number of clues indicate that she was indeed a woman who learned to trust in the Lord's divinity and enabling power. She openly declared those truths to others and was blessed that God would consecrate her testimony as a witness to all. Therefore, Hannah may properly be considered a prophetess.

Through her humility, faith in the Lord, and tremendous sacrifice, Hannah bore a son whom she quickly returned to the Lord to be His servant forever. That son, Samuel, would become a prophet, priest, and judge at one of the most desperate times in Israel's history.

1 SAMUEL 1:1–2:21
LDS BIBLE DICTIONARY, 698

HISTORICAL SETTING

Throughout the era of the judges (1200–1000 B.C.), the most populous Israelite settlements were found in the central hill country, where the number of residents increased fourfold during this period of two hundred years. The Bible indicates that the centers of Israel's population at the time were Shiloh, Bethel, Ramah, Gilgal, and Mizpah. All of these communities are located within thirty miles of where the boundaries of the territories of Ephraim, Manasseh, and Benjamin meet. The sanctuary that housed the ark of the covenant was situated in Shiloh in Ephraim, suggesting that the tribe of Ephraim was still considered the leading tribe (Joshua 18:1).

Although three hundred years had passed since Joshua led the Israelites into the promised land, the tribes of Israel had yet to demonstrate that they could one day be sovereign in the land (Judges 11:26). In addition to persistent conflicts with their Canaanite and Philistine neighbors, the Israelites faced the displeasure of their God because of their wavering loyalty to His covenant and their outright rebellion against His laws. Rather than forge a united front among all twelve tribes, hegemony was held within individual family clans. Consequently, the Israelites tolerated life among the various peoples who inhabited adjacent

Photo by Susan Y. Porter

The ark of the covenant was housed in the sanctuary in Shiloh, where Hannah's family regularly visited. This stone engraving, found in New Testament Capernaum north of the Sea of Galilee, depicts the ark being transported on a cart.

lands, thereby further isolating themselves from their fellow Hebrews. By the end of the book of Judges, the twelve tribes were disintegrating into anarchy with little semblance of any social order remaining (Judges 21:25).

The Israelites not only lacked political and military direction but were bankrupt in spiritual leadership. At risk of destruction by the Philistines to the west, Israel's loosely organized tribal settlements desperately needed a strong, faithful, and visionary leader. Eli, the high priest at the sanctuary and a judge in Israel, was the feeble head of priesthood for the nation. Furthermore, his sons, Hophni and Phineas, took advantage of the permissive environment and the weakness in leadership by corrupting the sacred priesthood office (1 Samuel 2:12–17).

Not all of Israel, however, had forgotten God. A small portion of the people valued God's covenant and looked to His law and servants to bring them back into His favor. Elkanah's family, which included Hannah, was among this fraction of the people who

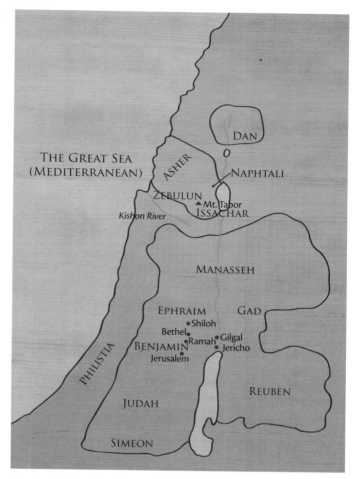

The land of Israel at the time of Hannah and near the end of the era of the judges.

continued to trust in God. One generation later, a dramatic turnaround in Israel's political strength and religious understanding occurred. Unknowingly, Hannah became an important catalyst for sweeping changes that would generate solidarity, military might, and repentance among the tribes of Israel.

During the lifetime of Hannah's son, Israel steadily advanced to become the greatest empire in the ancient Near East. As further evidence of the dramatic progress that the Israelites made as a nation in the generation after Hannah, we see that Samuel spent his childhood at the makeshift shrine that housed the ark of the covenant in Shiloh and before his death saw preparations for a splendid temple to be built in Jerusalem.

HANNAH'S HUSBAND

Although Hannah is unquestionably the central figure in this story, nothing about her ancestry or origins is mentioned. When Hannah married Elkanah, she became part of his family and tribal identity. Her husband's distinguished lineage, title, and geographical inheritance therefore introduce the account. Elkanah was descended from the Kohathite branch of the tribe of Levi (1 Chronicles 6:16, 22–28). More specifically, he was of the family of Zuph, or one of the "Zophim" (1 Samuel 1:1). There are four generations between Elkanah and Zuph (v. 1) and fifteen generations between Zuph and Levi (1 Chronicles 6:33–38). Elkanah is reported to be from "Ramathaim-zophim, of mount Ephraim" (1 Samuel 1:1), meaning he was a resident of the village of Ramah, which was located in the Zophim's land inheritance called Zuph near mount Ephraim (1 Samuel 9:5). According to Josephus, Elkanah was a Levite from Ramath, a village in Ephraim territory (*Antiquities,* 5.10.2). Later scholars have identified Elkanah's village with Ramah of Benjamin, a few miles northwest of Jerusalem (Keil and Delitzsch, *Commentary,* 2:372). Because the mountains of Ephraim extended south into Benjamin territory, Ramah of Benjamin was probably the same place as Ramah of Ephraim. Incidentally, the prophetess Deborah judged under a palm tree near this same village of Ramah, perhaps only a few decades before Hannah resided there (Judges 4:5). Possibly Hannah knew of Deborah and was strengthened and encouraged by her example of faith and determination to serve God.

ELKANAH'S TWO WIVES

Because Elkanah was a man of property and title, any woman he married would become significant whether or not she was capable of bearing children. Hannah was Elkanah's first and beloved wife according to 1 Samuel 1:8. He then married Peninnah, who was able to give him children when Hannah was not. Perhaps the only reason he took a second wife was because Hannah was barren.

According to a Jewish Midrash, Hannah and Elkanah were married ten years before Elkanah married Peninnah. This embellishment to the story probably resulted from a Mishnaic law that gives a man grounds for divorce or permission to take a second wife if his first wife does not conceive a child during the first ten years of marriage. Elkanah is therefore shown as a kind man for not divorcing Hannah, as was his right, and rather waiting the required ten years before taking a second wife. The same legend then surmises that it was yet another nine years after Peninnah joined the family before Hannah finally conceived (Ginzberg, *Legends,* 4:58–59; 6:215–16).

Scripture makes no mention of the number of years Hannah waited to become a mother or the length of time she was married to Elkanah before he took a second wife. It does indicate, however, that Elkanah did not share in Hannah's deep concern over her barrenness (1 Samuel 1:8). He felt that his love for her should satisfy her every need, even to exceed the blessing of having ten sons. On the other hand, Hannah's love for him was not sufficient to dissuade him from taking a second wife. Should he not have had any children by any wife, one wonders whether Elkanah would have been so unconcerned about Hannah's in-fertility. If Hannah were Elkanah's only wife, would he have been more like the New Testament priest

TIME LINE

1200–1020 B.C.	Judges provide leadership for Israel
1075 B.C.	Hannah gives birth to Samuel
1020 B.C.	Samuel anoints Saul as the first king of Israel (1 Samuel 13:1)
1005 B.C.	Samuel anoints David as the second king of Israel (2 Samuel 5:5)
	The site for the temple is identified
	Samuel dies
965 B.C.	Nathan (?) anoints Solomon the third king of Israel (1 Kings 11:42)

Zachariah, the husband of Elisabeth? In their case, not only the woman but also the man pleaded to God for a son (Luke 1:13).

Elkanah's recognition and sympathy for Hannah's depressed state of mind is evidenced by his questions to her: "Hannah, why weepest thou? and why eatest thou not? and why is thy heart grieved? am not I better to thee than ten sons?" (1 Samuel 1:8). Although well-meaning, Elkanah did not possess the solution for his wife's need; his love for her alone was not sufficient solace to fill the emptiness in her life. Hannah's responses to his questions, if she gave any, are not recorded. Perhaps Hannah knew that her husband could not understand her feelings and therefore wisely remained silent. Whatever the case, Hannah was reaching the conclusion that only God could understand and empathize with her feelings of isolation. Throughout her process of discovery, Hannah is shown as being always hopeful that she would one day give birth.

THE SANCTUARY AND PRIESTHOOD AT SHILOH

The religious center of the Israelites was in Shiloh from the time the twelve tribes conquered sufficient territory in the promised land until Solomon's temple in Jerusalem was completed more than two hundred years later (Joshua 18:1; Judges 18:31; 1 Samuel 4:3–4). Located about sixteen miles north of Ramah of Benjamin, Shiloh was the site for the enlarged, now-stationary tabernacle that was originally created during the Israelites' sojourn in the wilderness. Auxiliary structures, such as pillars or posts and a seat for the high priest, probably near the curtained entrance (1 Samuel 1:9), doors (1 Samuel 3:15), and accommodations for dining were among the additions that transformed the tabernacle into the Israelite sanctuary after its arrival at Shiloh. The Septuagint (LXX), or Greek translation of the Old Testament, indicates that women's quarters had also been added and were located on or near the temple premises (LXX 1 Samuel 1:18). Although neither elegant nor expansive, the sanctuary housed the ark of the covenant. Because it represented the dwelling place of God, the sanctuary at Shiloh was considered the most sacred place on earth for the Israelites.

When Elkanah and his family visited the tabernacle in Shiloh, Eli was the priesthood leader and a judge in Israel (1 Samuel 1:9; 4:18). Like Elkanah, Eli was from the tribe of Levi, but Eli was also from the lineage of Aaron, which qualified him to be a priest (1 Samuel 14:3). Eli's sons may have been mentioned early in the story (1 Samuel 1:3) because the high priest was elderly and unable to perform the duties required for sacrifices. His sons, therefore, would have served as officiators for Elkanah's sacrifices.

The law of Moses directed every Israelite man to offer sacrifices at the sanctuary three specific times every year (Exodus 23:14–17; Deuteronomy 12:5–7; 16:16–17). The first was Passover and the Feast of Unleavened Bread, which commemorated the Lord's deliverance of Israel from Egyptian slavery. This annual festival occurred during the first month of the Jewish calendar in the spring of the year. Seven weeks after Passover, the second holy festival, called the Feast of Weeks (or Pentecost, as it is called in Acts 2), was celebrated after the first harvest of the new year.

Finally, in the seventh month of the Jewish calendar, or late autumn, the Israelites observed the third sacrificial celebration. This final holy feast of the year was called Succoth, or the Feast of Booths or Tabernacles, to acknowledge God's bounteous harvest at the end of the growing season (Exodus 23:16) and to remind the Israelites of God's protecting care for their ancestors when they lived in tents or booths after the Exodus (Deuteronomy 8:7–18; Leviticus 23:40; Nehemiah 8:15). As another connecting point, the location of their first encampment was also called Succoth (Exodus 12:37). The Feast of Booths followed Yom Kippur, or the Day of Atonement, which was the most holy fast day and an annual reminder of Israel's need for God's pardon for their sins and uncleanness (Leviticus 16:33).

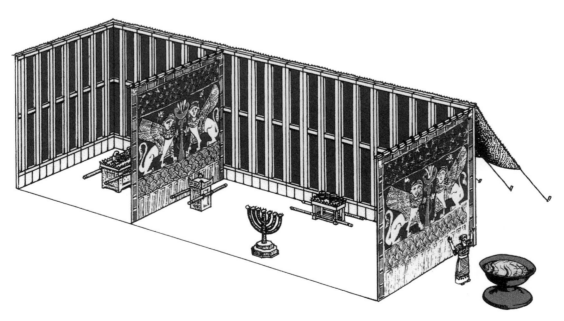

Artwork by Michael Lyon

The Israelites gathered around the sanctuary each year for the Feast of Tabernacles, camping in tents in remembrance of their ancestors' shelters during the forty years in the wilderness.

From the time of Moses until the kingdom of Judah was taken captive by the Babylonians in 586 B.C., every generation observed Succoth, or the Feast of Booths, in much the same way. Festival participants lived in tents or booths that were constructed of branches from fruit and palm trees during the week-long celebration.

In addition to the feast, family members joined the family patriarch in making sacred offerings to God at the sanctuary. Priests sacrificed the offerings and then returned parts of the offering to the family to enjoy for the feast. Bulls, rams, and lambs were sacrificed as burnt offerings each day of the holy week. As a supplement, a grain offering of fine flour and oil and a drink offering of undiluted wine from the ripest first fruits accompanied each of the animal sacrifices (Numbers 29:12–34).

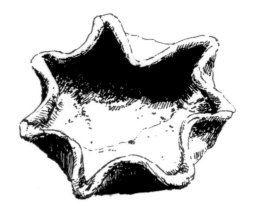

Artwork by Ashton Young

Thought to have been used for religious purposes in ancient Israel, the seven-spouted oil lamp may have been used to provide light in and around the tabernacle (1 Samuel 3). Each night, the lamp was filled with oil and a wick in each spout was lit to provide light until the oil was consumed the following morning.

The annual ritual sacrifice and holy familial meal in which Elkanah's family participated in Shiloh was likely the Feast of Booths. The scriptural narrative of Hannah's annual pilgrimages to Shiloh describes a holy feast that followed a fast, much like Succoth follows Yom Kippur. Hannah was fasting in preparation for her petition to God and waited until the other family members had feasted before advancing to the sanctuary (1 Samuel 1:8–9). Furthermore, during their visit a few years later, Hannah's family sacrificed a young bull along with offerings of flour and wine, which are indicative of sacrifices for the Feast of Booths (v. 24).

Elkanah gave both of his wives and each of Peninnah's children a portion of animal flesh during the celebration (1 Samuel 1:4–5). These portions may have been given to each person to offer as a sacrifice or as their share of the sacrificial animals that were to be eaten by the family who offered the animal for sacrifice. From Hannah's perspective, this general practice would only underscore the value of a woman with children over one who has no children. In an attempt to further communicate how important and dear she was to him, however, Elkanah apportioned more of the sacrifice to Hannah than to Peninnah (v. 5). Hannah's extra share may have simply been a double portion of flesh to sacrifice or perhaps even the equivalent of Peninnah and her children's portions combined. No matter how much Elkanah tried to allay Hannah's sorrow, however, these actions only reinforced her sense of inadequacy and diminished worth.

Another source of conflict for Hannah is suggested in the Hebrew or Masoretic Text (MT), from which our King James Old Testament was translated. "Her adversary," or *the other wife,* as clarified in Hebrew, "also provoked her sore, for to make her fret . . . therefore she wept" (1 Samuel 1:6–7). This brief observation evokes an image of a jealous Peninnah, who did not enjoy the same quality of love that

Elkanah had for Hannah, exciting Hannah's grief by telling her that God has greater love for women who give birth than for barren women.

In distress over our own areas of weakness and insecurity, it is easy to console ourselves by gloating to others over a part of our lives that is visibly successful without realizing the cruel judgment we consequently thrust on someone who does not share our success in that area. For example, a person who has lost a lot of weight can imply to a friend who has a weight problem that the friend is obviously lazy and undisciplined. Or those who come into money early in their careers may look down on those who continue to struggle financially even in their mature years. We tend to be more sensitive in areas where we know we have a weakness and boastful in areas where we perceive we have strength.

According to the prophet Mormon, our human weakness is God-given and a blessing to make us humble before Him (Ether 12:27). An important scriptural fact about Hannah is that "the Lord had shut up her womb" (1 Samuel 1:5). Remembering that at least some of our challenges in mortality are divinely designed can help us to avoid the temptation to condescendingly judge others.

Of importance, neither the Greek translation of the Old Testament, the Septuagint (LXX), nor Josephus the Jewish historian makes any mention of Peninnah taunting Hannah to tears. More specifically, the parallel Septuagint passage of verses 6–7 reads: "For the Lord gave her no child in her affliction, and according to the despondency of her affliction; and she was dispirited on this account, that the Lord shut up her womb so as not to give her a child. So she did year by year, in going up to the house of the Lord; and she was dispirited, and wept, and did not eat." According to this account, Hannah was not vexed by Peninnah, but depressed by her empty life. She had plenty of heartache because the Lord had closed up her womb without considering Peninnah as a source of conflict. The narrative provided by the Septuagint is a hopeful clarification to the traditional interpretation of the relationship between Peninnah and Hannah.

HANNAH'S PETITION

Preparing to commune with the Lord at His sanctuary, Hannah was fasting when she went to the annual sacrifice (1 Samuel 1:8–9). Like Zacharias, the New Testament priest who spent more time in the temple than was customary when he desired a son, disciples with burdens tend to stay longer at a sacred site (Luke 1:21).

Filled with emotion and deep anguish, Hannah approached God humbly but also confidently. Most likely, she already knew that God hears and answers prayers and that He does not ignore women as so many others in her life apparently did. She addressed God with, "O Jehovah of hosts," the first person in recorded scripture to do so (Keil and Delitzsch, *Commentary,* 2:375).

Most of Hannah's prayer is unknown except to God, but one part is recorded (1 Samuel 1:11). As we would expect, Hannah petitioned God that she could bear a child. In the Hebrew text, she did not specify that she wanted "a man child" (1 Samuel 1:11) but asked for "human seed" (Frymer-Kensky, *Reading*, 303). Then Hannah voiced her surprising promise to God. If she could just bear a child, she vowed to God that she would give him back to the Lord "all the days of his life" (v. 11). Surely this was not the first time Hannah had asked God for a child, but most likely it was the first time she had promised to return the child to the Lord. No longer looking for security in her old age or acceptance by the other women in the village, Hannah had learned more important lessons during her years of barrenness. Something greater than simply being like other women was driving Hannah to this heartfelt petition. The same Hebrew root *rhm* is used for both *womb* and *compassion*. When we allow the Savior's Atonement to fill our lives, compassion is produced. Hannah had already become fruitful and was able to reflect the Lord's mercy through her desires and actions.

Although all translations of the biblical text describe elements of the Nazarite vow in Hannah's petition, the parallel account in the Dead Sea Scrolls (4QSamª) clearly states that Hannah promised God that her son, should He grant her one, would be a Nazarite all of his life: "And I will [dedicate] him as a Nazarite forever" (1 Samuel 1:22; Parry, "Hannah," 14). Josephus also includes the fact that Hannah promised to dedicate her son to God (*Antiquities,* 5.10.3).

The Nazarite vow contained three requirements: A Nazarite abstained from grapes and any product of grapes, agreed not to shave his head for the entire length of the vow, and avoided any contact with the dead (Numbers 6:2–7; Judges 13:5).

Hannah is not so different from parents today who promise God they will rear their newborn child to serve the Lord. In official baby blessings in the Church, vows are frequently made to God that this babe will grow up to serve a mission for the Lord and spend his or her days participating in His work. Echoing the Nazarite vow, after a fashion, full-time missions for The Church of Jesus Christ of Latter-day Saints require restrictions in association, appearance, and diet. Like Hannah, mothers of missionaries can think of no better future for their children than to be in God's service.

That Hannah made this vow to God without first consulting her husband indicates that women had a right to choose their children's future. Her selfless promise also shows that she recognized that all children rightfully belong to God. She knew she could be His steward in bearing and rearing a babe but that her son would always belong to God.

ELI'S REBUKE

Eli, the priesthood leader, from his judgment seat near the entrance, observed Hannah when she entered the sanctuary. Apparently he saw nothing inappropriate or unusual in a woman coming alone to stand before the Lord. His motion to send her away did not occur until *after* Hannah completed her devotions. In other words, Hannah's manner of praying found disapproval in Eli's eyes, not her desire to worship in the holy site.

Because Hannah prayed silently and not audibly as was probably the norm in that day (Psalm 42:4; 62:8; Lamentations 2:19), Eli assumed that she was drunk. Perhaps he expected women to loudly ululate in prayer as professional mourners did, making Hannah's complete silence appear suspect. A Jewish Midrash explains that Hannah avoided the customary audible prayer because she feared that Peninnah would hear her and taunt her all the more. The same legend alleges that Eli assumed that Hannah was drunk because she came to pray at the sanctuary immediately after wine was served at the festival (Ginzberg, *Legends*, 6:217). Josephus attributed Eli's inaccurate judgment of Hannah to the fact that "she continued at her prayers a long time" (*Antiquities* 5.10.2). Whatever the cause of Eli's misjudgment, in his position of authority, the high priest charged Hannah to "put away thy wine from thee" (1 Samuel 1:14), or "go away and sleep off thine intoxication" (Keil and Delitzsch, *Commentary,* 2:378).

Once again, an important man in Hannah's life did not understand her plight. Giving evidence that she was filled with the Spirit, Hannah manifested no sign of being offended by Eli's scolding. Her explanation reminded the priest that prayers are directed not to priesthood leaders or family patriarchs but only to God. She defended herself as a respectable woman, not a "daughter of Belial" (1 Samuel 1:16), or a worthless woman.

Even when Eli failed to offer an apology for his mistake, Hannah was not thwarted in her petition. Making a word play on her name, which means grace, Hannah's hope was to find "grace" (1 Samuel 1:18), not the high priest's praises. She knew that only through the grace or enabling power of Jehovah could her desire be granted. Hannah's countenance also bore witness that God had heard her plea and would grant her heartfelt desire. She left the sanctuary "no more sad" (v. 18). No thoughtless or judgmental comment could cause her to weep for sorrow now. The cloud of despondency that previously surrounded her had been lifted. Hannah found the grace of Jesus Christ, which finally filled her emptiness that no other love or success could. In a sudden about-face, Eli changed his judgment of Hannah from a drunken daughter of Belial to a true disciple of the Lord, acknowledging that He would "grant thee thy petition" (v. 17).

THE MOTHER OF SAMUEL

God had closed Hannah's womb but was now ready to open it. All life is dependent on Him. When the Lord turns our weaknesses into strengths, we are more capable and have greater wisdom than we ever before imagined. That is the power of the infinite Atonement. Hannah's increased wisdom and strength are visible after her spiritual enlightenment in Shiloh.

Before the next year, when the family would return for the festival, Hannah had borne a son. True to His promise, "the Lord remembered her" (1 Samuel 1:19). In evidence of the rights of women in Israelite society, Hannah as the mother chose the name for the newborn son. In the great majority of Old Testament cases where children are named, the mother, not the father, had the right to decide the name. Hannah chose to name her son Samuel, which means, literally, "the name of God." With the name she selected for her son, Hannah began his preparation to remember the Lord and always serve Him. According to some rabbis, the fuller meaning of Samuel's name is, "his name is given to him by the Most High God" (Ginzberg, *Legends,* 6:218).

HANNAH AS PROPHETESS

On at least one subsequent visit to the tabernacle, Elkanah also made a vow to God (1 Samuel 1:21). Perhaps this was the vow that Elkanah made as a Levite, those who were assigned to serve the Lord from the age of twenty-five to fifty (Numbers 8:24–25). Elkanah's vow may have also been to support Hannah in her vow of returning their son Samuel to the Lord to serve Him not only for these twenty years but for all of his life.

At least the first year after the birth of Samuel, Hannah remained at home rather than accompanying the family for the annual sacrifice. Her explanation was that she would keep her son close to her until he was weaned and then take him to the sanctuary to "appear before the Lord, and there abide forever" (1 Samuel 1:22).

Before his departure, Elkanah communicated his support for Hannah's decision and then remarked, "only the Lord establish his word" (1 Samuel 1:23), indicating an understanding that Hannah was free to make daily decisions as she deemed best, except in cases that violated a promise to the Lord. Because Hannah could not return her son to God before the child was weaned, she was not violating her vow by remaining at home that year.

A far more interesting observation by Elkanah is recorded in the Septuagint and 4QSamᵃ, which records that he said to Hannah, "May the Lord establish that which cometh out of thy mouth" (1 Samuel 1:23). In the Greek translation, Elkanah is shown to be one who believes that his wife speaks the words of God and that God is working through her. The phraseology also assigns to Hannah characteristics of a prophetess.

The Septuagint supplies additional terminology in the Hannah narrative that is reminiscent of prophets. The phrase "Here I am" appears eighteen times in the Hebrew Old Testament, but the speaker is never a woman. Furthermore, ten of those eighteen times, the speaker is "in a temple setting or [is] part of a revelatory experience that involves God or his angels" (Parry, "Hannah," 9). In the Septuagint, Hannah, a woman, responded, "Here I am," when her husband called to her (1 Samuel 1:8). Like prophets in other times (see Genesis 22:1, 11; 31:11; 46:2; Exodus 3:4; 1 Samuel 3:4; Isaiah 6:8), Hannah responded, "Here I am," as she spiritually "stood before the Lord" in a temple setting to communicate a vow to God that would bless all of Israel (LXX 1 Samuel 1:9). Taken together, these details add credence to the suggestion that Hannah was a prophetess.

A Jewish Midrash also assigns a prophetic title to Hannah. It claims that Elkanah's forebears were prophets and that both Hannah and Elkanah were prophets (Ginzberg, *Legends,* 4:57). Although the

Midrash attempts to explain Hannah's importance through her husband's greatness and puts greater focus on Elkanah than does the biblical narrative, the fact remains in every version of the story that the Lord revealed Himself through Hannah and not through her husband. Hers is the active and critical role in every account.

RETURNING SAMUEL TO THE LORD

When she had weaned her son, Hannah prepared to take him to Shiloh and honor her vow to the Lord. The child's age at the time his mother took him to the high priest is not specified in scripture except that he was "young" (1 Samuel 1:24). Most likely, little Samuel was considerably older than babies are today when they are weaned. Considering the frequent spread of disease and high infant mortality rates in ancient days, a mother's prolonged nursing of her child may have been as great a protection against sickness as any other preventative measure. A document from the third century before Christ indicates that children were weaned at three years of age (2 Maccabees 7:27).

The reality and magnitude of Hannah's sacrifice are palpable in the brief scriptural narrative. It is one thing to promise God that you will rear your newborn to be His servant and quite another thing to leave that child at the Missionary Training Center for his full-time service. Mothers all over the Church who give their children to the Lord for two years know the pain that Hannah must have felt that day. The same mothers, however, also know God's compensatory power, which sustains them during their children's absence. At the time of her travel to Shiloh, Hannah gave no hint of having second thoughts about her promise to God.

Along with her only child, Hannah took abundant provisions to the tabernacle to be sacrificed, as required by the law to complete a vow (Numbers 15:8–10). Josephus explained that Hannah and Elkanah's sacrifice at the tabernacle was for the birth of their son and also to pay tithes (*Antiquities,* 5.10.3). The Septuagint offers more detail for this visit to the sanctuary, including that Hannah brought "a calf of three years old," rather than "three bullocks" as stated in the Hebrew Bible (1 Samuel 1:24). Furthermore, in the Septuagint and 4QSam^a, Elkanah accompanied Hannah to Shiloh and "slew the calf" that they brought for an offering (1 Samuel 1:25). In the MT, both Hannah and Elkanah "slew a bullock"

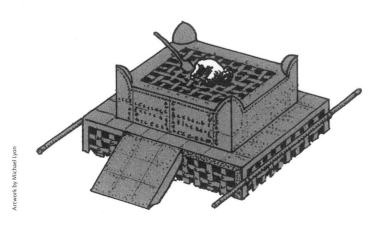

Artwork by Michael Lyon

To complete her vow to the Lord, Hannah brought a bullock to be sacrificed on the altar in front of the tabernacle.

(1 Samuel 1:25). Their sacrifice also included "one ephah of flour, and a bottle of wine" (1 Samuel 1:24). Hannah's grain or meat offering was an ephah of flour, about twenty-one quarts, and her drink offering was a skin of wine, which, in addition to the bullock as the burnt offering, satisfied the requirements (Numbers 15:8–10).

Facing the high priest who acted as representative for the Lord, Hannah held out her young son and reviewed the plea she had made to God "for this child . . . and the Lord hath given me my petition" (1 Samuel 1:26–27). She also repeated her promise to the Lord in return: "Therefore also I have lent [asked] him [from] the Lord; as long as he liveth he shall be lent [asked or of service] to the Lord" (1 Samuel 1:28). Replacing "asked" for "lent" in the translation may provide a clearer translation of the intent in the Hebrew.

HANNAH'S PSALM

In a clear indication of Hannah's unwavering faith in the Lord, she sang a song of rejoicing and praise to God *after* she returned her son to Him (1 Samuel 2:1–10). Some scholars have questioned Hannah's being the author of this psalm because it does not refer to Hannah's personal circumstances and it speaks of events that have not yet occurred, that is, the presence of a king in Israel (Berlin and Brettler, *Jewish,* 563; McCarter, *I Samuel,* 74–76). Others propose that Hannah was merely a "one-time prophetess," suggesting that this might have been the only moment of clairvoyant testifying in Hannah's life (Frymer-Kensky, *Reading*).

Considered from the perspective that Hannah had already received a spiritual witness to the reality of the Redeemer and a sense of her divine mission, she would naturally sing of broader principles and greater events than her immediate situation. When filled with the Spirit of the Lord, we profess doctrinal truths as directed by the Spirit. In other words, this psalm is a natural declaration of a prophet or prophetess. Furthermore, the Latter-day Saint Bible Dictionary points to Hannah's psalm as a "model of prayer" for any of us who have a similar testimony of Jesus Christ (s.v. "prayer," 752). Because of the similarities between these words and the Magnificat (Luke 1:46–55), Mary the mother of Jesus may have been influenced by the faith, message, and beauty of Hannah's psalm.

Considered verse by verse, Hannah's psalm as recorded in

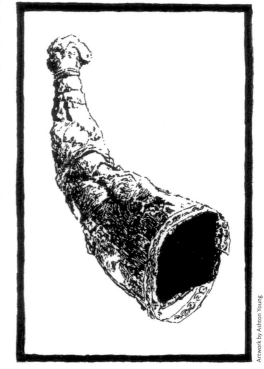

Artwork by Ashton Young

This drawing of a horn is based on an ivory horn found in the fourteenth-century B.C. palace at Megiddo. It may be similar to the horn that contained the oil Samuel used to anoint Saul and David to be kings of Israel.

The high priest's ephod and other sacred garments.

Artwork by Ashton Young

1 Samuel is a remarkable example of joy, wisdom, and inspired perspective amid life's trials. After she gave her all to the Lord, she could see only what great things He had done for her. A few explanations of terms and context can increase our appreciation of Hannah's teachings that she most likely expressed through song.

2:1 Hannah described her joy as though her "horn" were exalted or lifted up. When an animal raises its horns in the air, it communicates triumph, power, strength, and dignity (Deuteronomy 33:17). By knowing that salvation comes only from the Lord, Hannah's "mouth is enlarged over her enemies," or, she no longer fears her enemies. The Lord is her salvation.

2:2 Aware of people all around her who believed in other gods, Hannah definitively declared that "there is none beside [God]: neither is there any rock like our God." He is the Rock, as "broad as eternity" (Moses 7:53), upon which, if we build, we "cannot fall" (Helaman 5:12).

2:3–4 With new perspective gained through willing sacrifice and the knowledge that Christ is the only One to fill our void, Hannah learned true humility. None of us can speak with arrogance over our intellect or actions when we know the Lord. By contrast, we can only conclude that "man is nothing, which thing I never had supposed" after we have encountered true greatness (Moses 1:10).

2:4–9 Hannah could now sing with conviction that God gives us weakness and trials to help us gain strength in Him. In these six verses, Hannah described the cyclical patterns of life. With little or no warning, the sick are brought to good health and the healthy become sick; the poor find wealth while the rich fall into poverty; the fruitful become barren and the barren are filled.

Hannah's new perspective did not emerge because she bore a child but because she learned that only the Savior's perfect love fills our emptiness. She could then recognize that if we have been at the bottom of the wheel, we are less likely to forget the poor when we are on top. Another person who learned this lesson taught, "He that oppresseth the poor reproacheth his Maker: but he that honoureth him hath mercy on the poor" (Proverbs 14:31). The Lord tears down and He builds up, and with His restoration, He always brings us to a better place than we have ever been before (Alma 41). Everything that He does is "for the benefit of the world" (2 Nephi 26:24).

Hannah testified that God "will keep the feet of his saints," reminding those who have made a covenant with the Lord that He will never forget nor forsake them (1 Samuel 2:9; see Barker and Kohlenberger, *Commentary*, 383). Saints, however, will always remember that it is not by their strength that man prevails

A mosque sits on the traditional location of the burial place of Samuel the prophet, which is less than five miles north of Jerusalem.

but through the grace of God (1 Samuel 2:9). In the battles of life, it is not physical strength that brings victory but sincere reliance on God's enabling power.

2:10 Finally, Hannah prophesied of the Lord's strength and victory in the future. She announced that Israel would have a monarchy and that the kings would be "anointed." Interestingly, it would be Hannah's son Samuel who would anoint Saul and David as the first two kings of Israel. Under David's rule and that of his son Solomon, the nation of Israel would expand and fortify itself to become the most powerful empire in the ancient Near East.

With her concluding words, however, Hannah bore witness of the Judge of us all, the King of kings, the Anointed One. The definition of a prophet or prophetess is someone who possesses a "testimony of Jesus" (Revelation 19:10). Naturally, as a prophetess Hannah would testify of the Messiah, which in Hebrew means "the anointed one." If indeed Hannah's psalm prophesied of the Savior's coming, Hannah is also the first person in recorded scripture to speak of Him as "the Anointed One."

SAMUEL'S SERVICE

When she left little Samuel with the high priest, most likely Hannah did not envision the polluted environment that Eli's sons had created around the sanctuary (1 Samuel 2:12–17). Engaged in a form of ritual prostitution similar to that of the followers of Ba'alism, Hophni and Phineas callously administered their priesthood duties and misused the sacrificial meat. Their impudence and greed over the sacred meat broadcast to the faithful Israelites that, as sons of the high priest, their gluttonous desires preceded any devotion to God. In evidence of God's watchful care over young Samuel, the boy continued "in favour both with the Lord and also with men" (1 Samuel 2:26) despite the corruption that surrounded him. The scriptures do not indicate how much of Samuel's reverence for God is attributable to Hannah's influence. We only know that she visited him every year when the family went to Shiloh for the annual sacrifice, each time giving him another "coat," or robe or covering, that she had made (1 Samuel 2:19).

As an apprentice priest, Samuel "ministered before the Lord" wearing a "linen ephod," a garment that was worn over other clothing and tied around the waist (1 Samuel 2:18). The high priest wore an ornate ephod made up of fine-twined linen in the colors of scarlet, purple, gold, and blue. It had a strap over each shoulder that held an onyx stone engraved with the names of the twelve tribes of Israel (Exodus 28:4–12). Priests and apprentice priests wore simpler versions of the high priest's ephod. Perhaps the "coat" that Hannah made for her child each year was this ephod.

GOD REMEMBERED HANNAH

The story of Hannah contains multiple lessons for consideration today. Through the faith and prayers of Hannah, God prepared a remarkable young man to be a judge, a prophet, and the first priesthood official to anoint the divinely appointed kings of Israel. The Hannah narratives remind us that God will raise a righteous leader for His people and will not justify those who abuse and exploit their priesthood position.

The story of Hannah is also a reminder that reversals in fortune occur in everybody's life. God gives and He takes away. When we are down, the Lord raises us up with unimagined opportunities; and when we are puffed up with self-confidence and pride, He humbles us through challenges never anticipated.

Hannah petitioned God for a child, and He gave her four sons and two daughters (1 Samuel 2:21). The Lord's generosity and abundance of blessings exceeds anything we have imagined. It is like asking Him for a fork, and He gives us the whole house. The apostle Paul observed that because God "spared not his own Son" (Romans 8:32), he would not hold back anything from us.

Eventually, Hannah was blessed with several children; however, she was filled with the grace of the Lord before she bore any. When she found the power of the Atonement in her life, she was full and fruitful and could give back to the Lord all that she possessed. Without vanity or complacency, Hannah's sacrifice revealed her independence as well as her awareness of the need for God. Some of us will never bear children, some will never marry, some will never have a happy marriage, and some will never have good health in this life. But every one of us can be fruitful and filled with the power of Jesus Christ. When we find Him, like Hannah, we will lose our life in doing His work. That is His promise to all of us.

POINTS TO PONDER: APPLICATIONS FOR OUR LIVES

1. How may Hannah's response to family conflict and religious diversity assist you to a deeper relationship with your Father in Heaven in your life challenges?

2. How can Hannah help you increase in appreciation for someone in your neighborhood or work place whose life circumstances are different from your own? How can you show that increased appreciation?

3. Why do you think Peninnah might have taunted Hannah? What does that say about Peninnah?

4. In what ways is your life barren or void of the power and influence of the Savior? What can you give away so that the Lord can fill you?

5. How does your life verify Hannah's psalm? What evidence do you see in your life that the Lord takes away and then gives? Identify ways in which you are a stronger and wiser person because of this process.

6. What gospel principles do you see illustrated in this story? How could you use Hannah as an example in a lesson?

7. How does the story of Hannah lead you to a deeper testimony of Jesus Christ?

Treasure the Word

HULDAH

חֻלְדָּה

"Weasel"

$\mathscr{A}$s a trusted spiritual authority, Huldah was petitioned by Judah's king to identify God's call for repentance to his people. Her inspired testimony of impending destruction and consequence for sin motivated an extraordinary era of righteousness among the Israelites. Nevertheless, Huldah's story is easily lost in the larger biblical narrative. The greater saga focuses on Josiah, king of Judah, shortly before the Babylonian captivity. And like Huldah's, Josiah's influence and significance are frequently overlooked and underappreciated among biblical stories, even though their generation provides an important historical backdrop in Jerusalem for the Book of Mormon. Lehi and Sariah were among Josiah's subjects, so they might have known Huldah and her husband; it is even possible that they lived in the same quarter of Jerusalem.

Our glimpse of Huldah is in a few verses in two biblical accounts: one in 2 Kings, written from the perspective of exiled Judah in Babylon, and the other in 2 Chronicles, written to encourage the newly restored exiles as they rebuilt Jerusalem several decades later. Only by considering King Josiah's life and sovereign agenda, the competing political and religious policies embraced by the preceding kings, and the tragic consequences created through subsequent kings do we appreciate Huldah's role, courage, and prophetic voice at this dynamic period of biblical history (ca. 622 B.C.). A brief review of kings who preceded Josiah on the throne of Judah is therefore meaningful background for the era of Huldah and Josiah. Specifically, the religious reforms of King Hezekiah and the conflicting influences of his successors Manasseh and Amon provide information necessary for understanding King Josiah and his need for Huldah's prophetic wisdom. Her story within the national saga emerges as one of the most remarkable accounts of a woman in scripture.

THE REIGN OF KING HEZEKIAH (715–687 B.C.)

At the age of twenty-five, Hezekiah inherited the throne of Judah from his father, Ahaz, who had made Jerusalem

2 KINGS 22:12–20
2 CHRONICLES 34:22–28

politically and religiously dependent on the powerful Assyrian empire. While the Assyrians were conquering nations that surrounded the kingdom of Judah, including the northern kingdom of Israel, Ahaz paid heavy tribute to the Assyrians to allow the people of Judah to remain in their homeland (2 Kings 16:8). Hezekiah's attitude toward the Assyrians was markedly different from his father's.

During the first month of his twenty-nine-year reign, Hezekiah reopened the temple, which his father had closed, and ordered it repaired and rededicated to Jehovah. His plan to reconcile his people to the Lord included destroying images, worship sites for Canaanite and Assyrian deities, and even Moses' brazen serpent, which the people had begun to worship. Rather than battling for power over neighboring nations, Hezekiah focused on strengthening his people spiritually by reinstating the Passover celebration, the tithe, and their trust in God. Centralizing temple worship in Jerusalem, he dismantled all the small rural temples that had been originally built for worship of Jehovah but gradually merged pagan rituals with their worship, thus polluting the belief in the preeminent power of the Lord (2 Kings 18:1–8; 2 Chronicles 29–31).

During these reforms and confrontations with the Assyrians, Hezekiah fortified Jerusalem in the event of a siege. He established food storage areas and directed the digging of a tunnel seventeen hundred feet long through limestone bedrock to bring fresh water from the Gihon Spring inside the city walls. Hezekiah also fortified the walls surrounding Jerusalem and erected a new wall, twenty-three feet wide, to bolster the city's vulnerable northern defenses. Remains of Hezekiah's wall indicate that it was built on remnants of houses originally established on the outskirts of the city (2 Chronicles 32:2–5, 30; 2 Kings 20:20; Isaiah 22:11). These efforts certainly involved massive cooperation and effort by the city's inhabitants. At this time Jerusalem's population had swollen to some twenty thousand by an influx of refugees coming from the northern kingdom in the wake of the Assyrian invasion.

During the fourteenth year of Hezekiah's reign, the Assyrian king Sennacherib sent his armies to attack city after city in Judah, aiming to subdue the belligerent people of Hezekiah. According to Sennacherib's own records, the Assyrians captured forty-six walled cities of Judah at this time. With Jerusalem being the sole important city in the entire region that remained outside of Assyrian control, Hezekiah seems to have panicked and paid the Assyrians a huge tribute of gold and silver, taken from the temple, in an attempt to save the city and its people from destruction

Photo by Ruth Ann Hubbard

Hezekiah's Tunnel.

or deportation. But Sennacherib wanted more. He sent representatives to Judah to demand that the people surrender their loyalty to Hezekiah and his God and to submit to the Assyrian king (2 Kings 18:13–37; 2 Chronicles 32:1–19). In Huldah's day, the enemy was also a foreign power (Babylon) and the Israelites made it worse by trusting in foreign gods. Hezekiah, Huldah, and Josiah, however, found victory from the same ever-powerful Source.

Hezekiah's greatest contribution during this Assyrian threat

Hezekiah ordered that a wall be built to protect the vulnerable northern side of Jerusalem against Assyrian invasion. Remains of the wall are still visible in Jerusalem today. The Mishneh, where Huldah resided, is believed to have been bordered by this broad wall.

was rekindling reliance on prophets and appreciation for them. When the Assyrians taunted the people of Judah that their God could no more protect them from the king of Assyria than the pagan gods had protected those who had already fallen to the great empire, Hezekiah sought guidance from the prophet Isaiah (2 Kings 18:29–36; 19:5–6). Three generations later, Josiah turned to the prophetess Huldah for counsel.

Relaying God's words, "Be not afraid," Isaiah promised Hezekiah that the Lord would defend Jerusalem so that the Assyrians would not even be able to enter the city. When Sennacherib's massive army approached the walls of Jerusalem, "the angel of the Lord went out, and smote in the camp of the Assyrians an hundred fourscore and five thousand: and when they arose early in the morning, behold, they were all dead corpses" (2 Kings 19:35). Because of a miraculous show of Jehovah's power, the Assyrians failed to invade Jerusalem.

Isaiah further prophesied to Hezekiah that a remnant of Judah would not be destroyed but instead would flourish (2 Kings 19:30–31; Isaiah 37:31–32) although the greater part of Jerusalem's inhabitants and wealth would be carried away into Babylon, until "nothing shall be left" (2 Kings 20:14; Isaiah 39:6). Unfortunately, subsequent kings of Judah quickly forgot Isaiah's prophecy of warning.

THE REIGN OF MANASSEH (687–642 B.C.)

Although ten of the fifty-five years that Manasseh ruled Judah were as co-regent with his ailing father, he rejected his father's policies and reverted to pagan practices and homage to Assyrian power as his grandfather Ahaz had done. Co-regent at age twelve and sole monarch at age twenty-two, Manasseh would have had remarkable opportunities to be tutored by Hezekiah and influenced by the prophets, but instead he rejected them. Ruling Judah longer than any other monarch of the southern kingdom, Manasseh's loyal embrace of foreign gods, human sacrifice, and worship of the sun, moon, and stars quickly reversed all of Hezekiah's reforms and set Judah on a swift decline to destruction as Isaiah had prophesied. Disdainful of the prophets, he established a statue of the Canaanite fertility goddess Asherah in Solomon's temple and rebuilt the altars and high places for the worship of Ba'al (2 Kings 21:1–16; 2 Chronicles 33:1–17; Jeremiah 15:4). According to legend, Manasseh killed Isaiah the prophet (Ginzberg, *Legends,* 4:279). The clear distinctions of the gospel as preached and practiced during Hezekiah's reign were soon obscured in the immorality, pride, and gluttony associated with worshipping man-made gods and goddesses.

THE REIGN OF AMON (642–640 B.C.)

In what appears to have been a seamless transition, twenty-two-year-old Amon inherited the kingdom and continued his father's wicked policies and practices by sacrificing to his pagan gods (2 Kings 21:19–22; 2 Chronicles 33:21–23). Amon had served only two years when he was assassinated by his servants, who were in turn executed by the people of the land. The aristocrats and wealthy landowners were not those who now gave direction to the kingdom; rather, the common people chose Josiah, the eight-year-old son of Amon, to be their king, thus preserving the Davidic royal line and their potential to influence the boy monarch to reverence God in the face of a wicked royal precedent.

THE REIGN OF JOSIAH (640–609 B.C.)

The identity and actions of those who advised the young king and directed the nation's policies during Josiah's early years are not given. Likely, regents who came from the assembly of common people that selected Josiah as the new monarch temporarily governed and prepared the boy king for leadership. Josiah's early faith in Israel's God strongly indicates that these regents feared God and were observant of His commands.

According to the Chronicler, during the eighth year of his reign, sixteen-year-old Josiah began a quest to know God (2 Chronicles 34:3). The circumstances that led to this development are not mentioned. The people of the land, having suffered spiritually and financially under the rule of Josiah's father and grand-father, may have taught him to cherish a power greater than monarchy.

Another possibility is that the words of prophets in the area may have penetrated the palace. Zephaniah was one such prophet who ministered to the people of Judah early in Josiah's reign (Zephaniah 1:1). In warnings against the lingering influence of Manasseh's idolatry, Zephaniah rebuked those who simultaneously worshipped Abraham's God and their neighbors' false gods (Zephaniah 1:5, 12). Giving Josiah's people motivation to change, Zephaniah warned, "Before the fierce anger of the Lord come upon you, . . . seek ye the Lord, . . . seek righteousness, seek meekness: it may be ye shall be hid in the day of the Lord's anger" (Zephaniah 2:2–3). We might wonder whether Zephaniah's witness and warning instilled in Josiah humility before God and sufficient faith to heed the testimony of a prophetess some ten years later.

TIME LINE

722 B.C.	Northern kingdom (ten tribes) scattered by Assyrians
715–687 B.C.	Reign of Hezekiah, king of Judah
	Isaiah's ministry in Jerusalem
	Micah's ministry in the south
701 B.C.	Jerusalem is miraculously protected from the Assyrians
687–642 B.C.	Reign of Manasseh, king of Judah
642–640 B.C.	Reign of Amon, king of Judah
640 B.C.	Beginning of the reign of Josiah (8), king of Judah
	Zephaniah's ministry
632 B.C.	King Josiah (16) is converted
628 B.C.	King Josiah (20) begins cultic reforms
627 B.C.	Jeremiah begins his ministry
626 B.C.	Assyria is invaded and loses its hold on the Near East
623 B.C.	Repairs made on Solomon's temple
	The Scroll of the Covenant is discovered
	Huldah is consulted
	Josiah (26) leads his people to covenant with God
	The Passover is celebrated with people from all the tribes of Israel
612 B.C.	Nineveh falls to the Babylonians
609 B.C.	Josiah (39) is killed by Pharaoh Necho
605 B.C.	Babylonia takes control of Judah
600 B.C.	Lehi and Sariah leave Jerusalem
586 B.C.	Babylonia destroys Jerusalem and the temple

JOSIAH'S REFORMS AND GEOGRAPHICAL EXPANSION (628 B.C.)

Four years after his conversion to God, twenty-year-old King Josiah began his religious reformation. He eventually purged Judah of perverse religious practices and representations of Ba'alim (a collective term for false gods). Josiah destroyed all the high places and groves where Ba'al and his consort, the fertility goddess Asherah, were ritualistically petitioned and honored. He scattered the dust and fragments of broken images on idolaters' graves, bringing the fragments of idols into contact with the dead and thus rendering the idols unclean and repulsive. Similarly, he had the bones of dead false priests burned on pagan altars, thereby rendering the altars unacceptable for sacrifice to any god (2 Chronicles 34:4–5).

Josiah soon blotted out all the false priests, temple prostitutes, worship of the stars and the moon, and the practice of passing children through fire in reverence to the god Molech, practices which had been reintroduced by Manasseh. In place of this worship of false gods, Josiah reinstated and strengthened authorized men to be priests and Levites, thereby legitimizing their priesthood power (2 Kings 23:4–20). Exceeding even the reforms of Hezekiah, Josiah stretched his influence and political power through much of the former northern kingdom, indicating hopes of reuniting all the tribes of Israel.

A year after Josiah began his reforms, "in the thirteenth year of [Josiah's] reign," Jeremiah began his prophetic mission in Anathoth, a village about three miles northeast of Jerusalem (Jeremiah 1:1–2). Giving evidence that not all of Josiah's people rejoiced and embraced his religious reforms, Jeremiah chastised Israelites in the north for backsliding in their repentance and Judah in the south with even greater condemnation for being treacherous and feigning loyalty to the Lord (Jeremiah 3:6–11).

Coinciding with Josiah's ambitious reforms was Assyria's decline in power and presence. Likely spread too thin over their extensive empire, Assyrian armies gave little response to invasions from both the west and the east in 626 B.C. Plundering, seminomadic peoples from Armenia in the west stormed through Syria and the former northern kingdom about the same time that Babylonia in the east overthrew the Assyrian overlords. This combination of threats to Assyria's already crumbling hold on the ancient Near East created a power vacuum around Josiah's kingdom that freed Judah from paying tribute. The result was a final

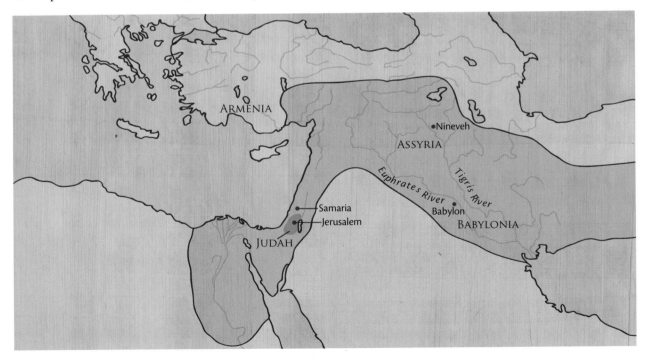

Assyrian Empire.

OVERSEERS OF THE TEMPLE REPAIRS

Hilkiah, the high priest. His grandson, as high priest, was killed by the Babylonians when they invaded Jerusalem (2 Kings 25:18–21).

Shaphan, the royal scribe, the ancient equivalent of the U.S. Secretary of State. The scribe's duties likely included domestic and foreign correspondence, sitting in council with the king, and accurately recording national decisions and policies.

Maaseiah, the mayor of Jerusalem. (2 Chronicles 34:8)

Joah, the son of the city recorder. (2 Chronicles 34:8)

Jahath and Obadiah, leaders of the Levite workmen. These men were priesthood officials who directed and paid the construction workers, all of whom would have been descendants of Levi. (2 Chronicles 34:12)

period of autonomy from foreign control for the kingdom of Judah and an unhampered opportunity for Josiah to return the nation's faith to Jehovah.

REPAIRING SOLOMON'S TEMPLE (623 B.C.)

Inspired by prophets, disgusted by Manasseh's decadence, and freed by Assyria's distraction and decline, Josiah continued reforms that would unify his people with God and restore the kingdom to the greatness it had enjoyed under King David. At age twenty-six, Josiah set out to repair and restore Solomon's temple to its former purity and holiness. Circumstances devolving from this temple reconstruction invited Huldah the prophetess into the story.

Many who assisted in repairing the temple are named in the biblical record, including city and priesthood leaders (2 Chronicles 34:8–9, 12). Suggesting that the reconstruction was planned and budgeted, sufficient funds had already been collected from the people. According to the Chronicler, Levites canvassed the kingdom amassing free-will donations for the temple project (2 Chronicles 34:9). The earlier account of 2 Kings reports that the people brought their contributions to officiating priests, who stood as "keepers of the door" at the temple gates in Jerusalem (2 Kings 22:4; see also 25:18). Josiah assigned three royal officials to supervise the transfer of these donations to the high priest. Priesthood authorities, in turn, drew from the funds to compensate the Levite carpenters, masons, and others who were the "doers of the work" (2 Kings 22:5).

THE SCROLL IS DISCOVERED

During the temple reconstruction, Hilkiah the high priest "found a book of the law of the Lord given by Moses" (2 Chronicles 34:14–15; see also 2 Kings 22:8). Discovered somewhere in Solomon's temple, the record had presumably been hidden in one of the storage areas that bordered the temple. Hilkiah quickly passed it on to the king's scribe, Shaphan.

The Hebrew term translated as "book" in this reference is better understood as a lengthy scroll. For both the Chronicler and the author of 2 Kings, the content and validity of the discovered document epitomize all that King Josiah accomplished in his reforms. His understanding of the scroll's contents would soon lead him to realize that the Lord required deeper and more extensive conversion to become His covenant people than what he had already accomplished in purging evil.

Several clues indicate that the scroll contained the entire book of Deuteronomy, or at least a significant portion of the book. The document's specific commands, the style in which it was written, and a reference to curses most closely reflect that book of scripture. Reactions from Josiah and his people when the scroll was read further indicate the dire circumstances pronounced on the disobedient that are recorded in the final book of Moses. Several chapters in Deuteronomy are especially poignant in this regard, namely Deuteronomy 12–13, 17, and 27–29. A rabbinic tradition claims that the scroll fell open to a specific verse when Shaphan reported the discovery to Josiah. According to the tradition, the first verse that Josiah heard as the scroll was read was Deuteronomy 28:36: "The Lord shall bring thee, and thy king which thou shalt set over thee, unto a nation which neither thou nor thy fathers have known; and there shalt thou serve other gods, wood and stone." Whichever passages were read, the message of the scroll did not bode well for Judah.

In response to hearing the scroll's contents, Josiah "rent his clothes," a cultural expression that reflects deep sorrow and concern (2 Chronicles 34:19; 2 Kings 22:11). He feared that all he had accomplished thus far in reform, repentance, and restoration were not extensive enough to avert the calamities prophesied in the document. In contrast to his father's sincere heart, Josiah's son, the future King Jehoiakim, later showed no fear or other sign of emotion when the dire warnings of the prophet Jeremiah were read to him (Jeremiah 36:24).

Without knowing the true significance and authority of the document found in the

Artwork by Michael Lyon

King Josiah's campaign of reparation and purification from practices of idolatrous worship in Judah included the reconstruction of Solomon's temple.

temple, Josiah called his top officials to "go, inquire of the Lord for me" to learn His counsel concerning the scroll and what they might do to turn away His wrath (2 Chronicles 34:20–21).

HULDAH THE PROPHETESS

For Hilkiah, Shaphan, and their colleagues, "Go, inquire of the Lord" meant to ask one who had the gift of prophecy to discern the Lord's will for Josiah and the kingdom of Judah. Whether the prophet was a man or a woman seemed irrelevant to them. Neither account of the story indicates surprise that men in official leadership positions conferred with a woman over the divine authority and application of the discovered book of the law. We simply read that they went to Huldah the prophetess (2 Chronicles 34:22; 2 Kings 22:14). Josephus indicates that Josiah himself identified Huldah as the one to consult (Josephus, *Antiquities,* 10.4.2).

Because Huldah was selected to authenticate the scroll, we assume that she could read and was therefore capable of studying the document. Hints from surviving samples of writing on stone, precious metals, and various forms of clay suggest that many Israelites, in addition to the scribes, could write. These sources, however, do not indicate the prevalence of literate women in the population, which makes it difficult to hypothesize about whether Huldah was unique in this regard.

Of added interest, the officials did not summon Huldah to come to them; they proceeded to her home

HULDAH'S MESSAGE TO THE KING

So Hilkiah the priest, and Ahikam, and Achbor, and Shaphan, and Asahiah, went unto Huldah the prophetess, the wife of Shallum the son of Tikvah, the son of Harhas, keeper of the wardrobe; (now she dwelt in Jerusalem in the college;) and they communed with her.

And she said unto them, Thus saith the Lord God of Israel, Tell the man that sent you to me, Thus saith the Lord, Behold, I will bring evil upon this place, and upon the inhabitants thereof, even all the words of the book which the king of Judah hath read: Because they have forsaken me, and have burned incense unto other gods, that they might provoke me to anger with all the works of their hands; therefore my wrath shall be kindled against this place, and shall not be quenched.

But to the king of Judah which sent you to enquire of the Lord, thus shall ye say to him, Thus saith the Lord God of Israel, As touching the words which thou hast heard; Because thine heart was tender, and thou hast humbled thyself before the Lord, when thou heardest what I spake against this place, and against the inhabitants thereof, that they should become a desolation and a curse, and hast rent thy clothes, and wept before me; I also have heard thee, saith the Lord. Behold therefore, I will gather thee unto thy fathers, and thou shalt be gathered into thy grave in peace; and thine eyes shall not see all the evil which I will bring upon this place. (2 Kings 22:14–20) to consult her. Furthermore, the king's officials did not question Huldah's response or look to another source for a second opinion. They conveyed her word immediately to the king.

Had it been unorthodox at the time to seek the advice of a prophetess while prophets were also in the land, we might expect a longer description of Huldah. As it stands, we receive one sentence of introduction: "Huldah the prophetess, the wife of Shallum the son of Tikvath, the son of Hasrah, keeper of the wardrobe; (now she dwelt in Jerusalem in the college:)" (2 Chronicles 34:22; see also 2 Kings 22:14). Following this introduction are six verses of scripture that cite Huldah's message to Josiah and the Israelites. Clearly, the focus of the story is not on her appearance, age, or lineage; the focus is on Huldah's words.

Mention of the ancestry of her husband, Shallum, indicates that his was an honorable lineage. Because Jeremiah had an uncle named Shallum, some scholars have posited that Jeremiah was the nephew of Huldah's husband (Jeremiah 32:7). No other scriptural clues either substantiate or negate this theory. Huldah's husband was also called the "keeper of the wardrobe," probably meaning that he was the servant responsible for either the king's royal clothing at the palace or the priests' vestments at the temple.

From this brief introduction, we learn that Huldah lived in "the college," or "Mishneh," in Jerusalem. Believed to be the newly developed area in the western quarter of the city bordered by Hezekiah's twenty-three-foot wall, the Mishneh became home to the city's more recent inhabitants. Refugees who fled the northern kingdom with the Assyrian invasion made up some of the original occupants of the Mishneh. Because Lehi and Sariah were descendants of the tribe of Manasseh, which was assigned land in the territories of what became the northern kingdom, they may have lived in this quarter along with other descendants of Israelite refugees—and, in 622 B.C., at the same time as Huldah.

Whereas the two biblical accounts (that is, the books of Chronicles and Kings) differ in chronology and many details when

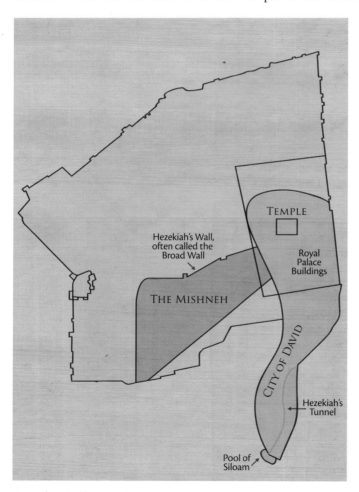

Jerusalem in the seventh century B.C.

WHY NOT JEREMIAH?

Many have wondered why Josiah consulted Huldah rather than Jeremiah or one of the other prophets. The following are some possible explanations.

According to rabbinic tradition, Josiah addressed Huldah rather than Jeremiah because he believed that "women are more easily moved to compassion" and would show greater mercy in her counsel (Ginzberg, *Legends*, 4:282).

Rather than conferring with anyone else for an interpretation, Josiah, the priest, and scribes did not pray directly to God or go to the temple themselves to commune with Him (Rasmussen, *Commentary*, 322).

Josiah may not have liked Jeremiah because he often spoke disparagingly about the government. Furthermore, Jeremiah's consistent message over the years would have made his response to Josiah in this case easy to guess. Another voice might have seemed to offer something more positive (Frymer-Kensky, *Reading*, 325).

Jeremiah's prophetic assignment was among the people outside Jerusalem, whereas Huldah may have been the court prophet consulted on matters pertaining to Josiah's reforms, as directed in the law (Deuteronomy 18:1–8) (Frymer-Kensky, *Reading*, 325).

Huldah was literate, whereas Jeremiah needed a scribe to record his messages (Phipps, "Woman," 15).

speaking of Josiah, his reforms, and even the finding of the scroll, the two narratives are nearly identical in their introduction to Huldah and her prophetic message.

The power of her words and confidence in her message indicate that Huldah was neither surprised nor uncomfortable with the royal request. With the witness of the Spirit that attends the communication of prophets and prophetesses, Huldah bore fervent testimony of the Lord's will (2 Chronicles 34:23–28; 2 Kings 22:15–20). Four times in her six-verse response to the scroll, Huldah boldly declared, "Thus saith the Lord" (2 Chronicles 34:23–24, 26–27).

Validating the authenticity of the document, Huldah applied the specific judgments in the scroll to the Judah of her day. The kingdom would not escape ruin, as it had escaped under King Hezekiah. Huldah's witness underscored the seriousness of Judah's predicament and drew attention to God's warnings to Moses (Deuteronomy 28:15–68) rather than to hopeful interpretations of the Davidic covenant (2 Samuel 7:18–29). For many people in Judah after their miraculous deliverance from the Assyrians, God's promise that David's throne would endure forever had come to be interpreted that God would never allow Jerusalem to be destroyed or its inhabitants taken.

Although God's patience and longsuffering are evident to all who desire to find Him, His warnings about the consequences are clear concerning those who persistently mock His standards and ignore His proffered mercy. Remarkable reigns and reforms carried out by two righteous kings could not undo the evils of wicked kings or prevent the dire consequences that God had prophesied (2 Chronicles 34:24–25). The time for present conditions had ended. Consequences would follow.

A similar situation occurred in Book of Mormon times. The prophet Abinadi warned the wicked people under King Noah that unless they repented, they would be brought into bondage (Mosiah 11:20–25). Two years later, he returned to find that the people showed no sign of changing. Although he preached repentance to them again, this time Abinadi gave the people no avenues for avoiding oppression. If the people did not repent after his second warning, they would be destroyed (Mosiah 12:1–8). Just as Abinadi prophesied, all the people were brought into bondage, but only those who persisted in their rebellion against God were eventually destroyed.

Huldah clearly communicated that Judah's destruction was now unconditional. Repentance would yet offer eternal blessings for Josiah and his believing people, but it would not reverse the imminent consequences for Jerusalem. The unparalleled gift of repentance removes the stain of sin and mistakes, but it does not necessarily erase the mortal repercussions of others' disobedient choices. The Lord in His mercy promises to heal broken hearts, not prevent them (Luke 4:18).

Huldah's prophetic message, however, contained a second part. Because the Lord recognized Josiah's sincere efforts to bring a humble people to Him, He would protect Josiah from witnessing the horrors

THE HULDAH GATES OF HEROD'S TEMPLE

Centuries after Huldah's proclamation to King Josiah, Herod the Great financed the expansion and beautifying of the Second Temple. On the southern side, accessed by stone steps that ran the length of the retaining wall, were sets of gates that led worshippers to enclosed stairways to the Temple Mount. The Mishnah refers to these gates collectively as the Huldah Gates. Although opinions vary as to why they were so named, one strong suggestion remains that the gates memorialized the great prophetess. Part of one of the original gates is still visible today, although the stairway opening was filled in by the Crusaders.

of Judah's fall. Huldah sent the message to Josiah that he would die, "gathered to [his] grave in peace," before Judah's devastating demise (2 Chronicles 34:28).

Huldah's courage and confidence in the Lord's word are striking in this context. She knew that kings had full power to command the death or banishment of any subject who displeased them, which would have given her good reason to fear. Certainly Josiah had been a wonderful king—the best Judah had ever known, according to one account (2 Kings 23:25)—but too many kings in Israel started out righteous and became incredibly wicked by the end of their reigns. Josiah's father was despicable, and his grandfather even worse. Still young at age twenty-six, Josiah could have reverted to his father's and grandfather's evil ways in reaction to the news Huldah relayed to him. Yet in the face of potential punishment for offending the monarch, Huldah was unflinching in her bold pronouncement of God's truth.

As difficult as it is for prophets or wise teachers and parents to deliver bad news—reminders of God's

King Josiah stood before the pillar of Solomon's temple to teach his people how to make a covenant with God.

displeasure, of broken dreams, or of other negative consequences that will surely come to their charges—failure to do so brings "the sins of the people upon our own heads if we [do] not teach them the word of God with all diligence" (Jacob 1:19). Similar in faith and courage to other prophets, Huldah did not shy away from her duty. Neither did God leave her to face her mission alone. As a prophetess, Huldah would have been bolstered by God's presence and confirming witness. Accompanied by the Spirit and the assurance of God's continued love, her words had the power to communicate hope and the will to persist in righteous efforts. As King Josiah found hope in Huldah's Spirit-filled message, so can we discover greater faith in Christ's atonement in times of chastisement. Repentance is an encouraging and hopeful doctrine. No matter how far we have strayed, His arm is stretched out still, providing us the way back.

THE RESULTS OF HULDAH'S TESTIMONY

Huldah's message, though stern and uncompromising, strengthened Josiah in his efforts toward greater reform. He now referred to the discovered scroll as "the book of the covenant," as evidence of his reverence for the law (2 Kings 23:2; 2 Chronicles 34:30). Encouraged by the knowledge that the Lord was

A model of the temple at the time of Christ clearly shows the Huldah Gates on the southern wall of the Temple Mount.

aware of him and his people and concerned with their lives, Josiah set out to involve all the people of his kingdom in his renewed commitment.

Much like King Benjamin in the Book of Mormon, who gathered his people to give them his stewardship report and lead them to make a collective covenant with God, Josiah called his people, "great and small," to Solomon's temple (2 Kings 23:2; 2 Chronicles 34:30). The "pillar" where he stood to address his people may have been one of the two pillars described during the temple's construction and named by Solomon. The first was named *Jachin,* meaning "He establishes"; the other was named *Boaz,* meaning "in him is strength" (1 Kings 7:15–22; LDS Bible Dictionary, 626).

At the temple, Josiah read "all the words of the book of the covenant" to his people. Then he invited them to join him in covenanting with God to keep His commandments with all their hearts and souls. According to the record, "all the people stood to the covenant" (2 Kings 23:3).

In this same year, Josiah commanded the people to hold the Passover, as required in the covenant document (Deuteronomy 16). The Chronicler praises Josiah's Passover celebration as the greatest one since the time of Samuel, at least in part because members of all the tribes of Israel were present (2 Chronicles 35:18–19). Echoing the new covenant they had just made with God, this Passover declared their independence from foreign power and their wholehearted and willing dependence on the Lord.

Even though Josiah knew that Jerusalem's destruction and his own death were imminent, he worked hard to strengthen his people. Bringing the entire community of Judah together in a covenant with God created a remarkable, although short-lived, taste of Zion.

THE DEATH OF JOSIAH (609 B.C.)

Josiah's tragic death in 609 B.C. at the hands of Pharaoh Necho leaves unanswered questions. Presumably, Pharaoh Necho of Egypt was leading his armies to assist the Assyrians against the increasingly powerful Babylonians. As the Egyptians traveled through Megiddo on their way to Carchemish, Josiah went out to challenge them, even though Pharaoh Necho had assured him that Josiah's kingdom was not in danger from them (2 Chronicles 35:20–24). Why did Josiah persist in his journey?

Three explanations have been offered. First, perhaps Josiah attempted to stop the Egyptians from assisting the struggling Assyrians against the Babylonians. Josiah may have feared reprisals from the Assyrians should they, as Israel's long-time nemesis, regain power. Second, in his continued hopes for territorial expansion, Josiah may have tried to forestall potential intrusion and occupation by the Egyptians. Third, the Chronicler, writing some two hundred years after Josiah's death, attributes the tragedy to Josiah's failure to heed God's words through Pharaoh Necho when he assured Judah of his nonhostility (2 Chronicles 35:21–22). The Chronicler implies that Josiah grew proud in the promises God had given him, leading him to think he was invincible. Jewish legend puts the blame on the people of Judah, who only feigned repentance and reverence for the covenant (Ginzberg, *Legends,* 4:282–83). Whatever the case, it is important to remember that many of God's promises are conditional: We can fall from His grace and lose opportunities that would have led us to unique blessings had we continued faithful to Him.

The manner in which Josiah died has also been a cause for speculation, because Huldah prophesied that he would die in peace. Being fatally shot by the pharaoh's archers does not sound like a peaceful way to die (2 Kings 23:29–30; 2 Chronicles 35:22–24). One explanation is that Huldah's prophecy was not about the manner of his death but about the peaceful conditions Judah enjoyed throughout Josiah's mortal life. Similarly, in our limited perspective, we often see the Lord's promises for our personal lives so narrowly that we fail to recognize a far greater blessing that He has in store for us. Fulfillment of God's

HULDAH'S INFLUENCE ON NINETEENTH-CENTURY WOMEN'S RIGHTS

In 1848, Lucretia Mott, a Quaker minister, and Elizabeth Cady Stanton, a devout Presbyterian, organized a women's rights convention in Seneca Falls, New York. Justifying their conference as an affirmation of the truer meaning of the Declaration of Independence: "We hold these truths to be self-evident: that all men *and women* are created equal," Elizabeth Stanton prepared a Declaration of Principles. In response to criticisms that she and other women defied the Bible's teachings that men are the only ones whom God commissions to lead in public, she wrote:

"The greatest character among the women thus far mentioned [in the Old Testament] is Huldah the prophetess, residing in the college in Jerusalem. . . . [She was] able not only to advise the common people of their duties to Jehovah and their country, but to teach kings the sound basis for a kingdom. Her wisdom and insight were well known to Josiah the king; and when the wise men came to him with the 'Book of the Law,' to learn what was written therein, Josiah ordered them to take it to Huldah, as neither the wise men nor Josiah himself could interpret its contents. . . . People who talk the most of what the Bible teaches often know the least about its contents" (Stanton, *Women's Bible,* 81–82; paragraphing altered; see also Phipps, "Woman," 15).

promises of health, success, and opportunity may not be immediately recognizable or obvious, but we will always have these miraculous blessings if we are willing to confess His merciful hand in our success.

Whatever the explanation for the king's tragic death, the prophet Jeremiah praised the works of Josiah by telling the people: "Weep ye not for the dead, neither bemoan him. . . . He judged the cause of the poor and needy; then it was well with him" (Jeremiah 22:10, 16).

There is no way to see peace, however, in events that soon befell Jerusalem. What became of the first part of Huldah's prophetic message? As Josiah's sons ruled struggling Judah, one by one, none showed any regard for the covenant, for their father's reforms, or for the words of the prophets. When the Babylonians swept through Judah in 605 B.C., the kingdom of Judah was forced to pay tribute to their new conquerors. In 601 B.C., King Jehoiakim, who was Josiah's son, ceased paying the tribute, gambling that the Egyptians would reassert themselves against Babylon and become Judah's protector. Instead, Babylon became stronger and answered Judah by besieging Jerusalem and deporting more of its inhabitants to Babylon in 597 B.C. By 586 B.C., Jerusalem had fallen, Solomon's magnificent temple had been destroyed, and huge numbers of Judah's people had been taken hostage to Babylon. The Babylonian captivity had begun.

But what of a golden era, initiated by the voice of the common people, carried by the conversion of a young king, and fueled by the unwavering witness of a prophetess? And what added reverence to all words of scripture did Huldah's testimony invite, she being "the first to declare scripture holy"? (Phipps, "Woman," 14). Huldah came on stage for one brief moment and left a lasting witness that continues to summon each of us to greater devotion to God.

POINTS TO PONDER: APPLICATIONS FOR OUR LIVES

1. How does Huldah's example inspire us to succeed in nontraditional roles? How does she remind us that being in tune with the Spirit and courageously bearing witness of God's word is not a gender role but a disciple's role?

2. What do you think gave such confidence to Huldah when the king's representatives consulted her? Why do we at times lack that confidence when faced with opportunities to bear witness?

3. Recognizing the importance that she placed on believing what God has given us in scripture, how does Huldah's story influence your own scripture study?

4. What added insights into the doctrine of repentance and consequences for our choices does Huldah's inspired message provide for you?

5. What additional gospel principles do you see illustrated in this story?

6. How does Huldah's experience enlarge or strengthen your testimony of Jesus Christ?

WOMEN WHO INFLUENCED LAW

*M*en wielded the power in the ancient Near East, and women exerted influence. Many women in the Old Testament approached problems from different angles than did men and opened a way for amicable solutions. More specifically, they inspired changes in the law of Moses, in laws of foreign occupiers of Israelite lands, and in the cultural laws of the larger society. Furthermore, these women did not wait for praise or recognition before speaking up or reaching out to make a difference.

Queens and the wives of other political authorities are easily recognized among those who influence law. Whether for good or evil, royal women in the Bible significantly changed the course of events that affected opportunities for future generations. They either preserved lives or immersed generations in apostasy, either secured greater rights for other women or hurled them deeper into oblivion and hardship. Examples include Potiphar's wife, the queen of Sheba, Solomon's foreign wives, Queen Jezebel of Israel and her daughter Queen Athaliah of Judah, and Esther and her predecessor, Vashti, in Persia.

Royal women who used their influence to destroy faith and freedom arguably surpassed their male counterparts in evil. During the ninth century before Christ, for example, Jezebel and Athaliah wreaked havoc among both Israelite kingdoms with their evil designs and idolatrous hearts. Jezebel, daughter of a Phoenician king, married Ahab, heir to the throne of the northern kingdom of Israel. Because of her wicked influence, Ahab did more to provoke God's anger than all of Israel's evil kings before him (1 Kings 16:31–33; 21:25). An ardent disciple of the Phoenician god Ba'al, Jezebel introduced and spread her idolatrous religion throughout the entire nation, curtailed the worship of the God of Israel, and hunted down and killed scores of "prophets of the Lord" (1 Kings 18:4, 13). Elijah the prophet feared Jezebel more than any other threat to truth and decency but was commanded by God to confront her and prophesy against her (1 Kings 19:1–3; 21:23).

Not satisfied with polluting the northern kingdom, Jezebel and Ahab arranged the marriage of their daughter Athaliah to Jehoram, son of King Jehoshaphat of the southern kingdom of Judah (2 Kings 8:18, 26;

For Such a Time As This (Esther)

2 Chronicles 21:6). When Jehoshaphat died and her husband became king, Athaliah began to exert her influence throughout Judah by promoting the cult of Ba'al.

Athaliah's greatest opportunity for influence, however, occurred after her husband's eight-year rule and the death of her royal son one year later. Before another male descendant could be named as king, Athaliah ruthlessly ordered the death of all the remaining royal offspring in order to seize the Davidic throne for herself (2 Kings 11; 2 Chronicles 22–23). She is noteworthy in the Bible for being the only woman to rule as monarch in either kingdom of Israel. In attaining such notoriety, however, Athaliah made no points for women in power. Her rule was cut short when one of her grandsons miraculously survived and assumed the throne at her execution.

Juxtaposed against these wicked women were the praiseworthy Vashti and Esther, who lived in Susa, the capital of Persia, during the fifth century before Christ. A bold and forthright queen of Persia, Vashti rebelled against her husband when his commands conflicted with her sense of propriety. Esther, who became queen after Vashti was removed, was a Jewess who saved her people from genocide through her royal position of influence.

The canonicity and historicity of the account of Esther are often challenged, both for what the story lacks and for what it contains. Because religious elements are absent, the account appears to emphasize the importance of Jewish nationalism rather than the faith and covenant practices of God's people. An aura of revenge, vindication, and persecution surrounds the story. Shifting values appear to justify revenge against anti-Semites in order to secure a position of influence (Esther 6:7; 8:11; 9:5, 13–14). Furthermore, the story contains passages that seem to indicate that adherence to God's laws is secondary to promoting a people's supremacy. For example, to be inducted into the king's harem, Esther hid her religious identity, submitted to a year-long beauty treatment, and spent a night in the king's bedchamber before being chosen as his favorite (Esther 2:8–17). Marriage outside the covenant seems to be excusable when it affords a position of power.

Aside from concerns about the authenticity of the book of Esther, Vashti and Esther present two likeable but very different women. Queen Vashti was not merely a trophy wife; she showed moxie. When the king summoned her to parade her beauty in front of his inebriated guests, she flatly refused. Fearing Vashti's influence would spread to their wives and all the other women in the court, the king's princely advisers counseled the king to regard her disobedience as a personal affront and to depose her (Esther 1:10–22).

Easily celebrated as a "woman's woman," Vashti defiantly stood up for her rights—but at what cost? She was stripped of her royal rank for her haughty example, deposed as queen, and possibly even executed for her bold refusal to obey the king's command. Could Vashti have found a better way to avoid compliance with her husband's inappropriate demands and at the same time retain her position of rectitude and royalty? Was Vashti's approach the best choice to preserve her principles, or was she too rash?

In contrast, Esther was coy, easily entreated, and quick to accommodate. Where Vashti was assertive and confrontational, Esther was passive and malleable. Vashti was defiantly unbending to demands that violated her sense of right and wrong. Esther was submissive to the king and presented the image of the ideal woman in the eyes of many men. As Mordecai's beautiful puppet, Esther appeared quite mild until she accepted her own power to act.

Learning of Haman's edict against all the Jews in Persia, Mordecai challenged Esther to forget about herself and do something to stop the destruction, reminding her, "Who knoweth whether thou art come to the kingdom for such a time as this?" (Esther 4:14).

Knowing that she risked losing her royal position and possibly even her life by approaching the king without being summoned, Esther resolutely accepted her mission, saying, "If I perish, I perish" (Esther 4:16).

Esther offered a feast to disarm and appease the king, creating an environment in which the king could feel he was making a moral decision. She patiently waited for the right moment to make her request. Because of her courageous and wise approach, the Jewish people were not hunted but instead were feared as the hunters. Elements in Esther's technique could likely be applied today to resolve conflict and promote peaceful relations in families and communities.

Every person in the story of Esther exhibits serious character flaws, but the account illustrates that God works through imperfect people to bring about His purposes. Furthermore, the story shows how God intervened through the subtle designs of a woman to protect His people. The story also gives a woman credit for creating a legal document that received the king's full support and saved the Jews in Persia from extinction (Esther 8:8). Finally, the record of Esther inspired the Jewish festival of Purim, which perpetuates her influence.

Even if the book of Esther is a work of historical fiction as many claim, it underscores how Esther and her exiled people specifically, and anyone who feels marginalized or powerless in society generally, can significantly influence the world for good. Using one's talents, wisdom, and divine inspiration, any woman or man can bring change by enlightening those who hold power and have the authority to make better laws. Assuredly, many women used their intelligence and charm in such positive ways throughout biblical history, but the stories of only a very few are recorded in scripture. As is often the case, such women used influence in quiet and humble actions rather than in public pronouncements and speeches—and were too often quickly forgotten by those who benefited from their actions. Nonetheless, the clear concern of such women was to protect and improve lives rather than to receive national acclaim.

Royal women receive attention for influencing law, but many other women exerted their influence without a political position. Less overt and without a royal title, these women have arguably had a more long-lasting and weighty influence on people today than did their royal counterparts. Abigail skirted her foolish husband's control, temper, and commands to save his estate and many lives and protect God's anointed king. The midwives Shiphrah and Puah ignored Pharaoh's murderous edict and quietly went about doing right to save numerous innocent lives. In a largely unknown biblical story, the daughters of Zelophehad effected a change in the law of Moses that more closely reflected the Lord's equal regard for His sons and His daughters. Working through existing priesthood channels, they expanded the perspectives of lawmakers to become more sensitive to the rights of women and to justice for all.

The following chapters explore the lives and influence of Old Testament women who lived among the common people. Their stories provide remarkable inspiration by showing the positive influence that one individual can have to make the immediate community and even the world a better place. More important, these stories show the enabling power of God when we fear Him more than we fear the worldly influences around us.

The Protector (Shiphrah)

SHIPHRAH AND PUAH

שִׁפְרָה   פּוּעָה

"Beauty," "Splendid"   *"Brilliant," "Shining One"*

As Jacob and his clan of seventy people left Canaan for Egypt, God told them He would there make them a great nation and be with them in that foreign land (Genesis 46:2–4). In an earlier prophecy, however, God had warned Abraham that his descendants would be oppressed in "a land that is not theirs" and afflicted by the inhabitants for four hundred years (Genesis 15:13). Near the end of that time of oppression lived two women of great integrity and high moral commitment. The women were midwives, an occupation that invited them to regularly witness the miracle of life while remaining in awe of God's creative power. Faced with a heinous edict ordered by the highest governing power of the great Egyptian empire, the midwives Shiphrah and Puah unflinchingly heeded a higher law in response.

The history of Jacob's clan during those four hundred years is largely lost. After seeing Israel's twelve sons happily situated in Goshen, the Bible narrative leaves us with news of Joseph's death during a time when the Israelites were honored in Egypt and subsequently "multiplied, and waxed exceeding mighty" (Exodus 1:7). Without explanation of time or governmental shifts, the account transitions to the era of oppression introduced by a "new king over Egypt, which knew not Joseph" (Exodus 1:8).

According to most biblical scholars, Joseph and his brothers were in Egypt while an outside people, the Hyksos, ruled the nation after the fall of the Middle Kingdom. The New Kingdom of Egypt emerged with the demise of the Hyksos, and the Egyptians again controlled their nation. By that time the Great Pyramid of Cheops was nearly a thousand years old. Shiphrah and Puah lived sometime during the first three hundred years of the renowned New Kingdom, when all traces of Hyksos domination had been erased but their influence was not completely forgotten.

THE HYKSOS

The Hyksos were a Semitic people from the same ethno-linguistic stock as Abraham's descendants. Entering Egypt from the north, these shepherd kings probably originated in Canaan, Syria, and Transjordan (east of

EXODUS 1:15–21

167

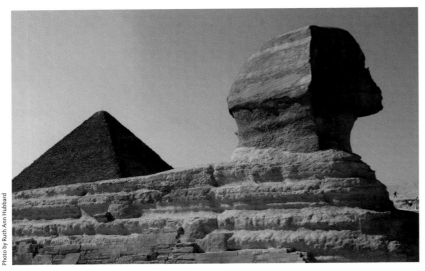

Photo by Ruth Ann Hubbard

The Great Pyramid of Cheops was a thousand years old and the Sphinx even older when Shiphrah and Puah lived in the Giza area of Egypt's delta. During the lifetime of these two midwives, Israelite slaves under harsh taskmasters were required to build treasure cities for Pharaoh.

the Jordan River) and settled mainly in Egypt's delta region. Although they were a minority in Egypt, their superior military equipment and organizational efficiency allowed them to rule Egypt for about 150 years, a time known as the second intermediate period (1720–1550 B.C.). The name "Hyksos" was probably assigned them by the Egyptians—it means "foreign rulers"—leaving us to wonder what they called themselves.

The Hyksos built their capital at Avaris in the eastern delta region. As evidence of their valuing literature and learning, the Hyksos copied and preserved many Egyptian texts, a contribution that has enlightened generations long after their expulsion.

When they allowed a measure of local autonomy in Upper Egypt, the Hyksos's hold over the country weakened. An Egyptian named Ahmes took advantage of his new freedom by leading a revolt against the Hyksos, commencing in Lower Egypt, eventually bringing down their capital in Avaris and forcing the foreign rulers out of the country.

Sometime during the Eighteenth Dynasty, the ruling Egyptians ceased to patronize foreigners in their land. They were particularly wary of outsiders in great numbers, fearing they might overpower their country as the Hyksos had done. Because the resurgent Egyptians lost or destroyed the history of the Hyksos and made no record that reflected any of their own losses or setbacks, no account remains

Photo by Ruth Susan Y. Porter

The Temple at Karnak was expanded during Egypt's Nineteenth Dynasty.

LATE BRONZE AGE (1550–1200 B.C.)

Egypt's Eighteenth Dynasty (1552–1306 B.C.)

Amosis (1552–1527 B.C.) drove out the Semitic Hyksos (ca. 1550) and opened the way for continued expansion in Asia.

Amenhotep I (1527–1507 B.C.)

Thutmosis I (1507–1494 B.C.) expanded the Egyptian empire north to the Euphrates River.

Thutmosis II (1494–1490 B.C.)

Thutmosis III (1490–1438 B.C.) came to power after Hatshepsut, his aunt and stepmother, who used the masculine title of pharaoh, ruled during the first eighteen years of his reign. Thutmosis III later brought Egypt to the zenith of its power by using slave labor in building projects and by extending Egyptian power from Nubia at the Fourth Cataract on the Nile River in the south to the Euphrates River in the north.

Amenhotep II (1440–1412 B.C.) undertook two military campaigns in Canaan to demonstrate his power.

Thutmosis IV (1412–1403 B.C.) made a treaty with the mighty Mitanni, or Hurrian, kingdom in northern Mesopotamia. The city of Haran in Padan-aram was part of the Mitanni kingdom.

Amenhotep III (1403–1364 B.C.) was ill during most of his reign.

Amenhotep IV, who renamed himself Akhen-aten (1364–1347 B.C.) changed the location of the capital from Thebes to Ahket-aten and changed the national religion to the worship of the sun or Aten, the Creator of all things. He was preoccupied with domestic affairs and was uninterested in foreign affairs. Tablets found at his capital, Ahket-aten (modern name Amarna), indicate great unrest in Canaan at the time.

Tutankhaten, who was later called Tutankh-amun (1347–1336 B.C.) was the son-in-law of Akhen-aten. He broke away from the worship of the sun and established his capital at Memphis.

Haremhab (1333–1306 B.C.) was the general who returned Egypt to stability and eradicated Akhen-aten's religious institutions.

Egypt's Nineteenth Dynasty (1306–1200 B.C.)

Sethos I (1305–1290) strengthened Egypt's unstable eastern empire. He rebuilt the Hyksos capital of Avaris as his capital and called it Rameses.

Rameses II (1290–1224) was a great warrior against the Hittites. His later reign saw peace and tremendous building. He invited Semitic influence and conscripted foreign slaves in building projects.

Merneptah (1224–1211) presided over a period of anarchy and weakness and the end of the Nineteenth Dynasty. The first mention of the nation of "Israel" in the Merneptah Stele during the fifth year of his reign (1220) shows that the people of Israel were inhabitants of the land of Canaan at the time.

TIME LINE

1750–1550 B.C.	Hyksos rule Egypt
	Death of Joseph

The Early Date Theory (see page 173)

1490–1438 B.C.	Thutmosis III
	Shiphrah and Puah save babies
	Moses is born
1440–1412 B.C.	Amenhotep II
1440 B.C.	The Exodus
1400–1350 B.C.	Israel's conquest of Canaan

The Late Date Theory (see page 174)

1317–1304 B.C.	Sethos I
	Shiphrah and Puah save babies
	Moses is born
1304–1237 B.C.	Rameses II
1280 B.C.	The Exodus
1237–1227 B.C.	Merneptah
1240–1200 B.C.	Israel's conquest of Canaan

Photo by Susan Y. Porter

The twin statues of Amenhotep III (1403–1364 B.C.) were carved out of stone quarried in Lower Egypt and transported to Upper Egypt. There they were erected in the vast temple complex at Karnak, which was expanded and beautified by the pharaohs of the Nineteenth Dynasty.

to validate either Joseph's existence and importance during the Hyksos reign or Moses' rise to greatness as a foreigner during the subsequent Egyptian domination.

EGYPT AFTER THE HYKSOS

The New Kingdom reached its height in 1469 B.C. under Thutmosis III, the greatest ruler during the Eighteenth Dynasty. As a result of his military campaigns, Egypt held all of Canaan from the Sinai peninsula to the Euphrates.

During the Nineteenth Dynasty, Rameses II reawakened Egypt's interest in the empire begun by Thutmosis III. His goal was to control the coastal highway west of Canaan. Known as the greatest builder in ancient Egypt, he established a series of forts in the Nile delta to secure Egypt's borders out of concern for a foreign invasion, evidence the Hyksos's influence was still felt. Archaeological clues link Rameses II to the ancient sites of Rameses and Pithom, storehouse cities where goods for trade and the military were stockpiled. His father, Sethos I, apparently built a summer palace at the Rameses site, and Rameses II greatly expanded it to become the empire's northern capital.

Merneptah, son and heir of Rameses II, is best known for commissioning the great Temple of Karnak and for historical clues inscribed on the Merneptah Stele, a stone slab that contains a commemorative message lauding Pharaoh Merneptah. More specifically, the stele claims Merneptah's victory over several nations, including "Israel" in the land of Canaan. A portion of the inscription reads: "Israel is laid waste, his seed is not." Although the precise period of Israel's exodus from Egypt and their conquest of Canaan is uncertain, the stele indicates that during Merneptah's reign, Israel was already a defined people facing challenges in Canaan that left them in a politically weakened state.

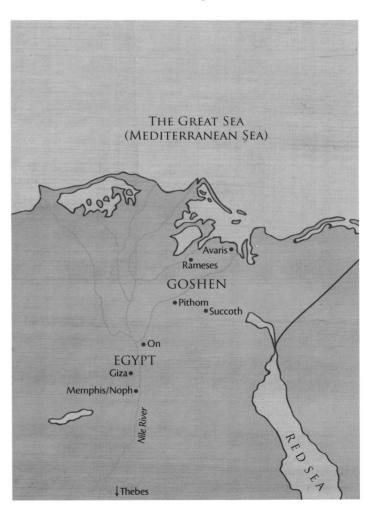

Map of Egypt during the Nineteenth Dynasty.

Choose You This Day (Puah)

WHO WAS THE PHARAOH OF THE OPPRESSION?

The Egyptian bondage, the Exodus, and the Israelites' first conquest of Canaan likely occurred during the Late Bronze Age (ca. 1550–1200 B.C.). Two schools of thought, each with compelling arguments, attempt to identify the pharaoh of the oppression and the pharaoh of the Exodus. One theory asserts that both pharaohs reigned during the Eighteenth Dynasty, the other that they ruled during the Nineteenth Dynasty. Because both theories have merit and invite serious consideration, each is briefly explained here.

2200	2100	2000	1900	1800	1700	1600	1500	1400	1300	1200	1100
Egyptian History											
		* Middle Kingdom (2040–1750)				* Hyksos Rule (1750–1550)		* New Kingdom (1550–1070)			
Early Date Theory											
	* Patriarchal period (2150–1870)				* Hebrews' Egyptian sojourn (1870 -1440)			* 40 years in wilderness (1440–1400)			
Late Date Theory											
		* Patriarchal period (1950–1710)			*Hebrews' Egyptian sojourn (1710–1280)					* 40 years in wilderness (1280–1240)	

THEORY 1: THE EARLY DATE THEORY

Placing the Exodus of Israel from Egypt at about 1430 B.C., the early date theory identifies Thutmosis III as the pharaoh of the oppression and his son Amenhotep II as the pharaoh of the Exodus. Queen Hatshepsut emerges as a plausible candidate for the daughter of Pharaoh who raised Moses as her own son.

This theory adequately corresponds with the chronology suggested in 1 Kings 6:1, which indicates that the Exodus occurred 480 years before the fourth year of King Solomon's reign over Israel. It also fits the biblical reference to Jephthah, one of Israel's judges, who lived 300 years after the children of Israel entered the promised land (Judges 11:26). A potential tie to the biblical account of Moses and the tenth plague is that a younger son of Amenhotep succeeded him on the throne because the eldest son had died very young.

This theory also explains the absence of interference from Egypt during Israel's conquest of Canaan. It identifies the pharaoh at the time as Amenhotep IV, the unusual leader who exclusively focused on religion at home while Canaan was in chaos. Expanding the time period between Moses and the Israelite monarchy by about 150 years, this theory also suggests that Joshua entered the promised land about 1390 B.C. and that the era of the judges extended from about 1370 to 1050 B.C.

THEORY 2: THE LATE DATE THEORY

According to the late date theory, the Exodus occurred about 1280 B.C., when Rameses II was pharaoh. His father, Sethos I, was therefore the pharaoh of the oppression, who ordered the death of all the male Hebrew babies. An alternative suggestion to this later date identifies Rameses II as the pharaoh of the oppression and Merneptah as the pharaoh of the Exodus, pushing back the date of the Exodus even later, to about 1195 B.C.

The strengths of this theory include archaeological evidence of a late-thirteenth-century destruction in numerous Canaanite cities that corresponds to stories of conquest in the book of Joshua, the biblical notation that the children of Israel built a treasure city named "Rameses" (Exodus 1:11), and 400 years between the time of the Hyksos rule and Moses (see Galatians 3:17).

Rameses II is known as the builder of the two biblical treasure cities, Pithom and Rameses (Exodus 1:11). He established the treasure city called Rameses in the northeast delta near the former Hyksos capital of Avaris. The city became the delta residence for all the succeeding kings of the Nineteenth and Twentieth Dynasties (1250–1050 B.C.). The two cities were strategically situated to protect Egypt against invasion. A stele found at Beisan commemorates the city of Rameses that Rameses II built with the labor of "Apiru" slaves, a term that refers to or includes the Hebrews, according to some scholars.

Another connection is a result of discoveries made by the 1883 Edouard Naville archaeological expedition in the delta of Egypt. Naville identified the remains of one city as ancient Pithom after analyzing the composition of the ancient mud bricks that made up the city and finding parallels with the biblical account of building Rameses and Pithom (Exodus 5:6–10). The lowest course of bricks had straw as a binding agent, the middle course had a variety of materials, and the top layer had no straw or other binding materials.

The late date theory considers the 480 years noted in 1 Kings 6:1 as a symbolic date, suggesting that 480 is a multiple of 40 and 12, both highly symbolic numbers among biblical peoples. Likewise, the 300 years noted in the time of the judges can be seen as a rounded number, not to be taken literally.

EGYPT'S FOREIGN SLAVES

For centuries, many people, like Jacob and his family, migrated to Egypt during times of famine, including during the Hyksos rule. Ancient Near Eastern texts indicate that others were taken to Egypt as slaves captured by the Egyptian army during later Egyptian raids through Canaan and Syria. Pharaoh Amenhotep II (1438–1412), for example, is recorded as having taken thirty-six hundred "Apiru" prisoners of war from Canaan. These "Apiru" (possibly Hebrew) prisoners were listed as distinct from other groups of prisoners taken from the Syro-Canaan region (Pritchard, *Ancient*, 247). Sethos I and Rameses II enslaved combinations of northwest Semitic people. Ancient records also indicate the absorption of hundreds of Semitic words into the Egyptian language during the Nineteenth Dynasty.

Most of these Semitic slaves lived in the delta region, an area about one hundred miles wide. This area can always depend on plenty of water to grow crops because of the annual flooding that occurs when the Nile River overflows its banks after heavy rains in central Africa. The Israelites settled in Goshen, most similar to the patriarchs' pastureland in Canaan and easiest to farm with the seasonal floodwaters, instead of residing in the more populated government center at Avaris.

Despite the number of generations that the Israelites lived in Egypt, they were still foreigners both in their customs and religious beliefs. These differences, combined with the explosive numbers of Israelites that "filled" the land (Exodus 1:7), excited Pharaoh's distrust. Haunting memories of an outside people ruling Egypt persisted. Specifically, Pharaoh feared that the Hebrew slaves would invite attack both from within and without Egypt (v. 10). His fear propelled him to establish a plan to curtail the numbers and collective strength of the Israelites.

Marked by four increasingly oppressive and drastic measures, Pharaoh aimed to halt the Israelites' proliferation. His initial act attempted to bend the Israelites' will and strength through forced labor: He made them slaves (Exodus 1:11–12). Second, believing that oppression would diminish the population, Pharaoh heaped bitter and hard labor upon them (vv. 13–14). Israelite slaves were forced to work with increased rigor that demanded all their strength and energy, particularly in the requirement to make bricks for building Pharaoh's great cities.

Slaves made mud bricks by mixing river mud or clay with straw that helped to hold each brick intact. They anchored dried bricks in place with mortar made with clay and sand or chalky lime mixed with water. The slaves also used the mortar as a plaster to cover the set bricks. Walls as high as sixty feet were successfully erected in this manner.

But as challenging and physically exhausting to the Israelite slaves as Pharaoh's measures were, his plan failed. The biblical narrative reads, "The more they [the Egyptians] afflicted them [the Israelites], the more they multiplied and grew" (Exodus 1:12).

Pharaoh's next measure to reduce the Israelite numbers and strength, however, showed far greater cruelty than the first two

If the early date of the Exodus is accepted and the pharaoh who declared the edict against the Hebrew babies was Thutmosis, the daughter of Pharaoh who saved Moses may have been the great Hatshepsut, the Eighteenth Dynasty princess who became queen of Egypt.

measures and depended on women for its success. He commanded midwives to kill all Hebrew boys at birth. In essence, he expected these women to reverence his royal law more than they feared God (Exodus 1:15–21). Pharaoh's edict of infanticide must have begun shortly before Moses' birth because it endangered Moses but not his brother Aaron, who was only three years older (Exodus 7:7).

DUTIES OF MIDWIVES

Midwifery was one of several occupations in biblical times in which women were the sole or chief professionals. Women were also weavers, such as those who designed and made the fabrics for the tabernacle (Exodus 35:25–26); cooks and bakers for the palace (1 Samuel 8:13); perfumers, including preparing holy anointing oil (Exodus 30:23–37; Luke 23:55; 24:1); musicians, particularly singers, dancers, and drummers (Exodus 15:20; 1 Samuel 18:6); makers of musical instruments (Psalm 68:26); and professional mourners (2 Samuel 1:24; 14:2; Jeremiah 9:17; Isaiah 32:11–12; 2 Chronicles 35:25; Ezekiel 32).

But midwifery was perhaps the earliest and most widespread profession for women. A midwife was highly regarded in ancient communities. As healthcare practitioners, women gained skills and were authorized to practice midwifery after a lengthy apprenticeship to seasoned midwives. Training their successors was an important responsibility for midwives. One tomb scene from the era of Egypt's Old Kingdom depicts a woman as the director of female physicians (Lesko, "Monumental," 5).

Midwifery is noted in numerous accounts of childbirth in the Bible. Twice in the patriarchal era midwives are mentioned. First, at Benjamin's birth, Rebekah's nurse Deborah was midwife to Rachel (Genesis 35:17). Second, a midwife attended Judah's daughter-in-law, Tamar, in her delivery of twins and properly identified the elder of the two sons by tying a scarlet string on the firstborn's hand (Genesis 38:28). This last example illustrates how a midwife held both clinical and legal authority in the ancient world.

A midwife's varied services were used over a lengthy period of time, often beginning before a prospective mother ever conceived and continuing throughout her baby's childhood. It was not unusual, for example, for a woman to consult a midwife to ascertain whether or not she was sufficiently healthy to bear a child. A midwife provided emotional and physical support to a client throughout her pregnancy, during her delivery, and after her baby was born, as would a child's pediatrician today. In times of such crisis as a miscarriage, stillbirth, or crib death, midwives assisted parents in their physical and emotional healing. Ezekiel outlined services a midwife rendered to grieving parents (Ezekiel 16:4–5).

A midwife was active in preparing for a baby's birth. First, she thoroughly cleaned the room where the birth would take place; banned men, children, or unmarried women from the room; and dusted the floor with flour to detect any intruder who could compromise the room's cleanliness. With a soothing voice, gentle hands, and music, the midwife massaged, sang softly, and spoke encouragement to the mother to control pain and calm fears throughout her labor. The rhythm and melody of the music were as important as the lyrics to set a proper pace for the mother's breathing. The mother's modesty was protected throughout the process.

During labor and delivery, the midwife positioned the mother in a squatting position on a birthing stool. The Hebrew term for *stool* is plural (*'obnayim*), suggesting that it consisted of more than one part. Archaeological findings suggest that the stool was probably two rocks pushed close enough together to support the mother's

In Egypt, life still depends on the Nile River, as it did in the time of Shiphrah and Puah.

weight as a midwife positioned the mother's hips for the baby's delivery. Discovered remains of birthing stools are often colorfully decorated rocks. Childbirth from a crouching position is easier for the mother, who has gravity on her side, but it is more demanding for the midwife. The much later practice of delivering babies while the mother is lying horizontally became popular not for the ease of the mother but for the greater comfort of the doctor.

After the delivery, the midwife cut the umbilical cord, tied off the stump, and rinsed away the placenta with a saltwater solution that also cleansed the baby. To protect the baby's skin from drying and cracking, a midwife massaged the little body with oil and wrapped him tightly in strips of cloth. Finally, she placed the baby in the mother's arms to be nursed (Ezekiel 16:4). A midwife's song of rejoicing after a healthy delivery reflected the jubilation of new birth, such as Eve seems to have sung after Cain was born: "I have gotten a man from the Lord; wherefore he may not reject his words" (Moses 5:16; see also Genesis 4:1).

In a theological sense, midwives helped their communities better understand God and His essential support of life as a result of their services. For example, birth and birthing frequently appear in scripture as metaphors for Christ as the Creator, Life-giver, and Redeemer. In a prayer, Isaiah referred to Jehovah as the true midwife during Judah's distress (Isaiah 26:16–19). The Israelites sang a hymn to Jehovah, calling Him their Rock that created them and sustained them (Deuteronomy 32:1–6, 30–31). Some translations of these lyrics link the role of midwife and the rocks of a birthing stool to the Savior's mission as the Rock of our salvation.

Among the rich biblical vocabulary for describing health and sickness of the body, terms denoting exceptional pain are most frequently reserved for the pains of childbirth (Isaiah 13:8; 21:3). Recognition of a woman's pain at childbirth provides an additional level of appreciation for the Savior's greater suffering in Gethsemane and on the cross (Isaiah 42:14; 53:11).

MURDEROUS ROYAL LAW

As those personally delegated by Pharaoh to implement his third stratagem for curtailing Israelite proliferation, Shiphrah and Puah were ordered into Pharaoh's presence to hear his charge to them. This encounter most likely occurred at Rameses, the palace city closest to Goshen.

As "Hebrew midwives," Shiphrah and Puah were commanded to kill Hebrew boy babies at birth and allow Hebrew girl babies to live (Exodus 1:15–16). The royal edict prompts questions concerning the decree itself as well as the midwives involved. For example, why were the boys targeted and not the girls? If one desired to limit population growth, wouldn't reducing the female population be more effective? Because Pharaoh's concern was war (Exodus 1:10), he may have reasoned that restricting the growth of the male population would eliminate a future military threat from the Israelites.

Pharaoh's edict may also reflect the tradition in many ancient cultures that the family line and identity were traced through the men. If that is the case, Pharaoh was as concerned about the Israelites' unique identity as about their numbers. He may have reasoned that if the boy babies were killed, he could soon eradicate the entire Hebrew culture. A Midrash explanation posits that Pharaoh commanded that Hebrew baby girls be kept alive because the Egyptians were naturally sensual in nature and desired to engage as many women as possible in their service (Ginzberg, *Legends,* 2:251).

Because the biblical narrative mentions only two midwives, Shiphrah and Puah, many questions arise. Were they the only midwives to serve the entire Hebrew slave population in Egypt, or were there others? Because midwifery was a profession taught to apprentices by experienced midwives, were Shiphrah and Puah the professional leaders who were expected to communicate Pharaoh's edict to the other midwives? From a different perspective, were Shiphrah and Puah the only midwives mentioned in the text because Moses knew of them and retained their names in his memory? Did they assist Jochebed in giving birth to her son Moses? Furthermore, did Shiphrah and Puah work as a team or did they work independently? Scripture supplies no additional clues to answer these questions.

Finally, were Shiphrah and Puah Hebrew women serving their own people, or were they Egyptian women working among foreigners? The Bible tells us simply that they were "Hebrew midwives" (Exodus 1:15). One Jewish Midrash suggests that Shiphrah and Puah must have been Israelite women because the Egyptians, fearing God's punishment, required Hebrew women to perform this murderous deed (Ginzberg, *Legends,* 2:251). Does this explanation, however, assume that the Egyptians shared the Israelites' beliefs about what would offend God? Conversely, Josephus assumed they were Egyptian, probably because the pharaoh would be less likely to rely on Israelite midwives to carry out his cruel plan among their own people (*Antiquities,* 2.9.2). The women's names, however, are Semitic, not Egyptian, which leads many

WOMEN'S COSMETICS IN THE ANCIENT WORLD

Women used cosmetics in the ancient world for both popular and practical purposes. Egyptian women were particularly fond of using cosmetics. They painted their upper eyelids and eyebrows black and the lower lids green. They stored their eye paint in a small horn or vase and applied it with a slender stick of wood, bone, or ivory. Composed of powdered mineral, the eye paint emphasized the shape of the woman's eyes, protected her eyes from the bright sun and pesky insects, and relieved eye ailments. The black paint, called *kohl*, came from galena, a lead ore. The green paint was derived from malachite, a copper ore.

At least some Israelite and Canaanite women wore eye makeup, too, although perhaps not as frequently or as universally as the Egyptians. One of Job's daughters was named Keren-happuch (Job 42:14), which means "horn of eye paint." Jezebel, the Phoenician princess who married the king of Israel, painted her eyes with kohl when news arrived that her political rival was coming (2 Kings 9:30). Women who used eye paint to emphasize their outward beauty while being inwardly corrupt were often chastised by the prophets (Jeremiah 4:30; Ezekiel 23:40).

scholars to believe they were Israelite women. With insufficient evidence, claims concerning the midwives' race remain assumptions and keep the debate open.

SHREWD HEBREW MIDWIVES

Because Pharaoh was considered a god by his people and by himself, he could order an execution without hesitation. Shiphrah and Puah's refusal to obey Pharaoh's law therefore put their lives in serious jeopardy. But they feared God rather than Pharaoh, suggesting that they knew obedience to Pharaoh's law would bring God's fierce displeasure. Was this understanding taught to them or instinctively known?

When evidence of the midwives' failure to eliminate male children from the Israelite population became undeniable, Shiphrah and Puah were commanded to give an accounting before the king. Their quick response to Pharaoh provides the highlight of this story (Exodus 1:18–19). In a remarkably inventive explanation, Shiphrah and Puah told Pharaoh that Israelite women were not like the delicate Egyptian women; Israelite women were full of life and vigor, giving birth without difficulty or need of assistance (Exodus 1:19). With their shrewd response the midwives seem to have succeeded in deceiving Pharaoh, saving the lives of countless Hebrew boys and protecting their own as a result. Pharaoh's ready acceptance of their explanation reveals his own gullibility, his ignorance of childbirth, and the blindness created by a desire to justify his cruelty to the Israelites because they were a different and perhaps inferior species to the Egyptians.

A Midrash claims that Pharaoh took an additional measure, not recorded in the Bible, to identify infant Hebrew boys after the Hebrew midwives failed to kill them. He ordered Egyptian women to spy on their Israelite neighbors by taking their Egyptian children to play at the homes of the Israelites and counting all the children in the home. The Midrash also claims that at this point Pharaoh assigned none but Egyptian midwives to attend Hebrew women in childbirth to be certain that the parents did not hide the baby boys and evade discovery (Ginzberg, *Legends,* 2:250–52, 257).

THE MIDWIVES' DIVINE BLESSING

In acknowledgment of their reverence for life and Him who gives that life, God "made houses" for Shiphrah and Puah (Exodus 1:21). The context of the story suggests a clear distinction between a physical building that the women could inhabit and a family or posterity. Because Shiphrah and Puah saved others' children, the Lord blessed them with their own children. Family, whether literal or adopted, is shown to be highly valued by God and scripturally referred to as a "house" (Ruth 4:11). In this same sense, God's people are often called the house of Israel, meaning the family of God (Ezekiel 20:5; 3 Nephi 16:13). The midwives' ability to protect their own children at birth suggests that there were other midwives with similar faith and courage.

Finally, God's blessing to Shiphrah and Puah also reveals something about the women's ages. The gift of childbirth may not have been given to Shiphrah and Puah before this time, perhaps indicating that Shiphrah and Puah were barren before God's reward. According to ancient custom, midwives were typically older women, but God's blessing to Shiphrah and Puah implies that they were young and yet working as skilled midwives during their childbearing years. Making them "a house" indicates that they bore more than one child, again implying relative youth. This insight shows that wisdom and courageous faith in God are not outside the grasp of young women.

PHARAOH'S FINAL SCHEME

In his fourth and final scheme to annihilate the young male Hebrew population, Pharaoh commanded all Egyptians to do their part to reduce the number of Hebrews in their nation. Specifically, he authorized the Egyptian public to perform acts of violence against the Israelites by drowning their baby boys in the river (Exodus 1:22). The Hebrew wording could be translated "expose" the babies in the Nile as much as "throw" them into the Nile, explaining the approach that Jochebed chose in sending her baby Moses down the Nile in a basket. Pharaoh must have counted on his people's regard for his law as a divine mandate, viewing him as one of the gods who ruled their lives.

Considering the recorded number of Israelites at the time of the Exodus as an indicator, whether that number is symbolic or literal, the Egyptians in general did not fully execute or long observe Pharaoh's final measure. As in every one of his other three schemes, Pharaoh's edicts seemed to incite an increase in the population rather than curtail it (Exodus 1:20). Did a popular movement arise in protest to Pharaoh's commands? Did the Egyptians' acquaintances with their Israelite neighbors instill an abhorrence to Pharaoh's mandate while they observed an innate law ordained by the only true God? Perchance Egyptians were emboldened by silent protests of such courageous Israelites as Jochebed and Amram (Exodus 2:2–3; Hebrews 11:23). Similarly, perhaps Shiphrah and Puah played a role, by their resilience and unflinching courage, in inspiring others to follow God's law rather than Pharaoh's.

Ironically, in the final two phases of Pharaoh's edict, both which involved infanticide, his murderous law led to the preservation of Moses, the Israelites' deliverer. In a scenario that could only have been appreciated after the fact, God was already working a miracle among His people. While Pharaoh planned the extermination of the Israelites, God was planning their deliverance and rapid rise to greatness. Shiphrah and Puah would have been among the first to acknowledge that God's miraculous deliverance from Egypt began decades before the parting of the Red Sea.

POINTS TO PONDER: APPLICATIONS FOR OUR LIVES

1. What symbolism do you see in childbirth that helps us better appreciate Christ's atoning sacrifice?

2. In what ways is the offering of a mother or a midwife like Christ's?

3. How is Christ the "rock" of your life?

4. If Shiphrah and Puah were indeed Hebrew women and still alive when Moses led the children of Israel out of Egypt, they likely would have departed with them. How does a consideration of such women as the two midwives aid your visualization of the Exodus?

5. Considering the numerous women they trained, their response to Pharaoh's edict, and the manner in which God blessed them, what potential legacy could Shiphrah and Puah have left their society?

6. How can Shiphrah and Puah inspire your own spiritual and professional legacy?

The Daughters of Zelophehad

DAUGHTERS OF ZELOPHEHAD

MAHLAH	NOAH	HOGLAH	MILCAH	TIRZAH
מַחְלָה	נֹעָה	חָגְלָה	מִלְכָּה	תִּרְצָה
"Sickness," "Song"	*Meaning uncertain*	*"Partridge," "Ruler," "Counsel"*	*"Delight," "Pleasure"*	*Musical instrument?*

*M*ahlah, Noah, Hoglah, Milcah, and Tirzah were born to Zelophehad and his wife during the Israelites' forty-year sojourn in the wilderness. The five daughters knew well the harshness of wilderness life and were reared amid frequent complaints against Israel's leaders. When legislation was proposed that ignored single women and parents without sons in regard to inheritances, the five sisters boldly stepped forward. Their approach, however, was strikingly different from the angry and whining appeals that Moses frequently heard in the camp. Demonstrating genuine respect for their leaders, Mahlah, Noah, Hoglah, Milcah, and Tirzah challenged the law with an articulate and unified voice. The Lord verified the justness of their request, and Moses granted them the right to inherit land in the name of their father, Zelophehad. This right, however, carried with it a restriction when they married.

The story of the daughters of Zelophehad considers women's roles outside the family domain, where they interact with men other than father, husband, or son. These young sisters illustrate how women can appropriately influence men in a church or community hierarchy to respect and receive their differing perspectives. In part because of their diplomatic manner and gracious attitude in questioning a policy, five young women inspired Israel's leaders toward a deeper understanding of God's love and awareness for all of His children. And through the sisters' willing acceptance of God's singular command to them, they preserved their father's name, inheritance, legacy, and family line.

THE DAUGHTERS' GENEALOGY

The daughters of Zelophehad were numbered with the tribe of Manasseh; six generations separated them from Joseph, son of Jacob and Rachel. Moses blessed Manasseh and Ephraim, the two tribes of Joseph, above the other tribes of Israel because of Joseph's birthright blessing of a double portion (Deuteronomy 33:13–17). In fact, Manasseh was the only tribe to inherit land on both sides

NUMBERS 26:33

NUMBERS 27:1–11

NUMBERS 36:1–13

JOSHUA 17:3–6

1 CHRONICLES 7:15

of the River Jordan when the Israelites were finally allowed to enter the promised land. As evidence of this inheritance, the territory of Manasseh east of the river carried the names of Manasseh's son Machir and grandson Gilead (Numbers 32:39–40; Deuteronomy 3:13–15; Joshua 13:29–31).

LIFE IN THE WILDERNESS

A hostile wasteland frequented by nomadic tribes and wild beasts was the only world that Mahlah, Noah, Hoglah, Milcah, and Tirzah knew. The Israelites' precise route of travel and the length of their stay at various sites in the wilderness cannot be definitively outlined because some of the places named in the book of Numbers are not known today, and the various accounts of their travels reported in the Bible do not always agree. The Israelite wilderness settlements, however, were likely beyond the limits of any other established community.

Notwithstanding, what is clear from scripture is that the Israelites' wasteland years were a disparaging time of scarcity and vulnerability. As a point of contrast, the Israelites wanted to return to slavery in Egypt after they escaped to the desert wilderness (Numbers 14:2–4), but they never desired to revisit the wilderness after they reached the promised land. Furthermore, the Bible contains no account of anyone desiring a portion of the wilderness for an inheritance or cherishing the years spent there. Although reverently recited throughout their long history, the events at Mount Sinai and the law that came out of those remarkable days never inspired the Israelites to make pilgrimages back to Sinai. Once the children of Israel left the desert and entered Canaan, as a body they never returned.

A high mortality rate among the Israelites further illustrates the hardships of wilderness living. Statistics from one tomb group in the general vicinity and era of the wilderness wanderings indicate that more than a third (35 percent) of the individuals in that ancient population died before the age of five. Nearly half lived only to the age of eighteen. Among the surviving adults, the average life expectancy for men was forty years and thirty for women. These data suggest that the mortality rate for childbearing women was higher than that of men who engaged in warfare (Meyers, "Roots," 95–96). Considering the frequency of battles mentioned in the Bible, the number of women who died in childbirth must have been staggering.

The daughters of Zelophehad lived a nomadic life in the harsh wilderness.

Disease was particularly rampant among ancient populations, including the Israelite community. About half of all deaths at any age were due to what the Bible calls pestilences and plagues. Some of these devastating diseases appear to have been regularly occurring endemic infections that routinely claimed about the same number of lives each year. Others were likely sporadic infectious epidemics that significantly devastated the Israelite population each time they struck.

Fifty miles south of Beersheba is the oasis of Kadesh-Barnea. The daughters of Zelophehad may have lived here for a time and perhaps were even born here.

The Bible indicates multiple outbreaks of disease and plagues sent by the Lord during the forty years the Israelites spent in the wilderness: an epidemic that killed many people who were associated with making the golden calf (Exodus 32:35); a plague that occurred in connection with gorging on quail (Numbers 11:31–34); pestilence on those who returned to Egypt (Numbers 14:12); a plague that afflicted the men who spied out the land of Canaan (Numbers 14:36–37); a plague that killed 14,700 Israelites after many murmured against Moses and Aaron (Numbers 16:46–50); and a disease that killed 24,000 after Israelite men participated with Midianite women in immoral rites of worship to the god of Moab (Numbers 25:8–18).

Perhaps Zelophehad had children who died young and were therefore not recorded in the Bible, but that he had five daughters who survived to at least their teenage years is somewhat miraculous, considering these numbers. If Mahlah's name does indeed come from the Hebrew word for "sickness" (ḥlh; see also Orr, *Encyclopaedia*, 3:1967), her name could be a reflection of the rampant plagues of the time.

The Bible suggests preventative measures the Israelites took to curtail the spread of disease. The area where the population was afflicted with a plague or pestilence was often sterilized by fire when a plague abated. Perhaps a similar health precaution led the Israelites to burn conquered cities in the promised land to control against an

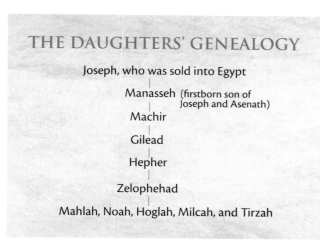

THE DAUGHTERS' GENEALOGY

Joseph, who was sold into Egypt
|
Manasseh (firstborn son of
Joseph and Asenath)
|
Machir
|
Gilead
|
Hepher
|
Zelophehad
|
Mahlah, Noah, Hoglah, Milcah, and Tirzah

MANNA

Although the Israelites occasionally had other sources of food in the wilderness (Numbers 21:5; see also 7:13, 19ff; Exodus 17:3), manna was a daily mainstay of their diet. They were sustained by it until their first harvest in the promised land (Exodus 16:35; Joshua 5:10–12).

Several characteristics of this primary food source are given in the Bible. A fine, white, flaky substance that resembled coriander seed, manna had a sticky, resinous texture and appeared on the ground like frost (Numbers 11:4–9; Exodus 16:1–36). It was sweet and tasted like wafers made with honey and oil. Each Israelite could gather an omer of manna (about two quarts) early in the day, but any manna left ungathered or stored longer than a day would go bad or quickly disappear after the sun warmed the ground. Manna could be boiled in pots or ground into meal and baked into cakes.

The name *manna* is best translated, "what is it?" Even today we are not able to definitively identify the substance and its origin. The most frequently accepted explanation was put forward by biblical scholar B. F. Bodenheimer. He observed that after feeding on the sap through the bark of the tamarisk tree, various insects expel a sweet, honey-like substance that accumulates through the night unless ants gather it. Called the "dew of heaven" and "hoarfrost" in some countries, the liquid secretions quickly solidify in the dry heat of day, forming small round, sticky granules on the tamarisk plants until either they fall to the ground because of their mass and waxy consistency or they are melted by the sun. The Israelites' manna may have been this substance. One insect known to excrete this substance is a small cicada that is locally called *man*, another tie to *manna*, the Israelites' label for their unusual food source (Bodenheimer, "Manna"; Drinkard, "Manna," 648).

The Israelites may have gathered manna from tamarisk trees.

Photo by David M. Whitchurch

outbreak of disease. In addition, those who were likely to have been exposed to potentially communicable diseases were quarantined for seven days before being allowed into camp, and their clothing and other articles made of animal skins and wood were thoroughly cleaned (Numbers 31:19–20).

In addition to the physical challenges associated with their harsh environment, Mahlah, Noah, Hoglah, Milcah, and Tirzah grew up in a social environment of criticism, complaints,

The Israelites camped where water could be found, as in this place, where a spring surfaces amid the rocks.

and defeatism. The Israelites often feared the worst and blamed their leaders for every discomfort. One might easily expect the five sisters to become insecure, distrustful, and bitter as a result.

But their forty years in the wilderness also provided important experiences and conditions to strengthen the Israelites spiritually and embolden them for their foreordained role as God's people. The harsh surroundings reminded them of their need for divine assistance; survival was impossible without God. Instead of becoming an unwieldy conglomerate of diverse peoples, the Israelites forged a faith in their God that proved to be a catalyst that bonded them to each other and attracted others to their society.

The lengthy time and circumstances in the wilderness also proved advantageous for physical preparation needed to conquer their future homeland. With their numbers significantly increasing over the years, the Israelites developed some military skills and created an irregular military force. United by their loyalty to Jehovah, the Israelites were motivated and inspired to conquer the land of Canaan for their inheritance.

Into this unique environment of hardship, opportunity, and the sustaining power of God, the daughters of Zelophehad confidently prepared to appeal an inheritance law while the Israelites organized themselves to enter the promised land.

POLICY FOR LAND INHERITANCE

Anticipation of a divinely reserved homeland kept the Israelites hopeful for their future. They already knew that special instructions and restrictions applied to their promised land. Previously the Lord had

CHRONOLOGY OF THE FORTY YEARS IN THE WILDERNESS

Year	
1	Depart Egypt; Red Sea miracle
1	The law given to Moses at Sinai
2	First census counts the men of the first generation (Numbers 1:1–3)
2	Camp at Kadesh in the wilderness of Paran (Numbers 10:11–12)
	Miriam's leprosy (Numbers 12)
	Of the spies sent to Canaan, only two return with a good report (Numbers 13–14)
	First generation told they will not enter the promised land (Numbers 14)
	Korah's rebellion (Numbers 16)
39?	Miriam dies (Numbers 20:1)
40	Aaron dies (Numbers 20:28; 33:38–39)
	Fiery serpents and the brazen serpent on the pole (Numbers 21:6)
	Victory over the Amorites, the people of Bashan (Numbers 21)
	Second census; inheritance policy announced (Numbers 26)
	Daughters of Zelophehad petition Moses (Numbers 27)
	Moses appoints Joshua as his successor (Numbers 27:18–23)
	Israelites defeat the Midianites (Numbers 31)
	Men of Manasseh appeal the inheritance law (Numbers 36)
	Moses' final instructions (Deuteronomy 1:3)
	Joshua leads the Israelites into the promised land

declared, "The land shall not be sold for ever; for the land is mine; for ye are strangers and sojourners with me" (Leviticus 25:23). Furthermore, the first generation, numbered in the first census shortly after Israel departed from Egypt, were not to enter the promised land because of their faithlessness (Numbers 14:29; 26:65).

At the end of the forty years, the Lord commanded Moses and Eleazar, the high priest, to number all the men, by tribe, who were at least twenty years old. These men survived their fathers, who had been counted in the first census nearly forty years earlier. Thirteen tribes are delineated in the census, including the two tribes of Joseph (Ephraim and Manasseh) in an acknowledgment of Joseph's double portion through the birthright. With the exception of Caleb and Joshua, none of the men numbered in the second census were among those counted in the first census (Numbers 26:64).

After the second census was taken, Moses assigned a portion of the promised land as a divine inheritance to the men listed in the second census, in the name of their fathers, who had been named in the first census. As stewards for God, the men were to forever keep the property in their family, passing the stewardship from generation to generation, retaining a memory of their fathers (Numbers 26:1, 52–56).

Evidence that family rights to the land and preservation of their divine stewardship were seriously safeguarded emerges later in the Bible. For example, in the northern kingdom of Israel in the ninth century before Christ, an Israelite named Naboth refused to sell his family's land for any price to the greedy king Ahab. On the advice of the wicked queen Jezebel, Ahab took possession of the property after falsely accusing Naboth and sentencing him to death (1 Kings 21:1–16).

Not all the descendants of the faithful children of Israel, however, were included in Israel's policy for land inheritance. The initial legislation that Moses and the elders of the tribes established ignored women and fathers who had no sons. Faithful Zelophehad, who had died in the wilderness without producing a male heir but having five daughters, is listed with the clans of Manasseh in the census as a case in point (Numbers 26:33). Under the proposed law, Zelophehad's family would become extinct when his daughters married because they would become members of their husbands' families, which might even be in a different tribe.

FIVE YOUNG WOMEN APPEAL THE INHERITANCE POLICY

Mahlah, Noah, Hoglah, Milcah, and Tirzah chose to petition their leaders concerning the inheritance of land because of their unique circumstance. If they could inherit in their father's name, the property would be included in their marriage dowry and perpetuated through their children and their children's children. A Jewish Midrash records a tradition of what the sisters discussed in preparing their petition to Moses. Believing that God extends His tender mercies to all of His creations and is not biased against His daughters, the five sisters are purported to have said, "God's love is not like the love of a mortal father; the latter prefers his sons to his daughters, but He that created the world extends His love to women as well as to men" (Ginzberg, *Legends,* 3:392).

EARLY EVIDENCES OF DAUGHTERS' INHERITANCE RIGHTS

In the eighteenth century before Christ, the Code of Hammurabi permitted a soldier to bequeath property to his daughter or to his wife (sections 38–39) and a father to designate a daughter as heir if she chose to become a priestess (sections 71–73). A hundred years earlier, in an area south of Babylon, the Code of Lipit-Ishtar allowed a priestess to inherit from her father because she would not have a husband to provide for her (section 22). Still earlier, Sumerian law allowed daughters to inherit in the absence of sons, but under no circumstance could daughters inherit in a Babylonian city just north of Sumeria. One scholar observed that "the inheritance rights for daughters appear to have been more of an aberration than a generally accepted practice" (Baker, Rights, 165; see also Ben-Barak, "Inheritance," 22–33).

The five daughters made their appeal to Moses, the high priest, and the elders of the tribes at the entrance to the tabernacle where Aaron's oldest son, Eleazar, served as high priest after Aaron's death. Apparently the doorway of the tabernacle served as a governing headquarters for Moses and was the place where individuals brought grievances to their leaders. Because the tabernacle proper represented the dwelling place of Jehovah, presenting a petition at the entrance symbolized taking one's concern to the Lord Himself. The Israelites were camped in Moab at the time, north of Mount Nebo and across the River Jordan from Jericho (Numbers 25:1; 27:12; 33:48–49).

The inheritance case of the five daughters of Zelophehad was not the first in history. Ancient texts from Mesopotamia, Egypt, and Syria attest to women inheriting property long before the time of Moses. The Bible indicates that women inherited wealth during the patriarchal era, although likely an inferior share compared to that of a male heir. For example, Leah and Rachel anticipated an inheritance, though not in real estate (Genesis 31:14–16). When such female heirs married, their children would inherit material goods from both parents. One practice that may have been required in any allowance of a female heir was that the father had to create a legal transfer of property to his daughter during his lifetime. If he died before making such arrangements, a daughter was left without recourse.

What made the Israelite law for inheriting land different from other laws was that it divinely bequeathed a stewardship to a family forever. The allocation of land was meant to be permanent. The property that God granted in the promised land was not to be alienated from the original family line and tribe.

Photo by Ruth Ann Hubbard

The daughters of Zelophehad may have looked similar to these Egyptian sisters.

In the case of the daughters of Zelophehad, the young women sought to be named heirs of this divine stewardship, and their request came after their father died.

The story of Mahlah, Noah, Hoglah, Milcah, and Tirzah, however, is remarkable in yet another way. Young, unmarried women appealing a law before national leaders is unprecedented in the Bible. A consideration of what their ages might have been when they approached Moses adds significance to their contribution. Although their specific ages are unknown, we assume they were young because none had yet married. Traditionally, marriages in ancient times were consummated when girls reached puberty. Rabbinic tradition considered that childhood ceased at age thirteen for boys and at age twelve for girls. Curiously, a Jewish Midrash reports that the youngest of the daughters was forty years old and that none had married (Ginzberg, *Legends*, 3:394). The probability of all five having never married and living beyond the age of forty is most unlikely in their culture. Because the census numbered men who would be at least twenty years old by the time the Israelites entered the promised land, this account- ing may suggest that at least one of Zelophehad's daughters might have been about twenty years old, but possibly most of them would have been younger.

Seeing the five sisters as young and fatherless intensifies their re-

Three Palestinian girls about the ages the younger daughters of Zelophehad may have been at the time of their appeal.

markable courage, conviction, and faith to share their unique perspective with authorities. In an interest- ing twist of the story, Josephus praised the men of the tribe of Manasseh for valiantly petitioning Moses in behalf of Zelophehad's daughters. In contrast, Mahlah, Noah, Hoglah, Milcah, and Tirzah are portrayed in Josephus's account as silent and helpless, standing in the background while courageous men represented their interests (*Antiquities*, 4.7.5). No amount of reinventing the story, however, can change the clarity of the biblical witness that five young women worked together to appropriately alter a law.

The daughters' wisdom and reverence for their forebears is underscored by their motive. The focus of their concern was not a selfish desire to secure their own land. They were not likely to have been con- cerned for their own economic status because those needs would have been met when they married and shared in their husbands' inheritances. No, the sisters' desire was that their father's name would be remem- bered. Without an inheritance in Zelophehad's name, the family line would become extinct. They asked Moses, "Why should our father's name be subtracted?" or as the question is translated in the King James Version, "Why should the name of our father be done away from among his family, because he hath no son?" (Numbers 27:4).

The daughters of Zelophehad focused their petition to obtain legislation that would protect the mem- ory of faithful Israelite families that lacked male descendants. A person's importance and worth in com- munities within the promised land depended on the survival of the family name at the time of the con- quest. If a man had no progeny, he was forgettable; without descendants, he would not be "immortal." The sisters feared that as far as the nation of Israel was concerned, the lineage of their father would die out and Zelophehad's name would be forgotten. They were not hoping to overthrow the general law of inheritance but to expand it to allow for special considerations and legitimate exceptions. Therefore, Mahlah, Noah,

Hoglah, Milcah, and Tirzah asked to be declared their father's legal heirs in the upcoming apportionment (Numbers 32–35).

The daughters' wisdom is notable in another significant way. Their manner of dealing with the problem they discovered in the law is commendable and exemplary. Rather than murmuring against the law, denigrating the leaders, or complaining to others of their plight, these young women took their cause directly to the governing body that held the authority to amend the law. Showing respect for their leaders, Mahlah, Noah, Hoglah, Milcah, and Tirzah presented themselves as capable citizens rather than as vulnerable victims.

KORAH'S REBELLION

With a unified voice and in just three sentences, Zelophehad's daughters clearly and succinctly articulated the void in the proposed law and suggested a solution (Numbers 27:3–4). They introduced their request by reminding Moses and the other leaders that their father had not been among those who rebelled with Korah and were subsequently destroyed (v. 3). Their father died as one of the doomed first generation. His "sins" were simply being part of the generation banned from entering the promised land and the misfortune of having no male heir. He had done nothing, however, that should preclude him from receiving an inheritance from the Lord.

Korah was a descendant of Kohath, a son of Levi. Korah and the rest of the Kohathites had the most important assignment in caring for the tabernacle: They disassembled and transported the furnishing of the Holy of Holies whenever the company moved (Numbers 4:4–20). Jealous of Aaron's exclusive rights as high priest, Korah apparently wanted even more authority and used deceitful methods in seeking to secure it in a manner that sharply contrasted with the approach used by Zelophehad's daughters.

Joined by 250 other leading men who nursed their own complaints against the Israelite leadership, Korah accused Moses and Aaron of setting themselves up as greater than the rest of the Israelites. "Ye take too much upon you," they complained, "seeing all the congregation are holy, every one of them, and the Lord is among them" (Numbers 16:3). When Korah's assembly refused to obey any of Moses' requests, Moses set up a trial by fire for the Lord to identify those He chose to lead (Numbers 16:44–50). The 250 Kohathite leaders were swallowed up in the earth and consumed in a fire that came from God. Many Israelites had been influenced by Korah, and after his dramatic death they complained that Moses had caused it. Subsequently, another 14,700 Israelites died in a plague.

Apparently, those who died in connection with Korah's rebellion also lost an inheritance in the promised land for their descendants. Zelophehad's daughters reminded Moses that their father was not involved with Korah, his death was not connected to the rebellion, and he retained the right to an inheritance.

REVISIONS IN THE LAW

Moses' response to the young women's request is a striking example of his wisdom and leadership. Without a hint of either impatience or condescending disregard, Moses took the young women's visit seriously and listened to their concerns. Likely he discussed the request with the other leaders and contemplated possible ramifications, but in the end, "Moses brought their cause before the Lord" (Numbers 27:5). Furthermore, the Lord heard the daughters' petition and instructed Moses to accede to their request (vv. 6–7).

We suppose that God could have made certain that the law initially included a provision for families without a male heir. Interestingly, He did not intervene to fix a law that was unfair but created an environment where women could act and take responsibility. Just as He led Adam and Eve to discover and choose truth, God allowed the daughters of Zelophehad the opportunity to learn greater freedom through disciplined choices.

Analytical, committed, and brave, Zelophehad's daughters voluntarily acted in appropriate ways to voice a perspective that had not been considered by Israel's leaders. Without waiting for someone else to speak for them or to see the injustice they had quickly ascertained or for God to intercede on their behalf, Mahlah, Noah, Hoglah, Milcah, and Tirzah stepped forward with faith and confidence that their request was righteous. In short, because of the young women's thoughtful petition, God modified the existing inheritance law and declared the daughters right in their request.

In the course of deciding the law for this particular case, the Lord also communicated general rules for succession in future exceptional cases. In regulating the order of God's inheritance in the promised land, the law was amended to delineate how the land would be passed down the family line in an accepted sequence in the absence of a son (Numbers 27:8–11). The general principle was to keep the inheritance as close as possible to the family line of the deceased man. No consideration was mentioned should a man abandon his inheritance claim or change clans through marriage or other reasons.

The revised law declared not that the inheritance given to Zelophehad's daughters would follow a female succession from then on but that it would be inherited by a son of each of the daughters and from them

ORDER OF THE RIGHT TO INHERITANCE (NUMBERS 27:8–11)

1. Son or sons
2. If no son, then a daughter or daughters
3. If no children, then a brother
4. If no brothers, then an uncle
5. If no uncle, then the next closest male relative

GENERATIONAL PATTERN FOR LINE OF INHERITANCE

Father	Zelophehad
Daughter(s)	Mahlah, Noah, Hoglah, Milcah, and Tirzah
Grandsons	sons of the five daughters

through a male succession. The law focused on the remembrance of the original generation who departed from Egypt and established a system to ensure that each inheritance remained with the original family.

CONCERNS OVER THE REVISED LAW

After Moses decided to amend the law to allow women without brothers to inherit property in the promised land, new questions arose. Men in Zelophehad's extended family approached Moses with their concern, much as Mahlah, Noah, Hoglah, Milcah, and Tirzah had done. These men did not dispute the decision Moses had rendered but recognized a loophole of considerable consequence for the tribe of Manasseh. Their question was about the subsequent land entanglements should the young women marry out of their family tribe. At issue was the continuity of the lines of inheritance within each tribe (Numbers 36:1–3).

THE JUBILEE YEAR

Of particular concern to the men of Manasseh were implications for the land deeded to Manasseh at the Jubilee year should any of the daughters marry a man from another tribe (Numbers 36:4). The year of Jubilee was the fiftieth year that occurred at the end of seven sabbatical cycles of seven years each (Leviticus 25:8–17, 23–55). Among other realignments, Jubilee was the time to resolve all problems with landed inheritance. All lands sold to others during the fifty years were to be returned to their ancestral owners.

The men of Manasseh foresaw that the property inherited by each of the five daughters could be permanently assigned at the next Jubilee to the tribe into which the heiresses married. Or if one or more of Zelophehad's daughters married into another tribe, the problem could remain unresolvable because of dual-line rights to the land or because the land was inherited and not sold. In any case, the intended plan for the property inherited in Zelophehad's name to remain in Manasseh territory would be jeopardized should any of his daughters marry outside their tribe.

SPECIAL RESTRICTIONS ON THE DAUGHTERS OF ZELOPHEHAD

As He did for the daughters of Zelophehad, the Lord responded to the concerns of the men of Manasseh. First the Lord reiterated that the daughters could inherit in their father's name but then added a restriction.

The young women were required to marry within the same tribe with which their father had been affiliated (Numbers 36:5–6). At issue was not their individual happiness but the solidarity of the larger family unit. The daughters were restricted from marriage outside the family's tribe to preserve the sacred stewardship of the land that the family was given forever (vv. 7–9). The revision safeguarded a balance of power among the tribes. The unstated alternative in this revision was that should one of these young women marry a man from a tribe other than Manasseh, her inheritance would go to another relative who remained in Zelophehad's tribal territory.

Although we could focus on the supposed unfairness of requiring the daughters to marry within the tribe of Manasseh, we should consider another perspective. Recognizing that the Lord has always given guidelines for selecting marriage partners, these young women faced the choice of putting trust in God's promises ahead of a larger pool of options in the men they would eventually marry. And

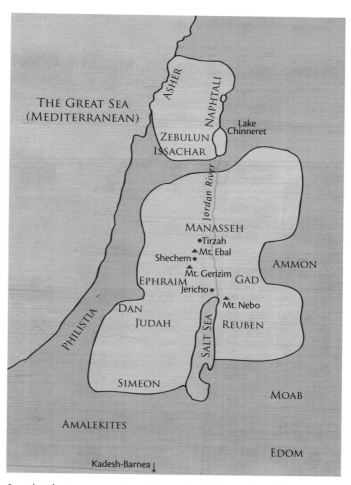

Land inheritances assigned to each of the tribes of Israel. The daughters of Zelophehad inherited land with the tribe of Manasseh.

even though the Lord directed the sisters not to marry outside their specific tribe, He did not restrict their choice within that tribe. They retained their freedom to accept the marriage offer of their choice among the men of Manasseh. Furthermore, their choice to follow the amended inheritance law indicated that they were sincere in their motive to retain a remembrance of their father.

ENDURING INFLUENCE

In an extraordinary tribute to their integrity and authenticity, the Bible lauds the young women for their obedience. "Even as the Lord commanded Moses," the record witnesses, "so did the daughters of Zelophehad" (Numbers 36:10). Obedience to the Lord was tied to receiving an inheritance in the promised land, which in turn symbolized God's promise of an eternal inheritance. The daughters' obedience in this situation, therefore, also significantly influenced eternal blessings for them and their children. The book of Numbers concludes with the verification that all five of Zelophehad's daughters married within the tribe of Manasseh and preserved their family's inheritance (vv. 11–12).

Direct and indirect reference to the legislation inspired by the five sisters appears later in the Bible. When the Israelites conquered enough of the land of Canaan for them to take occupancy, the promise to Zelophehad's daughters was redeemed and their story retold (Joshua 17:3–6). Still later, in the day of King Saul, the Chronicler included the daughters of Zelophehad in his genealogy of Abraham's descendants (1 Chronicles 7:15). In addition, the dispensation made to Mahlah, Noah, Hoglah, Milcah, and Tirzah became the rule for all families without sons and was permanently applicable (see page 235).

The legal decision inspired by Zelophehad's daughters has also directly influenced acceptance of women's inheritance rights in Judeo-Christian nations today. After reviewing various ancient inheritance laws, a legal scholar concluded that this ancient Israelite law, influenced by five young women, was "the oldest decided case that is still cited as an authority" (Clark, "Zelophehad," 133).

The account in Joshua 17:3–6 suggests that Zelophehad's daughters inherited land on the west side of the River Jordan, part of the second portion allotted to Manasseh (compare Numbers 32:33, 39–41, for Manasseh's share east of the Jordan). Possible traces of the family of Zelophehad in later material culture indicate that they settled with the tribe of Manasseh on the west side. For example, the female names "Noah" and "Hoglah" appear on pottery fragments from Samaria in the eighth century before Christ. About the same time a city called "Tirzah" was prominent in Manasseh territory in the northern kingdom of Israel. These records of their names suggest that the courageous young women themselves were not soon forgotten.

The story of Mahlah, Noah, Hoglah, Milcah, and Tirzah is important for many reasons. In an environment of sedition, pride, and rebellion, the story shows how five young women chose obedience to all that God said to Moses. Their story also provides a great example of how women working together can effectively communicate to a traditional male leadership to make important contributions to society. Additionally, their story invites us to reverence the memory of our ancestors, to discover a connection between our current opportunities and our forebears' sacrifices. Finally, their story reminds us of the Lord's watchcare and universal love for all of His children. He is sensitive to women and parents without sons. He is also interested in the laws of the land and temporal blessings for all His children.

Zelophehad's name would have continued in the land had he been blessed with a son, but it is doubtful whether that son would have been sufficiently distinguished from all the other inheritors in order to be recorded in the Bible. Zelophehad's name and its connection to a significant law is retained in scripture and known today because he had daughters. Furthermore, even though all five daughters are named in four different passages of scripture in the Bible, they are best known by the name of their father. They are most often called "the daughters of Zelophehad." Because of their righteous petition, his name has never been forgotten.

POINTS TO PONDER: APPLICATIONS FOR OUR LIVES

1. What can we learn from the five daughters' approach to male leaders to influence policies that may be biased against certain portions of the population? What noble characteristics did the young women possess?

2. What important characteristics of leadership does Moses exemplify in this story? How did his response to the five young women show his respect for women in general?

3. How do Zelophehad's daughters inspire you to greater courage and faith in facing a challenging situation in your life?

4. Why do you think God did not tell Moses of the void in the inheritance policy when it was first decided?

5. Who was influenced by the actions and decisions of Zelophehad's daughters? What difference would their influence make in their community? For future generations?

6. How may our spiritual inheritance be jeopardized by our marriage choices?

7. What gospel principles could be taught through the example of the daughters of Zelophehad?

8. How do Mahlah, Noah, Hoglah, Milcah, and Tirzah teach us about Christ?

A Lamp unto My Feet

ABIGAIL

אֲבִיגַיִל

"My father is my joy," "My cause is joy"

*A*bigail lived during the mid to late eleventh century before Christ, when King Saul of Israel was jealously pursuing the increasingly popular David, anointed to be Israel's next ruler. Nabal, a wealthy landowner and rancher, was married to Abigail, who possessed no recognized authority or important title. From the beginning of the story, through contrasting adjectives describing this couple, Abigail's unhappiness in her ill-matched marriage to Nabal becomes apparent. The Bible describes her as being attractive and having a keen intellect (1 Samuel 25:3). According to Jewish tradition, Abigail was one of the four most beautiful women in history, along with Sarah, Rahab, and Esther (Ginzberg, *Legends,* 4:117).

In striking contrast, Abigail's husband Nabal is described as "churlish and evil in his doings" (1 Samuel 25:3). Likely *Nabal* (meaning "fool") was not his proper name but an epithet earned through frequent foolish actions (v. 25). Nabal "was of the house of Caleb" (v. 3), suggesting that he was a descendant of the inspiring and faithful Caleb who was given the area of Hebron as an inheritance in the promised land (Numbers 14:24; Joshua 14:13–14). But in Hebrew, the name *Caleb* can mean "dog," which may be why both Josephus and the Septuagint concluded that the "house of Caleb" refers to one who is dog-like with a shameful character, or, as the Bible reports, "churlish and evil in his doings." Nabal's servants found him difficult to reason with or talk to and called him "a son of Belial," meaning a worthless, wicked, or lawless man (1 Samuel 25:17, 25; see also Deuteronomy 13:13).

Despite her challenging life, however, Abigail remained faithful and trusting in God. Her greatness emerges from the Bible not in one dramatic victory but through her Christlike response to daily conflicts. Forged over a lifetime of difficulties, Abigail's disposition had a gracefully calming effect on fearful and revengeful hearts. Courageous and gentle, she possessed exceptional wisdom and fortitude to disregard the law of her abusive husband and follow the laws of God. In defiance to her

1 SAMUEL 25:2–44; 27:3; 30:1–19

2 SAMUEL 2:2; 3:3

1 CHRONICLES 3:1

LDS BIBLE DICTIONARY, 601

husband, Abigail prepared a feast for David and his army. She saved Nabal's life and salvaged the character of the future king of Israel by using her cool head and following her God-fearing heart.

The scriptural description of Nabal being "very great" suggests that he was rich in land and material possessions (1 Samuel 25:2). Nabal lived in Maon, in the hill country of Judea, south of Hebron (Joshua 15:55). More specifically, his property and possessions were in Carmel, a short distance northwest of Maon, where there was good grazing land for Nabal's flocks. By contrast, the hilly land was not productive for farming. Nabal's three thousand sheep and a thousand goats had made him a wealthy man and likely involved him in the wool industry, an economic boon for early Israel.

DAVID IN EXILE

When Samuel was a judge in Israel, the Israelites wanted one king to rule over all their separate tribes. With the Lord's consent, Samuel anointed Saul, from the tribe of Benjamin, as Israel's first king. Saul's interests, however, soon shifted from giving reverence to God to receiving adulation from his people. For example, ignoring God's command to slay the Amalekites and "utterly destroy all that they have"

TIME LINE

ca. 1040 B.C.	Saul is made king over Israel
ca. 1035 B.C.	David is born
ca. 1020 B.C.	Samuel anoints David to be Israel's future king
	David slays Goliath
	David marries Saul's daughter Michal
	David is exiled from Israel
	Samuel the prophet dies
	Abigail dissuades David from retaliating
	Nabal dies
	David marries Abigail and Ahinoam
	David and his people live in Ziklag with the Philistines
	Ziklag is attacked; Abigail and Ahinoam are abducted
ca. 1000 B.C.	The Philistines kill Saul and Jonathan
	David (30) becomes king of Judah at Hebron (2 Samuesl 5:4–5)
ca. 990 B.C.	David becomes king over united Israel
ca. 980 B.C.	Bathsheba gives birth to Solomon
ca. 960 B.C.	David dies; Solomon (20) becomes king
ca. 929 B.C.	The kingdom of Israel is divided (Judah and Israel)

(1 Samuel 15:3), King Saul and his people spared the Amalekites' best livestock to sacrifice to the Lord, as Saul later explained to Samuel. We might wonder how many of the "best of the sheep, and of the oxen, and of the fatlings, and the lambs" (v. 9) were actually sacrificed and how many of them were added to the holdings of Israelite families. Because "to obey is better than sacrifice" (v. 22), the Lord rejected Saul as king over His people and sent Samuel to anoint young David as Saul's successor (1 Samuel 16).

As Saul's effectiveness in leadership and loyalty to God continued to falter, David became increasingly loved by the people and successful in his assignments from the king. Jealous and fearful, Saul engaged an army to eliminate his supposed rival. Finally, after surviving a number of Saul's attempts on his life, David fled the capital at Gibeah, four miles northwest of Jerusalem. For ten years David sought refuge in locations where Saul was not welcome, such as Philistia, Moab, and the hill country of Judea, where David's relatives lived.

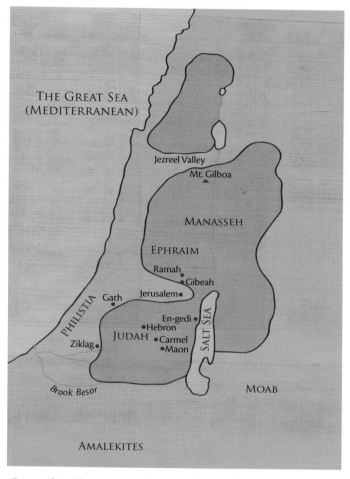

Geographical locations in the story of Abigail. Her husband owned good grazing land for his numerous flocks in Maon and Carmel.

The story of Abigail is located in the Bible between two chapters that chronicle separate encounters between Saul and David, when David could have killed his pursuer in self-defense. In the incident recorded in 1 Samuel 24, David wanted Saul to know that he could have killed him but refrained because he hoped to dispel rumors that he was seeking the king's life rather than the other way around. In 1 Samuel 26, David again came upon the king, but that incident was after he had met and married Abigail. Showing greater maturity and wisdom than he had manifested in the earlier chapter, David merely asked Saul why he was pursuing him and tried to reason with him to desist. A comparison of these two encounters with Saul show that the future king of Israel had increased in mercy, humility, and faith, whereas Saul had grown increasingly hardened and paranoid. One explanation for David's improved character may be Abigail's positive influence on him.

David encountered King Saul in En-gedi shortly before he met Abigail at Maon, a short distance farther south into the Judean wilderness.

Forming an army of six hundred supporters, David escaped from Saul and at the same time strengthened Israel's occupation of the land by protecting the southern boundaries from enemy invasion. For a time David and his men camped in the Judean wilderness near Carmel, the area where Nabal's flocks grazed. Protecting Israel's borders also meant shielding the property of Israelite families from predators and thieves. According to one of Nabal's servants, David's army was "a wall" of protection for them and was regarded as an exceptional blessing (1 Samuel 25:16).

While his army camped near Nabal's lands, David learned that Nabal's men were shearing the sheep. Traditionally, sheepshearing was a festive occasion, accompanied by a feast of celebration (Genesis 38:12). The feast, which generally coincided with the spring equinox, may have included the sacrifice of the firstborn male of the flock and was a formal time to pardon wrongs and settle debts (Wright, "Dumuze"; Geoghegan, "Israelite Sheepshearing"). If such suppositions are correct, the sheepshearing festival may have been established to point to and reverence the atoning sacrifice of Jesus Christ, the Lamb of God.

David sent ten of his men to greet Nabal and request a gift for him and his men, probably an invitation to their sheepshearing feast, in return for their service to his shepherds. David's men spoke with respect and deference to Nabal, even referring to David as "[Nabal's] son David," as though they were requesting Nabal's fatherly goodwill in their master's behalf. They explained to Nabal that they had not harmed his shepherds and made certain that nothing was taken from Nabal's servants while they were around (1 Samuel 25:4–9).

The customs of hospitality would have directed Nabal to answer favorably this request for food. Additionally, the Lord commanded His people to look after strangers so that they would remember that they had once been strangers: "But the stranger that dwelleth with you shall be unto you as one born among you, and thou shalt love him as thyself; for ye were strangers in the land of Egypt" (Leviticus 19:34).

NABAL'S INSULT

Contrary to custom and God's law, Nabal chose not to show David's army the hospitality they sought. In fact, he spoke against David in hateful tones when he heard their respectful request (1 Samuel 25:10–11). The Septuagint adds three small details to the story: Nabal's heated emotions were manifest in his actions as well as his words because he "sprang up" in reaction to the servants; Nabal's greed was the main reason for his refusal to honor David's request; and Nabal labeled David as an ingrate who had deserted his master, Saul.

Nabal's vehement reaction against David may appear surprising or curious during this time of relative peace. One may wonder how much Nabal would have known about David. It is uncertain how far David's fame had spread, but it is unlikely that Nabal could have remained unaware of the presence of an army on his land or that they were protecting his assets. Nabal's loyalty to Saul is also unexplained. Were greed and selfishness the only explanation for Nabal's spiteful response?

Consider a possible explanation for Nabal's allegiance to the king. The scene of Saul's rejection by the Lord after defeating the Amalekites occurred near Carmel (1 Samuel 15:12), the same place where Nabal's flocks grazed. This geographical area was also the location of Saul's great victory celebration, when the Israelites saved alive the Amalekites' good livestock against the Lord's commands. Saul explained to Samuel that he had disobeyed God "because I feared the people, and obeyed their voice" and that "the people took the spoil . . . to sacrifice" (vv. 21, 24). Was Nabal among "the people" who received of the victors' spoils? Had Nabal's wealth in sheep and goats grown from Saul's willingness to allow the best of the Amalekites' flocks to go to Nabal and others? Such a perk would inspire in Nabal great loyalty to King Saul and explain Nabal's adamant rejection of the king's nemesis and rival, David.

Armed with swords, David and four hundred of his men marched toward Nabal to take their revenge, while the remaining troops stayed behind to guard the army's "stuff" (1 Samuel 25:13). David's burst of violent passion against Nabal is in striking contrast to his disciplined restraint in the face of Saul's pursuit of him

In return for their protection of Nabal's servants and flocks, David asked Nabal to feed his men during the sheepshearing festival.

(1 Samuel 24). To use his God-given position of power for his personal battles is akin to priestcraft and echoes Saul's own weakness. No matter how foolish and arrogant it was, Nabal's baited insult did not justify a servant of God in retaliating with violence and bloodshed. Had David carried out his intent to destroy Nabal, he would have sinned against God and forfeited God's enabling power. The Lord, however, did not abandon David. He sent warning and counsel through the courageous and astute teachings of a woman: Abigail.

THE SERVANTS' TRUST IN ABIGAIL

In a striking show of loyalty, Nabal's servants broke with their master and trusted his wife for a solution to the problem Nabal had created for them. They rightly feared that his foolishness in having "railed" against David had invited danger for them all (1 Samuel 25:14) but recognized the futility of trying to reason directly with their employer. So they turned to Abigail. As matron of the estate, she directed the responsibilities and care for the hired help. This relationship would at least partly explain the servants' trust and openness with her, but Abigail was also approachable and a decisive woman of action. Most likely, the servants went to her rather than to Nabal when diplomacy and wise decisions were needed.

Abigail received a firsthand account of David's noble behavior toward her husband's servants. They reported that David's men had been "a wall" of protection for them against theft and attack from marauders (1 Samuel 25:16). But now David was on the warpath, prepared to take his revenge on Nabal and all of the men in Nabal's employ.

ABIGAIL'S FEAST

When placed at a crossroads where she had to decide between following her husband's unrighteous conduct and what she inherently knew was right, Abigail chose obedience to God. Like her servants, Abigail went against Nabal's directives. In a remarkable show of humility, diplomacy, and meekness, she devised a plan to appease David's anger and save innocent lives, and she did so immediately.

The word "haste" or "hasted" appears three times in the chapter to describe Abigail's perception that she had no time to delay in implementing her plan (1 Samuel 25:18, 23, 34). Her strategy included a means to assuage David's anger and deter him from his vow to destroy Nabal. It also included preparing a feast for an army and crafting a succinct and pithy petition for David, all the while keeping Nabal uninformed until the danger had subsided. She could not count on David to patiently endure an incoherent or emotional plea. Nor did she have time or, perhaps, the ability to calm her irrational husband of his buffoonery and the unrighteous dominion he would unquestionably exert to prevent her from carrying out her plan.

As an Israelite matriarch over a large household, Abigail was responsible to protect his vast assets and keep his estate running smoothly. Although she was free to travel as she chose, her various responsibilities would have kept her close to home. At the time, a woman's duties included hauling water from the closest well, grinding flour, cooking, and watching over the children and animals. Being mistress over a large estate would not have excused Abigail from heavy labor, although she would have been assisted by numerous servants in her household duties.

As mistress of Nabal's holdings, she had complete responsibility for food preparation and distribution. Abigail's feast for David's army was not a typical meal such as those usually planned for Nabal's household.

Abigail and her servants probably baked the "two hundred loaves" of bread in ovens similar to those used by these Arab women.

The foods themselves, however, were common in the Israelite diet and constituted a menu for a holy day or other special occasion.

Abigail prepared "five sheep ready dressed" for the feast (1 Samuel 25:18). The Israelites ate meat rarely because a living sheep was valuable for the wool and milk it produced. Once the sheep was killed, its value was limited to nourishment for a single day. Preparing a sheep for the feast involved slaughtering and dressing it, skinning it, and then salting and seasoning it. Next, a green tree branch was used to pierce the skinned animal lengthwise, and it rested on large rocks or forked sticks to allow the meat to cook on all sides as it turned. The animal's legs were bound to the sides to create uniform thickness for cooking. Roasted over a fire for several hours, the meat was considered cooked when it almost fell from the bones. No doubt several sheep were already roasting over fires in preparation for the sheepshearing feast when Abigail received word of David's threat.

The "bottles" of wine are more accurately translated "skins" of wine (1 Samuel 25:18), usually the skins of goats and sheep. Israelites removed the skins from slaughtered animals from the neck downward, retaining the top part of the skin from each of the limbs. The hair was cut as short as possible, the skin was tanned and turned inside out, with all the openings except one stitched closed with cords. Abigail's two wineskins could have held about ten gallons of wine each.

Abigail and her servants prepared five "measures," or seahs, of grain for the army. Because a "seah" is approximately two gallons, Abigail would have prepared some ten gallons of grain for the army's feast. Wheat and barley gave ancient peoples their basic nutrition. The grains could be eaten raw, stored for long periods of time, softened with water, ground for breadmaking, or used for seed for another season's crop.

Abigail may have heated the grain with a little water to gently soften and roast the kernels of wheat. This manner of preparation was preferable for traveling because the grain could be stored and served easily.

The fig cakes would have provided a natural source of sugar for quick energy. They were probably made by simply pressing figs and squeezing them together to form the "cakes."

Abigail ordered that all the food be laden on several donkeys and sent ahead of her. The initial strategy in her plan parallels Esther's approach to King Ahasuerus: present an array of savory and satisfying food to diffuse anger and encourage amiability. Abigail followed the traveling feast, prepared to meet David after he glimpsed the sights and savored the aromas of her banquet.

ABIGAIL MEETS DAVID'S WRATH

Abigail's initial encounter with David occurred by "the covert of the hill" (1 Samuel 25:20). Abigail may have approached a hidden hollow between two peaks in the hill country just as David and his army charged to the covert from the opposite direction. The juxtaposition of an army abruptly meeting a woman and her servants transporting a banquet laden on lumbering pack animals would have appeared surreal and near fantasy.

Despite the surprise of encountering a traveling feast, David rekindled his desire for vengeance against Nabal by repeating to Abigail his threat to destroy her husband and all his men because he had unabashedly rejected David's protection of his flocks and workers (1 Samuel 25:21). David's vulgarity in swearing that he would not leave alive any of the men of Nabal "that pisseth against the wall" (v. 22) employs startling imagery to portray the conflict between the two men. David's men were a wall of protection for Nabal's servants, and Nabal had manifested his disdain for David by symbolically relieving himself against that wall. Perhaps the author of 1 Samuel was also connecting *Nabal* to the Hebrew root of *Caleb* to suggest that Abigail's husband was no more than a dog that relieves himself wherever he chooses.

ABIGAIL'S WISDOM AND INFLUENCE

Upon meeting David and his men, Abigail "hasted, and lighted off the ass" she was riding (1 Samuel 25:23). She immediately bowed before David, falling at his feet in an act of complete humility and gratitude. Her speech to him was brilliant. In only a few words, she disarmed him and refocused him on his need for the Lord. Her brief message entailed five parts:

First, prostrated at David's feet, Abigail took Nabal's guilt upon herself (1 Samuel 25:24). Her introductory actions and words instantly began to diffuse the anger and soften a man intent on violence.

Second, she begged David to ignore Nabal. Apologizing for her husband, Abigail sought to cover his sinful insult against David by explaining that her husband was a fool who was not worth the wrath of such a great man as David. She further explained that she had been unaware of David's original request for food (1 Samuel 25:24–26).

Third, Abigail offered the army the banquet of food, a gift of gratitude for David's protection as well as restitution for Nabal's foolishness. Her blessing in the form of a feast was no doubt greater than David's army had hoped when they initially petitioned Nabal (1 Samuel 25:27).

Fourth, Abigail requested David's forgiveness while offering reminders of his importance to God in order to bring him to a conciliatory state of mind. Like a messenger from God, Abigail proclaimed her unshakable witness that David was chosen by God to lead Israel and to be made "a sure house," testifying God's promise to establish a royal legacy in David, a lineage that would rule the nation of Israel (1 Samuel 25:28–31; see also 2 Samuel 7:8ff). She also reminded him of his past obedience to God—that he had always put the Lord first—and pleaded with him not to disobey now by shedding blood.

Abigail bore witness that David's success was due to God's guidance and not to David's own intellect and strength. Her subtle message urged David not to let such a fool as Nabal become the stumbling block that prevented him from receiving God's glorious promises. If David trusted God in this matter, God would hurl David's enemies away from him, as a stone is flung from the cup of a sling (1 Samuel 25:29).

Finally, she asked David to remember her when he received the Lord's blessing by following her caution (1 Samuel 25:31). Her request for a personal blessing suggests that Abigail believed that her plan to preserve David's integrity was inspired and enabled by God.

In a sense, Abigail can be seen as a type of Christ in her reaction to David and Nabal. Without any sin or offense on her part, Abigail satisfied justice by taking upon her the sins of another, paying the debts of the sinner, and humbly bowing before her lord in righteousness. Furthermore, Abigail's own life was not in jeopardy, yet she put her life on the line to plead for the lives of numerous others. With a string of selfless actions and a fervent testimony of God, Abigail points us to Jesus Christ, who sacrificed His life for us, paid for our numerous sins and mistakes, and did it all because He loves us.

DAVID'S ACKNOWLEDGMENT

Abigail's speech softened David's heart. In reality, her sincere and inspired petition would have been difficult for any man with a conscience to refuse. David's response was that of a true disciple of the Lord. The vital importance of forgiving others and relinquishing to God personal vengeance against our enemies has always been a foundational tenet of discipleship of Christ (Romans 12:19; Mormon 3:19; D&C 64:8–11). How often do we compromise our integrity and lose the companionship of the Spirit because we assume that God's vengeance and judgments are ours to inflict upon our enemies? Too often the one who is wronged or abused is doubly hurt, first by the initial pain and then by the anger and resentment felt in response. For this reason, the Savior asks us to forgive those who have wronged us. Through this counsel, He is guiding us to let go of the anger, bitterness, and revenge that separates us from Him.

Expressing an immediate prayer of gratitude to God for sending Abigail to him, David admitted that he would have sinned against God in killing Nabal's men without hesitation had Abigail not intercepted him (1 Samuel 25:32–35). Then David thanked Abigail, communicating that he recognized her wisdom and accepted her counsel. Finally, David received her feast, assured her that he wholeheartedly forgave the insult, and invited her to return home without fear that his army would attack.

David and his men departed, devoid of vengeful emotions, satisfied with Abigail's apology, and grateful for her gifts. Nabal's servants likewise departed, relieved that through Abigail's swift intervention, their lives had been spared. And Abigail departed to confront the fool. She was now the one in great danger.

ABIGAIL'S ACCOUNTING TO NABAL

David's problems were resolved to his great satisfaction, Nabal's men were again safe from outside attack, but Abigail's situation became precarious. She faced the daunting task of confessing her actions to her arrogant and irrational husband. She had disobeyed his law to follow the law of the Lord.

Upon her return, Abigail found Nabal drunk from gorging himself on a kingly feast. Abigail must have known what he was like when he was in a drunken state and wisely waited until morning, when he was sober, to break the news of what she had done (1 Samuel 25:36). The scriptural text reports that upon hearing Abigail's report of her generous offering and agreement with David, Nabal "became as a stone" (1 Samuel 25:37). Did his shock reflect the terror he felt when he realized what might have happened had Abigail not intervened? Was it a reaction to his estimate of assets he had lost to feed David's army a feast? Or was it due to his wife disregarding his law and humiliating him in the face of his enemy? Whatever the cause, Nabal had what was likely a stroke. Ten days later, Nabal died from a second stroke or complications related to his weakened condition (1 Samuel 25:38).

In four ways, Nabal is a type of Saul: they both were threatened by David and desired to destroy him; both were wealthy and lived as kings; David protected and served both Nabal and Saul as "a wall"; and both Saul and Nabal reacted to David's generosity by refusing to recognize his service and seeking his death. With Abigail's tutelage, David was reminded that he was not divinely called to destroy individuals who disregarded and mocked those whom the Lord had called. He learned that the Lord will take care of that business in His own way and in His own time. As God took care of Nabal for David, so He would do the same with Saul.

In a different way, the Lord taught Abigail the same lesson. She could not change her husband. She could, however, trust in the Lord to find a solution to her perilous circumstances. The challenges of being married to a controlling, irrational, and hot-tempered husband were well known to Abigail. If his violent reaction to the request to feed David's army and the fear of his servants even to voice their life-threatening concerns to him are indicative of Nabal's typical temperament, it is not far-fetched to imagine abusive behavior in his relationship with Abigail, whether emotional or physical. Through God's intervention and inspiration, Abigail and other women in similarly troubled marriages can be guided to safety and a better

DAVID'S WIVES AND CHILDREN

Michal	Ahinoam	Abigail	Maacah	Haggith	Abital	Eglah	Bathsheba	other wives	concubines
	Amnon	Chileab	Absalom	Adonijah	Shephatiah	Ithream	Shimea	Ibhar	other sons
			Tamar?				Shobab	Elishama	
							Nathan	Eliphelet	
							Solomon	Nogah	
								Nepheg	
								Japhia	
								Elishama	
								Eliada	
								Eliphelet	

2 Samuel 3:2–5; 1 Chronicles 3:1–9; 2 Samuel 5:14–16; note slight differences in listings.

life when they trust in Him. Even when His enabling power is not recognized or when His rescue does not occur as soon as hoped, the Lord's watchful care never falters for those who love and serve Him.

DAVID'S MARRIAGE TO ABIGAIL

David was quick to attribute Nabal's death to God's promise that He would avenge the righteous when they trust in Him (1 Samuel 25:39). He also wasted no time in acknowledging Abigail's sudden status of widowhood. With no further explanation, David sent his servants to propose marriage to Abigail on his behalf (v. 40). The account gives no indication of what prompted David's desire to marry Abigail. He may have been motivated by her wisdom, her spiritual strength, or her physical beauty. On the other hand, he may have seen a marriage with the wealthy and wise widow as a means to garner greater political support in Judah.

With a reply that reflected the customs of hospitality in the ancient Near East, Abigail graciously consented to David's offer (1 Samuel 25:41). Her response essentially communicated that she would wash the feet of David's servants if that would communicate her profound esteem for him and his proposal. Abigail "hasted," wasting no time in putting her reply into action, again indicating her decisive nature and firm resolve (v. 42). That she traveled to David in the company of five maid servants is further evidence of the prosperous lifestyle she had known in Maon.

DAVID'S WIVES AND CHILDREN

About the same time as his betrothal to Abigail, David married a woman named Ahinoam and lost his first wife, Michal, to another man (1 Samuel 25:43–44). No account of Ahinoam appears in the Bible, except that she was from Jezreel, a community not far from Nabal's Carmel (Joshua 15:55–56). The Bible narrative does explain David's loss of Michal to her father's abuse of his kingly power. King Saul likely decided to take his daughter Michal from David and give her to another man because marriage to the reigning king's daughter would give David a claim to the throne. With this heartless edict, Saul probably hoped to eliminate an argument that David could have used to inherit Saul's power.

David eventually married several other women, who collectively gave him numerous sons and daughters, some of whom are named in scripture (2 Samuel 3:2–5; 5:14–16; 1 Chronicles 3:1–9).

THE AMALEKITES ABDUCT ABIGAIL AND AHINOAM

With Abigail, Ahinoam, and his army to support him, David turned to the nation of Philistia for refuge from Saul. Because the Philistines perceived that any enemy of Saul's was a friend to them, King Achish of Gath offered David sanctuary in the city of Ziklag, about twenty to twenty-five miles south of Gath (1 Samuel 26:5–6). The area of Ziklag was part of the inheritance of the tribe of Simeon when the Israelites conquered it under Joshua (Joshua 15:31; 19:1–5), but it had subsequently been recaptured by the Philistines.

During the year and four months that David remained in Ziklag as a fugitive from Saul (1 Samuel 26:7), he feigned support for Philistia in his attack on surrounding peoples. In reality, David was attacking Israel's enemies and clearing the land for his own future kingdom (vv. 8–12). Remembering God's covenant to give that land to the Israelites, David and his six hundred men attacked such other peoples as the Amalekites who encroached on "Israelite land." All the while David was being protected among the Philistines. At the same time, David strengthened his support base among the people of Judah by distributing booty from his raids to the inhabitants of the Negeb, or southern Judah.

David's ploy worked until the Philistines commissioned him to fight on their side against Saul and Jonathan and the Israelites at Mount Gilboa, a mountainous area east of the Jezreel plain in the territory of Issachar. On the eve of the battle, David escaped the dilemma when one of the Philistine

David's palace in Jerusalem was built in the City of David, near the site where the temple would be built during Solomon's reign. This three-dimensional map of Jerusalem, depicting the city at the time of Solomon, shows the temple area at the bottom right and the City of David in the enclosed area at the bottom left. The palace was built close to the temple but on a lower elevation.

princes questioned David's loyalty to Philistia and sent him and his men back to Ziklag (1 Samuel 29).

The journey from the battle site near the Jezreel Valley to Ziklag took David and his army three days (1 Samuel 30:1). Upon arriving at their city of refuge, David discovered that another people, the Amalekites, had invaded Ziklag. Descended from Esau, son of Isaac and Rebekah (Genesis 36:12, 16), the Amalekites had become a nomadic people over the centuries and were in continual conflict with the Israelites from the time they entered the land. While David and his army were away with the Philistines, the Amalekites burned the community of Ziklag and took captive all the women and children, including Abigail and Ahinoam (1 Samuel 30:1–5). As David and his men prepared to pursue the attackers and rescue their families and possessions, both King Saul and his son Jonathan were killed by the Philistines in battle at Mount Gilboa (1 Samuel 31).

DAVID RESCUES ABIGAIL AND AHINOAM

Facing his discouraged and angry men while tasting the bitterness of his own loss of family, David "encouraged himself in the Lord" (1 Samuel 30:6). How much of David's confidence in the Lord's enabling power was strengthened by Abigail's testimony and influence? Knowing that Abigail trusted in the grace of God, was David encouraged that God would empower him to rescue his wives and people? In response to David's prayer, God promised him that "thou shalt surely overtake [the Amalekites], and without fail recover all" (1 Samuel 30:8).

Crossing the brook Besor with four hundred of his men, David soon came upon an Egyptian mercenary who had fought with the Amalekites until he fell ill three days before. David's men fed him and returned him to better health. David vowed that he would spare the Egyptian's life and not return him to the Amalekite captain if the man would lead them to the Amalekite camp (1 Samuel 30:11–15).

When David's army came upon their enemies, the Amalekites were spread out over a large area and heavy with victory celebration due to their lucrative raids. They were an easy target. David's surprise attack garnered a complete recovery of their possessions and the safe rescue of all of their women and children, including David's wives, Abigail and Ahinoam (1 Samuel 30:16–19). The scriptures also suggest that David's men recovered not only all that had been taken from them but also additional loot taken by the Amalekites, which David subsequently shared with Israelites in various cities of Judah (1 Samuel 30:26–31). The Amalekites disappear from the biblical narrative after this defeat at the hands of David's army.

ABIGAIL'S LATER YEARS

Although very little further mention of Abigail is chronicled in the Bible, her whereabouts and some of her general activities may be deduced. Abigail and Ahinoam accompanied David to Hebron when he was named and anointed king of the tribe of Judah (2 Samuel 2:1–4). David was "thirty years old when he began to reign," and he ruled over Judah in Hebron for seven and a half years of his forty-year reign (2 Samuel 5:4–5). While living in Hebron as a wife of the king, Abigail gave birth to David's second son, whom they named Chileab (also called Daniel; 2 Samuel 3:3; Chronicles 3:1). That Chileab is not mentioned in the Bible beyond his birth hints that he died young.

When David was named king of all the tribes of Israel, he conquered Jerusalem and moved his capital there. Because he had taken his wives with him to Hebron, we assume that David took with him into Jerusalem his wives Abigail, Ahinoam, and others aligned with David during his reign in Hebron (2 Samuel 3:2–6). After establishing his palace in Jerusalem, David would add yet another wife to his household, Bathsheba, the wife of one of his "mighty men" (2 Samuel 11:26–27). Furthermore, after the death of King Saul, David used his royal position to demand the return of his first wife, Michal, much to the chagrin of her second husband (2 Samuel 3:13–16). Apparently, Michal was not happy with the decree to return to David, either; she was cloistered away in Jerusalem as punishment for her outspoken criticism against him when he made his celebratory entry into the city (2 Samuel 6:20–23). The scriptures are silent, however, about Abigail's life in Jerusalem as one of the king's wives.

Recent archaeological explorations in what would have been the ancient City of David have uncovered a large stone structure that appears to have been constructed shortly after David took Jerusalem from the Jebusites (2 Samuel 5:6–10). The structure sits above the well-known stepped-stone structure now believed to have been part of the same ancient edifice. From the material remains, archaeologists have posited that this may have been David's royal palace (Mazar). Did Abigail reside in this beautiful residence along with King David's other wives?

The six- to eight-foot wide walls, massive ashlars, and impressive design suggest that the building was a costly endeavor and an exquisite edifice. Of particular note is an elegant, five-foot-long, proto-Ionic capital that has survived to the present day. To imagine the column that must have supported the capital and the multiple replications of that column in an impressive hallway in the palace complex gives a hint of the grandeur that surrounded King David and may also have adorned Abigail's later life.

Yet after David's affair with Bathsheba, calamity and heartache followed him and perhaps every other member of his family. David's oldest son, Amnon,

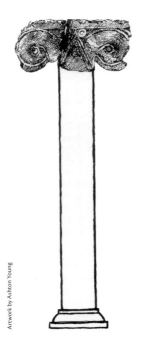

Artwork by Ashton Young

Explorations in the 1960s found this elegant proto-Ionic capital among ashlars at the base of what recent archaeologists believe may have been King David's palace.

raped his half-sister Tamar (2 Samuel 13:1–18). Absalom, David's third son and full brother to Tamar, killed Amnon in retaliation (2 Samuel 13:19–29). Did Amnon's death put Absalom next in line to the throne? Clearly, Absalom campaigned for popularity among the Israelites. After overtly taking his father's concubines, Absalom was killed by David's general, all before David was sixty-five years old (2 Samuel 16:20–23; 18:9–17).

A large stepped structure (perhaps the "Millo" of 2 Samuel 5:9; 1 Kings 11:27) was erected to fortify the side of a hill. Archaeologists excavating above the stepped structure believe they have found remnants of David's palace.

Because Abigail did not have a son who lived beyond childhood, her role and potential influence likely diminished. Life in the palace without family or responsibilities could have been lonely and unfulfilling. Seeing Abigail in her earlier years, however, suggests that her wisdom and resourcefulness would have assisted her to find much she could do to improve circumstances within the palace and in the growing city. Because they had shared unique experiences together early in their relationship with each other as David's wives, perhaps Abigail and Ahinoam became close friends and confidantes. That relationship and camaraderie alone could have made a significant difference in their later years.

In many ways, a comparison between Abigail and Bathsheba, a later wife of David, provides insight into Abigail's role and influence. Consider a few points of comparison. Both Abigail and Bathsheba were married to other men before they married David. Abigail's first husband was evil and irresponsible; Bathsheba's first husband was brave, good, and highly responsible. Abigail restrained David from killing unnecessarily; driven by his lust for Bathsheba, David ordered her husband's sure death. Abigail saw and certainly influenced David's rise to greater goodness, virtue, and faith in God; Bathsheba was the unfortunate witness of David's dramatic decline in virtue, restraint, and humility.

Abigail's story gains importance by showing God's hand in David's righteous reign. Through Abigail's prescient words, we hear the foreshadowing of David's legitimate rule and God's endorsement of David in that role. Through Abigail's wise approach to serious problems, David learned to control his anger and desire for revenge. He remembered to turn to God for protection and direction rather than confronting threats with destruction alone. Undoubtedly, David's future success in leadership and being loved by the people was, in part, due to Abigail's influence. Finally, Abigail's story brings out one of David's more endearing and remarkable qualities: He was willing to accept wise counsel from a woman.

But Abigail's importance vastly exceeds her rescue of David. Her story has the potential to inspire and encourage each of us in our daily struggles and devotion to the Lord. Abigail exemplifies the powerful influence of a wise woman's diplomacy in sidestepping one man's ignorant actions and another's vengeful pride to inspire the best in everyone. Far from living a dream life, Abigail remained an obedient and loving disciple of the Lord. Her pain and daily difficulties magnified for her the truth that only through reliance on the Savior could she find peace. She illustrates how a woman in pain can forgive enemies, compassionately serve others, and remain optimistic about the future. As one who trusted God and His laws over all others, Abigail can bolster our faith and willing dependence on the Only One who has power to save.

POINTS TO PONDER: APPLICATIONS FOR OUR LIVES

1. What can Abigail teach us about diffusing contention in times of conflict?

2. What characteristics can be found in Abigail that you would like to emulate? What would she include in a lesson about patience? About mercy? About wisdom? About God's providence?

3. The apostle John taught that "we are the sons of God . . . and when [God] shall appear, we shall be like him" (1 John 3:2). How was Abigail a type of Christ? How can she inspire women and men today to develop Christlike attributes to become more like Him?

4. How does Abigail's example give direction and hope to women who find themselves in a troubled marriage with no solution in sight? What legal protections and recourse do we have today that could have provided Abigail and her male servants additional options had they been available in her day?

5. What could Nabal's "double" death symbolize? (see page 208). How could Abigail inspire us to greater strength and faith even when God does not take away our adversary?

6. What principles of the gospel do we see taught through Abigail's story?

7. How does Abigail encourage us to more fully rely on Christ and trust in His command to forgive those who have hurt us?

UNNAMED WOMEN

In both the Bible and other ancient Near East literature, names often held important significance. A name reflected the essence of a person—his or her character, family connection and ancestry, religious affiliation, or even prophetic future. At times a name echoed society's view of an individual or the family's appreciation of the natural world around them.

Mothers were more likely than fathers in the Old Testament record to select names for their children. The preeminence of women in this important practice may be indicative of the intimacy that mothers and infants shared. It may also be evidence of the authority a woman continued to wield in domestic and family affairs throughout all biblical eras.

Recognizing the value that ancient societies placed on personal names, we are puzzled why so many men and women remain unnamed in scripture, especially when a significant aspect of their lives was recounted in the sacred text. Consider, in New Testament times, the Samaritan woman at the well who recognized that Jesus was the Christ and the Roman centurion whose faith was so great that the Savior immediately healed his beloved servant (John 4; Luke 7:1–10). In the Book of Mormon, the brother of Jared led the Jaredite people to the New World through his unshakable trust in the Lord, and King Lamoni's queen exemplified greater faith than all the Nephites—but their names are not recorded (Ether 1–3; Alma 19).

The same holds true in Old Testament writings. For example, we know the name of Naaman, the Syrian captain, but not the name of "the little maid" who inspired him to visit God's prophet to be healed (2 Kings 5). The name of the wicked queen Jezebel, who fought against the prophet Elijah, is recorded, but the name of the widow who sacrificed all to feed Elijah is not (1 Kings 17). Although the name of Elisha's servant Gehazi is known, we know only that Shunem was the hometown of the woman who sheltered and fed Elisha each time he traveled through the area (2 Kings 4).

No consistent practice is followed in either providing the names of women who played major roles in the biblical narrative or refraining from giving the names of ancillary characters. For example, Zeruiah is identified by name in twenty-five verses of scripture (e.g., 2 Samuel 2:13; 18:2; 1 Kings 1:7). The only facts communicated about her throughout them all, however, are that she is a sister to King David and the mother of at least three sons, one being Joab, captain of David's army. Each time one of her sons is mentioned, she is identified as his mother (e.g., 2 Samuel 18:2). Beyond those facts, she is not portrayed as doing or saying anything that influenced the course of events. But we know her name.

On the other hand, the story of the Egyptian seductress who attempted a tryst with Joseph when he was a slave in her husband's house has inspired many lessons on fleeing temptation and choosing moral cleanliness. She is known only by the name of her husband—the wife of Potiphar (Genesis 39). Similarly, the woman who could not let go of the world and persisted in looking back, against the Lord's directive, and was subsequently turned to salt is only known as the wife of Lot (Genesis 19:15–26). She has become an icon to warn latter-day believers to look to the future with faith and to trust the Lord's Atonement to cover the sins of our past.

In one of the most curious and troubling stories of the Old Testament, Jephthah sacrificed his daughter to keep a vow he had made to God (Judges 11:30–40). The details that are recorded generate more questions than answers. Why would Jephthah make such a rash vow, to sacrifice whatever emerged first from his house? Why was his daughter apparently complicit in allowing her father to keep his vow? Where was the girl's mother? Adding to the confusion of the story, the New Testament lists Jephthah among the faithful (Hebrews 11:32). The "daughters of Israel" mourned the daughter of Jephthah every year for four days, but her name and additional explanation are not found in scripture (Judges 11:40).

Many other unnamed women of the Old Testament lived in extraordinary times. We wonder, for example, what we could learn from the insights of Noah's wife in a postdiluvian world. We know simply that she and her family survived the destruction. Did Melchizedek have a wife? We assume so, although no mention is made of her. Certainly, her perspective and lessons from society at that unique time would be valuable to us today. What might have been said of Sarah's mother or one of two daughters of Adam and Eve? Innumerable stories in scripture are merely alluded to.

The Pearl of Great Price supplies additional glimpses of stories, such as Abraham's reports of the three daughters of Onitah (Abraham 1:11). Likening these nameless women to Shadrach, Meshach, and Abednego (Daniel 3), Elder Neal A. Maxwell observed: "Matching those three men are three young women whose names we do not have. They are mentioned in the book of Abraham, remarkable young women about whom I am anxious to know more. They were actually sacrificed upon the altar because 'they would not bow down to worship [an idol] of wood or stone' (Abraham 1:11). Some day the faithful will get to meet them" (*Not My Will,* 120). The anticipation of meeting these women one day promises opportunities to learn more from them, including their names.

Because groups of women are often referenced in the Old Testament, the number of nameless women cannot be estimated, let alone counted. Consider the "wise-hearted women" who spun with their hands the beautiful blue, purple, and scarlet linen for the tabernacle in the wilderness (Exodus 35:25–26). We cannot calculate the number of women artisans who gave their time and talents to weave and spin these striking colors to show reverence to the Lord (Exodus 35:35). The laver of the tabernacle was constructed using brass mirrors that women contributed, and women were part of the assembly of worshippers at the door of the tabernacle (Exodus 38:8). Although we know neither their number nor their names, we can recognize that each of them had a story. What had each learned through her sacrifices and hardships? What did the tabernacle come to mean to each woman because of her participation in its construction?

In many instances, unnamed individuals are arguably more noteworthy and inspiring than their named counterparts. So why were their names not recorded? One suggestion is that the omission was made consciously to protect the individual from being maligned. Because we *do* know the names of many remarkable and chosen women, such as Eve and Mary, the mother of Jesus, this suggestion rings hollow. By contrast, in one instance, the Lord specifically commanded that the names of the Three Nephites *not* be recorded (3 Nephi 28:25). Because their mission is to minister anonymously on the earth until the Savior returns, their being unnamed further assures their anonymity. Such a circumstance is unique, however, and does not fit other stories of unnamed individuals in scripture.

Perhaps the simplest explanation for the omission of names is that the author of the record did not know the name or did not perceive it was important to include. Most scholars estimate that many parts of the Old Testament were written centuries after the events occurred, suggesting that an individual's actions were remembered much longer than his or her name. One thing is certain, however. The unnamed individuals are as precious to the Lord as are the named ones.

Whatever the reason for the absence of names, unexpected benefits are derived from the lack of some names. First, studying the scriptural account of an individual's role, contribution, challenges, and victories without knowing the person's name invites us to place sharper focus on decisions made and actions taken rather than on the individual. Second, we often find ourselves more closely identifying with people in scripture who are not named than with those whose names are recorded. Finally, not knowing a person's name frequently directs us to see and praise God's influence in the story and avoid glorifying someone who has need of a Redeemer, as do we all.

This section will explore the choices, reactions, and manifestation of faith apparent in three unnamed women in the Old Testament: the widow of Zarephath, the Shunammite, and the Little Maid.

Charity Never Faileth

THE WIDOW OF ZAREPHATH
אַלְמְנַת צָרְפַת

The widow of Zarephath represents all of us who are poor in the eyes of the world. She was remembered by the Lord, however, as she was rich in spirit and in faith. Near death because of lack of food during a drought, she and her son lacked family support or other resources. Coupled with her profound poverty, she was a Phoenician, living in a community that belonged to the kingdom of Sidon, among a people who worshipped idols and rejected the God of Israel.

At the same time the widow was suffering for want of food, another woman of Phoenicia, Jezebel, daughter of the king of Sidon, was married to the king of Israel. Although they were contemporaries in the ninth century before Christ, growing up to adulthood in the same culture, and living within eight miles of each other, Jezebel was the opposite of the widow of Zarephath in every imaginable way. Jezebel knew only luxury; she had never known sacrifice except in performing self-aggrandizing rituals. She was reared in a king's palace and married to the heir to the throne of Israel. After she moved to the kingdom of Israel, she and her husband, Ahab, established an elaborate palace in their new capital of Samaria and embellished it with exquisite ivory inlays (1 Kings 22:39; Amos 6:4–6).

We have no evidence that the widow in Zarephath ever encountered Jezebel, but the prophet Elijah knew them both. Jezebel considered Elijah her mortal enemy, and he became the mortal savior of the widow of Zarephath. Their stories intertwined during a lengthy drought, which occurred as a direct response from God to Jezebel's wicked and pervasive religious practices. The Bible does not indicate whether Jezebel suffered during the famine, but the poor certainly did, including those north of Israel in Phoenicia. The prophets were also afflicted, including Elijah.

The story of the widow of Zarephath occurred after Elijah fled to the brook Cherith at the beginning of the drought and before the contest with Jezebel's idolatrous priests that ended the three-and-a-half-year famine. More than eight hundred years after these events, Jesus Christ

1 KINGS 17:8–24
LUKE 4:25–26

In contrast to the widow's extreme poverty, Jezebel lived in a palace filled with ivory embellishments. These representations of ancient ivory inlays suggest the opulence of Jezebel's surroundings.

reminded the Jews in Nazareth of the remarkable faith of this Gentile woman in Zarephath (*Sarepta* in the New Testament Greek) who put love of God before all others, including her son. There were many widows who lived in Israel and who were suffering from the drought, Jesus told them, but God sent Elijah (*Elias* in the New Testament Greek) to a Gentile widow.

The people of Nazareth had just heard Jesus give a powerful spiritual witness of His divinity, but they were searching for reasons to discount and deny it. The Savior indicated to the Jews of His hometown that Gentiles recognized and responded to the witness of the Spirit more readily than they did, even though they had been taught the ways of the Lord in their synagogue (Luke 4:25–28).

Presented as a foil for the believing widow of Zarephath, Jezebel is remembered today as the most wicked woman in the Bible. Ironically, we know the name of the evil one, but the name of the righteous one is known only to the Lord. Curiously, rabbinic literature contains various attempts to name the widow's son, even identifying him as Jonah, the prophet sent to preach repentance to the Assyrians in Nineveh a century later (Ginzberg, *Legends,* 4:197). By contrast, in rabbinic literature no suggestions were made for the boy's mother. She continues to be known simply as the widow of Zarephath.

Because the political environment and religious culture were responsible for the trying circumstances in Israel and Phoenicia, a discussion of the historical context and political dynamics surrounding the widow's story is important. A larger picture of the prophet Elijah's ministry is also presented to introduce his experiences in Zarephath.

POLITICAL CONDITIONS DURING THE OMRIDE DYNASTY

About fifty years after the northern tribes of Israel broke away from Judah to form their own kingdom, Omri, the captain of Israel's army, was crowned the monarch of the northern kingdom. Israel had certain advantages over the southern kingdom of Judah: more land (including the most fertile land), greater population, and key locations that offered control of important trade routes. Weakened by internal conflicts, evil kings, and poor leadership, however, Israel had lost its military dominance by the time Omri ascended to the throne. Especially vulnerable to the dangerous advances of King Ben-hadad of Syria, Israel was diminished through its loss of border towns in Transjordan and undermined by Ben-hadad's treaty with Phoenicia. When a flailing Israel welcomed the inexperienced Omri as king, Syria recognized an invitation to expand its territory.

Omri and his descendants, however, posed a greater threat to the Syrians than they anticipated. During the Omride dynasty (885–841 B.C.), Israel regained its military might, achieved internal peace, and made alliances with all of its neighbors. For example, Israel forged a loyal connection with Phoenicia when Ahab, the son of King Omri, married Jezebel, the daughter of the Phoenician king Ethbaal (1 Kings 16:31). This alliance offered Israel expanded commercial ventures to ship their products through the great Phoenician ports of Sidon and Tyre. Later, when Ahab became king of Israel, he nurtured the relationship with Judah by giving his daughter Athaliah in marriage to the son of Judah's king (2 Kings 8:18). Under the rule of Ahab and Jezebel, Israel even formed a coalition with Syria. A more dangerous peril was brewing in the East, heralding greater hazards for Israel in the future. Assyria, the rising power in Mesopotamia, was consuming every sovereign that opposed it. For a time, the coalition between Israel and its neighbors kept Assyria in check.

Israel's foreign policies and political clout may have been impressive under the Omrides, but conditions at home fell into a dire religious and economic oppression. Very few enjoyed luxuries and pleasures in ninth-century Israel, but the numbers of the poor and needy increased dramatically. Archaeological findings suggest that the royal court enjoyed tremendous material prosperity, as evidenced by

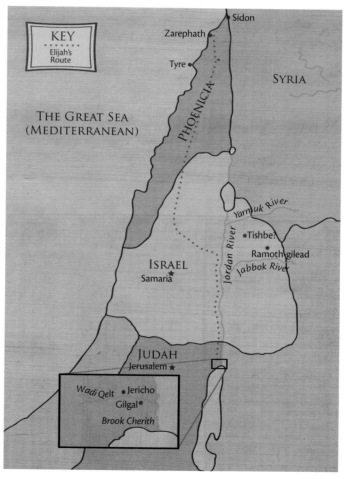

Geographical locations important to the ministry of the prophet Elijah.

THE OMRIDE DYNASTY

Omri (885–874 B.C.) began his rule from Tirzah, in the territory of Manasseh, and then purchased land to establish a new palace in Samaria (1 Kings 16:23–24).

Ahab (874–853 B.C.), son of Omri, was even more wicked than his father. Omri married Jezebel of Phoenicia and followed her worship of Ba'alim; he died from wounds suffered in battle against the Syrians (1 Kings 22).

Ahaziah (853–852 B.C.), son of Ahab and Jezebel, followed the evil ways of his parents but reigned only a few months before dying of wounds received in battle (1 Kings 22:51–53).

Joram/Jehoram (852–841 B.C.) was the son of Ahab and Jezebel; he rejected the worship of Ba'alim but promoted evil in other ways (2 Kings 3:1–3); his importance was overshadowed by the continued influence of Jezebel.

the superior workmanship of ivory carvings and inlays found in the remains of the Omride palace in Samaria. Impressive improvements in fortifications around key defense cities, sophisticated designs for water systems, and numerous stables for the horses meant to pull the massive fleet of chariots further suggest the wealth of the Omride dynasty. Moreover, Ahab and Jezebel saw nothing wrong in claiming property they desired for themselves, and they stooped to any depth of viciousness to secure it (1 Kings 21).

THE WORSHIP OF BA'ALIM

As oppressive to the people of Israel as the Omrides' economic policy was, the greater threat to Israel's security and progress came from the religious influence of Ahab's foreign wife. Although none of the kings of the northern kingdom proved loyal to the Lord, the Omride dynasty is best known for its unprecedented evil and wholesale rejection of Jehovah. Especially under Ahab and his lengthy twenty-two-year rule (ca. 874–853 B.C.), wickedness, including the worship of idols, flourished among the Israelites. Not content with having a temple and priests to facilitate her native religious practices in her new homeland, Jezebel sought to make her worship of Ba'alim the official religion of the Israelite court. (Collectively, all the gods in the Canaanite pantheon are referred to as Ba'alim.)

Together, Ahab and Jezebel worshipped the various Canaanite deities, including the god Ba'al and his consort, Asherah. As the storm god, Ba'al was believed to control the weather and send the needed rain. Asherah was the cult's fertility goddess. She was believed to make the earth fruitful and the harvest abundant when her followers performed erotic rituals that mocked everything that was sacred to Jehovah.

Jezebel succeeded in plunging Israel into the nadir of spiritual decline. Josephus described her as "active and bold" (*Antiquities,* 8.13.1). Interestingly, Ahab chose names for his sons that reflected the sacred Israelite worship: *Ahaziah* means "Jehovah upholds," and *Jehoram* means "Jehovah is high" (LDS Bible Dictionary, 605; Orr, *Encyclopaedia,* 3:1580).

On the other hand, Ahab willingly supported everything Jezebel sought to change in Israel. Still not satisfied when the people of the court were practicing Ba'alism, Jezebel sought to destroy any who opposed her religion. Specifically, Jezebel hunted down and killed any who professed and practiced the gospel of Jehovah (1 Kings 18:13). At the same time the Omrides were expanding their nation's military might and political clout, they were leading their people into moral filth and idolatry.

Encouraged by Jezebel's fervent idolatry, Ahab built a temple, an altar, and pillars to Ba'alim in their capital city of Samaria. The pillars were carved posts or trees that stood as fertility symbols in the worship of the goddess Asherah. For their licentious rituals, Ahab and Jezebel also established "high places," which were fertile elevations believed to be especially attractive to their gods and therefore inviting of divine approval in their petitions and practices.

Unfortunately, many in Israel forgot God and followed after the Ba'alim of Ahab and Jezebel. Presumably, many Canaanites with beliefs similar to Jezebel's had previously been absorbed into Israel during all the conquests and had become adherents of Israel's faith. Because of Jezebel, their conversions were likely in name only as they looked for ways to trans-

Artwork by Ashton Young

Considered the god of storms, Ba'al was an important deity in the Canaanite pantheon. As his name indicates, Ba'al was "lord" and master over the harvest. Many Iron Age depictions of Ba'al show him with a club in his right hand, representing strength, and a lightning rod in his left hand, indicating he was god over the elements.

form Israel's beliefs to include their own rituals of idol worship. One wonders how many descendants of Canaanite converts were waiting for an opportunity to shake off their feigned allegiance to Israel's "foreign" God and return to their religious heritage of Ba'al worship. Jezebel and Ahab afforded them an open invitation.

A prophet boldly challenged this mélange of wishy-washy disciples: "How long halt ye between two opinions? If the Lord be God, follow him: but if Baal, then follow him" (1 Kings 18:21). Emphasizing their spineless attitudes further, the Hebrew reads, "How long will you *limp* between two opinions?" Israel abandoned the Lord, and the Lord sought to humble them. He sealed up the heavens for more than three years, resulting in widespread drought and famine that reached at least as far as Jezebel's homeland. Yet the royal couple continued to mock Elijah and his God (Ginzberg, *Legends*, 4:196).

Meanwhile, the widow of Zarephath was caught in the pains of famine in Phoenicia.

ELIJAH'S PROPHETIC COUNSEL

In the midst of these dark days in Israel, God sent His prophet Elijah to warn the Israelites to remember their reverence of Him. The scriptural text introduces Elijah as a "Tishbite," a term that is generally accepted to mean someone who came from a town in Gilead called Tishbeh, between the Jabbok and Yarmuk Rivers on the east bank of the Jordan, although the exact location is uncertain.

Clad in hairy garments, Elijah resembled our first parents and the ancient patriarchs (2 Kings 1:8). Their similar animal-skin coverings prophetically pointed to the divine power of the Lamb of God, who would give His life to save the world. As Elijah's name indicates ("Jehovah is my God"; LDS Bible Dictionary, 664), his prophetic mission is remembered by the manner in which he made visible the reality and grandeur of Israel's God while at the same time exposing the futility of Jezebel's gods (1 Kings 17–19, 21; 2 Kings 1–2). He showed the wavering Israelites that Jehovah is the only true God and that Ba'alim possessed no power at all.

Centuries before, the Lord had warned the Israelites that an abundant harvest depended on their love and service to Him and that He would stop the rain if they worshipped other gods (Deuteronomy 11:13–17). According to one Jewish Midrash, Jezebel and Ahab considered the drought as evidence that Elijah's God was powerless to demand His people's devotion. Elijah's first illustration was therefore a perfect one to show that Ba'alim possessed no influence over the rainfall and harvest. Jehovah stopped the rainfall, which

TIME LINE

885 B.C.	Omri begins his reign as king of Israel
	Ahab, son of Omri, marries Jezebel.
874 B.C.	Ahab inherits the throne of Israel.
	Jezebel hunts the prophets of God.
	Elijah declares a drought of three and a half years.
	Elijah is nourished at the brook Cherith.
	The widow of Zarephath feeds Elijah.
	Elijah restores the widow's son to life.
	Elijah and the priests of Ba'al compete.
865 B.C.	Ahab's daughter, Athaliah, marries the heir to the throne of Judah.
	Ahab reaches the zenith of military success in the northern kingdom.
853 B.C.	Ahab dies in battle in Syria.
	Elijah is taken up in a chariot of fire; the mantle of prophetic power falls upon Elisha.
	Jezebel dies as Elijah foretold.

prevented a harvest and resulted in the widespread famine. Prayers to the storm god and rituals to the fertility goddess did not bring the needed water or abate the serious famine. Through a three-and-one-half-year drought, God showed that Baal does not control the weather or supply a bounteous harvest (Luke 4:25–26; James 5:17–18). Jehovah is God, and none other.

To prove that Ba'al was impotent, Elijah challenged the priests of Baal to a contest that required each side to call down help from their God. When Elijah's God proved to be the only One with power, the Israelites repented of their idolatry, and God restored precipitation and vegetation (1 Kings 18).

FINDING SUSTENANCE AT THE BROOK CHERITH

Although God caused the drought, Elijah the prophet was not spared the suffering, discomforts, and uncertainties of famine; neither were other followers of the Lord who lived under Ahab's rule. The scriptures recount only how the faithful Elijah was sustained, but no doubt other believers had their own miraculous experiences of divine deliverance. The obvious purpose for the famine was to warn the wicked Ahab and Jezebel and those who worshipped their gods of calamitous consequences if they did not repent. But through trials, God could also teach those who believed in Him valuable lessons of preparation and faith. Elijah and others learned to rely wholly on the Lord for divine sustenance and not look to the powers of the world.

The Lord prepared Elijah to go to Zarephath by sending him first to hide in the seclusion of the wilderness during the early stages of the drought. Subsisting on water that trickled down the brook (or wadi) Cherith and on food that was delivered by ravens, Elijah became completely reliant on the Lord for his survival.

A wadi is a narrow gorge through which water pours after heavy rains. The exact location of the brook Cherith is unknown but is thought to be one of the gorges that empties into the River Jordan. Cherith may have been near Elijah's hometown on the east side of the Jordan or as far away as the Wadi Qelt, near Jericho, on the West Bank. The area of the brook appears to have been within Israelite territory but outside King Ahab's influence.

Wadi Qelt cuts deep into the Judean wilderness, going east through Jericho to finally meet the Jordan River. Elijah was sustained by water from one of the gorges, or wadis, that empties into the Jordan River.

A Jewish Midrash posits that the righteous Jehosaphat, who was king of Judah at the time, sent the ravens carrying food from his royal larder in Jerusalem to nourish and support Elijah (Ginzberg, *Legends*, 4:196). The prophet was safe from Ahab and Jezebel as long as he remained near the brook Cherith, but prolonged hiding was not the Lord's ultimate mission for Elijah. Therefore, the brook dried up and the Lord told a Phoenician woman to prepare for a visitor (1 Kings 17:7–9).

RECEIVING LIFE-GIVING SUSTENANCE FROM THE WIDOW

It was one thing to camp near a stream of water and wait for ravens to deliver food, but quite another to travel into the heart of enemy territory in order to survive. Specifically, God sent Elijah to a Phoenician town called Zarephath, about eight miles south of Sidon and twelve miles north of Tyre. His assignment was to search out a particular widow whom God had already chosen to care for him. The peculiarity of this command could not have escaped Elijah. Jezebel was from the Ba'al-worshipping stronghold of Sidon. Now God was asking Elijah to go to a town that belonged to Sidon and ask a woman there to take care of him (1 Kings 17:9).

Scripture often links widows with orphans, the poor, and strangers while at the same time acknowledging God's particular compassion for them (Deuteronomy 10:18; 26:12; Malachi 3:5; James 1:27; D&C 83:6). The "stranger" in Israelite societies specifically included Gentiles, or those whose faith differed from the worship of Jehovah and who were not culturally related to the people of Israel. God commanded the Israelites to love strangers, remembering that they also were once "strangers in the land of Egypt" (Deuteronomy 10:19). The woman whom God called to assist Elijah represented every category of defenseless ones: she had lost her husband, her son was fatherless, and she was a Gentile, a stranger to the Israelites.

The widows, the fatherless, and strangers were the vulnerable and unprotected in society. They were the ones without family connection, without anyone to champion their cause or care for their needs. Therefore, the law of Moses specifically provided for their care and threatened curses on those who hurt or neglected them (Exodus 22:21–22; Deuteronomy

Artwork by Ashton Young

The gate to a city was closed at night for the protection of the inhabitants, but during the day the area around it was bustling with activity.

24:17–21). Prophetic counsel given during the era of the divided kingdoms indicates that the law was often ignored, resulting in widows, fatherless, and strangers being oppressed (Ezekiel 22:7; Jeremiah 7:8; Isaiah 1:17).

Furthermore, as God's prophet and Jezebel's mortal enemy, Elijah could easily have been viewed as the most powerful person in the kingdom of Israel at the time. On the other hand, the widow of Zarephath could just as easily have been seen as the least

Iron Age gate into the city of Dan, with chambers for sitting and conversing. It is from approximately the same time period when Elijah met the widow at the gate to the city of Zarephath, which may have had similar chambers.

important to Israel: She lacked any recognizable power, was an outsider to Israel, and had no resources of material worth. Yet, the Lord sent the greatest to depend on the least. What a magnificent lesson in humility and added faith in the One who is "least in the kingdom of God" and yet "greater" than all others (Luke 7:28).

As in all of God's challenging circumstances, this lesson was not just to prepare and fortify Elijah. The Lord had something to teach the widow as well. Her encounters with the Israelite prophet would be life changing, faith building, and empowering.

Of all the people who were likely in view in Zarephath, how did Elijah recognize this one woman as the widow whom God had prepared to nourish him? Did she wear dark and particularly plain clothing or some other specific type or color of dress that designated her as a widow? (2 Samuel 14:2). Was her plight apparent in the effort it took her to walk or by her weakened condition as she bent to gather sticks? Was Elijah expecting her to be an elderly woman, as is often assumed of a widow? Because the Lord revealed to Elijah that He had already commanded the woman to sustain His prophet, did she share in the responsibility to recognize Elijah when he came to town? If so, how would she recognize a man of God, perhaps the first she had ever seen?

Elijah first encountered the widow at the gate, or entrance, to the town of Zarephath. She was there gathering sticks to make the fire that would cook the last food she had reserved for her young son and herself (1 Kings 17:10). Perhaps the widow hoped to find a compassionate soul who would offer to help her and therefore elected to gather sticks at the city gate. In peacetime, the city gate would have been a hub of activity nearly every day. Town meetings, public speaking, and merchants with their wares displayed in the alcoves created from the elaborate zigzag construction of a city's entrance were frequent occurrences. The gates' high walls provided shade for conversation, business transactions, begging, and simply for a pleasant place to rest.

THE CRUSE OF OIL AND BARREL OF MEAL

Anticipating what the relationship between the prophet and the widow might be, we would expect Elijah to be the provider and the poor woman to be the one provided for. Again, she may have gone to the city gate to seek for help. But in this case, the Lord turned the tables. He commanded the one who had nothing to give as if she had everything. In like manner, God required the one who had been so blessed and richly endowed to ask for help from the lowest in the social, religious, and economic order.

Elijah greeted this woman, whom he had never before met, by asking for a drink of water (1 Kings 17:10). Without any hesitation, she turned to accommodate him as though she had forgotten how priceless water had become during the drought. As if testing her willingness to share her water was not egregious enough, Elijah added a petition for some bread (1 Kings 17:11). This time the widow could not hold back her desperation. "As the Lord thy God liveth," she cried, "I have not a cake, but an handful of meal in a barrel, and a little oil in a cruse." She was going home to cook it "for me and my son, that we may eat it, and die" (1 Kings 17:12).

In the Old Testament era, few commodities could be kept for long periods of time. Stored in large clay barrels, wheat and barley were the staff of life and constituted at least half of a person's daily caloric intake. Bread-making skills were essential for survival throughout the ancient Near East. As the members of society who practiced these skills, women may have therefore had more prestige than is typically imagined. For a daily ration of bread, about two cups of grain were ground into flour on a large basalt grinding stone. Because of the climate, a woman ground the grain within a day or two of baking bread. The flour was stored in a smaller jar about the size of a modern day gallon jug. The Hebrew word translated

Photo by Jeffrey R. Chadwick; Tell es-Safi/Gath Archaeological Project

Remains excavated from an Iron Age II (1000–586 B.C.) kitchen-bakery area of a home in biblical Gath. Notice the large grinding stone (right), a broken pot with handles, which could have stored grain (lower left), and a small cruse that likely held oil (far left, with the opening facing down). Smashed remains of other storage jars are also visible.

"barrel" in the King James Version (1 Kings 17:12) more accurately describes a smaller vessel than we think of when we read "barrel" (Chadwick, "Daughters"). Because it is more flavorful, wheat was more expensive than barley and therefore more likely eaten by the rich. In her meager circumstances, the widow's last ration was probably barley.

Olive oil had a long shelflife and was very versatile in food preparation, making it a storage staple. Oil was kept in smaller clay jars, or cruses, about the size of salad dressing bottles today (Chadwick, "Daughters").

This photo of the Iron Age II (1000–586 B.C.) kitchen suggests the size of the workplace a woman had for grinding grains and cooking. Student archaeologist Renee Chadwick points to the oil juglet.

Elijah met the widow's report of abject poverty with a seemingly selfish and insensitive request. "Fear not," he said, "but make me thereof a little cake first, and bring it unto me, and after make for thee and for thy son" (1 Kings 17:13). With only enough food to make one last morsel of nourishment for herself and her child, the widow heard this stranger tell her to do the seemingly impossible—"Fear not." He then directed her to go home and cook the precious final meal but give food to him first: "For thus saith the Lord God of Israel, The barrel of meal shall not waste, neither shall the cruse of oil fail, until the day that the Lord sendeth rain upon the earth" (v. 14).

Specifically, Elijah requested the widow to make him "a little cake" (1 Kings 17:13). Derived from the Hebrew word meaning round, a cake was one type of biblical bread that was round, flat, and cooked on a hot, flat stone or in an enclosed oven made from stone. A biblical cake was not sweet but looked and tasted much like modern pita bread.

With only an Israelite's word that her supply of oil and grain would inexplicably continue throughout the duration of the drought, the widow of Zarephath faced a decision that ultimately revealed where her greatest loyalties lay. Would she provide for her little boy, who would surely die without her care? Or would she trust in the promise of a stranger from a foreign land and the power of his God? Interestingly, the widow's oath for assuring Elijah that she was speaking honestly was not founded in her beliefs in the Phoenician and Canaanite gods but in Elijah's God; the widow declared, "As the Lord *thy* God liveth"

(1 Kings 17:12; emphasis added). What knowledge did she already have of Jehovah? In the midst of Ba'al worshippers, this Gentile woman had gained a certain level of reverence for the Israelites' God.

With no hint of indecision, the widow put her trust in Elijah's God. She gave Elijah her family's last morsel of food with faith that his God would sustain them until the famine abated. The scriptural text simply reports that God did exactly that (1 Kings 17:15–16). The length of time that Elijah remained with the widow and her son in Zarephath is not specified, but it was likely most of the first three years of the three-and-a-half-year drought (1 Kings 18:1).

THE WIDOW'S SON RESTORED TO LIFE

As though the widow's faith had not been tried sufficiently, the Lord had yet another test that would stretch and fortify her faith beyond what she had thus far experienced. After receiving daily replenishing of her jar of flour and cruse of oil for three years, the widow saw her son become ill and die (1 Kings 17:17). Her son was her only family and security for the future. The widow's accusations against Elijah indicate a fear that God was now punishing her for all of her past sins by taking away her son (1 Kings 17:18). Her faith cracked. She accused Elijah and the Lord of abandoning her.

We can become complacent with God's daily miracles. During times of peace and prosperity, we may gradually lose the awe we initially experienced when His grace dramatically sustained us beyond our natural abilities. Because of His constant gifts, we may begin to expect God's enabling power as something we deserve or have even earned. In the case of the widow of Zarephath, she may have felt forsaken by the Lord when He took her son's life away, perhaps because she had begun to pride herself on the daily service she rendered to Elijah by cooking his meals and providing him shelter. Had she therefore falsely assumed that God would shield her from future trials as His gratitude for her service?

Amid the cacophony of emotions and attempts to understand, the widow cried out to Elijah, "What have I to do with thee, O thou man of God?" (1 Kings 17:18). Here was the greater test of her faith in the Lord. Was her love and trust in God dependent on the absence of pain, difficulties, and loss, or was she loyal to Him without condition? Could she be stretched to wholeheartedly accept and understand that everything God does for His children is for their benefit—even painful situations?

After Elijah removed the dead boy from his mother's embrace and laid him on the bed in an upstairs room, his own

Photo by Jeffrey R. Chadwick; Tell es-Safi/Gath Archaeological Project

The cruse, or oil juglet, found in the Iron Age II (1000–586 B.C.) kitchen in Gath. The vessel for oil used by the widow of Zarephath may have resembled this container.

INCONVENIENT SACRIFICE

A member of the Quorum of Seventy, Elder Lynn G. Robbins spoke of a principle taught in this story: "Now doesn't that sound selfish, asking not just for the first piece, but possibly the only piece? Didn't our parents teach us to let other people go first and especially for a gentleman to let a lady go first, let alone a starving widow? Her choice—does she eat, or does she sacrifice her last meal and hasten death? Perhaps she will sacrifice her own food, but could she sacrifice the food meant for her starving son?

"Elijah understood the doctrine that blessings come after the trial of our faith (see Ether 12:6; D&C 132:5). He wasn't being selfish. As the Lord's servant, Elijah was there to give, not to take. . . .

"One reason the Lord illustrates doctrines with the most extreme circumstances is to eliminate excuses. If the Lord expects even the poorest widow to pay her mite, where does that leave all others who find that it is not convenient or easy to sacrifice?" (*Ensign*, May 2005, 35).

pain and confusion became apparent. Pouring his heart out to God, Elijah asked how such evil could have befallen this unselfish and faithful woman. Much like the widow's own interpretation of the tragedy, Elijah told the Lord that this good woman clearly did not deserve such hardship (1 Kings 17:20).

In a different manner than the widow experienced, the death of the young boy was a test for the prophet as well. As a mouthpiece for God, Elijah would have appreciated the power to protect from pain those whom he loved. That power, however, is God's alone. Similarly, how often are priesthood leaders tempted to excuse a family in deep poverty from the command to pay tithing? Yet, how many bishops bear witness to the profound ways that God uniquely blesses faithful individuals and families who respond to God's commandment to sacrifice when their circumstances are the darkest.

Reverence for God is important during peaceful and prosperous times, but how do we respond when a crisis erupts? Where do we turn when everyone around seems to abandon us? Do our hearts become hardened and bitter or soft and pliable by turning unflinchingly to God for the solace that only He can give? A Book of Mormon king wisely taught that turning to the Lord in times of loss was not enough. We must also continue to trust Him when no solution seems possible and actively serve Him even when we don't know how He will rescue us (Mosiah 7:33).

In the King James Version of the Bible, Elijah *stretched* himself on the boy three times as he petitioned God to return him to life (1 Kings 17:21). The Hebrew reads

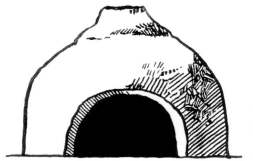

Bread "cakes" (KJV) were often baked in ovens that were made of clay, or a mixture of clay and straw, and shaped like large, upside-down bowls. To allow the smoke to escape, most ovens were located in the open court of the home.

Artwork by Ashton Young

literally, "he *measured or extended* himself three times upon or over the boy" as he prayed. This reading appears nowhere else in the Hebrew Bible. A likely meaning of the passage is that three times Elijah extended himself to God in a prayer, perhaps with his hand stretched heavenward, on behalf of the boy.

GOD'S CARE FOR THE ONE

The Lord loved and cared for this widow in Zarephath. He went to great lengths to show her that she was known to Him, that she had a unique mission to accomplish for Him, and that she was just as precious in His sight as His prophet. If God knew her—a woman without title, without status, without believing lineage, and without a name recorded—He certainly knows each of us. His promise to her is also given to all those who become His children. "Fear thou not," the Lord tells us, "for I am with thee: be not dismayed: for I am thy God: I will strengthen thee: yea, I will help thee; yea, I will uphold thee with the right hand of my righteousness" (Isaiah 41:10).

As He did for the widow and Elijah, God often teaches us through counterintuitive means. He often requires us to do or say or consider something that appears to contradict a favorable solution. Comparable to tests of faith in this biblical story, God may ask us to put our trust in a stranger from enemy territory, to give away all that we have to gain infinitely more, or to obey God when His command will deprive our family of what they desire most. Despite the obstacles, trials, and dangers that Elijah or the widow faced, the Lord showed His power and compassion to bring them through victorious. In similar ways today, no matter how ferocious the enemy, God will champion and never forget His own.

A restored ancient jar excavated at biblical Gath in Israel. This is the type of jar in which freshly ground flour would have been kept before being made into dough for baking. The widow's "barrel" (KJV) in Iron Age II (1000–586 B.C.) Zarephath probably was a jar like this one.

The widow's story concludes with a testament of her fortified faith in God and His prophet after the loss and return of her young son. "Now by this I know that thou art a man of God," the widow declared to Elijah, "and that the word of the Lord in thy mouth is truth" (1 Kings 17:24). We are left with an image of a woman who had been born again through times of uncertainty and pain and who became an unshakeable witness for the God of the Israelites. Although nothing more is reported in scripture concerning the widow's later years, we perceive her as a beacon of light to her son as he grew to manhood and to her idol-worshipping neighbors whenever pains and uncertainties faced them.

Although details of her later life are unknown, the widow's example is evident in Elijah's continued mission. Before the contest with Ahab and Jezebel over whose god was truly

God, Elijah had witnessed the unselfish faith and generosity of a Gentile widow for whom God manifested genuine compassion. How could he fear Jezebel's Ba'al when Elijah had experienced Jehovah's tender mercies for a poor widow? As Israel's monarchs, Ahab and Jezebel ruled over many of God's chosen people, but the Lord showed Elijah that His people are "those who hear [His] voice and harden not their hearts," whether they be Israelite or Gentile (D&C 29:7).

The Lord promises each of us the same blessing that He gave to the widow and Elijah. "Trust in the Lord, and do good; so shalt thou dwell in the land, and verily thou shalt be fed. Delight thyself also in the Lord; and he shall give thee the desires of thine heart" (Psalm 37:3–4). Because of the Atonement of Jesus Christ, the way is opened for every person, Israelite or Gentile, to find Him and receive His greatest blessings. Praise the memory of the widow from Zarephath for showing us that truth.

POINTS TO PONDER: APPLICATIONS FOR OUR LIVES

1. How does God view wealth differently from the way the world sees it? Who are the poor and who are the rich to the Lord?

2. What can we learn from the widow about true sacrifice?

3. How does God's instruction to the "have-nots" to serve the "haves" strengthen and ennoble those who "have"? What does it afford those who "have not"?

4. How were the trials of the widow also trials for Elijah? How did the widow's example prepare him to face Ahab and Jezebel again?

5. Why may the Lord have chosen the Phoenician widow to help Elijah rather than an Israelite widow?

6. How can pain, loss, and uncertainties lead us to greater faith in Jesus Christ? How do trials from God illustrate the scriptural truth that all that God does is for the benefit of His children? (2 Nephi 26:24)

7. The New Testament counsels us to "be not forgetful to entertain strangers: for thereby some have entertained angels unawares" (Hebrews 13:2). How did acceptance of this advice bless the widow of Zarephath?

8. What does the story of the widow of Zarephath teach us about the Atonement of Jesus Christ?

9. What gospel principles do you find illustrated in the widow's story?

What Is to Be Done for Thee?

THE SHUNAMMITE
הַשּׁוּנַמִּית

$\mathcal{K}$nown only by her connection to the village of Shunem, an Israelite woman chose to use her abundant resources to care for a prophet. The Lord's miraculous blessings and trials in response to her selfless service strengthened her faith in God and exceeded her expectations. Called simply "the Shunammite" in the Bible, the woman was married, but she behaved differently from other married women portrayed in scripture. Independent and decisive, the woman appeared to lack nothing in material wealth and have everything to give. Through a series of challenges and tragedies, however, she would come to recognize that she had nothing without the Lord and that life and redemption are only the Savior's to give. The woman also learned how completely and miraculously the Lord will provide for those who trust in Him, selflessly care for others, and act in faith.

The events described in 2 Kings 4 cover a period of some five to eight years, from the time the Shunammite learned that she would bear a son until the son had grown old enough to accompany his father to the fields. The biblical narrative returns to the Shunammite in 2 Kings 8, following a seven-year famine. By combining these events, we are able to follow the life of this extraordinary woman for at least a dozen years.

Because reference to the king of Israel is made in 2 Kings 4 and the king was present during the event recounted in 2 Kings 8, a brief discussion of the political setting in the kingdom of Israel, of which Shunem was a part, is helpful. At times rulers in both kingdoms of Israel were known by the same name, so a chance for greater confusion is manifest during this era of biblical history.

POLITICAL BACKGROUND

After the death of the wicked king Ahab (853 B.C.), the political stability in the northern kingdom of Israel steadily declined, beginning with the brief rule of his son Ahaziah (1 Kings 22:40). Ahaziah's reign lasted only

2 KINGS 4:8–37
2 KINGS 8:1–6

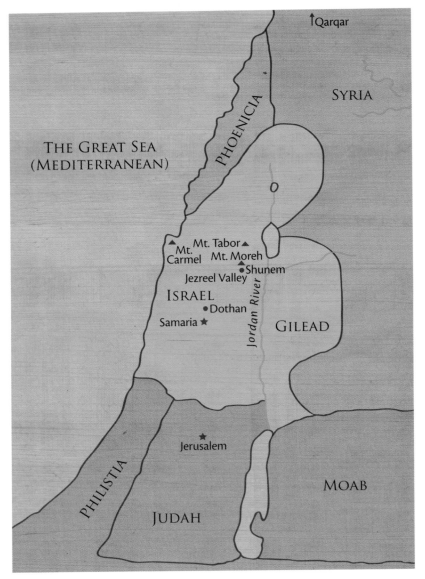

The village of Shunem was at the foot of the southern slope of Mount Moreh, about twenty-five miles north of Samaria, capital of the northern kingdom of Israel.

for a few months when complications from a fall took his life (2 Kings 1:17). But Ahab's wicked influence continued through two more of his children, a son, Joram/Jehoram, and a daughter, Athaliah.

Not only does the biblical narrative refer to the king of Israel as both Joram and Jehoram but it reports the same names for the king of Judah who ruled at the same time. Therefore, to distinguish Ahab's second son who became king of Israel from a king of the southern kingdom of Judah who had the same name, I will refer to Ahab's son as Joram and the king of Judah as Jehoram.

Inheriting the throne of Israel after his brother Ahaziah died, Joram ruled for eleven years (852–841 B.C.). His rule differed from his father's and his brother's evil leadership only in that he "put away the image of Baal that his father had made" (2 Kings 3:2). Perhaps in an effort to gain greater allegiance from the common people, Joram removed the cult objects and tried to initiate a semblance of reform, but that was of little use with Jezebel still in the palace.

At the same time Joram began his reign in the northern kingdom, Ahab's daughter Athaliah was married to Jehoram, heir to the throne of Judah. As Jezebel had done in Samaria, the capital of the northern kingdom of Israel, Athaliah gradually turned the southern kingdom of Judah toward idolatry and immorality (2 Kings 8:18). Judah experienced some of its most unsettled years after the death of Jehoshaphat (ca. 848 B.C.) during the reigns of his son Jehoram (848–841 B.C.), his grandson Ahaziah (841 B.C.), and his daughter-in-law Athaliah (841–835 B.C.).

Frustrated by the ineffectiveness and gluttony of the Omrides in the northern kingdom, the disgruntled citizens, led by Israel's general named Jehu, undertook a revolution against the monarchy. About this same time, the prophet Elisha arranged for Jehu to be anointed king over Israel, instructing him, "And thou shalt smite the house of Ahab thy master, that I may avenge the blood of my servants the prophets, . . . for the whole house of Ahab shall perish" (2 Kings 9:7–8).

Jehu began purging the house of Ahab by finding Joram, king of Israel, while he was convalescing in Jezreel from wounds sustained in a battle with the Syrians. Coincidentally, the king of Judah, Ahaziah (son of Athaliah), was visiting his uncle during his recovery (2 Kings 9:15–16). Jehu killed them both (2 Kings 9:20–27). Next, Jehu traveled to the palace in Samaria, where he confronted the dowager queen Jezebel. She had been warned that he was coming, and she taunted him from her upper story window. At Jehu's command, Jezebel's servants threw her out the window to her death (2 Kings 9:30–37). The bloodbath continued until every descendant of Ahab in the kingdom of Israel was dead, thereby ending the Omride dynasty (2 Kings 10).

The village of Shunem was located at the southern slope of Mount Moreh, in the tribal territory of Issachar.

The story of the Shunammite occurred during the reign of Joram and perhaps during the early years of Jehu's rule. For more than fifty years Elisha was the principal prophet. He ministered throughout most of Joram's reign, all of Jehu's twenty-eight-year rule, Jehoahaz's seventeen-year-rule, and into the reign of Joash/Jehoash.

PROPHETS IN THE NORTHERN KINGDOM

During the time of Elijah and Elisha, groups of prophets lived communally (2 Kings 2:3, 5), with one prophet appointed as leader (2 Kings 6:1–7). Supported by believers, prophets were loyal to their nation. They frequently followed the military and encouraged the king to fight when God so commanded (1 Kings 20:13–21; 2 Kings 3:11–19). Prophets were as zealous for Israel's political success as any king and showed no hesitation in criticizing the monarchy should the king follow a plan that was contrary to God's purposes. Prophets were often distinguished by unique characteristics (see 1 Kings 20:41), such as a mantle of animal skin (2 Kings 1:8), reminiscent of the covering the Lord gave to Adam and Eve. Neither ashamed of their message nor their lifestyle, prophets were often mocked and misunderstood in their efforts to bring their nation closer to God (2 Kings 2:23–25). At other times deeply appreciated, prophets were mourned when they died. For example, at Elisha's death, even the evil king Joash wept and compared him in value to an army, calling him "the chariot of Israel, and the horsemen thereof" (2 Kings 13:14).

Like his predecessor Elijah, Elisha cared for the oppressed and the vulnerable. He was the son of a farmer from the area just south of the Sea of Galilee, perhaps near Dothan. He appears to have regularly traveled around Israel and at times, especially on holy days and the Sabbath, received visitors at such religious centers as Bethel, Gilgal, and Mount Carmel. People went to him for counsel or instruction or to participate in a worship service. Much as Elisha had served Elijah in his prophetic mission, Gehazi served Elisha and assisted him in his travels and ministry.

THE WIDOW OF OBADIAH

In introducing Elisha's sensitivity and compassion to the Shunammite, the biblical narrator recounts the story of another woman in need (2 Kings 4:1–7). The unnamed woman was the widow of one of Elisha's followers, a man known as one of the "sons of the prophets" (2 Kings 4:1) and perhaps one who was killed during Jezebel's campaign against prophets (1 Kings 18:4, 13). The widow approached Elisha, carrying the threat that she would lose her children to servitude if she could not pay off her debt. Under the law of Moses a creditor had the right to take possession of the debtor and his or her children as hired servants in payment for the debt (Leviticus 25:39–43; Isaiah 50:1).

Both Josephus and rabbinic tradition identify the woman as the widow of Obadiah, the righteous steward of the wicked king Ahab (1 Kings 18:3–6). Both sources explain that the widow's debt had been incurred by Obadiah when he borrowed money to feed and sustain "an hundred prophets" during the reign of Ahab and Jezebel (1 Kings 18:4; Josephus, *Antiquities,* 9.4.2; Ginzberg, *Legends,* 4:241–42). Certainly, to "fear the Lord greatly" at the time when the royal court espoused the worship of Ba'al required particular valor and courage (1 Kings 18:3).

Elisha's initial response to the widow's plight suggests that he was unsure what he could do to help her (2 Kings 4:2). The biblical narrative discloses the humanness of Elisha as

TIME LINE

874–853 B.C.	King Ahab's reign
853–852 B.C.	King Ahaziah's reign
852 B.C.	Elijah is translated, and the mantle falls upon Elisha
	The widow's oil is multiplied
852 B.C.	Joram becomes king
	Elisha meets the Shunammite
849 B.C.	The Shunammite's son is restored to life
842 B.C.	The famine ends
841 B.C.	Joram dies; Jehu becomes king

further evidence of the infinite power of God. In searching for a possible way to begin to help her, Elisha asked the widow what valuables she still retained in her home. Her answer reinforced her pitiful predicament—she had nothing "save a pot of oil" (v. 2). Typically, earthenware containers for storing oil were narrow, pointed at the bottom, and kept upright by being inserted into wooden or stone stands or by being anchored in the earth.

Putting everything she had on the line, the widow had to rely completely on the Lord. The prophet directed her to borrow empty containers from her neighbors and then, behind closed doors, fill them from her single container of oil (2 Kings 4:3–4). Miraculously, the oil continued to flow until every vessel was filled (2 Kings 4:6). She now had a commodity she could sell. Olive oil was valuable for cooking, medicine, fuel for lamps, anointing, and in some sacrificial offerings to God. Elisha did not directly rescue the widow from her distress but required her to act in faith during every step of the process.

The account of the widow whose oil was multiplied invites us to likewise act in faith to personally experience the wonder of God's daily miracles in our lives. The instructions that He gives through His prophets may at times feel disconnected and not directly applicable to our concerns, but by trusting that their counsel is inspired by God, we are placed in a similar position to see solutions that only He can provide.

THE WOMAN OF SHUNEM

The scriptures next direct us to the woman in the village of Shunem whose situation was very different from that of the widow whose oil was multiplied. The Shunammite's husband was living, she had no children, and she was "great" (2 Kings 4:8). The Hebrew word translated "great" can communicate greatness in any sense, including power, status, wealth, age, or size. Considering that the house and property belonged to the Shunammite (2 Kings 8:3), she lived among her "own people" (2 Kings 4:13), and she was not in need of help, financially or otherwise, indicates that the Shunammite's greatness was in status and wealth in Shunem.

The village of Shunem was in the tribal territory of Issachar, along an important trade route, about twenty-five miles north of the Israelite capital of Samaria. The village sat at the foot of the southern slope of Mount Moreh. Apparently, the prophet Elisha often traveled through Shunem on his way from his home on Mount Carmel through the Jezreel Valley and back without advertising his purpose or importance.

After several journeys that took Elisha through Shunem, this unnamed "great" woman recognized that among all the travelers who passed along the route, Elisha was a "holy man" (2 Kings 4:9). Interestingly, some of the ancients attempted to explain what there was about Elisha that set him apart in the eyes of the Shunammite. Among the Jewish legends is the suggestion that Elisha was distinguishable for two reasons: "not even a fly dared approach close to the holy man" and a glorious "fragrance" attended him (Ginzberg, *Legends,* 4:242). A more believable idea is that the Shunammite heeded the whisperings of the Spirit to reach her conclusion.

A Jewish Midrash suggests an unlikely connection with another biblical woman from Shunem. Some rabbis claimed that the Shunammite was a sister to Abishag, King David's last wife (1 Kings 1:8). The more than one hundred years that separate the stories make that claim highly suspect, however. The same Midrash asserts that the Shunammite's husband was Iddo, a man from the school of the prophets. Yet the story we have is about the wife, not the husband, whether he was a prophet or not. Unfortunately, Josephus does not mention the Shunammite's story or the other miracles that Elisha performed that are recorded in 2 Kings 4–9, leading some scholars to believe that a few of Josephus's original writings were lost (*Antiquities,* 9.4.3, footnote). Josephus's account of the Shunammite might have supplied support to the rabbis' claims that, on their own, do not appear plausible.

Like the women who assisted Jesus and His apostles in their travels (Luke 8:1–3), the Shunammite used her resources to support the prophet Elisha. She suggested to her husband that they construct and furnish an extra room in their home to accommodate Elisha whenever he visited the village (2 Kings 4:10). Her husband complied with all his wife's requests.

The Shunammite is unique among other women in scripture. Known neither as her father's daughter nor as her husband's wife, the Shunammite was identified by the name of her village, where *her* people lived, rather than where her husband's clan resided. Independent and decisive, the Shunammite was more like a woman without the protection or support of a man than a married woman. She was free to act without receiving her husband's permission or blessing. By contrast, Abigail feared her husband's fierce reaction when she countermanded his offense to David and fed David's army (1 Samuel 25). In another comparison, Abraham asked Sarah to fix a meal for their visitors (Genesis 18:6), but the Shunammite said to her husband, "Let us make a little chamber" for Elisha (2 Kings 4:10). In the latter story, the Shunammite made the decisions and was free to use the family resources as she deemed appropriate. The Shunammite chose to host Elisha because her own recognition and faith told her he was a holy man.

THE SHUNAMMITE'S HOUSE

Much can be inferred about the construction and floor plan of the Shunammite's house because a four-room house was ubiquitous among the Israelites during the Iron Age period (1200–586 B.C.). Hundreds of such buildings have been found, making it distinctly recognizable even when some variations occur. This standardization in a nation's building construction, whether for the rich or the poor, may have represented the value the Israelites placed on equality, order, and unity (Bunimovitz and Faust, "Ideology").

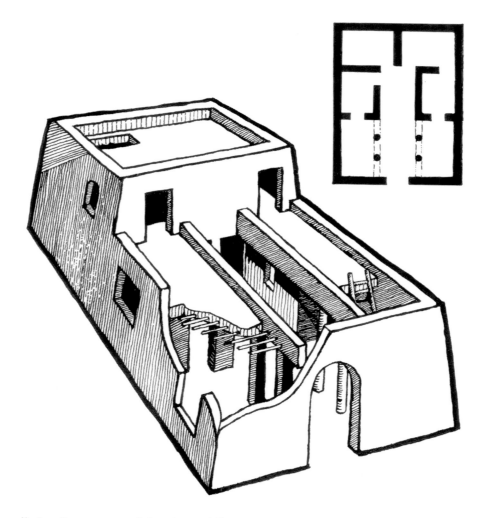

Almost universally Israelites constructed their homes following this general four-room design. The central courtyard, on the ground and upstairs levels, was used for cooking, eating, and sleeping quarters. The covered rooms were likely used for storage, for individuals who were sick, and for protection from the elements during inclement weather.

A container for oil, such as that used in the Shunammite's house.

Archaeological findings therefore provide clues about the general appearance and function of the various parts of the houses. The ground floor had a low ceiling, the overall height of the building's two stories not exceeding fifteen feet. The roof was frequently used for sleeping (1 Samuel 9:25–26), and walls or fences were added around the roof for safety (Deuteronomy 22:8). The second story could be accessed by steps or a ladder.

The main floor opened to a courtyard, which was probably used as a communication center. The courtyard was surrounded on three sides with rooms used for storage, food preparation, and animal shelter. Light and air came primarily from the entrance; however, spaces between the building materials that made up the first floor roof were deliberately created to allow light and air to filter through.

The upper floor included a central space that was left unroofed to invite more light and air into the lower floor. The main living quarters were probably on the upper floor. The Shunammite's husband likely created a private room for Elisha on this second floor. The biblical description of a "little chamber . . . on the wall" (2 Kings 4:10), however, likely holds more than one possible meaning. The term could mean walls built with brick rather than of wood, an upper room built on the wall of the house, or a walled area set on the flat roof of the house (Keil and Delitzsch, *Commentary,* 3:219; Cogan and Tadmore, *II Kings,* 56–57; Chadwick, "Daughters"). Wherever the exact location of Elisha's room, he would have had privacy, which the general floor plan of the house abundantly offered. Access to individual rooms was available only from the central room or by a ladder or stairway directly to an upper room.

The homes were constructed of mud-bricks on a stone foundation. Ceilings and roofs were framed with crossbeams and then covered with branches or reeds. The walls and roof were plastered over with a coating that required frequent reapplication because of erosion caused by wet weather.

The Shunammite requested that Elisha's room be furnished. In addition to the customary bed and small table was "a stool." The Hebrew word here translated "stool" is elsewhere translated in the Bible as "throne," suggesting a seat of honor and indicating the finer furnishings that the Shunammite could provide for Elisha. The "candlestick" that completed the furnishings for the room is in Hebrew a *menorah,* or a lamp, probably made of clay.

THE BLESSING OF A CHILD

It appears that in many ways Elisha remembered his mentor, Elijah, and desired to follow his example in his ministry. As Elijah showed his appreciation to the widow of Zarephath by securing food for her throughout the famine, Elisha may have searched for a way to reward the Shunammite. Identifying a gift for a woman who was affluent and independent would not be as easy as finding a way to help an indigent widow. At first Elisha initiated conversations with the Shunammite through his servant, Gehazi (2 Kings 4:13). But the practice did not endure during the woman's greatest trial. Later, when she needed divine assistance, she spoke directly to the prophet, and he addressed her without an intermediary.

Elisha asked whether she had some wish or petition that he could communicate to the king or chief captain (2 Kings 4:13). The Shunammite was content, and her explanation simple: "I dwell among mine own people" (2 Kings 4:13). Her family or clan supplied all the support she needed. How unusual it must have been for Elisha to encounter someone who was completely satisfied with life. The Shunammite's actions exemplified the Savior's later admonition to His apostles, "Freely ye have received, freely give" (Matthew 10:8). She acknowledged her blessings from God and simply wanted to give to others in return.

The woman's satisfaction did not dissuade Elisha from desiring to help her. He turned to his servant, Gehazi, for his observations. Gehazi mentioned that the woman had no children. The absence of a child, particularly a son, was a serious lack for a family and even more so for a woman. Without a son, the family name and line would end. Of more immediate concern, without a son, a woman had no one to provide for her when her husband died. Remarkably, the Shunammite was not worried and had not mentioned this unfortunate circumstance when given the opportunity.

Gehazi also observed that the Shunammite's husband was old (2 Kings 4:14). To mention only her husband's age as an impediment against her conceiving a child indicates that she was considerably younger than her husband and still in her childbearing years. Her marriage to an older man when she was young may suggest that she had known the possibility that she would never bear a child. Additionally, the age difference presented a higher chance that she would be left a widow for a significant number of years, and, lacking offspring, she would be without a provider or protector.

The promise of a son within a year's time seemed to be the greatest possible blessing for the woman. But she responded, "Nay, my lord"

Women stored oil in juglets, such as this one, or in containers that came to a point at the base and that could be anchored by burying the bottom half in the ground.

Artwork by Ashton Young

(2 Kings 4:16). Rather than a lack of faith in the prophet's power, the woman revealed a fear of disappointment when she declined Elisha's proffered gift. For how long had she learned to accept the probability that she would never bear or rear a child? Now, even the mention of the possibility seemed to reopen wounds and portend greater pain.

Manifesting the grace of Jesus Christ, the Shunammite was miraculously blessed with a son in a year's time. In our day of instant gratification, we can learn from the Lord's blessing to the Shunammite. God works great miracles in the life of each one of us, but they often occur later than we anticipate. Blessings that are long in coming are frequently all the more precious for the waiting. The delay affords greater opportunity to realize His awareness of us and appreciation that the miracle actually occurred at the right time. That is why the reader feels as surprised as the Shunammite must have been when her miracle son was taken from her just a few years later. Her faith was initially stretched to conceive the child, but through the trial of the boy's death, the Shunammite received an even greater demonstration of God's power and mercy.

DEATH OF THE CHILD

The scriptural account of the little boy's death indicates that he may have suffered sunstroke while working in the fields with his father (2 Kings 4:18–20). A servant helped the ailing boy back to the house and into the arms of his mother. The pain that the Shunammite feared in never having a child intensified as she watched her little boy die without being able to prevent it. She may have reasoned that it would have been better never to have borne a child than to enjoy the blessing of a son and soon afterward lose him. A Jewish Midrash quotes her as saying, "O that the vessel had remained empty, rather than it should be filled first, and then be left void" (Ginzberg, *Legends,* 243). Struggling to understand why God would take the gift that He had bestowed without her asking for it, the Shunammite faced her greatest test of faith.

Placing her son's body in Elisha's room and closing the door, the Shunammite concealed the boy's death from the rest of the household as she quickly put together a plan of action (2 Kings 4:21). She did not tell the boy's father of the child's death or the specifics of her plan. She told her husband only that she was going to see Elisha (2 Kings 4:22). Her husband was surprised at her plan, not because she was traveling some distance to consult the prophet, but that she was going "today" (2 Kings 4:23).

Apparently, it was customary for many Israelites, including the Shunammite, to visit the holy man on worship days, such as the Sabbath and the first day of the month (Leviticus 23:3; Numbers 28:11–15; Isaiah 66:23). In the absence of official priests in the apostate northern kingdom, prophets became essential for regular worship services. Because that day was not one of the days for worship, the Shunammite's husband was confused at her announcement of where she planned to go. To her husband's surprised reaction, the woman simply responded, "It shall be well," as it is translated in the King James Version. In

Hebrew, the woman answered, "Shalom," communicating something similar to "everything is fine" or "don't worry" (2 Kings 4:23).

The narrative paints a picture of the woman speedily riding to find the prophet at his home on Mount Carmel without interruption or delay (2 Kings 4:24). Her son was dead, but the Shunammite's profound faith impelled her to seek the prophet's help to restore him to life. She knew that God had miraculously given her the son and that He was mindful of her. Riding on an ass was the preferable mode of transportation for a woman of means in biblical times. A servant attended the woman by running alongside or behind her and driving the animal with a whip or stick to maintain the desired speed. The Shunammite was completely focused on the task at hand as she traveled the approximate twenty miles from Shunem to Mount Carmel.

PETITION TO ELISHA

From Mount Carmel, Elisha recognized the Shunammite from a distance, again suggesting that she had visited him before (2 Kings 4:25). He sent Gehazi to intercept her in an effort to save her the need to travel farther. When Gehazi met her and made his inquiries, however, the Shunammite again answered, "Shalom" (Hebrew for "It is well"; 2 Kings 4:26). Gehazi was an impediment to her mission, so she quickly brushed him aside. She was determined to discuss her heartache and plea for help only with the prophet.

The Lord did not reveal the Shunammite's problems to Elisha. Rather, she was required to articulate her need for help—something she was not accustomed to doing. In contrast to her typically confident and controlled demeanor, when she finally reached Elisha, the Shunammite fell down and grasped Elisha's feet (2 Kings 4:27). This emotional outburst before the prophet was apparently unusual or disconcerting because Gehazi tried to prevent the woman from such close contact. Elisha quickly overruled. The Shunammite finally let out her pent-up pains and fears as she cried to the prophet (2 Kings 4:28). She had not asked for a son. In fact, she had been reluctant and even protested when Elisha offered the gift to her. Now the child was dead. Therefore, did not Elisha have a responsibility to help?

Elisha directed Gehazi to return quickly to attend to the boy. His directive, "Gird up thy loins," was an instruction to tie up his robes so they did not trip him up and to run back to Shunem as swiftly as possible (2 Kings 4:29). Elisha also offered his staff to Gehazi to accompany him in ministering to the dead boy. The staff was tangible evidence of Elisha himself. But the woman was not satisfied with a substitute. The Shunammite insisted that Elisha return with her himself to attend the boy (2 Kings 4:30).

RESTORATION OF LIFE

Upon reaching the Shunammite's son, Elisha prayed before attempting any action to resuscitate the boy (2 Kings 4:33). His actions indicate his understanding that he did not hold power of himself but was dependent on God, the only source of power. Power to resuscitate the boy did not come from a staff or from any individual who attended the boy. The power of the Lord was activated through sincere faith in Christ, prayer, and the authority God granted to the prophet Elisha. Apparently, Gehazi needed to learn that lesson, too. In his behavior we may sense his desire for greater acceptance and importance, perhaps even jealousy for the reverence people held for Elisha (2 Kings 4:31). Did Gehazi expect to assume leadership of the prophets when Elisha was gone, as Elisha had done after Elijah was taken up? This story is one of a few incidents that suggest an unrighteous ambition in Gehazi.

Elisha did not allow the boy's mother into the room during his ministrations. The process and time required for the boy to regain consciousness may have been as important for Elisha's faith as for the Shunammite. The biblical account suggests that Elisha was alone with the boy for a considerable time, as Elisha paced the room and "stretched himself upon the child." The Hebrew word here is different from that used to describe the manner in which Elijah raised the son of the widow of Zarephath (2 Kings 4:34–35; 1 Kings 17:21). In this story of the Shunammite's son and Elisha, the scriptures clearly state that Elisha prostrated himself on the dead boy.

The narrator describes a slow return to life in the boy. More than once Elijah lay on the child before the boy sneezed "seven" times (2 Kings 4:35). Because seven symbolizes perfection, completion, and wholeness in Hebrew, the unusual detail of the boy's sneezes may signify that the child was made completely whole. Some scholars have linked Elisha's method of healing to a Mesopotamian procedure to ward off evil spirits. The Mesopotamian healer touched his head to the head of the patient, hand to hand, and foot to foot (Berlin and Brettler, *Jewish*, 713). Elisha's mode of resuscitating the boy may point to the ultimate victory of the Savior. By lying prostrate on the dead boy, Elisha typified the Savior's unique ability to take upon Himself all of our sicknesses. Furthermore, when both Elisha and the boy rose again, the miracle testified that not only would Jesus Christ be resurrected but also that all the children of God will live again because of His sacrifice.

The Shunammite's response to the miracle revealed her deepest gratitude and reverence for the power of the Lord (2 Kings 4:36–37). She had made room for a prophet of God in her life, and God poured out His blessings upon her.

RESTORATION OF PROPERTY

The Shunammite's story resumes in the Bible four chapters later when the Israelites were on the brink of a long famine. Many scholars have argued, reasonably, that the later incident pertaining to the Shunammite, recorded in 2 Kings 8:1–6, does not appear in the Bible in its proper chronological order. The proper context for these verses is more likely just before 2 Kings 5 and therefore before the Syrian siege and Elisha's encounter with Naaman (Keil and Delitzsch, *Commentary*, 3:218). One observation for this argument is that in chapter 5, Gehazi was struck with leprosy and offended Elisha, but in chapter 8 he was clearly free from leprosy and in good standing with Elisha. If this theory is correct, the famine referred to in chapter 8 was possibly the same one introduced in 2 Kings 4:38, commencing shortly after the Shunammite's son was brought back to life.

That the "Lord had called for" the famine suggests it was another divine judgment sent upon the Israelites on account of their wickedness (2 Kings 8:1). Elisha warned the Shunammite that the famine would last seven years and advised her to relocate her family until the famine abated (v. 2). It is worthy of note that this famine lasted twice as long as the one that occurred during the reign of Ahab and Jezebel (1 Kings 17–18).

The Shunammite and her family moved to the Mediterranean coast in the land of Philistia (2 Kings 8:2). The area contains ample productive farmland, natural springs, and grasslands for grazing to produce sufficient food even during times of famine. When the famine ended in seven years, the Shunammite's family returned to Shunem. Their homecoming was marred, however, by the discovery that the Shunammite's home and property had been confiscated in their absence (2 Kings 8:3). The monarch might have assumed ownership of her land because of her long absence, or perhaps an unknown party had illegally appropriated it.

Years before, the Shunammite had declined help when Elisha offered to petition the king on her behalf. Now, in her homeless condition, she went "to cry unto the king for *her* house and for *her* land" (2 Kings 8:3; emphasis added). Two aspects of this statement are unusual considering the customs of the day. The Mosaic law allowed citizens of Israel to bypass local magistrates and appeal directly to the king (Deuteronomy 16:18). Customarily, however, a man would have petitioned the king for *his* home and *his* land. According to the Israelite law, property went to a man's sons who then were responsible to care for their widowed mother. In applying this law to the case of the Shunammite, we would expect the property to belong to the Shunammite's husband if he still lived, or to their son, if her husband was dead. In either case, a man would have represented her before the king and the property would never have been called *hers*.

The Shunammite's entrance to the court coincided with Gehazi's telling the king of Elisha's mighty miracles wrought by the power of God, including the miracle of the Shunammite's son being restored to life (2 Kings 4:4–5). There is some uncertainty concerning the identity of the king in this event. For the king to ask Gehazi to recount Elisha's great works assumes he was unfamiliar with the prophet's ministry. Certainly, after his encounter with the Syrian captain Namaan in 2 Kings 5, Joram would have known about Elisha. If this story occurred some seven years after the Shunammite's son was raised from the dead, Joram was probably still ruling. On the other hand, if this incident is chronologically placed in the Bible, the king was likely Jehu, Joram's successor. In other words, Gehazi's report of Elisha's greatness occurred either before Namaan encountered Joram or shortly after the new king, Jehu, had assumed the throne.

After hearing of the Shunammite's own testimony of Elisha's power from God and then seeing her son, very much alive, beside her, the king graciously responded to the woman's plea. In another example of unusual verbiage associated with the Shunammite, the king gave the command to "restore all that was *hers,*" not her husband's or son's property but property that belonged to the woman (2 Kings 8:6; emphasis added). In addition to restoring her home and land, the king ordered that all that the land had produced in her absence be restored, a restitution not required by law. Furthermore, the king assigned an officer of the court to accompany the Shunammite to ensure that his orders were enforced (2 Kings 8:6).

UNIQUE CHARACTERISTICS OF THE SHUNAMMITE

The combined incidents involving the Shunammite reinforce our idea that she was not typical of Israelite women at the time. A careful consideration of the anomalies included in her story suggests that she was in an exceptional situation with unique opportunities for a woman. Recall the following about the Shunammite:

1. Without hope of bearing a child, she neither asked for nor yearned for a baby.
2. She showed no anxiety for her future because of her childless condition.
3. She lived among "her people," not her husband's people.
4. She did not ask her husband's permission and gave no explanation for her actions.
5. The land belonged to her, not to her father, husband, or son.

The only situation that answers all of these anomalies was proposed by biblical scholar Tikva Frymer-Kensky, who suggests that the Shunammite was a beneficiary of that part of the Mosaic law that was influenced by the daughters of Zelophehad. Each of Zelophehad's daughters inherited property and lived among her own people, specifically because Zelophehad had no sons. Applying the law to the story of the Shunammite, we could conjecture that she was likely the daughter of a wealthy landowner who had no sons, thus making his daughter his heir. Therefore, the land and house were hers, she lived among her people to keep the inheritance within the larger family, and she was not dependent on a son to support her if she should become widowed.

When given the privileges of inheritance and complete discretion in the use of her wealth, the Shunammite acted responsibly, unselfishly, and with great faith in God. The recipient of unusual opportunities for women of her era, the story of the Shunammite illustrates that wealth and privilege do not necessarily reduce a woman's compassion and faith in the Lord. It also reminds us that no amount of status and prosperity diminishes our need for the Redeemer.

The Shunammite received the miracle of a child, at his birth and again when he was restored to life, only through the power of God. Against all odds, her inheritance was likewise restored through a miraculous chain of events. Echoing the divine gifts of being born again through repentance and faith in the Lord and the resurrection of our bodies from the grave, the Shunammite's story bears witness that restoration occurs only because of the Atonement of Jesus Christ.

POINTS TO PONDER: APPLICATIONS FOR OUR LIVES

1. From your experience, how do you think the Shunammite recognized that Elisha was a "holy man of God?"

2. How does the Shunammite's example contribute to the meaning and blessings of "barrenness" discussed elsewhere in this book?

3. In your estimation, what made the Shunammite "great"?

4. What might Elisha have learned from his association with the Shunammite?

5. What gospel principles are illustrated in this story?

6. How can the Shunammite strengthen our testimony of Jesus Christ and inspire us to be more obedient to Him?

The Seed of Faith

THE LITTLE MAID
נַעֲרָה קְטַנָּה

With faith in the boundless power and mercy of God, an Israelite girl whose name was never recorded showed courage to proclaim the power of Israel's God to the Syrians who had taken her captive. Naaman, the military captain of Syria, took the Little Maid from her family in Israel to be a servant to his wife in Damascus. At the time, Naaman was unaware that his success in battle was due to the enabling power of Israel's God. Only through the spirit-filled example and counsel of a young slave did he learn the identity of God and choose to follow his Redeemer. With the simple and steadfast faith of a child, the girl also gave a great Syrian military captain a reason to hope when he and his family despaired because of his disease.

The larger story that is introduced by the Little Maid illustrates how individuals of higher status become humble and strong when they accept inspired counsel and help from those of lesser status. In this single chapter of scripture, a military captain wisely heeds the advice of his wife and later his servants; a victorious king graciously condescends to plead for help from the king he has recently defeated; and a proud and vengeful king is saved from an international disaster by a prophet who comes to his rescue before the king realizes the danger. The catalyst that inspired each of these situations and invited proud souls to become humble in the sight of God was the lowest of them all—the Little Maid. Only three verses in all of scripture directly refer to her (2 Kings 5:2–4), yet an entire chapter is the result of her testimony and influence (2 Kings 5).

The absence of additional information about the captive girl may be one reason that the account of Naaman's spiritual conversion is often told without any mention of her. The omission may also be due to her having no name or significant position in society whereas the Syrian man has both a name and a title. This chapter considers the story of Naaman and the prophet Elisha by remembering the Little Maid and her influence, even when she was not present. By considering the political dynamics between Israel and Syria and

2 KINGS 5:1–27

251

attempting to understand the lifestyle and challenges of a girl enslaved by a foreign people, we can more easily recognize the Little Maid's role throughout the entire story of Naaman's conversion to the God of Israel.

ISRAEL'S RELATIONSHIP WITH SYRIA

Because the Bible is unclear about when the Syrians took the Little Maid captive, a brief review of reported invasions and conflicts between the two peoples offers important background and a possible time frame for her story.

The northern kingdom of Israel had a long history of conflict and brief alliances with their neighbors to the north. Known as Syria in the Bible, the land was also called Aram. Its capital was Damascus, a major trade and transportation center on the trade route through the Fertile Crescent. Aramaic, the Syrian language, influenced the language of the Israelite peoples down through the time of Jesus Christ, reflecting the strength of their interaction historically. The two nations were often involved in border skirmishes and extended wars, with only brief periods of peace interspersed.

During one year of the reign of Ahab, king of Israel (874–853 b.c.), God gave the northern kingdom

The Moabite Stone, or Mesha Stele

victory over the Syrians two different times to teach one clear message. God wanted to remind Ahab that "I am the Lord" and to show the Syrians that Israel's God was not merely another local deity (1 Kings 20:13). The Syrian king Ben-hadad II (860–843 b.c.) led both attacks with an army that "filled the country" in contrast to the small number of Israelites who were "like two little flocks of kids" (v. 27).

Archaeological evidence of additional fortifications and improved water shafts in Megiddo and Hazor probably date to the time when Ahab strengthened his key cities in response to the Syrian threat. Israel repulsed both Syrian attacks and took Ben-hadad II prisoner (1 Kings 20:32–33). Contrary to the Lord's will, Ahab then set the Syrian king free in exchange for the return of captured Israelite cities and trading privileges for Israel in Damascus (v. 34). The pact led to three years of peace between the two nations (1 Kings 22:1).

It was probably during these three years that Israel allied itself with Syria to confront and diffuse the greater

TIME LINE

856 B.C.	God gives Israel victory during two Syrian attacks (1 Kings 20)
	Peace between Israel and Syria
853 B.C.	Syrians kill Ahab during the battle at Ramoth-Gilead (1 Kings 22)
	Elijah is translated; the mantle falls on Elisha (2 Kings 2)
852 B.C.	Joram becomes king of Israel (2 Kings 3)
	Syrian hosts randomly raid Israelite cities (2 Kings 6)
	The Little Maid testifies to Naaman's wife (2 Kings 5)
	Naaman journeys to Israel to be healed (2 Kings 5)
	Elisha leads the blinded Syrian invaders to Samaria (2 Kings 6)
	Syria besieges Samaria but flees without battle (2 Kings 6)
841 B.C.	Syria defeats Israel at Ramoth-Gilead for control of the area; the "house of Ahab" (2 Kings 9–11) is destroyed
800 B.C.	Elisha dies (2 Kings 13:14)

Assyrian threat from the east. Not mentioned in the Bible but documented in Assyrian inscriptions, a major battle at Qarqar, north of Israel, between a coalition of Semitic states (including Israel and Syria) and the Assyrians temporarily checked the Assyrian advance. Perhaps because their pride was stoked from their success against the Assyrians, Israel turned against Syria in the hope of regaining territory east of the Jordan River. The story of this latter confrontation is reported in scripture.

Ahab's quest to recapture Ramoth-Gilead from the Syrians broke the alliance with the northern neighbor (1 Kings 22:2–40). Ramoth-Gilead was an important city in Transjordan on the trade route from Damascus. Despite warnings of doom from the prophet Micaiah, Ahab persisted in his plan and rallied assistance from Jehoshaphat, king of Judah. Not only did Israel fail to reconquer the land but Ahab was killed in the attempt (vv. 34–40). This war against Damascus continued off and on for the next eight years, perhaps with Israel finally succeeding in regaining the Transjordan territory (2 Kings 9:14).

Scriptural hints of Syrian raids into Israelite territory likely extended the conflict over these next several years. In one such attack, the prophet Elisha revealed to King Joram places of safety to thwart the Syrian threat (2 Kings 6:8–23). When they learned that Elisha was the source of their failure, the invaders attempted to take him by force from his home in Dothan, some ten miles north of Samaria (v. 13). Surrounded by a host of Syrian soldiers, chariots and horses, Elisha and his servant prayed to the Lord (vv. 14–17). In response, the Lord smote the invading army with blindness and showed Elisha and his servant the heavenly army that was there to support them (vv. 17–18). Elisha easily led the blinded enemy to

Samaria, where he presented them to Joram with the request that he feed and shelter the prisoners of war before turning them back to their homeland (vv. 19–23).

Not to be defeated, King Ben-hadad II of Syria then led another army to Samaria to besiege the city during a famine (2 Kings 6:24–25). When the suffering in Samaria became so severe that some Israelite mothers ate each other's babies, King Joram blamed the Israelites' starvation on the Lord and turned on Elisha (vv. 26–33). In response, Elisha prophesied that on the morrow, the people of Samaria would have an abundance of food for a minimal cost. The next morning, Israelite scouts found the abandoned Syrian camp. Because the Syrian army mistakenly thought noises in the night were Egyptian and Hittite troops arriving to assist the Israelites, they fled before sunrise. In their hasty retreat, they left a trail of food, clothing, and supplies that were quickly taken to Samaria and sold for a pittance (2 Kings 6:24–7:20).

In the twelfth year of Joram's reign, the king of Israel again warred against Syria and their king named Hazeal (843–805 b.c.) for control of Ramoth-Gilead (2 Kings 8:25–28). Wounded in the battle, Joram handed over command of the Israelite army to Jehu, his general, and returned some fifty miles to his winter palace in Jezreel to convalesce. During his days of recovery, the newly anointed king of Israel, Jehu, broke in upon Joram and killed him before going on to kill almost all the other descendants of Ahab (2 Kings 9).

No further altercations between Israel and Syria are recorded in the Bible until the end of Jehu's reign as king of Israel (841–814 b.c.), when Hazeal, king of Syria, extended Syrian control in Transjordan as far south as the Dead Sea and again posed a serious threat to Israel.

The exact chronology of events between 2 Kings 4–8 is uncertain. The story of the Israelite maid and the Syrian military captain logically fits during the eight years of skirmishes after Ahab's death. Because the strongest mention of these conflicts appears in 2 Kings 6, Naaman probably visited Elisha the prophet after events described in 2 Kings 6:23–24 or even after events in 2 Kings 7. Another key to placing the story chronologically is to set it within those eight years when Israel was subject to Syria and Naaman could travel at will anywhere in Israel. Likely the king of Israel at the time was Joram, son of Ahab, and the Syrian king was Ben-hadad II.

NAAMAN, THE SYRIAN CAPTAIN

Because we are introduced to the Little Maid in the home of Naaman, a better understanding of his character and circumstances adds helpful context. As captain of the Syrian army, Naaman would have been distinguished among the Syrians as a man of high regard and prestige (2 Kings 5:1). He was sharp in intellect and strong in physical ability. The biblical narrative gives no background to explain how he came to be appointed to such a high position, but the Jewish historian Josephus does. He called Naaman a "nobleman," even when he was young, and identified him as the young Syrian soldier who gave King Ahab his fatal wound in battle over Ramoth-Gilead (*Antiquities,* 8.15.5; see also 1 Kings 22:34–40).

This great, strong man, however, was a leper. Naaman had one of a variety of skin diseases that collectively are called leprosy in the Bible. His disease appeared to be incurable. Because he was not ostracized from the royal courts, military leadership, or Syrian temple rituals, as he probably would have been in Israel, a few explanations are possible. Perhaps Naaman's leprosy did not disfigure him or cause an offensive appearance, or, possibly, his case was not as serious as those who were outcast from society. It may be, too, that leprosy in Syria was not a cause for segregation and quarantine as it was in Israel (for more information on leprosy in the Bible, see page 102).

The Bible states that Naaman was "honourable," even so much that God enabled him to be successful in battle (2 Kings 5:1). At this point, however, the Syrian hero did not recognize this divine help or the God who empowered him. All of us are like Naaman when we fail to acknowledge the Lord's hand in our lives. His help often comes in such natural ways that we look beyond Him as though we did it all ourselves. In a most unexpected way, however, the Lord would lead Naaman to know Him. Through a captive Israelite girl, this great non-Israelite hero came to revere the God of Israel as the only true God.

Artwork by Ashton Young

This representation of an ancient Syrian nobleman is reminiscent of Naaman, the captain of Syria's army.

THE TESTIMONY OF THE LITTLE MAID

Only part of the Little Maid's background can be deduced from the few details given in the scriptural text. She could have become a slave in a foreign country for a number of reasons. She might have been born to Israelites who were already enslaved in that country, or she might have been sold by her parents to pay a debt, as was almost the case with the Israelite widow's children (2 Kings 4:1–7). The scriptures, however, do record what happened to this particular slave. She was captured and carried back to Damascus by a Syrian "company" after an attack or a marauding expedition in Israel (2 Kings 5:2). Because she became the maid to his wife, Naaman probably led the attack that occurred near the Little Maid's community, or perhaps he was given the maid as a gift by one of his subordinate officers who led a raid.

The servant girl is described as "little," the translation of a Hebrew term used to indicate either age or size. The same Hebrew word was used by Solomon to express his feelings of inadequacy after being made king: "I am but a *little* child: I know not how to go out or come in" (1 Kings 3:7; emphasis added); to describe the size of the last little cake that the widow of Zarephath made with her remaining ingredients (1 Kings 17:13); and to depict Naaman after he came up out of the river water, his skin being "like unto the flesh of a *little* child" (2 Kings 5:14; emphasis added). The indication in the story, therefore, is that the Israelite slave girl in Naaman's house was young and diminutive in size.

The Bible also reports that the girl "waited upon" Naaman's wife (2 Kings 5:2). The Hebrew term translated here as "waited upon" is rendered "in his presence" in 1 Samuel 19:7. In all likelihood, the Little Maid personally attended Naaman's wife, who was the mistress of his estate, being often at her side. Her duties and living conditions were, feasibly, more desirable than those of most other servants who were taken captive and were probably quite luxurious in comparison to her family's modest home and heavy labors necessary to survive in Israel. When slave girls grew to childbearing age, they often became concubines to their mistresses' husbands.

Taken far from her home to be made a servant, it would have been understandable had the Little Maid been vindictively delighted when news spread of her master's serious disease. As merely one of countless Israelite captives taken by the Syrians at the time, she could easily have justified herself as unable to make a difference, telling herself she was too young, too helpless, and too insignificant to have an influence. She might have felt hatred for Naaman's household and bitterness for her plight at one time, but if she had, that time was past. Manifesting the spirit of the Savior's instructions for living the higher law—"love your enemies, . . . do good to them that hate you" (Matthew 5:44)—the Little Maid desired to see her master restored to health.

There is no scriptural evidence that Elisha or another prophet at that time had ever healed a "leper," yet the Little Maid believed a true prophet of God could. One wonders what circumstances she had observed, heard about, or experienced to lead her to this unshakeable faith in priesthood power. Had she or someone she knew been sick, discouraged, or lost, only to be found or healed by a power not of this world? Once we possess a solid testimony of the power of God, our understanding can stretch to accept the truth that nothing is impossible for the Lord. Whatever her previous experience with priesthood power, this little girl bore witness to Naaman's wife that a prophet in Samaria, the capital of Israel, could cure him, if he would just inquire (2 Kings 5:3).

The word in the King James Version that refers to healing Naaman is "recover" (2 Kings 5:3). The corresponding Hebrew word means "to gather, or restore" or

The age of the Israelite maid is not specified, only that she was "little," perhaps like this young Arab girl.

Photo by Ruth Ann Hubbard

"to take away or remove." The Little Maid desired that Naaman's disease be "taken away," perhaps so that he could be "gathered" or readmitted to society. Although not specifically implied in the Hebrew, but reflected in the English translation, the Little Maid's testimony promised that Naaman would be "covered again" by the Atonement of Jesus Christ if he would visit the prophet in Israel. Naaman had already been "covered"—protected and enabled to succeed in battle through the grace of the Lord's sacrifice—but now he was being invited to be healed physically and spiritually through the Lord's infinite Covering. And that remarkable invitation came from the lips of a little girl!

The Bible does not specify who told Naaman what the Little Maid said, but that he listened and acted positively in response indicates that the spirit and power of the truth in her words were transferable through at least one other person (2 Kings 5:4). Naaman's wife could have told him after hearing the stirring testimony of the slave girl; another servant might have been present, heard the testimony, and then reported it to Naaman; or the words of hope and promise may have circulated among others before they finally were told to Naaman. The fact remains that the words of the Little Maid carried stunning power.

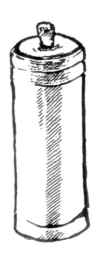

Artwork by Ashton Young

As a personal servant to Naaman's wife, the Little Maid may have applied her mistress's cosmetics that were kept in a container like this one. She may also have dressed her mistress's hair with combs and had responsibility to care for her valuables.

NAAMAN'S VISIT TO THE KING OF ISRAEL

The recitation of the Little Maid's testimony of God's power did not stop with Naaman. The leprous warrior repeated it in Damascus to Ben-hadad II, king of Syria. Showing that he believed the girl's promise of a cure, this pagan king responded positively. He wrote a letter to the king of Israel requesting that Naaman be healed and quickly amassed a generous and valuable gift as payment for the deed. Ben-hadad mistakenly assumed, however, that Elisha's healing power was at the Israelite king's command and that God's power could be purchased (2 Kings 5:5). Along with gold and multiple changes of clothing, the king gave Naaman ten talents of silver to give to Elisha as payment for the Syrian captain's recovery. As a measure of the value that Ben-hadad put on his military captain's health, consider that Omri (885–874 B.C.) bought the hill of Samaria for his capital for ten talents of silver, which was only part of the payment Naaman carried to Israel (see 1 Kings 16:24). Obviously, the king highly valued Naaman and held him in great esteem.

The king of Syria assumed the king of Israel had power to command prophets. Apparently, he made no mention of Elisha or a prophet in his letter. When Joram, king of Israel, read the letter, he failed to recognize how he or his nation could "recover" anyone of leprosy, because only God could do that (2 Kings 5:6–7). Interestingly, a little Israelite girl knew about a prophet's greatness and power from God, but the king of Israel did not. Joram did know, however, that he had power to control armies but none to heal the sick. Perhaps the void in his memory stemmed back to an incident when Elisha voiced his disregard for the king and Joram showed distrust for the prophet (2 Kings 3:13–14).

After reading the letter, Joram feared that the Syrians were presenting him with an impossible demand as a pretext to recommence a war. Extremely upset, shown by his rending his clothes, Joram accused the Syrians of seeking occasion to fight (2 Kings 5:7).

No indication is given of how Elisha learned of both the letter and King Joram's fearful response. Perhaps he had loyal friends in the royal court who knew he could resolve the crisis by helping Naaman and averting a war. The scriptures report only that when Elisha heard of Joram's panic attack, he wrote to the king to send Naaman "to me, and he shall know that there is a prophet in Israel" (2 Kings 5:8). The Syrian captain was about to learn the source of his victories and the promise of greater successes to come.

NAAMAN'S HEALING

What a scene Naaman's entourage must have created as they approached Elisha's home (2 Kings 5:9). In contrast to a military captain's impressive domicile, filled with multiple servants in addition to the Little Maid, Elisha's house must have looked very humble. What crossed the mighty Naaman's mind as he stood in front of Elisha's door to ask for help that no one else could provide? The Hebrew text even implies that the prestigious Syrian was required to wait for a while before the door was opened. He probably was not accustomed to being treated as an ordinary person. Being willing to follow advice from a young Israelite girl, however, is evidence that he had already commenced along the path to humility and recognition that God sees worth in different ways than the world measures it.

Naaman washed seven times in the River Jordan, south of the Sea of Galilee.

Photo by Ruth Ann Hubbard

Israelite girl, however, is evidence that he had already commenced along the path to humility and recognition that God sees worth in different ways than the world measures it.

When the prophet's servant appeared at the door to relay Elisha's instructions instead of the prophet himself appearing, Naaman's pride broke through, manifested by his anger (2 Kings 5:10–11). Articulating what he had thought would happen—"he will surely come out to me"—the Syrian revealed the cause of his lost humility (2 Kings 5:11). How often do we lose our tempers when things happen in some way other than we expect? By assuming we know what God thinks and how He will solve our problems, we set ourselves up to be disappointed and unrighteously judge others.

Naaman's inaccurate expectations continued. He was also dissatisfied that Elisha did not perform a ritual to heal him, as was likely the way "healers" in his culture approached the sick (2 Kings 5:11). Far from exhibiting fear of becoming unclean through association with a leper or some other selfish concern, Elisha remained hidden, perhaps to break down Naaman's false assumptions about healing power.

The absence of the prophet also placed greater focus on his directives to Naaman. Rather than performing an idol-worship dance or ritual to heal someone, we might have expected Elisha to direct the Syrian to do something clearly faith-promoting, such as being consistent in prayer and gospel study.

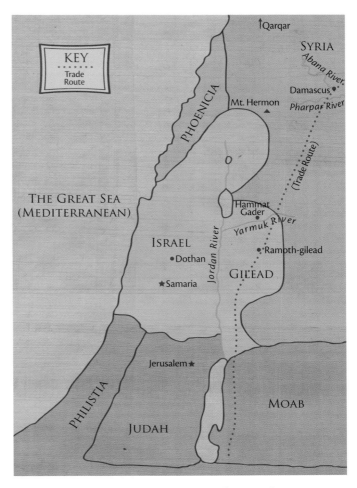

Before Assyria conquered Israel, the trade route from Damascus along the east bank of the Jordan River was often contested by neighboring kingdoms.

Instead, the prophet required him to manifest his trust in God's messenger by performing an unusual act of faith—washing seven times in the Jordan River.

One look at the murky Jordan River probably added intensity to Naaman's fury. The two rivers that flow through and around Damascus were visibly superior to Israel's river, so Naaman figured he could have stayed home to perform the healing rather than condescend into inferior Israel (2 Kings 5:12). The river called the Abana in the biblical account is probably the river known today as the Barada. Its transparent waters descend from surrounding mountains to flow through the city of Damascus and water the surrounding plains. The Pharpar is thought to be the river known today as the el-A'wai, which flows east from Mount Hermon and travels just south of the city of Damascus. These two rivers made Damascus a fertile

Naaman was familiar with the mighty Euphrates River (above) and was impressed with the Pharpar and Abana Rivers of Damascus. By comparison, the River Jordan appeared quite inconsequential.

oasis in the middle of the desert. Their waters were cleaner than the clay-colored waters of the Jordan (Keil and Delitzch, *Commentary,* 225).

As Naaman "turned and went away in a rage," his servants gave him reason to heed the prophet's directives (2 Kings 5:12–13). Exhibiting an unusual loyalty and concern for their master, they referred to the captain as "my father" and counseled him to not reject Elisha's instructions merely because they directed the mighty Syrian to do something simple and unsophisticated. Naaman's situation echoes the predicament and opportunity that the children of Israel faced when they were threatened by poisonous snakes in the wilderness. When invited merely to look on the brazen serpent—an emblem of the Savior—to be healed, many of the Israelites died "because of the simpleness of the way" (1 Nephi 17:41).

Remarkably, and to Naaman's credit, he listened to his servants' counsel and chose to obey precisely Elisha's instructions (2 Kings 5:14). Perhaps the counsel of the Little Maid back home had opened Naaman's ears to hear what his other servants advised. A fifth-century Byzantine tradition claimed that fourteen hundred years before, lepers were healed by Hammat Gader in the River Jordan near where it leaves the Sea of Chinnereth in the Yarmuk Valley (Cogan and Tadmor, *II Kings,* 65).

Naaman's recovery from leprosy in inferior waters reinforced the message that healing and cleansing do not occur by washing in water, whether it be crystal clear or muddy, but through the power of God. The act of faith that Elisha required symbolized baptism for Naaman. As the Israelites had done when Joshua led them into the promised land by crossing through the Jordan, Naaman also entered a spiritual promised land through the Jordan. Likewise, when we are baptized, the baptismal waters do not wash away our sins. Only through the mercy, merits, and grace of Jesus Christ are we made clean.

Before his cleansing, Naaman demonstrated his faith in the God of Israel through an act of obedience and trust. The healing power of God occurred only after Naaman exhibited faith and obeyed the Lord's representative. Naaman was thereby saved by God's grace. Healed of his leprosy and of his idolatry, he was born again both physically and spiritually. The Syrian captain had been introduced to the Atonement of Christ.

NAAMAN'S CONVERSION AND SYRIAN WORSHIP

Recognizing that all the gold and silver he had carried with him from Syria would never pay the debt he owed for being healed, Naaman returned to Elisha in gratitude and a willingness to confess his new faith. "Now I know that there is no God in all the earth, but in Israel," he testified (2 Kings 5:15). God had given the Syrian captain infinitely more than he would ever be able to repay; Naaman would be Jehovah's servant forever. In his mind, however, the blessing of a testimony of the living God did not excuse him from giving Elisha the generous payment from the king of Syria.

Without hesitation, Elisha viewed himself in relation to God and gave the only correct answer to Naaman's generous offer: "I will receive none" (2 Kings 5:16). Elisha's refusal for payment reinforced his testimony of the source of his power and avoided the temptation of priestcraft (2 Nephi 26:29). Naaman's healing occurred through the grace and power of God, not because of any power inherent in Elisha.

A belief among many polytheists of the day was that no deity could be worshipped except in his own nation. Even the future king David became distressed about being exiled from Israel because he feared he would be required to "serve other gods" (1 Samuel 26:19). Therefore, Naaman wanted to transport sufficient soil to allow him to worship Israel's God when he returned to Syria (2 Kings 5:17).

The Syrian convert to Jehovah had one question before he departed. He knew that when he was back in Damascus, at the temple built for the Syrian storm god, that his master, King Ben-hadad II, would expect him to worship with him there. Rimmon, or Hadad-rimmon (Zechariah 12:11), was the god of thunder in Syria, similar to the Phoenician and Canaanite god of thunder called Ba'al. The awkward repetitiveness in Naaman's explanation in 2 Kings 5:18 reflects his nervousness in apologizing for his continuing to worship Rimmon, which he knew would be offensive to Israel's God.

In contrast to Naaman's rambling, Elisha was succinct: "Go in peace" (2 Kings 5:19). Although simple, the response gave Naaman no direct answer to his dilemma of giving the appearance of worshipping an idol while in his heart worshipping the God of Israel. The prophet's modest answer reinforced to Naaman that God, not Elisha, provided both the miracle of his healing and held the answer to Naaman's concern. With the sustaining power of God, Naaman would likely be a true, albeit secret, follower of Israel's God when he returned home to Syria. Having forsaken his master's god, Naaman now added his testimony to that borne by the Little Maid.

CONFLICTING RESPONSE FROM GEHAZI

The Syrian company began their return to Damascus but had not traveled far when Gehazi, Elisha's servant, ran after them. The Syrian-offered gift of tremendous wealth may not have tempted Elisha, but it consumed Gehazi (2 Kings 5:20–21). In a concocted tale, Gehazi claimed that Elisha had sent him to accept a small gift of silver and clothing to provide for two poor pupils of the prophets. Gehazi had likely never before seen so much wealth in his life, let alone heard it offered in a gesture of gratitude. But that was no excuse for one who claimed allegiance to the Creator of all.

The Little Maid and Naaman discovered that no material wealth exceeds the value of a testimony of the living God. In a tremendous evidence of his own weakness and lack of faith, Gehazi chose greed and selfishness rather than appreciation for God's abundant blessings.

Gehazi took his dishonestly acquired loot to the safety of a house on the elevated part of the city, the "tower" or citadel, before returning to Elisha (2 Kings 5:24). To Elisha's inquiry of where Gehazi had been, his servant responded with what he unquestionably knew was a lie.

Elisha was already aware that Gehazi had chosen to make merchandise out of the sacred power of God. The prophet's poignant response echoed the Lord's own remorse for the fallen disciple, "Went not mine heart with thee?" (2 Kings 5:26). The possessions Elisha named are likely an indication of what Gehazi hoped to purchase with the two talents of silver he secured from Naaman.

Punished for his avarice and for tainting the prophet's true motive, Gehazi was cursed with leprosy. In a remarkable reversal of roles, the greedy and disloyal Israelite Gehazi was afflicted with the disease that cuts off the victim from God, whereas the humble pagan Naaman acted in faith and became a clean and welcomed servant of Jehovah. Becoming "a leper as white as snow" (2 Kings 5:27) suggests that the pallor of his skin was the color of snow or that the affected skin cells dried up and fell away like flakes of snow. The harshest consequence for willing disobedience to God is being cut off or separated from His presence. That is the symbolism of leprosy (see page 102). Perhaps the greatest tragedy is that such a "curse" often passes to future generations, as it appears to have done in Gehazi's family.

WHAT HAPPENED WHEN NAAMAN RETURNED?

No more is told about the Little Maid after she encouraged Naaman to seek a prophet of God. The absence of information, however, does not preclude our asking questions and formulating possible scenarios about what happened to her after Naaman returned home. Although Naaman would have responded to the amazement and curiosity of his transformation from his wife and associates, his possible encounter with the Little Maid could have been the most dramatic.

Although the Syrian captain probably had not addressed the Israelite slave in the past, he might have sought her out when he returned home. Visualizing the scene is an interesting exercise. Who would have shown greater respect for the other? Who would have been the stronger of the two? Who would have been the more uncomfortable, not knowing the right words to communicate deep gratitude? The unusual reversal of roles, with the great and powerful captain outranked by the diminutive servant, is a reminder of how God often chooses the small and weak to turn a lost soul to Him. The absence of the girl's name further underscores her humility in serving solely out of love and concern for another, without any thought for herself.

Other questions search for hints of what life was like for Naaman and the Little Maid years later. In his gratitude for the maid's gift of testimony, would Naaman have freed the girl from slavery and even escorted her home? Would she have elected to stay as a member of his household, finding in Naaman and his wife something akin to second parents? Would Naaman's testimony, in turn, have strengthened the Little Maid in times of difficulty that she would surely face in the future? Would Naaman have been emboldened to share his witness of God to others in his family and among his associates because of the courage and faith of the little Israelite girl? These questions are not answerable, of course, but we can with some certainty conclude that because Naaman had been born again, his daily life would have borne witness of his mighty change of heart, much like the life of the Little Maid. Like her, the great Syrian would be a witness "of God at all times and in all things, and in all places" (Mosiah 18:9).

On the other hand, Naaman might never have thought to thank the girl. She could have remained unnoticed and insignificant. But not by God or in the series of events and lives that she influenced. Through the Atonement, Jesus Christ takes bad things caused by foolish or wicked people and makes good things happen. He did not cause or approve of enslavement, but through it, He blessed the lives of a little girl, a great Syrian captain, and so many others. She should never have been in her predicament in faraway Syria, but there she was. Through the magnanimous power and mercy of the Savior, He enabled her to grow beyond her natural abilities and reach out to strengthen others as He does. That is the gift that all disciples of Christ desire.

The story's larger message is a warning to Israel. God's covenant is made with any person who accepts and heeds Him as God, whether that person is a literal descendant of the sons of Jacob or is from outside of Israel, whether that person is surrounded by other believers or is alone among unbelievers. A captive Israelite girl and the gentile Naaman were steadfast in their faith in Jehovah, which contrasted sharply with the fear and selfishness shown by Gehazi and by the king of Israel.

Much like Gehazi, the Jews in Nazareth rejected the Savior after they were blessed to see, hear, and experience His teachings and miracles. To this privileged group, the Savior spoke of Naaman: "And many lepers were in Israel in the time of [Elisha] the prophet; and none of them was cleansed, saving Naaman the Syrian" (Luke 4:27).

Vulnerable and far from home, the Little Maid was not alone. She knew her God was always with her. In simple ways, she exemplified much of what Jesus Christ has asked of us. She recognized the worth of a soul and knew that the atoning blood of Christ is available to every individual. Freely she had received, and freely she was willing to give (Matthew 10:8). With nothing to gain and much to lose by offering her master unsolicited advice, her bold witness of a prophet in Israel stands as a remarkable act of faith and charity.

POINTS TO PONDER: APPLICATIONS FOR OUR LIVES

1. How does the Little Maid help us find the Lord's enabling power in the face of others' unrighteous actions? How can "opposition in all things" (2 Nephi 2:11) help us find God's perfect love for ourselves?

2. What principles of effective missionary service are exemplified by the Little Maid?

3. How can being "recovered" from an illness or other challenge typify the Atonement of Christ?

4. What does the story of the Little Maid teach about the value of social status in God's eyes? Who did He say was the greatest? What would the Savior say to Naaman because he received the testimony of a little girl? (Matthew 18:1–5).

5. How does the story of the Little Maid engender confidence to influence those not of our faith to believe in Christ? Was advanced education, training, high social status, or material wealth required for her to succeed? What did she have?

6. In what ways was the Little Maid a type of Christ?

7. How does the Little Maid encourage us toward greater faith in the Savior's Atonement?

CONCLUSION

Without thinking, we can portray scriptural women in two-dimensional terms: we may either elevate them to occupy pedestals or demote them as pitiful swamp dwellers. Naturally, none of us wants to live in the swamp, but I do not think that any of us really desires to be put on a pedestal, either. What is there to do on a pedestal? Sit up there and look pretty—or fall off.

Because the scriptures typically give only one or at most a few snapshots of a woman's life, the temptation is to make a judgment and assign a label to define the woman's entire life. That is especially true when two women with different challenges appear together in a biblical story, such as Sarah and Hagar, Rachel and Leah, or Deborah and Jael. If the passage exposes a weakness in a woman, we can easily conclude that everything about her was weak or evil. If we find evidence of strength and goodness in a biblical woman, we may hastily conclude that she was a sinless, perfect woman, who never became discouraged or doubted.

Careful observation of women then and now reveals that none is a pedestal dweller and few spend their lives in the swamp. We can readily detect imperfections in the women of the Old Testament, but we can also find much to admire and emulate in their imperfect lives. Their challenges and struggles have led me to feel that I belong with them. Not one is exactly like me, but individually and collectively they help me face my challenges and recognize the tender mercies of the Lord in my life.

As a result of studying these women, we remember that the purpose of scripture is to bear witness of Jesus Christ, not to define the level of righteousness of the various individuals portrayed therein. As is true for all of us today, none of these biblical women was without weakness, and all had a divine potential to contribute to the Lord's work. That is why careful gospel study never confuses the Savior with anyone else in scripture. He alone is without sin; everyone else has a desperate need for the Redeemer.

By acknowledging that God performed some of His work in ancient times through a variety of women with a broad diversity in personalities, strengths, life circumstances, and opportunities, we are less likely to fear diversity in those same areas among today's women who likewise love the Lord and desire to serve

Him. In other words, it would be difficult for a modern-day disciple of Christ to see herself as an outlier if she were acquainted with the women in scripture. We would all feel more included in the Church, for example, if we acknowledged that God has always worked His miracles through women and men who differ dramatically from each other. It is the Atonement of Jesus Christ that unites us, not our physical appearance, talents, cultural background, or comparative gospel knowledge.

We live in a day when scriptures are readily available and when we can regularly read or hear the counsel of prophets, seers, and revelators. These tremendous opportunities do not signal that we need Christ less than did the women in ancient days. We need Him every bit as much as they did. One day we will have an opportunity to meet these women. They were ordinary women who made extraordinary contributions despite their challenges and foibles—because of the grace of the Lord. They are waiting to teach us that we, as ordinary individuals, can also do extraordinary things to make the world a better place and bring people to Christ when we follow their examples by turning our lives over to Him.

APPENDIXES

Appendix A, Old Testament Time Line. Specific years cannot be assigned to major events and main characters in the Old Testament, and even estimates for the century during which they lived can vary considerably, particularly before Israel's monarchy was instituted. Yet recognizing the general flow of biblical history is essential to understanding its stories and teachings. This time line identifies the major Old Testament eras, including events, prophetic and royal leaders, and the women discussed in this volume. The assigned dates are approximate.

Appendix B, Women Identified in the Old Testament. A complete listing of every woman who is named or described in the Old Testament is provided to encourage and assist further study of women of the Old Testament. Because of potentially parallel reports of the same incident in which a woman or women are named, it is occasionally uncertain whether the various names reported indicate one woman or two. Such circumstances are noted in this appendix. Also included are the meaning of each name, as well as references in scripture and the LDS Bible Dictionary where applicable.

Appendix C, The Artists and the Paintings. Elspeth Young, the primary artist for the paintings used in this volume, introduces herself and gives some background for her involvement in this project. Her brother, Ashton, provided line drawings that appear throughout this book. Elspeth and her father, Al R. Young, describe their respective paintings, including symbolism and details that were used to communicate additional insight for each woman depicted. The scriptural accounts of each woman in the series were the primary sources of inspiration to the artists. In addition, insight for certain costume elements, settings, and flora and fauna were artistic interpretations of artifacts still surviving from ancient cultures. Research sources for these artifacts, as well as sources that describe the manners and customs of daily life in Bible times, are listed after the description of each painting.

Appendix A

TIME LINE

Era	Century before Christ	Event
		The Creation
		The Flood
The Patriarchs	2000	The Abrahamic Covenant
	1900	
	1800	
	1700	Jacob's family moves to Egypt
Egyptian captivity	1600	
	1500	
	1400	
Wilderness wanderings	1300	Exodus from Egypt
The judges	1200	Entering the promised land
	1100	
United monarchy	1000	Saul's reign (1040–1000 B.C.)
		David's reign (1000–960 B.C.)
		Solomon's reign (960–930 B.C.)
Divided monarchy	900	The kingdom divides (929 B.C.)
	800	
	700	Assyria scatters northern kingdom (722 B.C.)
Babylonian empire	600	Josiah's reign (640–609 B.C.)
		Babylonia captures southern kingdom (586 B.C.)
Persian empire	500	Persia allows Judah to return
	400	
Greek empire	300	Alexander conquers the Persians (332 B.C.)
	200	
Hasmonean rule	100	The Maccabees rule Israel (166–63 B.C.)
Roman rule	1	Rome appoints Herod to rule Palestine (40 B.C.)

Prophet	Women
Adam	Eve
Enoch	
Noah	
Abraham	Sarah, Hagar, Keturah
Isaac	Rebekah
Jacob	Leah and Rachel, Bilhah and Zilpah
Joseph	Asenath, Tamar
Moses	Shiphrah and Puah, Miriam, Zipporah
Joshua	Daughters of Zelophehad, Rahab
	Deborah, Ruth
	Hannah
Samuel	
Nathan	Michal, Abigail, Ahinoam, Bathsheba, Abishag
Elijah	Widow of Zarephath, Jezebel
Elisha	Shunammite, Little Maid, the woman whose oil was multiplied
Isaiah	
Jeremiah	Huldah
Malachi	Vashti, Esther
Jesus Christ	Mary

Appendix B
WOMEN IDENTIFIED IN THE OLD TESTAMENT

Women in the Old Testament can be identified with only partial certainty. On occasion the name or the identity of the woman is vague. Some of the meanings of the names are likewise tentative. Superscript numbers refer to different women sharing the same name.

WOMEN WHO ARE NAMED

Abi "My father is Jehovah"

  2 Kings 18:2

  2 Chronicles 29:1 (called Abijah)

Abiah "Jehovah is father"

  1 Chronicles 2:24

Abigail[1] "Father of joy"

  1 Samuel 25; 26:3; 27:3; 30:1–20

  2 Samuel 2:2; 3:3

  1 Chronicles 3:1

  LDS Bible Dictionary, 601

Abigail[2] "Father of joy"

  2 Samuel 17:25

  1 Chronicles 2:16–17

  LDS Bible Dictionary, 601

Abihail[1] "Father of strength"

  1 Chronicles 2:29

Abihail[2] "Father of strength"

  2 Chronicles 11:18

Abishag "My father wanders"

  1 Kings 1:1–4, 15; 2:13–25

Abital "Father of dew"

  2 Samuel 3:4

  1 Chronicles 3:3

Achsah "Anklet"

  Joshua 15:16–19

  Judges 1:12–15

  1 Chronicles 2:49

Adah[1] "Ornament"

  Genesis 4:19–24

  Moses 5:44–47

Adah[2] "Ornament"

  Genesis 36:2, 4, 10, 12, 16

  (May be the same person as Bashemath[2])

Ahinoam[1] "Brother is good"

  1 Samuel 14:50; 20:30

Ahinoam[2] "Brother is good"

  1 Samuel 25:43; 27:3; 30:1–20

2 Samuel 2:2; 3:2

1 Chronicles 3:1

LDS Bible Dictionary, 605

Ahlai "Wishful"

1 Chronicles 2:31

Aholibamah "My tabernacle is exalted"

Genesis 36:2, 5, 14, 18, 25

Anah "One who answers"

Genesis 36:2, 18 (vv. 20–29 describe a man)

Asenath (of Egyptian origin)

Genesis 41:45–52; 46:20

LDS Bible Dictionary, 615

Atarah "Crown"

1 Chronicles 2:26

Athaliah "Afflicted of the Lord"

2 Kings 8:26; 11

1 Chronicles 8:26

2 Chronicles 22:2–12; 23:12–21; 24:7

Ezra 8:7

LDS Bible Dictionary, 617

Azubah¹ "Forsaken"

1 Chronicles 2:18–19

Azubah² "Forsaken"

1 Kings 22:42

2 Chronicles 20:31

Baara "Burning"

1 Chronicles 8:8

(May be the same person as Hodesh in v. 9)

Bashemath¹ "Fragrant"

Genesis 26:34

(May be the same person as Adah²)

Bashemath² "Fragrant"

Genesis 36:3, 4, 10, 13, 17

(May be same person as Mahalath¹)

Basmath "Fragrant"

1 Kings 4:15

Bathsheba "Daughter of the covenant"

2 Samuel 11; 12:1–24

1 Kings 1:15–31; 2:12–25

1 Chronicles 3:5 (Bath-shua)

Psalm 51

Matthew 1:6

Doctrine & Covenants 132:39

LDS Bible Dictionary, 620

Bilhah "Timid"

Genesis 29:29; 30:3–7; 35:22, 25; 37:2; 46:25

1 Chronicles 7:13

Doctrine & Covenants 132:38

LDS Bible Dictionary, 625

Bithiah "Daughter of Jehovah"

1 Chronicles 4:18

Cozbi "Deceitful"

Numbers 25:6–18

Deborah¹ "Bee"

Genesis 24:59; 35:8

LDS Bible Dictionary, 655

Deborah² "Bee"

Judges 4–5

LDS Bible Dictionary, 655

Delilah "Delicate"

Judges 16:4–20

LDS Bible Dictionary, 655

Dinah "Justice"

Genesis 30:21; 34; 46:15

LDS Bible Dictionary, 657

Eglah "Heifer"

2 Samuel 3:5

1 Chronicles 3:3

Elisheba "God is my oath"

    Exodus 6:23

Ephah "Gloomy"

    1 Chronicles 2:46

Ephrath "Fruitful land"

    1 Chronicles 2:19, 50; 4:4 (called Ephratah)

Esther "Star"

    Book of Esther

    Ezra 4:6

    LDS Bible Dictionary, 667; also 673, "Feast of
        Purim"

Eve "Life"

    Genesis 2:21–25; 3; 4:1, 25

    2 Corinthians 11:3

    1 Timothy 2:13–15

    1 Nephi 5:11

    2 Nephi 2:18–21; 9:9

    Alma 12:21–26

    Doctrine & Covenants 138:39

    Moses 2:27; 3:22–25; 4:6–30; 5:1–27;
        6:2–6, 9

    Abraham 5:16–19

    LDS Bible Dictionary, 668

Gomer "Complete"

    Hosea 1:3

Hagar "Flight"

    Genesis 16:1–16; 17:20; 21:9–21; 25:12

    Galatians 4:22–31 (spelled Agar)

    Doctrine & Covenants 132:34, 37, 65

    LDS Bible Dictionary, 698

Haggith "Festive"

    2 Samuel 3:4

    1 Kings 1:5, 11; 2:13

    1 Chronicles 3:2

Hammoleketh "Queen"

    1 Chronicles 7:18

Hamutal "Akin to dew"

    2 Kings 23:31; 24:18

    Jeremiah 52:1

Hannah "Grace"

    1 Samuel 1; 2:1–11, 18–21

    LDS Bible Dictionary, 698

Hazelelponi "Deliver me, O God"

    1 Chronicles 4:3

Helah "Necklace"

    1 Chronicles 4:5, 7

Hephzibah "My delight is in her"

    2 Kings 21:1

    LDS Bible Dictionary, 700

Hodesh "New moon"

    1 Chronicles 8:9

    (May be the same person as Baara)

Hodiah "Splendor of Jehovah"

    1 Chronicles 4:19

    (May be the same person as Jehudijah)

Hoglah "Partridge"

    Numbers 26:33; 27:1–11; 36

    Joshua 17:3–6

    1 Chronicles 7:15

Huldah "Weasel"

    2 Kings 22:12–20

    2 Chronicles 34:22–28

Hushim "Who makes haste"

    1 Chronicles 8:8, 11

Iscah "Observant"

    Genesis 11:29

Jael "Wild goat"

    Judges 4:17–22; 5:6, 24–27

    LDS Bible Dictionary, 709

Jecholiah "Strong through Jehovah"

2 Kings 15:1–3

2 Chronicles 26:3 (spelled Jecoliah)

Jedidah "Beloved of Jehovah"

2 Kings 22:1

Jehoaddan "Whom Jehovah adorns"

2 Kings 14:2

2 Chronicles 25:1

Jehosheba "Jehovah's oath"

2 Kings 11:2

2 Chronicles 22:11 (spelled Jehoshabeath)

Jehudijah "The Jewess"

1 Chronicles 4:18

(May be the same person as Hodiah)

Jemima "Little dove"

Job 42:14–15

Jerioth "Tents"

1 Chronicles 2:18

Jerushah "Married"

2 Kings 15:33

2 Chronicles 27:1

Jezebel "Chaste"

1 Kings 16:31; 18:4–19; 19:1–3

2 Kings 9

LDS Bible Dictionary, 713

Jochebed "Jehovah is glory"

Exodus 2:1–10; 6:20

Numbers 26:59

Hebrews 11:23

LDS Bible Dictionary, 714

Judith "Jewess"

Genesis 26:34–35

Keren-Happuch "Horn of beauty"

Job 42:14–15

Keturah "Perfumed" or "Incense"

Genesis 25:1–6

1 Chronicles 1:32–33

Doctrine & Covenants 132:37

LDS Bible Dictionary, 721

Kezia "Cassia"

Job 42:14–15

Leah "Weary"

Genesis 29; 30; 31; 33; 34:1; 35:23, 26;
46:15,18; 49:31

Ruth 4:11

Doctrine & Covenants 132:37

LDS Bible Dictionary, 723

Lo-Ruhamah "Not having obtained mercy"

Hosea 1:6–7

Maachah[1] "Oppression"

2 Samuel 3:3

1 Chronicles 3:2

Maachah[2] "Oppression"

1 Kings 15:2, 10, 13

2 Chronicles 11:20–22; 13:2 (called
Michaiah); 15:16

Maachah[3] "Oppression"

1 Chronicles 2:48–49

Maachah[4] "Oppression"

1 Chronicles 7:15–16

Maachah[5] "Oppression"

1 Chronicles 8:29; 9:35

Mahalah "Sickness"

1 Chronicles 7:18

Mahalath[1] "Sickness"

Genesis 28:9

(May be the same person as Bashemath[2])

Mahalath[2] "Sickness"

2 Chronicles 11:18

Mahlah "Sickness"

    Numbers 26:33; 27:1–11; 36:1–11

    Joshua 17:3–6

    1 Chronicles 7:15

Matred "Pushing forward"

    Genesis 36:39

    1 Chronicles 1:50

Mehetabel "God does good"

    Genesis 36:39

    1 Chronicles 1:50

Merab "Increase"

    1 Samuel 14:49; 17:25; 18:17–19

    2 Samuel 21:8 (probably Merab)

Meshullemeth "Friend"

    2 Kings 21:19

Michaiah "Who is like Jehovah"

    2 Chronicles 13:2 (may be the same person as Maachah²)

Michal "Who is like Jehovah"

    1 Samuel 14:49; 18:20–28; 19:11–17; 25:44

    2 Samuel 3:13–16; 6:16–23; 21:8 (probably Merab)

    1 Chronicles 15:29

    LDS Bible Dictionary, 732

Milcah¹ "Counsel"

    Genesis 11:29; 22:20, 23; 24:15, 24, 47

Milcah² "Counsel"

    Numbers 26:33; 27:1–11; 36:1–13

    Joshua 17:3–6

    1 Chronicles 7:15

Miriam¹ "Bitterness" or "Exalted"

    Exodus 2:4–8; 15:20–21

    Numbers 12:1–16; 20:1; 26:59

    Deuteronomy 24:8–9

    1 Chronicles 6:3

    Micah 6:4

    LDS Bible Dictionary, 733

Miriam² "Bitterness" or "Exalted"

    1 Chronicles 4:17

Naamah¹ "Pleasant"

    Genesis 4:22

    Moses 5:46

Naamah² "Pleasant"

    1 Kings 14:21, 31

    2 Chronicles 12:13

Naarah "Maiden"

    1 Chronicles 4:5, 6

Naomi "Pleasant" (calls herself Mara, "Bitterness")

    Ruth 1–4

    LDS Bible Dictionary, 737

Nehushta "Brass"

    2 Kings 24:8

Noadiah "Whom Jehovah meets"

    Nehemiah 6:14

Noah "Comfort"

    Numbers 26:33; 27:1–11; 36:1–13

    Joshua 17:3–6

    1 Chronicles 7:15

Orpah "Stubborn"

    Ruth 1:4, 14

Peninnah "Pearl"

    1 Samuel 1:1–7

Puah "Splendid"

    Exodus 1:15–21

Rachel "Ewe"

    Genesis 29–35; 46:19, 22, 25; 48:7

    Ruth 4:11

    1 Samuel 10:2

    Jeremiah 31:15 (spelled Rahel)

    Matthew 2:18

Doctrine & Covenants 132:37

LDS Bible Dictionary, 759

Rahab "Spacious"

Joshua 2:1–21; 6:17–25

Matthew 1:5 (spelled Rachab)

Hebrews 11:31

James 2:25

LDS Bible Dictionary, 759

Rebekah "Ensnarer"

Genesis 22:23; 24–29; 35:8; 49:31

Romans 9:10–13 (spelled Rebecca)

Doctrine & Covenants 132:37

LDS Bible Dictionary, 760

Reumah "Elevated"

Genesis 22:24

Rizpah "Live coal"

2 Samuel 3:7; 21:8–11

Ruth "Friend"

Ruth 1–4

Matthew 1:5

LDS Bible Dictionary, 764

Sarah "Princess"

Genesis 11:29–32; 12–24; 49:31

Isaiah 51:2

Romans 4:19; 9:9 (spelled Sara)

Galatians 4:23–31

Hebrews 11:11 (spelled Sara)

1 Peter 3:6–7

2 Nephi 8:2

Doctrine & Covenants 132:29, 34–37;
     137:5–6

Abraham 2

LDS Bible Dictionary, 769

Serah "Lady"

Genesis 46:17

Numbers 26:46 (spelled Sarah)

1 Chronicles 7:30

Shelomith[1] "Peaceful"

Leviticus 24:10–12

Shelomith[2] "Peaceful"

1 Chronicles 3:19

Sherah "Kinswoman"

1 Chronicles 7:24

Shimeath "Fame"

2 Kings 12:21

2 Chronicles 24:26

Shimrith "Vigilant"

2 Kings 12:21 (called Shomer)

2 Chronicles 24:26

Shiphrah "Brightness"

Exodus 1:15–21

Shua "Wealth"

1 Chronicles 7:32

Shuah "Wealth"

Genesis 38:2, 12

1 Chronicles 2:3 (spelled Shua)

Tahpenes "Head of the age"

1 Kings 11:18–20

Tamar[1] "Palm tree"

Genesis 38

Ruth 4:12

1 Chronicles 2:4

Matthew 1:3 (spelled Thamar)

LDS Bible Dictionary, 780

Tamar[2] "Palm tree"

2 Samuel 13

1 Chronicles 3:9

LDS Bible Dictionary, 780

Tamar³ "Palm tree"

2 Samuel 14:27

LDS Bible Dictionary, 780

Taphath "Drop of myrrh"

1 Kings 4:11

Timna "Restraint"

Genesis 36:12, 22

1 Chronicles 1:39

Tirzah "Delight"

Numbers 26:33; 27:1–11; 36:1–11

Joshua 17:3–6

1 Chronicles 7:15

Vashti "Beautiful"

Esther 1:9–19

LDS Bible Dictionary, 787

Zebudah "Bestowed"

2 Kings 23:36

Zeresh "Gold"

Esther 5:10, 14; 6:13

Zeruah "Leprous"

1 Kings 11:26

Zeruiah "Balm from Jehovah"

1 Samuel 26:6

2 Samuel 2:13, 18; 3:39; 8:16; 14:1; 16:9–10; 17:25; 18:2; 19:21, 22; 21:17; 23:18, 37

1 Kings 1:7; 2:5, 22

1 Chronicles 2:16; 11:6, 39; 18:12, 15; 26:28; 27:24

Zibiah "Female gazelle"

2 Kings 12:1

2 Chronicles 24:1

Zillah "Shadow"

Genesis 4:19–23

Moses 5:44–53

Zilpah "A trickling"

Genesis 29:24; 30:9–13; 35:26; 37:2; 46:18

Doctrine & Covenants 132:37

Zipporah "Sparrow"

Exodus 2:16–22; 4:20, 25, 26; 18:2

LDS Bible Dictionary, 793

WOMEN WHO ARE NOT NAMED

DAUGHTERS OF

Adam Genesis 5:4; Moses 5:2, 3, 12; Moses 6:5, 6, 11

Seth Genesis 5:7; Moses 6:14

Enos Genesis 5:10; Moses 6:18

Cainan Genesis 5:13; Moses 6:18

Mahalaleel Genesis 5:16; Moses 6:20

Jared Genesis 5:19; Moses 6:21

Enoch (of Zion) Genesis 5:22; Moses 6:21

Methuselah Genesis 5:26

Lamech Genesis 5:30

"Men" Genesis 6:2

Shem Genesis 11:11

Salah Genesis 11:13

Eber Genesis 11:15

Peleg Genesis 11:19

Reu Genesis 11:21

Serug Genesis 11:23

Nahor Genesis 11:25

Lot Genesis 19:8, 15, 30–38

Pharaoh Exodus 2:5, 7–10; Acts 7:21; Hebrews 11:24

Priest of Midian Exodus 2:16, 20 includes Zipporah

Putiel Exodus 6:25

Priest Leviticus 21:9

Jephthah Judges 11:34, 35, 40

Ibzan Judges 12:9

Peninnah and Elkanah 1 Samuel 1:4

Hannah and Elkanah 1 Samuel 2:21

Philistines 2 Samuel 1:20

Machir 1 Chronicles 2:21

Sheshan 1 Chronicles 2:35

Shimei 1 Chronicles 4:27

Heman 1 Chronicles 25:5

Barzillai Ezra 2:61; Nehemiah 7:63

Foreigners Ezra 9:2

Shallum Nehemiah 3:12

Sanballat Nehemiah 13:28

King Psalm 45

"As cornerstones" Psalm 144:12

"Zion" Isaiah 3:16–26

King (Zedekiah) Jeremiah 41:10

King of the south Daniel 11:6

WIFE OF

Cain Genesis 4:17; Moses 5:28, 42

Noah Genesis 6:18; 7:7, 13; 8:16, 18; Moses 8:12

Noah's sons Genesis 7:7, 13; 8:18

Lot Genesis 19:26; Luke 17:32; Abraham 2:4

Judah Genesis 38:2–5, 12

Potiphar Genesis 39:7–9, 12, 19

Moses (Ethiopian woman) Numbers 12:1

Gideon Judges 8:30

Gilead Judges 11:2

Manoah Judges 13:2, 11, 19–23

Samson Judges 14:15–20

Levite's concubines Judges 19, 20

Four hundred young wives Judges 21:12–23

David (ten concubines) 2 Samuel 15:16; 16:20–23; 20:3

Solomon 1 Kings 3:1; 7:8; 11:1–8

Hadad 1 Kings 11:19–20

Jeroboam 1 Kings 14:2–6, 17

Naaman 2 Kings 5:2

Machir 1 Chronicles 7:15

Artaxerxes Nehemiah 2:6

Job Job 2:9; 19:17; 31:10

Isaiah Isaiah 8:3–4

Wives who burned incense to gods Jeremiah 44:15

Ezekiel Ezekiel 24:16–18

WIDOW

Women of Midian Numbers 31:9

Of Zarephath 1 Kings 17:8–24; Luke 4:25–26

Whose oil was multiplied 2 Kings 4:1–7

MOTHER OF

Shaul the Canaanite Genesis 46:10; Exodus 6:15

Sisera Judges 5:28

Abimelech Judges 9:1, 3

Micah Judges 17:2–4

Ichabod 1 Samuel 4:19–22

David 1 Samuel 22:3, 4

Two mothers judged by Solomon 1 Kings 3:16–28

Hiram 1 Kings 7:13–14

Elisha 1 Kings 19:20

Two mothers who agreed to eat their sons 2 Kings 6:26–30

Jabez 1 Chronicles 4:9

Machir (the Aramitess, concubine of Manasseh) 1 Chronicles 7:14

Lemuel Proverbs 31:1–9

Isaiah Isaiah 49:1; 1 Nephi 21:1

Jeremiah Jeremiah 15:10

Belshazzar Daniel 5:10–12

OTHERS

Wise-hearted women Exodus 35:25

Women assembled at tabernacle Exodus 38:8

Patriot at Thebez Judges 9:53

Harlot of Gaza Judges 16:1

Young maidens going out to draw water 1 Samuel 9:11

Women with tabrets 1 Samuel 18:6

Witch of Endor 1 Samuel 28:7–25

Nurse of Mephibosheth 2 Samuel 4:4

Wise woman of Tekoa 2 Samuel 14:1–20

Wench of En-Rogel 2 Samuel 17:17

Bahurim woman 2 Samuel 17:19

Wise woman of Abel 2 Samuel 20:16–22

Queen of Sheba (the south) 1 Kings 10:1–13; 2 Chronicles 9:1–12; Matthew 12:42; Luke 11:31

The little maid 2 Kings 5:2–4

Women of the proverbs Proverbs 2, 5, 6, 7, 9, 11, 14, 18, 19, 21, 25, 27, 29, 30, 31

Woman whose heart is snares and nets Ecclesiastes 7:26

Careless women at ease Isaiah 32:9–12

Queen of heaven Jeremiah 7:18; 44:17–19

Women weeping for Tammuz Ezekiel 8:14

Women who sew pillows to armholes Ezekiel 13:18

Appendix C
THE ARTISTS AND THE PAINTINGS
Elspeth Young

As I look back over the artworks created for this project, I see women of faith—women who exemplify every aspect of the power and vitality and influence which faith in the Lord Jesus Christ engenders. These women came unto Christ despite their imperfections and weaknesses, worries and fears, doubts and despair. As they stepped into the light available through the word of the Lord, they were able to overcome the darkness and fear they faced. Indeed, faith is the fiber that weaves these images together.

Each painting seeks to capture the beauty of light, not just the temporal light that separates the day from the night but the beauty of the light offered to each of us by the Light and the Life and the Truth of the world—the living Christ. His word, His works, His very Spirit permeate the darkness of eternity and provide a path for us to follow. These paintings testify that there is no place so dark, no trial so formidable, no difficulty so great that the Master is not there. His Light can always reach us and envelop us in the comfort of His peace.

Perhaps the most exciting discovery I made during this project was learned from the models for each painting. They are ordinary women from all walks of life and circumstances. They all share a faith in Jesus Christ and a goodness that echoes the devotion of the women they are meant to portray. These noble, "unnamed" women who live here and now—family members, neighbors, and friends—have taught me that the kind of discipleship shown in the heroes we look to in the scriptures lives on in the ordinary individuals who humbly follow the Savior through everyday discipleship. They may not walk the streets of Palestine, but they follow in the footsteps of the Master just as surely as did His disciples of old.

My father, Al Young, graciously joined me in this project, adding his testimony of the truth through his images of Mother Eve. My brother Ashton also willingly contributed his unique gifts to create the numerous pen-and-ink illustrations throughout this volume. Sister Olson has been my teacher, my mentor, my friend. Her influence for good stretches far beyond the pages of this book. She and her husband touch the lives of countless individuals through their selfless sacrifices. My dear family has also planted, nurtured, and cultivated the seeds of faith in my own life and stretched my view heavenward. For these and all others along my path who have blessed my life through their faithfulness, I express my deepest thanks.

THE MOTHER OF ALL LIVING, BY AL R. YOUNG

EVE

And Adam called his wife's name Eve; because she was the mother of all living. (Genesis 3:20)

THE STORY IN THE PAINTING

The Mother of All Living portrays the enduring faith, hope, and charity of Eve. In the painting, she is not merely looking upward from the darkling clouds of a fallen world but is contemplating the Fountainhead of light and being. Her countenance is portrayed so that we understand she is seeing not just with her eyes but also with her mind and heart. And because the light above her and around her is kindred to the light within her own soul, we sense that she is a daughter of God and that the light within her is kindred to the Light upon which she looks.

Eve was a mother in a fallen world. Being in a fallen world is challenge enough to an individual, but to be a mother in such circumstances is to bring one's children into darkness. Thus, Eve had the choice that belongs to every mother, indeed, to motherhood: She could focus on the sad and sorry state of things and thus set a sorrowing example of selfish recrimination, or she could look to the Light, to the future, and to all the goodness yet to come. She chose faith, hope, and charity—the qualities of character by which the goodness and the brightness of that future will be made.

Who could have had more reason to be sad than the mother of all living? Nevertheless, she was profoundly happy, as we see her here. The only way she could have such happiness is through the gospel of Jesus Christ. The placement and orientation of the figure of Eve raise her above the darkness of the world, and as we look at her, our own souls are lifted heavenward. Thus, as the mother of all living, she lifts not only her own gaze but also the gaze of her children. She lifts our minds and hearts as well as hers. She lifts the world.

Eve is contemplating, or remembering, the great things of God—not only those that have been but also the great promises God is bringing to pass. Remembering is one of the most important things we do toward helping to build that promised future when once again the earth will be renewed and receive its paradisiacal glory.

Adam and Eve were cast out of the Garden of Eden and shut out from the presence of the Lord, but neither they nor any of their children have ever been beyond His reach. Therefore, the light in the painting can best be understood as the Father's hand resting gently, lovingly, on a daughter's sunlit head.

THE JOY OF OUR REDEMPTION, BY AL R. YOUNG

EVE

And in that day Adam blessed God and was filled, and began to prophesy concerning all the families of the earth, saying: Blessed be the name of God, for because of my transgression my eyes are opened, and in this life I shall have joy, and again in the flesh I shall see God.

And Eve, his wife, heard all these things and was glad, saying: Were it not for our transgression we never should have had seed, and never should have known good and evil, and the joy of our redemption, and the eternal life which God giveth unto all the obedient

And Adam and Eve blessed the name of God, and they made all things known unto their sons and their daughters. (Moses 5:10–12)

THE STORY IN THE PAINTING

Knowing *The Joy of Our Redemption* to be a painting of Eve, some could think she is looking back at Eden, perhaps even longingly. But in reality she is looking ahead, looking out across the darkness surrounding this life, and focusing on the brightness of the future that God has promised and prepared.

Eve is profoundly hopeful and full of faith. She had fallen into spiritual darkness and taken a world with her in the tumble. Engulfed by the consequences of her choice, she likely felt the blame and self-recrimination that follows whenever we give in to temptation. The darkness in which she appears in the painting is the chasm into which her world has fallen. And, yet, in the midst of everything that has come upon her and upon everyone she would ever love in this world, she finds the salvation that God had prepared for her to be more than sufficient to abolish all her problems. She is looking toward the Light and the Life and the Truth of the world.

IS ANYTHING TOO HARD FOR THE LORD? BY ELSPETH YOUNG

SARAH

I will certainly return unto thee according to the time of life; and, lo, Sarah thy wife shall have a son. . . .
Therefore Sarah laughed within herself, saying, After I am waxed old shall I have pleasure . . . ?
And the Lord said unto Abraham, Wherefore did Sarah laugh . . . ?
Is any thing too hard for the Lord? (Genesis 18:10–14)

THE STORY IN THE PAINTING

The painting *Is Anything Too Hard for the Lord?* shows Abraham's wife Sarah tenderly kissing her newborn son, Isaac. This precious child was miraculously provided by the Lord, despite Sarah's old age and previous inability to bear children (Genesis 18:10–11). That miracle is portrayed through the juxtaposition of ages within this image, emphasizing the Lord's ability to fulfill His promises to the faithful, no matter how seemingly difficult or impossible their circumstances.

Years before the scene depicted here, Abraham was promised seed as numerous as "the dust of the earth" (Genesis 13:16) or the stars in the heavens (Genesis 15:5), yet Sarah remained barren until the Lord appeared to Abraham in the patriarch's ninety-ninth year and promised that Sarah would have a son (Genesis 17:16).

Genesis 21:6 tells us Sarah rejoiced (the Hebrew root *tzachak* used there means both to "laugh" and to "rejoice"). As she holds her newborn infant, she enjoys the fulfillment of the Lord's promise to Abraham. She understands that "all that hear will laugh [or rejoice] with [her]" (v. 6). This statement by Sarah invites all of us to rejoice in the Lord's willingness and ability to fulfill the covenants He makes with us. Therefore, this painting seeks to be a visual reminder of what Sarah discovered—that nothing is too hard for the Lord to accomplish.

Sarah's hands are the central element of the painting. Every other element radiates from her strong, beautiful hands. Such a composition represents the strength, beauty, and loving care of motherhood.

SIGNIFICANT ELEMENTS IN THE PAINTING

Sarah is positioned in front of two wall hangings in her tent. Scholars believe such hangings were used to separate rooms within the goatskin tents used by the families of the patriarchs (Kamm, *Israelites,* 111). One of the hangings painted here is based on a fragment from the oldest known rug. The animal in the border of this tapestry is a ram, used here to symbolize the ram in the thicket provided by the Lord when Abraham was willing to sacrifice his miracle son, Isaac (Genesis 22).

The gold embroidery on Sarah's tunic is based on motifs in a facsimile from the book of Abraham, a papyrus containing drawings by Abraham that was discovered in Egyptian tombs during the nineteenth century. The costly materials used in her clothing also denote Abraham's abundant wealth (Genesis 13:2).

Baby Isaac is wrapped in a soft blue covering. A blue like this was frequently employed in Egyptian tomb paintings (Walch, *Color,* 16). Thus, the Egyptian "Nile blue" blanket represents the time and experiences Abraham and Sarah had in Egypt.

Sarah wears a gold wedding band, typical of early Hebrew wedding rings (Fielding, *Customs,* 27). The wedding band is known to have been used in ancient Egypt and was worn on the third finger of the left hand, just as it is today.

REFERENCES

Cansdale, George. *All the Animals of the Bible Lands.* Grand Rapids, Mich.: Paternoster Press, 1970.

Fielding, William J. *Strange Customs of Courtship and Marriage.* Philadelphia: Blakiston, 1942.

Kamm, Anthony. *The Israelites: An Introduction.* London and New York: Routledge, 1999.

Matthews, Victor H. *Manners and Customs in the Bible.* Peabody, Mass.: Hendrickson, 1991.

Millard, Alan. *Treasures from Bible Times.* Oxford: Lion Publishing, 1985.

Walch, Margaret. *Color Source Book.* New York: Charles Scribner's Sons, 1971.

GOD LIVETH AND SEETH ME, BY ELSPETH YOUNG

HAGAR

And the angel of the Lord found [Hagar] by a fountain of water in the wilderness. . . .

And the angel of the Lord said unto her, I will multiply thy seed exceedingly, that it shall not be numbered for multitude.

And the angel of the Lord said unto her, Behold, thou art with child, and shalt bear a son, and shalt call his name Ishmael; because the Lord hath heard thy affliction. (Genesis 16:7–11)

THE STORY IN THE PAINTING

In *God Liveth and Seeth Me,* we see Abraham's Egyptian wife, Hagar, at the fountain she named Beer-lahai-roi (Hebrew for "The well of him who liveth and seeth me"). This well is believed to have been in the wilderness on the edge of the Negev desert.

In the painting, Hagar is looking heavenward. She hears the voice of the Lord speaking to her, promising that her seed "shall not be numbered for multitude" (Genesis 16:10). The Lord instructs Hagar to give her future son the name *Ishmael,* which literally means "God hears" (v. 11, note *a*).

The light and beauty of Hagar's countenance reflect her testimony that the voice she has heard is indeed the voice of Jehovah (Genesis 16:13). From this experience, she gains the courage and resolve to return and submit herself to Sarah despite their previous quarrel (v. 9).

This painting reflects Hagar's testimony of the Savior and reminds us that the Lord sees and hears all of His children.

SIGNIFICANT ELEMENTS IN THE PAINTING

The basket just behind the figure of Hagar represents her hasty flight into the wilderness. She might have taken such a container with some needed provisions during her journey back to Egypt, but the basket here is empty, symbolic of the need she experiences during her wilderness flight. It is this need that leads her to the well, where she is visited by the angel of the Lord.

The well behind Hagar symbolizes the "living water" of testimony of the Savior, Jesus Christ (John 4:10). The vine above her head symbolizes the Savior, who is the "true vine" in whom we are to abide (John 15:1).

REFERENCES

Blaiklock, E. M., ed. *The Zondervan Pictorial Bible Atlas.* Grand Rapids, Mich.: Zondervan, 1975.

Corson, Richard. *Fashion in Hair: The First Five Thousand Years.* London: Peter Owen, 1965.

Freeman, James. *Manners and Customs of the Bible.* Plainfield, N.J.: Logos International, 1972.

Houston, Mary G. *Ancient Egyptian Mesopotamia and Persian Costume and Decoration.* London: Adam and Charles Black, 1920.

THE STRUGGLE WITHIN, BY ELSPETH YOUNG

REBEKAH

And they blessed Rebekah, and said unto her, Thou art our sister, be thou the mother of thousands of millions.

And Isaac intreated the Lord for his wife, because she was barren: and the Lord was intreated of him, and Rebekah his wife conceived.

And the children struggled together within her; and she said, If it be so, why am I thus? And she went to enquire of the Lord.

And the Lord said unto her, Two nations are in thy womb . . . ; and the one people shall be stronger than the other people; and the elder shall serve the younger. (Genesis 24:60; 25:21–23)

THE STORY IN THE PAINTING

The painting of Rebekah in *The Struggle Within* depicts Isaac's wife as she inquires of the Lord concerning the babies struggling within her womb. Symbolically, however, this moment in Rebekah's experience represents the future of her two sons, who, as the Lord states, will be "two nations . . . two manner of people" (Genesis 25:23). Even in their mother's womb, the strife between Jacob and Esau for blessing and birthright was apparent.

The theme of this painting is that the Lord answers our prayers when we come to Him in faith. His word is the ultimate solution to all the struggles we may face, at times, within.

SIGNIFICANT ELEMENTS IN THE PAINTING

Rebekah stands at the door of her tent, looking toward the barren landscape beyond. She is also, symbolically, looking toward the Light, the Savior, as she prayerfully contemplates the children struggling within her womb. Because Genesis 25:11 tells us that Isaac "dwelt by the well Lahai-roi," believed to be in the Negeb desert bordering Egypt (Blaiklock, *Pictorial,* 53), a desert landscape is shown beyond the tent door. Rebekah was childless for twenty years before she bore Esau and Jacob (Genesis 25:20, 26), and so, even though we do not know Rebekah's exact age, she is depicted here in middle age.

According to biblical scholar James Freeman, Arab tents were made of camel or goat skins draped over poles that varied in number according to the size and shape of the tent. These structural poles were "made useful by having hooks driven into them from which [were] suspended clothes, baskets, saddles, weapons, and various other articles of daily use" (Freeman, *Manners,* 245). Accordingly, baskets and fabrics are draped along the tent pole behind the figure of Rebekah.

Rebekah's costume is loosely based on the design of costumes worn by the women in the wall painting of the Beni Hasan tomb (Robinson, *History,* 15). The blue dye of the fabrics she wears could have been produced from indigo, a plant dye dating back to Egypt in 2500 B.C. (Robinson, *History,* 24).

The plant to the right of the figure of Rebekah is the lentil (*lens culinaris*), used here to symbolize the event when Esau sells Jacob his birthright for a "pottage of lentiles" (Genesis 25:29–34).

REFERENCES

Blaiklock, E. M., ed. *The Zondervan Pictorial Bible Atlas.* Grand Rapids, Mich.: Zondervan, 1975.

Cook, J. Gordon. *Handbook of Textile Fibres.* 5th ed. Durham, England: Merrow Publishing, 1984.

Freeman, James. *Manners and Customs of the Bible.* Plainfield, N.J.: Logos International, 1972.

Hepper, F. N. *Illustrated Encyclopedia of Bible Plants: Flowers and Trees, Fruits and Vegetables, Ecology.* Leicester, England: Inter Varsity Press, 1992.

Robinson, Stuart. *A History of Dyed Textiles.* Cambridge, Mass.: MIT Press, 1969.

WITH HER FATHER'S SHEEP, BY ELSPETH YOUNG

RACHEL

Behold, Rachel his daughter cometh with the sheep. . . .
And while he [Jacob] yet spake with them, Rachel came with her father's sheep: for she kept them. (Genesis 29:6–9)

THE STORY IN THE PAINTING

The Old Testament prophet Jacob heeded his father's charge: "Arise, go to Padan-aran, to the house of Bethuel thy mother's father; and take thee a wife from thence of the daughters of Laban" (Genesis 28:1–2). His journey from his father's home in Beer-sheba to his mother's family in Haran was approximately fourteen hundred miles (Barnes, *Atlas,* 61). He received a promise from the Lord that, like Abraham and Isaac, his "seed shall be as the dust of the earth . . . and in thee and in thy seed shall the families of the earth be blessed" (Genesis 28:14).

Upon reaching his destination, Jacob found shepherds waiting with their flocks for the approach of his cousin Rachel with her father's sheep (Genesis 29:1–3, 7–8). The painting *With Her Father's Sheep* depicts this moment in the life of Rachel—we see Rachel as Jacob might have first seen her, leading her father's flocks to the well for water.

SIGNIFICANT ELEMENTS IN THE PAINTING

A famous painting from the Egyptian tomb of Beni Hasan (believed to be from the nineteenth century before Christ) depicts a caravan of Semitic people journeying to Egypt (*World,* 114, 130). Rachel's clothing, as depicted in this painting, is based loosely on the style and color of the dresses worn by the women in the tomb painting. In addition, Rachel is shown wearing a lovely shawl woven from the wool provided by her father's sheep.

Aside from the visual interest they provide and their significance in the biblical account of Jacob's family (Genesis 29–30), the sheep in this painting contribute to the theme of the artwork itself, reminding us that we are each to seek after the Father's "sheep" and care for those within our own sphere of influence. The scriptures make it clear that not only are we expected to follow the Good Shepherd but we are also to act as shepherds ourselves by caring for our fellowmen.

After His resurrection, the Savior repeatedly instructed Peter to "feed my sheep" (John 21:15–17); this admonition is still in force today (D&C 112:14). Each of us is, like Rachel, a keeper of our Father's sheep, instructed to "mourn with those that mourn; yea, and comfort those that stand in need of comfort" (Mosiah 18:9), leading others to "the fountain of all righteousness" (Ether 12:28), who offers each of us "living water" (John 4:10). Therefore, the sheep depicted here are not just part of Rachel's story but a reminder that feeding the "sheep" in our midst, by leading them to Christ, demonstrates our love for Him.

REFERENCES

Barnes, Ian. *The Historical Atlas of the Bible.* London: Cartigraphica Press, 2006.

Cansdale, George. *All the Animals of the Bible Lands.* Grand Rapids, Mich.: Paternoster Press, 1970.

The World of the Bible. 2 vols. New York: Educational Heritage, 1964.

BLESSED, BY ELSPETH YOUNG

LEAH

And Leah said, Happy am I, for the daughters will call me blessed. (Genesis 30:13).

The Lord make the woman that is come into thine house like Rachel and like Leah, which two did build the house of Israel. (Ruth 4:11)

THE STORY IN THE PAINTING

This simple portrait, entitled *Blessed,* favorably portrays Jacob's wife Leah. Though unfortunate contentions between her and her sister are generally associated with her in the Old Testament account, the book of Ruth gives us a little glimpse into her true character and the work which she, together with Jacob and Rachel, performed. Ruth 4:11 extols Leah and Rachel as the builders of the house of Israel. Surely this accolade speaks of Leah's ultimate goodness, despite weaknesses and difficulties with which she wrestled.

Leah's words in Genesis 30:13 also show us that she understood that the "daughters will call me blessed" because she was a mother in Israel. This image depicts a mother who is blessed with the understanding of her sacred role in Heavenly Father's plan.

BY THE RIVER'S BRINK, BY ELSPETH YOUNG

MIRIAM

And when [Jochebed] could not longer hide him, she took for him an ark of bulrushes, and daubed it with slime and with pitch, and put the child therein; and she laid it in the flags by the river's brink.

And his sister stood afar off, to wit what would be done to him. . . .

Then said his sister to Pharaoh's daughter, Shall I go and call to thee a nurse of the Hebrew women, that she may nurse the child for thee? (Exodus 2:3–7)

THE STORY IN THE PAINTING

Jochebed, the mother of Moses and Aaron, entrusted her daughter with the care of her younger brother Moses. Jochebed placed the infant Moses in an ark among the bulrushes and charged Miriam to watch over her brother. *By the River's Brink* seeks to portray Miriam's faith, even as the child she must have been. It shows the courage this little girl must have had, courage desperately needed to preserve her brother from destruction (Exodus 1:22). The painting also conveys another lesson: Even the faith and obedience of a small child can help build the Lord's kingdom and accomplish His purposes.

SIGNIFICANT ELEMENTS IN THE PAINTING

Biblical scholars believe that the bulrushes "in the flags by the river's brink" (Exodus 2:3) were reed mace, which grows in sheltered places along the Nile. Rooted in the mud, it quickly multiplies through seeds dispersed upon the wind. The plant seems a particularly appropriate companion for young Miriam as she maintains her patient vigil, the sole guardian of her tiny brother's life. At this point in Old Testament history, the children of Israel were indeed rooted in the mud of their bleak, brick-making lives, but they were growing in awesome strength, soon to cast their power far beyond the rivers of Egypt.

The same caring, motherly hands that fashioned an ark of bulrushes to hold a treasured son have carefully embroidered a tunic for a treasured daughter. Its bright indigo would have been a well-known plant-based dye available in ancient times. It echoes the vivid colors of sun and sky in the Nile region as well as the coloration suggested in the tomb of Beni Hasan, whose paintings are thought by some scholars to depict the clothing of Semitic peoples. The vibrant embroidery further reflects ancient Egypt's brilliant tomb paintings.

Miriam's braided hair is a simplified, childlike version of the much more elaborate Egyptian hairstyles of the day.

REFERENCES

Cansdale, George. *All the Animals of the Bible Lands.* Grand Rapids, Mich.: Paternoster Press, 1970.

Corson, Richard. *Fashion in Hair: The First Five Thousand Years.* London: Peter Owen, 1965.

Freeman, James. *Manners and Customs of the Bible.* Plainfield, N.J.: Logos International, 1972.

Hepper, F. N. *Illustrated Encyclopedia of Bible Plants: Flowers and Trees, Fruits and Vegetables, Ecology.* Leicester, England: Inter Varsity Press, 1992.

I AROSE A MOTHER IN ISRAEL, BY ELSPETH YOUNG

DEBORAH

And [Deborah] sent and called Barak . . . and said unto him, Hath not the Lord God of Israel commanded, saying, Go and draw toward mount Tabor, and take with thee ten thousand men of the children of Naphtali and of the children of Zebulun?

And I will draw unto thee to the river Kishon Sisera, the captain of Jabin's army, with his chariots and his multitude; and I will deliver him into thine hand.

And Barak said unto her, If thou wilt go with me, then I will go: but if thou wilt not go with me, then I will not go.

And she said, I will surely go with thee. (Judges 4:6–9)

Then sang Deborah and Barak the son of Abinoam on that day, saying,

Praise ye the Lord for the avenging of Israel. . . .

. . . I, even I, will sing unto the Lord; I will sing praise to the Lord God of Israel. . . .

The inhabitants of the villages ceased, they ceased in Israel, until that I Deborah arose, that I arose a mother in Israel. (Judges 5:1–7)

THE STORY IN THE PAINTING

In the painting entitled *I Arose a Mother in Israel,* the prophetess Deborah stops for a moment during her preparations to accompany the Israelite captain Barak and his troops to battle. Deborah knows that the

Lord is ready to deliver the Israelites from the mighty oppression experienced at the hand of the Canaanites (Judges 4:3). She shares the Lord's promise with Barak that the Lord "will deliver [Sisera] into thine hand" (v. 7).

This valiant "mother in Israel" shows her great faith by relying on the word of the Lord, putting her faith into action by encouraging Barak to do as the Lord desires, and praising the Lord in song after the Israelites achieve victory. She is an example of the courage exemplified by many mothers who are willing, pioneer-like, to step into the wilderness of difficulty to guide those they love out of spiritual darkness by holding fast to the word of the Lord.

SIGNIFICANT ELEMENTS IN THE PAINTING

Deborah holds a sword in this painting not because she is going to fight with it but because it symbolizes the word of God. The apostle Paul teaches, "The word of God is quick, and powerful, and sharper than any two-edged sword" (Hebrews 4:12). Deborah represents all who, in faith, use the word of the Lord and His promise of deliverance as the means of victory in the spiritual battles of life.

The mountains behind her symbolize both the challenges the Israelites face from their oppression and the tender mercies of a loving Father in Heaven. Isaiah declares, "For the mountains shall depart, and the hills be removed; but my kindness shall not depart from thee, neither shall the covenant of my peace be removed, saith the Lord that hath mercy on thee" (Isaiah 54:10). As a covenant mother in Israel, Deborah relies on the Lord's promises that despite mortality's rocky terrain of trials and thorns and thistles, He will never leave us comfortless (John 14:18).

Deborah's clothing is based loosely on the costume of a figurine from about the time the Israelites conquered Canaan. The artifact shows a woman with a simple head wrap and long, flowing fabrics from neck to foot (*Emergence,* 79). Deborah's richly ornate and detailed costume also reminds us of Isaiah's invitation to Israel: "Awake, awake; put on thy strength, O Zion; put on thy beautiful garments" (Isaiah 52:1).

Deborah's choice to arise as a mother and a judge in Israel clothed her in the beauty of faith, courage, and devotion.

REFERENCE

The Emergence of Man: The Israelites. New York: Time Life Books, 1975.

FOR THIS CHILD I PRAYED, BY ELSPETH YOUNG

HANNAH

And [Hannah] vowed a vow, and said, O Lord of hosts, if thou wilt indeed look on the affliction of thine hand-maid, and remember me, and not forget thine handmaid, but wilt give unto thine handmaid a man child, then I will give him unto the Lord all the days of his life. . . .

Wherefore it came to pass, when the time was come about after Hannah had conceived, that she bare a son, and called his name Samuel, saying, Because I have asked him of the Lord. . . .

And when she had weaned him, she took him up with her . . .

. . . and brought the child to Eli.

And she said, O my lord, as thy soul liveth, my lord, I am the woman that stood by thee here, praying unto the Lord.

For this child I prayed; and the Lord hath given me my petition which I asked of him:

Therefore also I have lent him to the Lord; as long as he liveth he shall be lent to the Lord. And he worshipped the Lord there. (1 Samuel 1:11–28)

THE STORY IN THE PAINTING

For This Child I Prayed celebrates the joy of motherhood, depicting Hannah in the life-renewing role of nurturer.

Grieved because she was childless, Hannah petitioned the Lord for a son, promising that she would give the child to the Lord to be His servant. Her request was blessed by Eli, the high priest, and she gave birth to a son and named him Samuel. Hannah kept young Samuel only until he was weaned, when he would likely have been about three years old (Keil and Delitzsch, *Commentary,* 26).

In the few years between the infant's birth and his presentation at the tabernacle, Hannah cared for him and planted seeds of faith and devotion through her nurturing influence. Her care of Samuel through his early years is apparent from the "little coat" she made for him "from year to year, when she came up with her husband to offer the yearly sacrifice" (1 Samuel 2:19). Hannah's testimony of the Savior, as evidenced in her beautiful prayer (1 Samuel 2:1–10), shows her trust in the "rock" of Israel (1 Samuel 2:2).

When she prayed to the Lord, Hannah declared, "My heart rejoiceth in the Lord . . . ; because I rejoice in thy salvation" (1 Samuel 2:1). The happiness in Hannah's expression in *For This Child I Prayed* is a reflection of the joy she felt because of the blessings of the Lord. The "Lord remembered her," as he had remembered Rachel and also blessed Hannah with the righteous desire of her heart. In addition, the Lord, through Eli, promised more children to Hannah and her husband, showing us that, indeed, the Lord "crowneth thee with lovingkindness and tender mercies" (Psalm 103:4).

SIGNIFICANT ELEMENTS IN THE PAINTING

The Levites were "to wait on the sons of Aaron for the service of the house of the Lord, in the courts, and in the chambers, and in the purifying of all holy things, and the work of the service of the house of God" (1 Chronicles 23:28). Joshua 18:7 also makes it clear that the "inheritance" of the Levites was the "priesthood of the Lord." Elkanah, father of the prophet Samuel, was a Levite (1 Chronicles 6:16–28), so his son Samuel could serve with Eli at the tabernacle.

Because of their work, or "inheritance," of priesthood obligations and duties, the Lord instructed Moses to give the Levites forty-eight cities for their dwelling. Hence, Hannah and Samuel are depicted with a stone building visible behind the figures. The dwelling here also symbolizes Hannah's words in her beautiful prayer of thanksgiving: "There is none holy as the Lord: for there is none beside thee: neither is there any rock like our God" (1 Samuel 2:2).

Her words of praise echo the words of the Lord to the prophet Enoch when He declared: "I am Messiah, the King of Zion, the Rock of Heaven, which is broad as eternity; whoso cometh in at the gate and climbeth up by me shall never fall; wherefore, blessed are they of whom I have spoken, for they shall come forth with songs of everlasting joy" (Moses 7:53). Likewise, the Savior declared in the Sermon on the Mount that the wise man "built his house upon a rock . . . and it fell not: for it was founded upon a rock" (Matthew 7:25). Therefore, the stone edifice behind Hannah and her child symbolizes the way in which they are built "upon the rock of [their] Redeemer, who is Christ, the Son of God" (Helaman 5:12).

The fabric directly behind the figure of Hannah on the left side of the painting recalls many artists' renderings of Old Testament prophets, who are often shown in striped clothing. The fabric is meant, therefore, to symbolize Samuel's prophetic mission and the priesthood power given to the tribe of Levi (1 Chronicles 23).

Samuel wears a white tunic trimmed in gold, representing the "linen ephod" he would later wear while he "ministered before the Lord, being a child" (1 Samuel 2:18). The scriptural account also tells us that Hannah "made [Samuel] a little coat" (1 Samuel 2:19) as he grew year by year. Whatever Samuel's clothing may have actually looked like, the details of a carefully and lovingly crafted garment shown here symbolize the central importance of purity in the life of both mother and child. The whiteness of his clothing symbolizes Samuel's "faith, patience, integrity, and self-sacrifice" (LDS Bible Dictionary, 768).

Hannah also wears white, symbolic of her faith and purity. A brightly colored wrap warmly enfolds her and visually "touches" the child as well, symbolizing the influence of a righteous mother in the life of her child.

REFERENCES

Keil, Carl Friedrich, and Franz Delitzsch. Translated by James Martin. *Commentary on the Old Testament*. Edinburgh: Clark, 1872.

LDS Bible Dictionary. Salt Lake City: The Church of Jesus Christ of Latter-day Saints, 1987.

TREASURE THE WORD, BY ELSPETH YOUNG

HULDAH

And whoso treasureth up my word, shall not be deceived. (Joseph Smith–Matthew 1:37)

THE STORY IN THE PAINTING

During the reign of righteous King Josiah, the temple was cleansed after long years of idolatry and apostasy. During this time the "book of the law of the Lord given by Moses" was discovered by Hilkiah, father of the prophet Jeremiah (2 Chronicles 34:14; Jeremiah 1:1). This book (or scroll) was read to the king, who greatly mourned because the people had not been living according to to its teachings. Josiah desired to know the Lord's will concerning the writings and instructed his servants to "enquire of the Lord" (2 Chronicles 34:21). They in turn spoke with the prophetess Huldah, and she prophesied concerning the words written in the book and also provided a beautifully comforting prophecy about King Josiah's future.

SIGNIFICANT ELEMENTS IN THE PAINTING

Treasure the Word depicts Huldah in a rich setting with hanging carpets and a stone enclosure. Accounts of this prophetess tell us that she lived in the "second quarter" of Jerusalem, an area added to the city two centuries earlier during the reign of King Hezekiah. Called the Mishneh, this residential area was near the palace and Solomon's temple. The background of this painting depicts the rich architecture and surroundings that might have been part of the second quarter.

The scroll Huldah is reading and the scroll on the table before her represent both the word of the Lord as revealed through Moses and all scripture available to us today. As we treasure up the word (Joseph Smith–Matthew 1:37; D&C 6:20), we, like Josiah, will be blessed of the Lord.

The water vessel represents the "living water" of truth (John 4).

REFERENCES

Hepper, F. N. *Illustrated Encyclopedia of Bible Plants: Flowers and Trees, Fruits and Vegetables, Ecology*. Leicester, England: Inter Varsity Press, 1992.

Ogden, Kelly D., and Jeffrey R. Chadwick. *The Holy Land: A Geographical, Historical, and Archaeological Guide to the Land of the Bible.* Jerusalem: HaMakor, 1990.

Olmert, Michael. *The Smithsonian Book of Books.* New York: Wings Books, 1992.

Rogerson, John, ed. *The Oxford Illustrated History of the Bible.* Oxford: Oxford University Press, 2001.

FOR SUCH A TIME AS THIS, BY ELSPETH YOUNG

ESTHER

Think not with thyself that thou shalt escape in the king's house, more than all the Jews. . . .

. . . and who knoweth whether thou art come to the kingdom for such a time as this?

Then Esther bade them return Mordecai this answer,

Go, gather together all the Jews that are present in Shushan, and fast ye for me . . . : I also and my maidens will fast likewise; and so will I go in unto the king . . . : and if I perish, I perish. (Esther 4:13–16)

Now it came to pass on the third day, that Esther put on her royal apparel, and stood in the inner court of the king's house. . . .

. . . and the king held out to Esther the golden sceptre. . . .

Then said the king unto her, What wilt thou, queen Esther? . . . it shall be even given thee to the half of the kingdom. (Esther 5:1–3)

THE STORY IN THE PAINTING

For Such a Time As This depicts Queen Esther at the conclusion of her three-day fast, which was a preparation for her supplication before the Persian king Ahasuerus. The theme of the painting is the power and efficacy of fasting when coupled with prayer. Indeed, as Isaiah states, "Is not this the fast that I have chosen? to loose the bands of wickedness, . . . and to let the oppressed go free, and that ye break every yoke? . . . thy righteousness shall go before thee; the glory of the Lord shall be thy rereward. Then shalt thou call, and the Lord shall answer" (Isaiah 58:6–9).

Esther's plea was heard by the king, and her people were released from the wicked edict inspired by the king's servant Haman. Although prayer itself is not mentioned in Esther's request to the Jewish people (Esther 4:16), the Book of Mormon makes clear the vital link between prayer and fasting (Alma 6:6; 17:9; 30:2; Helaman 3:35). Thus, Esther is shown here in an attitude of prayer and supplication.

SIGNIFICANT ELEMENTS IN THE PAINTING

The figure of Esther wears a richly embroidered tunic with surcoat and vest, an interpretation of a Persian costume from the fifth century before Christ (Houston, *Ancient,* 156, 165). The purples, reds, and golds of her robe symbolize her royalty and also the luxury of her circumstances. They remind the viewer that

Esther is willing to forgo these worldly pleasures, and even her very life, for the sake of her people, the Jews. The style of her hair is based loosely on a Persian bas-relief from this era that depicts figures with crimped hair pulled back from the face.

The carpet on which the figure kneels features geometric designs and motifs known as *guls,* which are characteristic of carpets from Central Asia created by the Turkmen tribes north of modern-day Iran (Curatola, *Oriental,* 103, 106, 196). This element, therefore, symbolizes the extent of the Persian empire during Ahasuerus's reign: It "stretched from India to Ethiopia and from the Caucasus Mountains to the Arabian Sea" (*Great People,* 264).

The small blooms of narcissus (*Narcissus tazetta*) scattered before Esther symbolize her purity. They are native to Palestine and could be what Solomon refers to as the "rose of Sharon" (Hepper, *Illustrated,* 46). Therefore, in this painting they symbolize that she is Jewish, a fact she had concealed prior to her interview with Ahasuerus (Esther 2:10).

The figure's surroundings include marble pillars (Esther 1:6) and black marble flooring that stretches out in front of her (v. 6). The palace at Shushan where Esther lived at this time was famous for its "hall of pillars" (*World,* 196).

The verdant landscape beyond the palace represents Isaiah's promise that those who fast "shalt be like a watered garden" (Isaiah 58:11).

REFERENCES

Curatola, Giovanni. *The Simon and Schuster Book of Oriental Carpets.* New York: Simon and Schuster, 1981.

Great People of the Bible and How They Lived. Pleasantville, N.Y.: Reader's Digest, 1974.

Hepper, F. N. *Illustrated Encyclopedia of Bible Plants: Flowers and Trees, Fruits and Vegetables, Ecology.* Leicester, England: Inter Varsity Press, 1992.

Houston, Mary G. *Ancient Egyptian Mesopotamia and Persian Costume and Decoration.* London: Adam and Charles Black, 1920.

Pfeiffer, Charles F. *The Wycliffe Historical Geography of Bible Lands.* Chicago: Moody, 1967.

Rasmussen, Carl G. *Zondervan NIV Atlas of the Bible.* Grand Rapids, Mich.: 1989.

The World of the Bible. 2 vols. New York: Educational Heritage, 1964.

THE PROTECTOR, BY ELSPETH YOUNG

SHIPHRAH

And the king of Egypt spake to the Hebrew midwives, of which the name of the one was Shiphrah, and the name of the other Puah:

And he said, When ye do the office of a midwife to the Hebrew women, and see them upon the stools; if it be a son, then ye shall kill him: but if it be a daughter, then she shall live.

But the midwives feared God, and did not as the king of Egypt commanded them, but saved the men children alive. (Exodus 1:15–17)

THE STORY IN THE PAINTING

Shiphrah and Puah were midwives among the Hebrews during the time of Moses. Pharaoh commanded these women to kill at birth the male children born to the Hebrews. Shiphrah and Puah, as recounted in Exodus 1, quietly refused to carry out the edict. In *The Protector,* Shiphrah is a solitary figure surrounded not only by darkness but by the loneliness in which an act of courage cloaks an individual. She holds a newborn babe, protecting the child from fear, darkness, and death. Her gentle caress enfolds the babe in love and hope, despite the void in which she and the child appear.

The scriptural account tells us that Shiphrah chose to defy Pharaoh because she feared God. Proverbs 14:26 tells us that "fear of the Lord is strong confidence: and his children shall have a place of refuge." It is this confidence, born of faith, that gave Shiphrah the courage to defy Pharaoh. Her righteousness in this moment, which surely tested her character and faithfulness, resulted in the Lord's blessing her and Puah with "houses" (Exodus 1:21). Just as the Savior promises that He will "prepare a place" for His disciples (John 14:2), so He provided a "place" for these noble women because of their courageous actions.

SIGNIFICANT ELEMENTS IN THE PAINTING

Light in the image does not come from anything we can see. Consequently, the light could emanate from a candle or a lamp or perhaps from a protective Providence. For just as Shiphrah holds the infant safe in the midst of peril, so Providence stands in the void to light such unseen acts of quiet courage.

The almost minimalist treatment of Shiphrah's costume and adornment emphasizes her act of courage. Our eyes are drawn directly to the child and Shiphrah's tender expression rather than to her clothing. Both midwife and child are bathed in a warm, ochre light, rather than a pale or silvery light, symbolizing the watchful eye of the Lord and the rewards He had in store for these righteous women.

REFERENCE

Nowell, Irene. *Women in the Old Testament.* Collegeville, Minn.: Liturgical Press, 1997.

CHOOSE YOU THIS DAY, BY ELSPETH YOUNG

PUAH

And if it seem evil unto you to serve the Lord, choose you this day whom ye will serve; whether the gods which your fathers served that were on the other side of the flood, or the gods of the Amorites, in whose land ye dwell: but as for me and my house, we will serve the Lord. (Joshua 24:15).

And the king of Egypt spake to the Hebrew midwives, of which the name of the one was Shiphrah, and the name of the other Puah:

And he said, When ye do the office of a midwife to the Hebrew women, and see them upon the stools; if it be a son, then ye shall kill him: but if it be a daughter, then she shall live.

But the midwives feared God, and did not as the king of Egypt commanded them, but saved the men children alive. (Exodus 1:15–17)

THE STORY IN THE PAINTING

Choose You This Day depicts the heroic midwife Puah after her interview with Pharaoh, as described in Exodus 1:15–16. Pharaoh commanded Puah and Shiphrah to kill all Hebrew male children at birth and thereby play a key part in his plan to destroy the children of Israel. Puah and Shiphrah were, therefore, forced to choose between fear of God and fear of man. Their decision would affect the entire Israelite nation for good or ill and also affect their own lives. Nonetheless, these two valiant women "feared God, and did not as the king of Egypt commanded them, but saved the men children alive" (Exodus 1:17).

We see Puah as she makes this vital decision between good and evil. Her countenance evidences her concern, but her resolute choice to do what is right despite her fears is mirrored in her confident posture. Despite peril, she is quietly courageous, looking forward with faith and trust in the Lord. She and Shiphrah nobly choose to serve the Lord, just as the prophet Joshua firmly declared almost 150 years later: "As for me and my house, we will serve the Lord" (Joshua 24:15). Puah's choice saved countless lives and enabled the children of Israel to "wax very mighty" (Exodus 1:20).

Shiphrah and Puah were not left to face evil alone, however. The biblical account tells us that because the women feared God, He "dealt well with the midwives" and "made them houses" (Exodus 1:20–21), meaning posterity. Shiphrah and Puah were also blessed with an inspired answer to give Pharaoh regarding their inability to carry out his commands (Exodus 1:19). Consequently, Pharaoh spared the women's lives.

Biblical scholars have endeavored to interpret what kind of blessing "houses" might indicate. The Hebrew word used in verse 21 is *bayith,* possibly derived from the root *banah* (Strong, *Exhaustive,* 20, 22). Both words embody a variety of meanings that could combine to connote the repair or building up of a house, family, palace, or temple. Whatever the precise blessing conferred by the Lord upon these faithful women, the words remind us of the blessings of eternal families, available in holy temples, where covenants "build up" and "repair" family ties so that they may last throughout eternity. These blessings are available to those who, like Shiphrah and Puah, overcome evil's insidious invitations. If we "fear God," the Lord promises to extend his arm to support us against the "fiery darts of the adversary" and to be with us "in every time of trouble" (D&C 3:7–8). "Houses" also suggests the promise of the Lord to the faithful Book of Mormon prophet Enos that "there is a place prepared for you in the mansions of my Father" (Enos 1:27).

SIGNIFICANT ELEMENTS IN THE PAINTING

Elements of ancient Egyptian costume are suggested in the painting of Puah. A simplified semicircular gold pectoral adorns Puah's throat, and a white linen wrap falls in pleats from her shoulder. Colorful rust and royal blue fabrics are also part of her costume. These elements are an interpretation of Egyptian and Canaanite clothing depicted in a fourteenth-century B.C. tomb painting from Thebes. The sharp visual contrast created by the white wrap immediately draws our eye, reminding us of Puah's purity and faith.

The pillars behind the figure of Puah are incised with hieroglyphics and echo ancient Egyptian architectural detailing. They are, however, crumbling visibly. Not only do the crumbling pillars symbolize Pharaoh's fear of losing his political power because of the rise of the Israelite nation (Exodus 1:7–10) but they also represent the way our lives and futures crumble when we choose to serve man rather than God. The palm tree beyond the pillars, on the other hand, symbolizes the renewal of life and eternal continuance afforded those who choose to serve the Lord.

REFERENCES

Strong, James. *The Exhaustive Concordance of the Bible.* New York: Abingdon Press, 1890.
The World of the Bible. 2 vols. New York: Educational Heritage, 1964.

THE DAUGHTERS OF ZELOPHEHAD, BY ELSPETH YOUNG

THE DAUGHTERS OF ZELOPHEHAD: MAHLAH, NOAH, HOGLAH, MILCAH, AND TIRZAH

And [the daughters of Zelophehad] stood before Moses . . . saying,
Our father died in the wilderness. . . .
Why should the name of our father be done away from among his family, because he hath no son? Give unto us therefore a possession among the brethren of our father.
And Moses brought their cause before the Lord.
And the Lord spake unto Moses, saying,

The daughters of Zelophehad speak right: thou shalt surely give them a possession of an inheritance among their father's brethren; and thou shalt cause the inheritance of their father to pass unto them. (Numbers 27:2–7)

THE STORY IN THE PAINTING

Mahlah, Noah, Hoglah, Milcah, and Tirzah, the daughters of Zelophehad, were five sisters who appealed to Moses for an inheritance in Israel, just before Israel entered the promised land. Their father's death in the wilderness left his name without remembrance, and these faithful daughters took their plea to Moses, who in turn inquired of the Lord about the matter. The Lord granted their petition, blessing these daughters with an inheritance.

The Daughters of Zelophehad shows three of the daughters inside their tent during the time of their wilderness journey (Numbers 11:10). The girls are eating the manna they have collected that day. Milcah is seated, enjoying her basket of manna, while Mahlah is offering a bowl to the youngest, Tirzah, who is seated on the floor of their tent.

SIGNIFICANT ELEMENTS IN THE PAINTING

The elements in *The Daughters of Zelophehad* symbolize the inheritance the Lord promises all His faithful children. Such promises include fruitfulness in lands, fruits, grains, and endeavors; freedom from fear; safety, strength, covenant, and the Lord's presence (Leviticus 26). In this painting, these promises are represented by such visual elements as the large basket at the rear of the painting. It represents the storage basket the Lord might have meant when He instructed the Israelites to "take of the first of all the fruit of the earth, . . . and . . . put it in a basket" (Deuteronomy 26:2). This kind of coiled basket was made using a method dating back to Egypt thousands of years before the daughters of Zelophehad would have lived (Hepper, *Illustrated,* 174–75).

The smaller baskets held by two of the daughters contain manna, the food provided by the Lord during the forty-year journey in the wilderness (Exodus 16:31). We understand from Exodus 16 that manna represents God's goodness and was used to test the people's obedience. In a larger sense, this manna symbolizes not only the miraculous power of the Lord to provide for the children of Israel temporally during their journeyings but the inheritance of eternal life prepared by the Savior for the faithful. He has promised, "I go to prepare a place for you" (John 14:2). The Savior declares that He Himself is the "bread which cometh down from heaven, that a man may eat thereof, and not die" (John 6:50). His atoning sacrifice makes possible His promise of eternal life (2 Nephi 2:25–28), another kind of inheritance awaiting the faithful followers of Jesus Christ.

Even the abundant detailing and richness of material within the tent, such as the striped canvas, detailed carpet, and the rich clothing, symbolize the blessings of the promised land. The skill with which the embroidery is done on the girls' clothing is a visual reminder of the "needlework" wrought on the hanging for the tabernacle (Exodus 26:36).

The strong light in the tent symbolizes the Savior's presence, for He promises, "And I will walk among you, and will be your God, and ye shall be my people" (Leviticus 26:12).

REFERENCES

Curatola, Giovanni. *The Simon and Schuster Book of Oriental Carpets*. New York: Simon and Schuster, 1981.

Hepper, F. N. *Illustrated Encyclopedia of Bible Plants: Flowers and Trees, Fruits and Vegetables, Ecology*. Leicester, England: Inter Varsity Press, 1992.

Robinson, Stuart. *A History of Dyed Textiles*. Cambridge, Mass.: MIT Press, 1969.

Sentance, Bryan. *Art of the Basket*. London: Thames and Hudson, 2001.

A LAMP UNTO MY FEET, BY ELSPETH YOUNG

ABIGAIL

[Abigail] was a woman of good understanding, and of a beautiful countenance. . . .
Abigail made haste, and took two hundred loaves, and two bottles of wine, and five sheep ready dressed, and five measures of parched corn, and an hundred clusters of raisins, and two hundred cakes of figs. . . .
But she told not her husband Nabal. (1 Samuel 25:3–19)

THE STORY IN THE PAINTING

A Lamp unto My Feet depicts Abigail gathering foodstuffs to take to David's army after her husband foolishly refused to succor the men despite their sore need. This noble woman's act of courage in defying her unrighteous husband and taking food to David's army saved her and her entire household.

Abigail is enveloped in the darkness surrounding her at the time of her decision, for David's wrath meant that their deaths were imminent (1 Samuel 25:13). Any fear, whether great or small, envelops us in darkness; however, the light of Jesus Christ is the way out of such difficulties—following his words, no matter how dark or perilous the circumstance, is a "lamp" unto our feet and a "light" unto our path (Psalm 119:105). It is this light that leads Abigail to do what is right, despite the trying circumstance in which she finds herself. That is why she is depicted here in the light provided by a nearby lamp. The blankets and ropes and the basket filled with foodstuffs show her determination to make her faith in God active by supplying what David's troops requested. She will not sit by and wait to be overcome by fear but takes the hand of the Lord, as it were, and steps into the darkness, knowing He will light her way.

The biblical account describes Abigail as "a woman of good understanding, and of a beautiful countenance" (1 Samuel 25:3). She has both beauty and wisdom in her countenance, augmented by the light framing her face. Behind the figure is a table covered with food and containers for the loaves, parched corn, figs, and other foods she will offer David. She wears a head wrap because a journey is ahead of her (1 Samuel 25:19). Her clothing is rich in pattern and material because Nabal was very wealthy (1 Samuel 25:2), and her foods and jars are therefore also of the very finest.

SIGNIFICANT ELEMENTS IN THE PAINTING

An ornate candlestick appears in the lower left of the work, symbolic of the Savior's admonition from the Sermon on the Mount to "let your light so shine before men" (Matthew 5:16) by putting the candle on a candlestick so that it "giveth light unto all that are in the house" (v. 15). Abigail's behavior is a light to her household because of her foresight and righteousness in providing a means of saving them from death. The candles have burned down so that only a flame appears, indicating that Abigail's time is running out for completing the task at hand.

The biblical account states that Abigail rode a donkey to meet David. Traditionally, blankets such as those on Abigail's arm were tied onto a donkey's back as a sort of makeshift saddle (Cansdale, *Animals*, 72). Therefore, she carries both thick blankets and ropes to prepare for her ride.

REFERENCES

Achtemeier, Paul J. *Harper's Bible Dictionary.* San Francisco: Harper and Row, 1985.

Cansdale, George. *All the Animals of the Bible Lands.* Grand Rapids, Mich.: Paternoster Press, 1970.

Freeman, James M. *Manners and Customs of the Bible.* New York: Logos International, 1972.

Matthews, Victor H. *Manners and Customs in the Bible.* Peabody, Mass.: Hendrickson, 1991.

Strong, James. *The Exhaustive Concordance of the Bible.* New York: Abingdon Press, 1890.

CHARITY NEVER FAILETH, BY ELSPETH YOUNG

THE WIDOW OF ZAREPHATH

> *And she went and did according to the saying of Elijah. . . .*
> *And the barrel of meal wasted not, neither did the cruse of oil fail, according to the word of the Lord, which he spake by Elijah.* (1 Kings 17:15–16)

THE STORY IN THE PAINTING

The widow of Zarephath feeds the prophet of the Lord in faith during a famine that almost took her and her son's life. Because of her incredible faith, the Lord feeds her, her son, and Elijah for "many days"

(1 Kings 17:15), providing for her throughout the remainder of the famine. The painting itself depicts the fulfillment of the Lord's word to her because of her act of faith.

Perhaps as important a lesson as any we can learn from this account is that the Lord fulfills His promises. *Charity Never Faileth* expresses the joy that awaits all who trust in the Lord and "lean not unto [their] own understanding" (Proverbs 3:5). Indeed, the faithful will always find that no matter the circumstances, "charity never faileth" (1 Corinthians 13:8).

SIGNIFICANT ELEMENTS IN THE PAINTING

Later in the account of this faithful widow, Elijah raises her son from the dead in an upper room. Such rooms are believed to indicate wealth, and so it is likely this widow was wealthy before the famine. Indeed, perhaps the widow was still surrounded by signs of outward wealth, such as the carpet on the stone wall behind her or the rich robes and jewelry she wears even when she and her son are starving.

Charity Never Faileth teaches us that having money does not spare us from spiritual starvation. Only charity never fails. Relying on anything other than the Savior and His restored gospel to save us will eventually come to naught. As an angel teaches King Benjamin in the Book of Mormon, "there shall be no other name given nor any other way nor means whereby salvation can come unto the children of men, only in and through the name of Christ" (Mosiah 3:17). If, like this widow, we trust in the words of the prophets, heed their counsel, and rely upon the Savior's infinite atoning sacrifice, we will always find within us a "well of water springing up into everlasting life" (John 4:14).

The woman holds a "cruse of oil" (*tsappachath,* the Hebrew word translated here as "cruse," may also be translated as "saucer"). Near the figure is the "barrel" of meal whose contents were also miraculously extended. Both are a visual representation of the Lord's love, or charity.

When the widow went to gather "two sticks" to build a fire for her last meal, she met the prophet Elijah, who directed her to make him "thereof a little cake first," with the Lord's promise that "the barrel of meal shall not waste, neither shall the cruse of oil fail, until the day that the Lord sendeth rain upon the earth" (1 Kings 17:12–14).

Likewise, if we willingly give first the little that the Lord asks of us in tithing, he will open "the windows of heaven" (Malachi 3:10) and provide for us both temporally and spiritually.

REFERENCES

Freeman, James. *Manners and Customs of the Bible.* Plainfield, N.J.: Logos International, 1972.

Gower, Ralph. *The New Manners and Customs of Bible Times.* Chicago: Moody Press, 1987.

Hepper, F. N. *Illustrated Encyclopedia of Bible Plants: Flowers and Trees, Fruits and Vegetables, Ecology.* Leicester, England: Inter Varsity Press, 1992.

Matthews, Victor H. *Manners and Customs in the Bible.* Peabody, Mass.: Hendrickson, 1991.

Ogden, Kelly D., and Jeffrey R. Chadwick. *The Holy Land: A Geographical, Historical, and Archaeological Guide to the Land of the Bible.* Jerusalem: HaMakor: 1990.

Rawlinson, George. *History of Phoenicia.* New York: Longmans, Green, 1989.

Strong, James. *The Exhaustive Concordance of the Bible.* Nashville and New York: Abingdon Press, 1890.

WHAT IS TO BE DONE FOR THEE? BY ELSPETH YOUNG

THE SHUNAMMITE

Behold, thou hast been careful for us with all this care; what is to be done for thee? (2 Kings 4:13)

THE STORY IN THE PAINTING

The noble woman of Shunem known as the Shunammite provided a place in her home for Elisha, who offered her help in return for her kindness and care. She asked nothing for herself, but Elisha's servant observed to the prophet that she was childless. The prophet then extended to her the Lord's promise that she would "embrace a son," a promise that was fulfilled (2 Kings 4:16–17).

The moment depicted in *What Is to Be Done for Thee?* is the time before she receives the promise. She is in what appears to be an empty room. The room is as empty as she must have felt without a child of her own. She appears in the dark, but there is warm light just beyond her, waiting to envelop her as soon as she walks toward it. The light within the image, on the other hand, is meant to represent the blessings the Lord has in store for the faithful. As Paul states, "Eye hath not seen, nor ear heard, neither have entered into the heart of man, the things which God hath prepared for them that love him" (1 Corinthians 2:9). The blessing of a child awaits her because she has been selfless and faithful, and it is just beyond the emptiness she currently surveys.

As recounted in 2 Kings 4 and 8, the Shunnamite runs straight to the prophet in her sore need at the death of her son, and she witnesses the miraculous raising of her son from the dead by the Lord's prophet. Later, she heeds the prophet's counsel to leave her home before a famine. Upon her return at the famine's end, her lands are restored to her, along with all the increase her seven years away would have given her. These miracles combine to give us a little taste of the "things which God hath prepared for them that love him" (1 Corinthians 2:9) if we, like the Shunammite, "run" to the words and counsel of the Lord's prophet in our time of need and provide a place for his words in our hearts.

SIGNIFICANT ELEMENTS IN THE PAINTING

The light on the large curtain behind the Shunammite represents the light the prophet of the Lord offers her. The Lord, who is "the true Light, which lighteth every man that cometh into the world" (John 1:9), holds all the solutions to her difficulties and personal tragedies, ultimately making her life beautiful.

REFERENCES

Bunimovitz, Shlomo, and Avraham Faust. "Ideology in Stone: Understanding the Four-Room House." *Biblical Archaeology Review* 28, no. 4 (July/Aug. 2002): 32–41.

Freeman, James. *Manners and Customs of the Bible.* Reprint. Plainfield, N.J.: Logos International, 1972.

Matthews, Victor H. *Manners and Customs in the Bible.* Peabody, Mass.: Hendrickson, 1991.

THE SEED OF FAITH, BY ELSPETH YOUNG

THE LITTLE MAID

Now Naaman, captain of the host of the king of Syria, was a great man with his master, and honourable, because by him the Lord had given deliverance unto Syria: he was also a mighty man in valour, but he was a leper.

And the Syrians had gone out by companies, and had brought away captive out of the land of Israel a little maid; and she waited on Naaman's wife.

And she said unto her mistress, Would God my lord were with the prophet that is in Samaria! for he would recover him of his leprosy.

And one went in, and told his lord, saying, Thus and thus said the maid that is of the land of Israel. . . .

And Elisha sent a messenger unto [Naaman], saying, Go and wash in Jordan seven times, and thy flesh shall come again to thee, and thou shalt be clean. . . .

Then went [Naaman] down, and dipped himself seven times in Jordan, according to the saying of the man of God: and his flesh came again . . . and he was clean. (2 Kings 5:1–14)

Verily I say unto you, If ye have faith as a grain of mustard seed, ye shall say unto this mountain, Remove hence . . . and nothing shall be impossible unto you. (Matthew 17:20)

THE STORY IN THE PAINTING

In *The Seed of Faith* the young girl known as "the little maid" is seated in Naaman's palace, looking into the distance—looking toward home, reflecting on her testimony of the Israelite prophet Elisha and his power to heal her master of his leprosy. She knows that "the prophet that is in Samaria" has the priesthood power to heal Naaman, and she is considering communicating that knowledge to her mistress, Naaman's wife. Her willingness to speak out indicates her fearless faith and courage—the kind of faith the Savior taught his disciples.

SIGNIFICANT ELEMENTS IN THE PAINTING

The biblical account in 2 Kings 5 uses the Hebrew word *naarah* to describe the Israelite servant. Because the Hebrew is perhaps better rendered "girl" than "maid" in translation (Strong, *Concordance,* Hebrew and Chaldee Dictionary), the painting depicts a young child. She wears a simple tunic-like overdress, reminiscent of the costume worn by a serving girl in an eighth-century B.C. Syrian relief (*World*, 270). The tunic's whiteness symbolizes her faith and purity. It is as simple as the testimony burning within her: "Would God my lord were with the prophet that is in Samaria! for he would recover him of his leprosy" (2 Kings 5:3).

Second only in importance to the young girl in the painting is the bowl of orchids blooming close by. Its symbolism is twofold. First, and most important, it represents the faith of this young girl who is willing to step forward and bear her testimony of the prophet, despite her living without her family in a strange land. It also symbolizes the faith of Naaman, who is willing to humble himself by listening not only to an obscure servant girl but also to the word of Elisha by accepting the "trial" of his faith (Ether 12:6).

When the Savior spoke to His disciples about faith, as recorded in Matthew 17:20, He compared faith to a grain of mustard seed. One scholar observes that "at the time of Christ mustard seed was one of the smallest of all known seeds" but points out that "orchid seeds, as infinitesimal as fine dust, are today considered to be the smallest [seed] in the plant kingdom, but these were not familiar to Jesus' audience in Galilee" (Rosengarten, *Spices*, 300).

Therefore the orchids represent the faith spoken of by Christ. They are a reminder that despite her relative insignificance as a household slave, her testimony is of lasting significance to the captain of the Syrian host. Just as an exquisite orchid grows and blooms from the smallest of seeds, so the simple, faith-filled testimony of the little maid produces bounteous blessings for Naaman and his household.

The orchids also symbolize the little maid's own captivity. Just like the little maid, these orchids are out of place, away from their native homeland, but blossoming beautifully nonetheless. Similarly, the little maid does not allow her difficult circumstances to blight the energy and vitality of her faith.

Archaeological evidence confirms the use of pillars in homes throughout Palestine and surrounding countries well before the story of the little maid (Mazar, *Archaeology*, 343). The capitals of the pillars, as rendered here, are based on carved lotus blossoms found on an ivory inlay of the king of Syria from about 950 B.C. (*World*, 264).

When Elisha's servant first counsels Naaman to "wash in Jordan seven times" (2 Kings 5:10), Naaman is "wroth" and asks: "Are not Abana and Pharpar, rivers of Damascus, better than all the waters of Israel?" (2 Kings 5:12). His statement is represented in the painting by the waters that stretch out into the distance. They symbolize our need to follow the words of the living prophet despite any misgivings we might have concerning the counsel we receive.

REFERENCES

Barnes, Ian. *The Historical Atlas of the Bible.* London: Cartigraphica Press, 2006.

Hepper, F. N. *Illustrated Encyclopedia of Bible Plants: Flowers and Trees, Fruits and Vegetables, Ecology.* Leicester, England: Inter Varsity Press, 1992.

Mazar, Amidai. *Archaeology of the Land of the Bible 10,000–586 B.C.E.* Doubleday, New York. 1990.

Meyers, Carol L. *Women in Scripture: A Dictionary of Named and Unnamed Women in the Hebrew Bible, the Apocryphal/Deuterocanonical Books, and the New Testament.* Grand Rapids, Mich.: Eerdmans, 2000.

Rosengarten, Frederick, Jr. *The Book of Spices.* Philadelphia: Livingston, 1969.

Strong, James. *The Exhaustive Concordance of the Bible.* New York: Abingdon Press, 1890.

The World of the Bible. 2 vols. New York: Educational Heritage, 1964.

SOURCES

DESCRIPTION OF ANCIENT TEXTS CITED

Code of Hammurabi. Dated to circa 1750 B.C., this list of laws for the people of Babylonia was presumably used to pass judgment on a transgressor. Customs concerning marriage, wages, slaves, children, and inheritance are included in the code. Inscribed on a seven-foot-high black diorite stele, the code contains 282 laws and a scene portraying the sun god Shamash delivering the laws to King Hammurabi. The stele is located in the Louvre Museum in Paris.

Dead Sea Scrolls. Multiple scrolls and scroll fragments that date from circa 250 B.C. to A.D. 70, they include the oldest existing copies of every book in the Old Testament with the exception of the book of Esther. Discovered between 1947 and 1956 in caves west of the Dead Sea in Palestine, the scrolls also preserve various law codes of the religious society that inhabited the area near the caves. The modern name that scholars give to each document includes the cave in which it was found and the scroll's general content, and the name is then abbreviated. For example, 4QSama signifies the scroll was found in Cave 4 of Qumran and preserves a copy of 1 and 2 Samuel.

Flavius Josephus (A.D. *37–ca. 100).* A Jewish historian and eyewitness to the destruction of Jerusalem by the Romans in A.D. 70, Josephus published his longest work, *The Antiquities of the Jews,* to educate a non-Jewish audience about the remarkable legacy of the Jews. His history begins with the biblical creation and ends with his own era, when the Jews were under Roman rule. It draws heavily from the Septuagint and extrabiblical Jewish traditions. It should be remembered that although these writings are ancient and authentic, many of Josephus's sources are unknown and untested. Additionally, Josephus wrote the history of the Jewish people to attract sympathy from his readers, whether they were pagan Greeks and Romans or Hellenized Jews. That being said, these writings are valuable communications of how Jews living about the time of Christ understood stories of the Old Testament. Josephus's writings become additionally interesting when they intersect or coincide with scriptural commentary received through modern revelation.

Midrash (*"scriptural interpretation"; **plural, Midrashim).*** An assortment of rabbinic writings from a variety of sources, Jewish Midrashim include the multivolume Jerusalem and Babylonian Talmuds, the Genesis Rabba, Leviticus Rabba, Midrash Tanhuma, and others that relay traditional explanations for many Old Testament stories. At times they differ dramatically from accepted scholarly commentary, but often they suggest ways of considering the story from a different angle. Many of these assorted commentaries were collected and arranged by Louis Ginzberg as a parallel to the biblical text in a seven-volume work entitled *The Legends of the Jews.*

Masoretic Text **("transmission").** The traditional Hebrew text of the Old Testament was produced between the sixth and tenth centuries after Christ. The King James translators used the Masoretic Text as they translated the books of the Old Testament. Abbreviated MT, it was preserved by Jewish grammarians, who added notes to protect the text from inadvertent changes.

Nag Hammadi texts. Discovered in Lower Egypt in 1945, the Nag Hammadi collection consists of thirteen leather-bound books containing forty-five religious works that were translated from Greek to Coptic in the fourth century after Christ. This eclectic library was amassed by a Christian community whose theology differed substantially from that of the fourth-century Roman Catholic Church. Among the various texts is literature relaying "hidden" knowledge purported to have been written by the early apostles, along with other versions of the Garden of Eden story.

Nuzi texts. Dating to the fifteenth century before Christ, the Nuzi texts were created by a people called the Hurrians, who left behind thousands of cuneiform tablets from their northeastern Mesopotamian city of Nuzi. The tablets contain a variety of documents, including marriage certificates, wills, inheritance laws that allowed the bequeathing of property to individuals other than sons, bills of sale, and adoption agreements. Because the Hurrians occupied the area near where the patriarchs in the Genesis narrative often resided, these texts are valuable in lending insight into the possible culture and society during the patriarchal era.

Septuagint ("seventy"). This Greek translation of the Old Testament dates back to the third century before Christ. When the Ptolemies ruled the ancient Near East, all the major works of the peoples they had conquered were commissioned to be translated into Greek and housed in a great library in Alexandria, Egypt. The Jewish contribution to this library was their scriptures. Abbreviated LXX, the Septuagint was purportedly translated in seventy days by seventy-two Jewish scribes who were brought to Egypt by Ptolemy II Philadelphus (285–246 B.C.). Sometimes agreeing more with the Dead Sea Scrolls than with the Masoretic Text, the Septuagint stands today as another witness of the preservation of the Hebrew scriptures.

SELECTED SOURCES

EVE

Barker, William P. *Everyone in the Bible.* Old Tappan, N.J.: Fleming H. Revell, 1966.

Benson, Ezra Taft. "What I Hope You Will Teach Your Children about the Temple." *Ensign,* Aug. 1985, 6–10.

———. "The Book of Mormon and the Doctrine and Covenants." *Ensign,* May 1987, 83–85.

Campbell, Beverly. "Mother Eve: Mentor for Today's Woman: A Heritage of Honor." *Collegium Aesculapium,* April 2, 1993, 37–49.

Freedman, R. David. "Woman, a Power Equal to Man." *Biblical Archaeology Review,* Jan./Feb. 1983, 56–58.

Ginzberg, Louis. *The Legends of the Jews.* 7 vols. Translated by Henrietta Szold. Baltimore: Johns Hopkins University Press, 1998.

Hafen, Bruce C., and Marie K. Hafen. "Crossing Thresholds and Becoming Equal Partners." *Ensign,* Aug. 2007, 25–29.

Hinckley, Gordon B. *Standing for Something: Ten Neglected Virtues That Will Heal Our Hearts and Homes.* New York: Random House, 2000.

———. "Daughters of God." *Ensign,* Nov. 1991, 97–100.

Hunter, Howard W. "Being a Righteous Husband and Father." *Ensign,* Nov. 1994, 49–51.

McConkie, Bruce R. *Doctrinal New Testament Commentary.* 3 vols. Salt Lake City: Bookcraft, 1973.

Mead, G.R.S., trans. *Pistis Sophia: A Gnostic Miscellany.* London: John M. Watkins, 1921.

Meyers, Carol. "Eve." In Carol Meyers, ed., *Women in Scripture: A Dictionary of Named and Unnamed Women in the Hebrew Bible, the Apocryphal/Deuterocanonical Books, and the New Testament.* Grand Rapids, Mich.: Eerdmans, 2000.

Nelson, Russell M. "Constancy amid Change." *Ensign,* Nov. 1993, 33–36.

Nibley, Hugh. *The Collected Works of Hugh Nibley: Volume I. Old Testament and Related Studies.* Salt Lake City: Deseret Book, 1986.

Oaks, Dallin H. "The Great Plan of Happiness." *Ensign,* Nov. 1993, 72–75.

Packer, Boyd K. "The Relief Society." *Ensign,* May 1998, 72–74.

Parry, Donald W. "Eve's Role as a 'Help' ('ezer) Revisited." Manuscript. Paper delivered at Society of Biblical Literature, San Diego, CA, Nov. 2007.

Ricks, Stephen D. "The Garment of Adam in Jewish, Muslim, and Christian Tradition." In Donald W. Parry, ed., *Temples of the Ancient World: Ritual and Symbolism.* Salt Lake City: Deseret Book and Provo: FARMS, 1994.

Robinson, James M., ed. *The Nag Hammadi Library in English.* San Francisco: HarperCollins, 1990.

Sawyer, Deborah F. "Resurrecting Eve? Feminist Critique of the Garden of Eden." In Paul Morris and Deborah Sawyer, eds., *A Walk in the Garden: Biblical, Iconographical and Literary Images of Eden.* Sheffield, England: Sheffield Academic Press, 1992.

Schneider, Tammi J. *Mothers of Promise: Women in the Book of Genesis.* Grand Rapids, Mich.: Baker Academic, 2008.

Smith, Joseph. *History of The Church of Jesus Christ of Latter-day Saints.* 2d ed., rev. Edited by B. H. Roberts. 7 vols. Salt Lake City: The Church of Jesus Christ of Latter-day Saints, 1932–51.

Smith, Joseph Fielding. *Doctrines of Salvation: Sermons and Writings of Joseph Fielding Smith.* Compiled by Bruce R. McConkie. 3 vols. Salt Lake City: Bookcraft, 1954–56.

———. *Seek Ye Earnestly. . . .* Salt Lake City: Deseret Book, 1970.

Terrien, Samuel, ed. *The Interpreter's Bible.* 12 vols. New York: Abingdon Press, 1952–57.

Tvedtnes, John A. "Priestly Clothing in Bible Times." In Donald W. Parry, ed., *Temples of the Ancient World: Ritual and Symbolism.* Salt Lake City: Deseret Book and Provo: FARMS, 1994.

Young, Brigham. *Journal of Discourses.* 26 vols. London: Latter-day Saints' Book Depot, 1854–86.

WIVES OF THE PATRIARCHS

Baker, James R. *Women's Rights in Old Testament Times.* Salt Lake City: Signature, 1992.

Barker, Kenneth, ed. *Zondervan KJV Study Bible.* Grand Rapids, Mich.: Zondervan, 2002.

Berlin, Adele, and Marc Zvi Brettler, eds. *The Jewish Study Bible.* New York: Oxford University Press, 2004.

Bright, John. *A History of Israel.* 4th ed. Louisville, Ky.: Westminster John Knox Press, 2000.

Harris, Roberta L. *The World of the Bible.* London: Thames and Hudson, 1995.

Hoerth, Alfred J. *Archaeology and the Old Testament.* Grand Rapids, Mich.: Baker Books, 1998.

Matthews, Victor H. *Manners and Customs in the Bible.* Rev. ed. Peabody, Mass.: Hendrickson, 1996.

Pritchard, James B., ed. *Collins Atlas of the Bible.* Ann Arbor, Mich.: Borders Press, 2003.

———. *Ancient Near Eastern Texts Relating to the Old Testament.* Princeton, N.J.: Princeton University Press, 1969.

SARAH AND HAGAR

Baker, James R. *Women's Rights in Old Testament Times.* Salt Lake City: Signature, 1992.

Barker, Kenneth, ed. *Zondervan KJV Study Bible.* Grand Rapids, Mich.: Zondervan, 2002.

Berlin, Adele, and Marc Zvi Brettler, eds. *The Jewish Study Bible.* New York: Oxford University Press, 2004.

Bright, John. *A History of Israel.* 4th ed. Louisville, Ky.: Westminster John Knox Press, 2000.

Falk, Ze'ev W. *Hebrew Law in Biblical Times.* Provo, Utah: Brigham Young University Press, 2001.

Freeman, James. *Hand-book of Bible Manners and Customs.* Cincinnati, Ohio: Hitchcock and Walden, 1877.

Frymer-Kensky, Tikva. *Reading the Women of the Bible.* New York: Schocken Books, 2002.

Genesis Apocryphon.

Ginzberg, Louis. *The Legends of the Jews.* 7 vols. Translated by Henrietta Szold. Baltimore: Johns Hopkins University Press, 1998.

Harris, Roberta L. *The World of the Bible.* London: Thames and Hudson, 1995.

Hoerth, Alfred J. *Archaeology and the Old Testament.* Grand Rapids, Mich.: Baker Books, 1998.

Hoskisson, Paul Y. "Where Was Ur of the Chaldees?" In H. Donl Peterson and Charles D. Tate Jr., eds., *The Pearl of Great Price: Revelations from God.* Provo, Utah: Religious Studies Center, Brigham Young University, 1989.

————. "Research and Perspectives: Where Was the Ur of Abraham?" *Ensign,* July 1991, 62–63.

Hunter, Howard W. "All Are Alike unto God." In *1979 Devotional Speeches of the Year.* Provo, Utah: Brigham Young University Press, 1979.

Jackson, Kent P. *The Restored Gospel and the Book of Genesis.* Salt Lake City: Deseret Book, 2001.

Josephus, Flavius. *Antiquities of the Jews.* In *The Works of Josephus, Complete and Unabridged.* Translated by William Whiston. Peabody, Mass.: Hendrickson, 1987.

Kimball, Spencer W. *Faith Precedes the Miracle.* Salt Lake City: Deseret Book, 1979.

Lundquist, John M. "Was Abraham at Ebla? A Cultural Background of the Book of Abraham." In Robert L. Millet and Kent P. Jackson, eds. *The Pearl of Great Price.* Vol. 2 of Studies in Scripture series. Salt Lake City: Randall Book, 1985.

Mace, David R. *Hebrew Marriage: A Sociological Study.* London: Epworth Press, 1953.

Matthews, Victor H. *Manners and Customs in the Bible.* Rev. ed. Peabody, Mass.: Hendrickson, 1996.

Maxwell, Neal A. *All These Things Shall Give Thee Experience.* Salt Lake City: Deseret Book, 1980.

Nibley, Hugh. *Abraham in Egypt.* 2d ed. Salt Lake City: Deseret Book and Provo, Utah: FARMS, 2000.

————. *Old Testament and Related Studies.* Salt Lake City: Deseret Book, and Provo, Utah: FARMS, 1986.

Pritchard, James B., ed. *Collins Atlas of the Bible.* Ann Arbor, Mich.: Borders Press, 2003.

Rogers, Mary Eliza. *Domestic Life in Palestine.* Cincinnati: Poe and Hitchcock, 1869.

Schneider, Tammi J. *Mothers of Promise: Women in the Book of Genesis.* Grand Rapids, Mich.: Baker Academic, 2008.

Speiser, E. A. *Genesis.* The Anchor Bible Series. New York: Doubleday, 1962.

Thompson, John L. *Writing the Wrongs: Women of the Old Testament among Biblical Commentators from Philo through the Reformation.* New York: Oxford University Press, 2001.

REBEKAH

Barker, Kenneth, ed. *Zondervan KJV Study Bible.* Grand Rapids, Mich.: Zondervan, 2002.

Berlin, Adele, and Marc Zvi Brettler, eds. *The Jewish Study Bible.* New York: Oxford University Press, 2004.

Bright, John. *A History of Israel.* 4th ed. Louisville, Ky.: Westminster John Knox Press, 2000.

Freeman, James. *Hand-book of Bible Manners and Customs.* Cincinnati: Hitchcock and Walden, 1877.

Frymer-Kensky, Tikva. *Reading the Women of the Bible.* New York: Schocken Books, 2002.

Ginzberg, Louis. *The Legends of the Jews.* 7 vols. Translated by Henrietta Szold. Baltimore: Johns Hopkins University Press, 1998.

Hoerth, Alfred J. *Archaeology and the Old Testament.* Grand Rapids, Mich.: Baker Books, 1998.

Hunter, Howard W. "Commitment to God." *Ensign,* Nov. 1982, 57–58.

Ivins, Anthony W. "Asenath, Wife of Joseph." *Improvement Era,* Aug. 1931, 571.

Jackson, Kent P. *The Restored Gospel and the Book of Genesis.* Salt Lake City: Deseret Book, 2001.

Jessee, Dean C., ed. *Personal Writings of Joseph Smith.* Salt Lake City: Deseret Book, 1984.

Josephus, Flavius. *Antiquities of the Jews.* In *The Works of Josephus, Complete and Unabridged.* Translated by William Whiston. Peabody, Mass.: Hendrickson, 1987.

Journal of Discourses. 26 vols. London: Latter-day Saints' Book Depot, 1854–86.

Köhler-Rollefson, Ilse. "Camels and Camel Pastoralism in Arabia." *Biblical Archaeologist* 56, no. 4 (1993): 180–88.

Mace, David R. *Hebrew Marriage: A Sociological Study.* London: Epworth Press, 1953.

McConkie, Bruce R. "Our Sisters from the Beginning." *Ensign,* Jan. 1979, 61–63.

Nibley, Hugh. *Abraham in Egypt.* 2d ed. Salt Lake City: Deseret Book, 2000.

Ripinsky, Michael. "The Camel in Dynastic Egypt." *Journal of Egyptian Archaeology* 71 (1985): 134–41.

Sasson, Jack M. "The Servant's Tale: How Rebekah Found a Spouse." *Journal of Near Eastern Studies* 65, no. 4 (2006): 241–65.

Schneider, Tammi J. *Mothers of Promise: Women in the Book of Genesis.* Grand Rapids, Mich.: Baker Academic, 2008.

Smith, Joseph. *History of The Church of Jesus Christ of Latter-day Saints.* Edited by B. H. Roberts. 2d ed. rev. Salt Lake City: The Church of Jesus Christ of Latter-day Saints, 1932–51.

Smoot, Mary Ellen. "We Are Creators." *Ensign,* May 2000, 64–65.

Speiser, E. A. *Genesis.* Anchor Bible Series. New York: Doubleday, 1962.

LEAH AND RACHEL

Baker, James R. *Women's Rights in Old Testament Times.* Salt Lake City: Signature, 1992.

Barker, Kenneth, ed. *Zondervan KJV Study Bible.* Grand Rapids, Mich.: Zondervan, 2002.

Berlin, Adele, and Marc Zvi Brettler, eds. *The Jewish Study Bible.* New York: Oxford University Press, 2004.

Bright, John. *A History of Israel.* 4th ed. Louisville, Ky.: Westminster John Knox Press, 2000.

Draffkorn, Anne E. "Ilani/Elohim." *Journal of Biblical Literature* 76, no. 3 (Sept. 1957): 216–24.

Dresner, Samuel H. "Barren Rachel." *Judaism* 40, no. 4 (Fall 1991): 442–51.

Freeman, James. *Hand-book of Bible Manners and Customs.* Cincinnati: Hitchcock and Walden, 1877.

Ginzberg, Louis. *The Legends of the Jews.* 7 vols. Translated by Henrietta Szold. Baltimore: Johns Hopkins University Press, 1998.

Greenberg, Moshe. "Another Look at Rachel's Theft of the Teraphim." *Journal of Biblical Literature* 81, no. 3 (Sept. 1962): 239–48.

Hellerstein, Kathryn. "A Word for My Blood: A Reading of Kadya Molodowsky's 'Froyen-Lider.'" *AJS Review* 13, no. 1/2 (Spring–Autumn 1988): 47–79.

Hoerth, Alfred J. *Archaeology and the Old Testament.* Grand Rapids, Mich.: Baker Books, 1998.

Hunter, Howard W. "Commitment to God." *Ensign,* Nov. 1982, 57–58.

Josephus, Flavius. *Antiquities of the Jews.* In *The Works of Josephus, Complete and Unabridged.* Translated by William Whiston. Peabody, Mass.: Hendrickson, 1987.

Kennedy, Charles A. "Dead, Cult of." In *Anchor Bible Dictionary.* Edited by David Noel Freedman. 6 vols. New York: Doubleday, 1992.

Mace, David R. *Hebrew Marriage: A Sociological Study.* London: Epworth Press, 1953.

Nibley, Hugh. *Abraham in Egypt.* 2d ed. Salt Lake City: Deseret Book, 2000.

———. *Old Testament and Related Studies.* Salt Lake City: Deseret Book, 1986.

Neusner, Jacob. *Genesis Rabbah: The Judaic Commentary to the Book of Genesis.* 3 vols. Atlanta: Scholars Press, 1985.

Pritchard, James, ed. *Collins Atlas of the Bible.* Ann Arbor, Mich.: Borders Press, 2003.

Schneider, Tammi J. *Mothers of Promise: Women in the Book of Genesis.* Grand Rapids, Mich.: Baker Academic, 2008.

Spanier, Ktziah. "Rachel's Theft of the Teraphim: Her Struggles for Family Primacy." *Vetus Testamentum* 42, fasc. 3 (July 1992): 404–12.

Speiser, E. A. *Genesis.* The Anchor Bible Series. New York: Doubleday, 1962.

PROPHETESSES

Hinckley, Gordon B. "Ten Gifts from the Lord." *Ensign,* Nov. 1985, 86–89.

Kimball, Heber C. *Journal of Discourses.* 26 vols. London: Latter-day Saints' Book Depot, 1854–86.

Oaks, Dallin H. "Scripture Reading and Revelation." Address to BYU Studies Academy, Provo, Utah, 29 Jan. 1993.

Smith, Joseph. *Teachings of the Prophet Joseph Smith.* Selected by Joseph Fielding Smith. Salt Lake City: Deseret Book, 1976.

Talmage, James E. *Articles of Faith.* 12th ed. Salt Lake City: The Church of Jesus Christ of Latter-day Saints, 1924.

MIRIAM

Bach, Alice. "With a Song in Her Heart: Listening to Scholars Listening for Miriam." In Alice Bach, ed., *Women in the Bible.* New York: Routledge, 1999.

Berlin, Adele, and Marc Zvi Brettler, eds. *The Jewish Study Bible.* New York: Oxford University Press, 2004.

Bright, John. *A History of Israel.* 4th ed. Louisville, Ky.: Westminster John Knox Press, 2000.

Freedman, David Noel, ed. *The Anchor Bible Dictionary.* 6 vols. New York: Doubleday, 1992. S.v. "Leprosy" and "Miriam."

Ginzberg, Louis. *The Legends of the Jews.* 7 vols. Translated by Henrietta Szold. Baltimore: Johns Hopkins University Press, 1998.

Hales, Robert D. "With All the Feeling of a Tender Parent: A Message of Hope to Families." *Ensign,* May 2004, 88–91.

Hoerth, Alfred J. *Archaeology and the Old Testament.* Grand Rapids, Mich.: Baker Books, 1998.

Josephus, Flavius. *Antiquities of the Jews.* In *The Works of Josephus, Complete and Unabridged.* Translated by William Whiston. Peabody, Mass.: Hendrickson, 1987.

Keil, C. F., and F. Delitzsch. *Commentary on the Old Testament.* 10 vols. Peabody, Mass.: Hendrickson, 1996.

Meyers, Carol L. "Of Drums and Damsels: Women's Performance in Ancient Israel." *Biblical Archaeologist* 54, no. 1 (Mar. 1991): 16–27.

Oaks, Dallin H. "Criticism." *Ensign,* Feb. 1987, 68–73.

Ogden, D. Kelly, and LaMar C. Barrett. *Discovering the World of the Bible.* 3d ed. Provo, Utah: Grandin, 1996.

Richards, George F. Conference Report, Apr. 1947, 23–28.

Trible, Phyllis. "Bringing Miriam Out of the Shadows." *Bible Review* 5 (Feb. 1989): 14–25, 34.

Walton, John H., and Victor H. Matthews. *The IVP Bible Background Commentary: Genesis-Deuteronomy.* Downers Grove, Ill.: Inter Varsity Press, 1997.

DEBORAH

Ackerman, Susan. "Digging Up Deborah: Recent Hebrew Bible Scholarship on Gender and the Contribution of Archaeology." *Near Eastern Archaeology* 66, 4 (Dec. 2003): 172–84.

Berlin, Adele, and Marc Zvi Brettler, eds. *The Jewish Study Bible.* New York: Oxford University Press, 2004.

Boling, Robert G. *Judges.* The Anchor Bible Series. Garden City, N.Y.: Doubleday, 1975.

Bright, John. *A History of Israel.* 4th ed. Louisville, Ky.: Westminster John Knox Press, 2000.

Gates, Susa Young, ed. "Mothers in Israel." *Relief Society Magazine* 3, no. 1 (1916), 3–5.

———. "The Mother of Mothers in Israel: Eliza R. Snow." *Relief Society Magazine* 3, no. 4 (1916), 183–90.

Ginzberg, Louis. *The Legends of the Jews.* 7 vols. Translated by Henrietta Szold. Baltimore: Johns Hopkins University Press, 1998.

Hoerth, Alfred J. *Archaeology and the Old Testament.* Grand Rapids, Mich.: Baker Books, 1998.

Jamieson, Robert. *Eastern Manners Illustrative of Old Testament History.* Philadelphia: Presbyterian Board of Publication, 1838.

Josephus, Flavius. *Antiquities of the Jews.* In *The Works of Josephus, Complete and Unabridged.* Translated by William Whiston. Peabody, Mass.: Hendrickson, 1987.

Frymer-Kensky, Tikva. "Deborah 2" and "Jael." In *Women in Scripture: A Dictionary of Named and Unnamed Women in the Hebrew Bible, the Apocryphal/Deuterocanonical Books, and the New Testament,* edited by Carol Meyers. Grand Rapids, Mich.: Eerdmans, 2000.

Orr, James. "Judge," "Kenites," and "Milk." In *The International Standard Bible Encyclopaedia.* 4 vols. Grand Rapids, Mich: Eerdmans, 1956. Reprint, Peabody, Mass.: Hendrickson, 2002.

Pritchard, James, ed. *Ancient Near Eastern Texts Relating to the Old Testament.* Princeton, N.J.: Princeton University Press, 1969.

Ricks, Stephen D., and Donald W. Parry. "The Judges of Israel." In *The Old Testament,* edited by Kent P. Jackson and Robert Millet. Studies in Scripture series. Salt Lake City: Deseret Book, 1985.

HANNAH

Achtemeier, Paul J., ed. "Festivals." *HarperCollins Bible Dictionary.* San Francisco: HarperCollins, 1996.

Barker, Kenneth L., and John R. Kohlenberger III. *The Expositor's Bible Commentary, Abridged Edition: Old Testament.* Grand Rapids, Mich.: Zondervan, 1994.

Berlin, Adele, and Marc Zvi Brettler, eds. *The Jewish Study Bible.* New York: Oxford University Press, 2004.

Bright, John. *A History of Israel.* 4th ed. Louisville, Ky.: Westminster John Knox Press, 2000.

Cross, Frank Morre, Donald W. Parry, Richard J Saley, and Eugene Ulrich. *Qumran Cave 4: Discoveries in the Judean Desert, XVII.* Oxford: Clarendon Press, 2005.

Frymer-Kensky, Tikva. *Reading the Women of the Bible.* New York: Schocken Books, 2002.

Ginzberg, Louis. *The Legends of the Jews.* 7 vols. Translated by Henrietta Szold. Baltimore: Johns Hopkins University Press, 1998.

Harris, Roberta L. *The World of the Bible.* London: Thames and Hudson, 1995.

Hoerth, Alfred J. *Archaeology and the Old Testament.* Grand Rapids, Mich.: Baker Books, 1998.

Herrmann, Siegfried. *A History of Israel in Old Testament Times.* Philadelphia: Fortress Press, 1981.

Josephus, Flavius. *Antiquities of the Jews.* In *The Works of Josephus, Complete and Unabridged.* Translated by William Whiston. Peabody, Mass.: Hendrickson, 1987.

Keil, C. F., and F. Delitzsch. *Commentary on the Old Testament.* 10 vols. Peabody, Mass.: Hendrickson, 1996.

Klein, Lillian R. "Hannah." In Carol Meyers, ed. *Women in Scripture: A Dictionary of Named and Unnamed Women in the Hebrew Bible, the Apocryphal/Deuterocanonical Books, and the New Testament.* Grand Rapids, Mich.: Eerdmans, 2000.

McCarter, P. Kyle, Jr. *I Samuel.* The Anchor Bible Series. Garden City, N.Y.: Doubleday, 1980.

Meyers, Carol. "The Hannah Narrative in Feminist Perspective." In *"Go to the Land I Will Show You": Studies in Honor of Dwight W. Young,* edited by Joseph E. Coleson and Victor H. Matthews. Winona Lake, Ind.: Eisenbrauns, 1996.

Ochs, Vanessa L. *Sarah Laughed: Modern Lessons from the Wisdom and Stories of Biblical Women.* New York: McGraw-Hill, 2005.

Parry, Donald W. "Hannah in the Presence of the Lord." Publication forthcoming.

Unger, Merrill F. "Festivals." In *The New Unger's Bible Dictionary.* Edited by R. K. Harrison. Chicago: Moody Press, 1988.

HULDAH

Berlin, Adele, and Marc Zvi Brettler, eds. *The Jewish Study Bible.* New York: Oxford University Press, 2004.

Borowski, Oded. *Daily Life in Biblical Times.* Atlanta: Society of Biblical Literature, 2003.

Bright, John. *A History of Israel.* 4th ed. Louisville, Ky.: Westminster John Knox Press, 2000.

Camp, Claudia V. "Huldah." In Carol Meyers, ed. *Women in Scripture: A Dictionary of Named and Unnamed Women in the Hebrew Bible, the Apocryphal/Deuterocanonical Books, and the New Testament.* Grand Rapids, Mich.: Eerdmans, 2000.

Cogan, Mordechai, and Hayim Tadmor. *II Kings.* The Anchor Bible Series. Garden City, N.Y.: Doubleday, 1988.

Frymer-Kensky, Tikva. *Reading the Women of the Bible.* New York: Schocken Books, 2002.

Ginzberg, Louis. *The Legends of the Jews.* 7 vols. Translated by Henrietta Szold and Paul Radin. Baltimore: Johns Hopkins University Press, 1998.

Hoerth, Alfred J. *Archaeology and the Old Testament.* Grand Rapids, Mich.: Baker Books, 1998.

Josephus, Flavius. *Antiquities of the Jews*. In *The Works of Josephus, Complete and Unabridged*. Translated by William Whiston. Peabody, Mass.: Hendrickson, 1987.

Myers, Jacob M. *II Chronicles*. The Anchor Bible Series. Garden City, N.Y.: Doubleday, 1965.

Phipps, William E. "A Woman Was the First to Declare Scripture Holy." *Bible Review*, Apr. 1990, 14–16.

Rasmussen, Ellis T. *A Latter-day Saint Commentary on the Old Testament*. Salt Lake City: Deseret Book, 1993.

Stanton, Elizabeth Cady. *The Woman's Bible*. Amherst, N.Y.: Prometheus Books, 1999.

SHIPHRAH AND PUAH

Berlin, Adele, and Marc Zvi Brettler, eds. *The Jewish Study Bible*. New York: Oxford University Press, 2004.

Bright, John. *A History of Israel*. 4th ed. Louisville, Ky.: Westminster John Knox Press, 2000.

Ginzberg, Louis. *The Legends of the Jews*. 7 vols. Translated by Henrietta Szold. Baltimore: Johns Hopkins University Press, 1998.

Josephus, Flavius. *Antiquities of the Jews*. In *The Works of Josephus, Complete and Unabridged*. Translated by William Whiston. Peabody, Mass.: Hendrickson, 1987.

Keil, C. F., and F. Delitzsch. *Commentary on the Old Testament*. 10 vols. Peabody, Mass.: Hendrickson, 1996.

King, Philip J., and Lawrence E. Stager. *Life in Biblical Israel*. Louisville: Westminster John Knox Press, 2001.

Lesko, Barbara S. "Women's Monumental Mark on Ancient Egypt." *Biblical Archaeologist* 54, 1 (Mar. 1991): 4–15.

Matthews, Victor H., and Don C. Benjamin. *Social World of Ancient Israel 1250–587 B.C.E.* Peabody, Mass.: Hendrickson, 1993.

Pritchard, James B. *Ancient Near Eastern Texts Relating to the Old Testament*. 3d ed. Princeton, N.J.: Princeton University Press, 1969.

DAUGHTERS OF ZELOPHEHAD

Baker, James R. *Women's Rights in Old Testament Times*. Salt Lake City: Signature Books, 1992.

Ben-Barak, Zafrira. "Inheritance by Daughters in the Ancient Near East." *Journal of Semitic Studies* 25 (1980): 22–33.

Berlin, Adele, and Marc Zvi Brettler, eds. *The Jewish Study Bible*. New York: Oxford University Press, 2004.

Bodenheimer, F. S. "The Manna of Sinai." *Biblical Archaeologist* 10, 1 (1947): 2–6.

Borowski, Oded. *Daily Life in Biblical Times*. Atlanta: Society of Biblical Literature, 2003.

Clark, Henry C. "And Zelophehad Had Daughters." *American Bar Association Journal* (Feb. 1924): 133–34.

Drinkard, Joel F. "Manna." In Paul J. Achtemeier, ed. *HarperCollins Bible Dictionary*. San Francisco: HarperCollins, 1996.

Falk, Ze'ev W. *Hebrew Law in Biblical Times*. Provo, Utah: Brigham Young University Press, 2001.

Ginzberg, Louis. *The Legends of the Jews*. 7 vols. Translated by Henrietta Szold. Baltimore: Johns Hopkins University Press, 1998.

Josephus, Flavius. *Antiquities of the Jews*. In *The Works of Josephus, Complete and Unabridged*. Translated by William Whiston. Peabody, Mass.: Hendrickson, 1987.

Meyers, Carol. "The Roots of Restriction: Women in Early Israel." *Biblical Archaeologist,* Sept. 1978, 91–103.

Ochs, Vanessa L. *Sarah Laughed: Modern Lessons from the Wisdom and Stories of Biblical Women.* New York: McGraw-Hill, 2005.

Orr, James, ed. *The International Standard Bible Encyclopaedia.* 4 vols. Grand Rapids, Mich: Eerdmans, 1956. Reprint, Peabody, Mass.: Hendrickson, 2002.

ABIGAIL

Berlin, Adele. "Abigail." In Carol Meyers, ed. *Women in Scripture: A Dictionary of Named and Unnamed Women in the Hebrew Bible, the Apocryphal/Deuterocanonical Books, and the New Testament.* Grand Rapids, Mich.: Eerdmans, 2000.

Geoghegan, Jeffrey C. "Israelite Sheepshearing and David's Rise to Power." *Biblica* 87, 1 (2006): 55–63.

Ginzberg, Louis. *The Legends of the Jews.* 7 vols. Translated by Henrietta Szold. Baltimore: Johns Hopkins University Press, 1998.

Harris, Roberta. *The World of the Bible.* London: Thames and Hudson, 1995.

Hoerth, Alfred. *Archaeology and the Old Testament.* Grand Rapids, Mich.: Baker Books, 1998.

Klinck, Arthur W. *Home Life in Bible Times: A Study of Biblical Antiquities.* St. Louis, Mo.: Concordia Publishing, 1966.

King, Phillip J., and Lawrence E. Stager. *Life in Biblical Israel.* Louisville, Ky.: Westminster John Knox Press, 2001.

Leithart, Peter J. "David's Threat to Nabal: How a Little Vulgarity Got the Point Across." *Bible Review* 18, 5 (Oct. 2002): 18–23, 59.

———. "Critical Note: Nabal and His Wine." *Journal of Biblical Literature* 120, 3 (2001): 525–27.

McCarter, P. Kyle, Jr. *I Samuel.* The Anchor Bible Series. New York: Doubleday, 1980.

Mazar, Eilat. "Did I Find King David's Palace?" *Biblical Archaeology Review* 32, 1 (Jan./Feb. 2006): 16–27.

Radin, Max. *The Life of the People in Biblical Times.* Philadelphia: Jewish Publication Society of America, 1948.

Vamosh, Miriam Feinberg. *Food at the Time of the Bible.* Herzlia, Israel: Palphot, 2004.

Wright, George R. H. "Dumuzi at the Court of David." *Numen* 28, 1 (1981): 54–63.

THE WIDOW OF ZAREPHATH

Ackerman, Susan. "Digging Up Deborah: Recent Hebrew Bible Scholarship on Gender and the Contribution of Archaeology." *Near Eastern Archaeology* 66, 4 (Dec. 2003): 172–84.

Berlin, Adele, and Mark Zvi Brettler, eds. *The Jewish Study Bible.* New York: Oxford University Press, 2004.

Borowski, Oded. *Daily Life in Biblical Times.* Atlanta: Society of Biblical Literature, 2003.

Bright, John. *A History of Israel.* 4th ed. Louisville, Ky.: Westminster John Knox Press, 2000.

Chadwick, Jeffrey R. "Baking in the Bible." Paper presented at the Annual Meeting of the American Schools of Oriental Research (ASOR), San Diego, California, Nov. 16, 2007. Publication forthcoming.

Ginzberg, Louis. *The Legends of the Jews.* 7 vols. Translated by Henrietta Szold. Baltimore: Johns Hopkins University Press, 1998.

Gower, Ralph. *Manners and Customs of Bible Times.* Chicago: Moody Press, 1987.

Josephus, Flavius. *Antiquities of the Jews.* In *The Works of Josephus, Complete and Unabridged.* Translated by William Whiston. Peabody, Mass.: Hendrickson, 1987.

Meyers, Carol. "Material Remains and Social Relations: Women's Culture in Agrarian Households of the Iron Age." In William G. Dever and Seymour Gitin, eds. *Symbiosis, Symbolism, and the Power of the Past: Canaan, Ancient Israel, and Their Neighbors, from the Late Bronze Age through Roman Palestina.* Winona Lake, Ind.: Eisenbrauns, 2003.

Orr, James, ed. *The International Standard Bible Encyclopaedia.* 4 vols. Grand Rapids, Mich: Eerdmans, 1956. Reprint, Peabody, Mass.: Hendrickson, 2002.

Robbins, Lynn G. "Tithing—a Commandment Even for the Destitute." *Ensign,* May 2005, 34–36.

Vamosh, Miriam Feinberg. *Food at the Time of the Bible.* Herzlia, Israel: Palphot, 2004.

THE SHUNAMMITE

Berlin, Adele, and Marc Zvi Brettler, eds. *The Jewish Study Bible.* New York: Oxford University Press, 2004.

Borowski, Oded. *Daily Life in Biblical Times.* Atlanta: Society of Biblical Literature, 2003.

Bright, John. *A History of Israel.* 4th ed. Louisville, Ky.: Westminster John Knox Press, 2000.

Bunimovitz, Shlomo, and Avraham Faust. "Ideology in Stone: Understanding the Four-Room House." *Biblical Archaeology Review* 20, no. 4 (July/Aug. 2002): 32–41.

Chadwick, Jeffrey R. "The Ancient Israelite in the Bible." Paper presented at the Annual Meeting of the American Schools of Oriental Research (ASOR), San Diego, California, Nov. 16, 2007. Publication forthcoming.

Cogan, Mordechai, and Hayim Tadmor. *II Kings.* The Anchor Bible Series. New York: Doubleday, 1988.

Freeman, James M. *Hand-book of Bible Manners and Customs.* Cincinnati: Hitchcock and Walden, 1877.

Frymer-Kensky, Tikva. *Reading the Women of the Bible.* New York: Schocken Books, 2002.

Ginzberg, Louis. *The Legends of the Jews.* 7 vols. Translated by Henrietta Szold. Baltimore: Johns Hopkins University Press, 1998.

Josephus, Flavius. *Antiquities of the Jews.* In *The Works of Josephus, Complete and Unabridged.* Translated by William Whiston. Peabody, Mass.: Hendrickson, 1987.

Keil, C. F., and F. Delitzsch. *Commentary on the Old Testament.* 10 vols. Peabody, Mass.: Hendrickson, 1996.

Robbins, Lynn G. "Tithing—a Commandment Even for the Destitute." *Ensign,* May 2005, 34–36.

THE LITTLE MAID

Barker, Kenneth, ed. *KJV Study Bible.* Grand Rapids, Mich.: Zondervan, 2002.

Berlin, Adele, and Mark Zvi Brettler, eds. *The Jewish Study Bible.* New York: Oxford University Press, 2004.

Bright, John. *A History of Israel.* 4th ed. Louisville, Ky.: Westminster John Knox Press, 2000.

Cogan, Mordechai, and Hayim Tadmor. *II Kings.* The Anchor Bible Series. New York: Doubleday, 1988.

Ginzberg, Louis. *The Legends of the Jews.* 7 vols. Translated by Henrietta Szold. Baltimore: Johns Hopkins University Press, 1998.

Greenfield, Jonas C. "The Aramaen God Ramman/Rimmon." *Israel Exploration Journal* 26 (1976): 195–98.

Hulse, E. V. "The Nature of Biblical 'Leprosy' and the Use of Alternative Medical Terms in Modern Translations of the Bible." *Palestine Exploration Quarterly* 107 (1975): 87–105.

Josephus, Flavius. *Antiquities of the Jews.* In *The Works of Josephus, Complete and Unabridged.* Translated by William Whiston. Peabody, Mass.: Hendrickson, 1987.

Keil, C. F., and F. Delitzsch. *Commentary on the Old Testament.* 10 vols. Peabody, Mass.: Hendrickson, 1996.

Orr, James, ed. *The International Standard Bible Encyclopaedia.* 4 vols. Grand Rapids, Mich: Eerdmans, 1956. Reprint, Peabody, Mass.: Hendrickson, 2002. S.v. "Jordan."

Pritchard, James, ed. *Collins Atlas of the Bible.* Ann Arbor, Mich.: Borders Press, 2003.

SCRIPTURE INDEX

SUBJECT INDEX

Page numbers in italics indicate paintings and other visual images.